Neo-Confucianism

Neo-Confucianism

Metaphysics, Mind, and Morality

JeeLoo Liu

California State University, Fullerton
CA, USA

This edition first published 2018
© 2018 John Wiley & Sons, Inc.

All rights reserved. No part of this publication may be reproduced, stored in a retrieval system, or transmitted, in any form or by any means, electronic, mechanical, photocopying, recording or otherwise, except as permitted by law. Advice on how to obtain permission to reuse material from this title is available at http://www.wiley.com/go/permissions.

The right of JeeLoo Liu to be identified as the author of this work has been asserted in accordance with law.

Registered Offices
John Wiley & Sons, Inc., 111 River Street, Hoboken, NJ 07030, USA

Editorial Office
350 Main Street, Malden, MA 02148-5020, USA

For details of our global editorial offices, customer services, and more information about Wiley products visit us at www.wiley.com.

Wiley also publishes its books in a variety of electronic formats and by print-on-demand. Some content that appears in standard print versions of this book may not be available in other formats.

Limit of Liability/Disclaimer of Warranty

While the publisher and author have used their best efforts in preparing this book, they make no representations or warranties with respect to the accuracy or completeness of the contents of this book and specifically disclaim any implied warranties of merchantability or fitness for a particular purpose. It is sold on the understanding that the publisher is not engaged in rendering professional services and neither the publisher nor the author shall be liable for damages arising herefrom. If professional advice or other expert assistance is required, the services of a competent professional should be sought.

Library of Congress Cataloging-in-Publication Data

Names: Liu, JeeLoo, author.
Title: Neo-Confucianism : metaphysics, mind, and morality / JeeLoo Liu,
 California State University Fullerton, CA, US.
Description: First edition. | Hoboken : Wiley, 2018. |
 Includes bibliographical references and index. |
Identifiers: LCCN 2017016337 (print) | LCCN 2017017858 (ebook) |
 ISBN 9781118619322 (pdf) | ISBN 9781118619186 (epub) |
 ISBN 9781118619148 (hardback) | ISBN 9781118619414 (paper)
Subjects: LCSH: Neo-Confucianism. | BISAC: PHILOSOPHY / Eastern.
Classification: LCC B127.N4 (ebook) | LCC B127.N4 L574 2017 (print) |
 DDC 181/.112–dc23
LC record available at https://lccn.loc.gov/2017016337

Cover image: (Texture) © Lightspring/Shutterstock; (Caligraphy) Yue Feng (岳峰); (Text) Wang Fuzhi, translating to "The Six Classics make it incumbent upon me to break a new path and present a new facet."
Cover design by Wiley

Set in 10/12pt Warnock by SPi Global, Pondicherry, India

10 9 8 7 6 5 4 3 2 1

This book is dedicated to my mother Chu-Wei Lin Liu (劉林祝闈), whose high standards made me who I am today.

Contents

Preface *ix*
Acknowledgments *xi*

Introduction *1*

Part I Neo-Confucian Metaphysics: From Cosmology to Ontology *29*

1 From Nothingness to Infinity: The Origin of Zhou Dunyi's Cosmology *31*

2 The Basic Constituent of Things: Zhang Zai's Monist Theory of *Qi* *61*

3 Cheng–Zhu School's Normative Realism: The Principle of the Universe *85*

4 Wang Fuzhi's Theory of Principle Inherent in *Qi* *103*

Part II Human Nature, Human Mind, and the Foundation of Human Morality *123*

5 Zhu Xi's Internal Moral Realism: Human Nature Is Principle *125*

6 Lu Xiangshan and Wang Yangming's Doctrine of Mind Is Principle *139*

7 Wang Fuzhi's Theory of Daily Renewal of Human Nature and His Moral Psychology *157*

Part III The Cultivation of Virtue, Moral Personality, and the Construction of a Moral World *181*

8 Zhang Zai on Cultivating Moral Personality *183*

9 The Cheng Brothers' Globaist Virtue Ethics and Virtue Epistemology *205*

10 Zhu Xi's Methodology for Cultivating Sagehood: Moral Cognitivism and Ethical Rationalism *227*

11 Wang Yangming's Intuitionist Model of Innate Moral Sense and Moral Reflexivism *245*

12 Constructing a Moral World: Wang Fuzhi's Social Sentimentalism *265*

References *285*
Index *301*

Preface

This book is not about the history of Chinese philosophy, and it does not confine neo-Confucianism to its historical contexts. Instead, it aims to extract the philosophical core of neo-Confucianism in the Song-Ming era to make it relevant to contemporary philosophical discourse. The methodology of this book is comparative philosophy, and the angle of comparison is that of analytic philosophy. The analytic reconstruction of neo-Confucianism is chosen on the grounds of my philosophical training and expertise. It provides one credible analysis of neo-Confucianism among many other respectable approaches to Chinese philosophy. My intent behind writing this book is not to define what neo-Confucianism is, but to demonstrate how one could philosophically engage neo-Confucianism.

In this book, many contemporary philosophical theories in the analytic tradition are employed to provide a hermeneutic entry to the ancient philosophical ideas in neo-Confucianism. The claim is of course not that neo-Confucians of the eleventh to the seventeenth century did embrace these contemporary doctrines, since such a claim would result in anachronistic or Procrustean interpretation. The contemporary recontextualization, however, can liberate neo-Confucianism from its particular historical contexts and make it relate to contemporary readers. I believe that most philosophical ideas, though having their contextual roots, emerge out of shared human concerns, and can thus be recontextualized in different eras. A text should live on through its interpreters and readers.

At the same time, such a comparative approach, that is, using Western philosophical concepts to interpret Chinese philosophy, could incur the criticism of epistemological colonization, or the so-called reversed matching of meaning (*fanxiang geyi* 反向格義, borrowing Xiaogan Liu's terminology), to which many Chinese historians and Sinologists strongly oppose. Some Chinese scholars have vehemently argued against using any Western philosophical ideas to explicate Chinese thought, in that such Westernization would maim "the essence" of Chinese thinking. What I want to challenge in this book is exactly this kind of philosophical nationalism or essentialism that takes

Chinese philosophy to be exclusively of Chinese intellectual lineage, and intelligible only to Chinese readers. Using Western terminology to explicate Chinese philosophy is not necessarily to force the latter into the former's conceptual framework. If the interpretation remains true to the text, and does not distort the philosophical ideas of the philosophers, then the comparative angle can serve as a bridge for outsiders to gain intellectual access to Chinese philosophy. At the same time, scholars familiar with Chinese philosophy can also be motivated to learn more about Western philosophical theses. By reconstructing neo-Confucianism with the terminology of contemporary analytic philosophy in this book, I hope to render these philosophical ideas accessible and philosophically inspiring. To be true to the philosophical import of neo-Confucianism, the reconstruction is based on careful textual analysis, in consultation with other relevant interpretations both in English and Chinese secondary sources.[1] What I hope to present to the readers is a refreshing, innovative and perspicuous articulation of the philosophical dimension of neo-Confucianism.

---

1 Unless otherwise specified, all translations from Chinese into English are my own.

Acknowledgments

This book was made possible by a generous grant from the John Templeton Foundation. I wish to thank its past and present directors Hyung Choi, Michael J. Murray, and John Churchill for their assistance.

   This book serves as the sequel to my first book, *An Introduction to Chinese Philosophy: From Ancient Philosophy to Chinese Buddhism* (Blackwell, 2006). I am deeply indebted to the former philosophy editor of Wiley-Blackwell, Jeff Dean, for helping launch my writing career. In the late 1990s, when I was a junior assistant professor at SUNY Geneseo with little writing credentials, I approached Jeff with my idea of writing an introduction to Chinese philosophy with an analytic approach. He embraced the idea enthusiastically and provided me with helpful feedback along the way. I am very grateful to Jeff for trusting me to write the book the way I wanted to write it. We agreed at the time that an introduction that spans into neo-Confucianism would have made the book too long, so neo-Confucianism would have to wait for the second volume. It took me nearly 10 years to complete this project. With this book, Jeff was again welcoming and encouraging, and offered his shrewd editorial suggestions including the current title for this book. I was sorry that Jeff left Wiley-Blackwell before the book could be completed; however, I am thankful that the current editor Marissa Koors took over the project for publication. I would also like to thank the two reviewers of this book for their friendly and very helpful suggestions for improvement.

   Neo-Confucianism has always been my passion. When I was an undergraduate at National Taiwan University, I loved reading neo-Confucian writings on the rooftop balcony at my parents' apartment. Watching the sunsets and beautiful clouds, I often thought that this was the same sky that these neo-Confucians shared hundreds of years ago and felt connected with them. The person who instilled this passion in me was my undergraduate professor and later my master's thesis advisor, Yongjun Zhang 張永儁. He is a living neo-Confucian in our times, dedicated to learning, teaching, and passing on the torch of *Dao*. I am extremely grateful to him for opening the door to neo-Confucianism for me.

In 2009, when my idea for writing this book first emerged, I was invited to conduct an experimental summer course on the same topic at National Chengchi University in Taiwan. I would like to thank the Philosophy Department of National Chengchi University for giving me this great opportunity to develop my thoughts through engaging discussions with students. I must credit the participants for helping make this book possible: my teaching assistant Zili Zhang 張子立, the fellow scholars as well as the students in this class. I am also grateful to the Philosophy Department of the Chinese University of Hong Kong for providing a sponsored sojourn during the final stage of my manuscript revision.

Last, but most important, I also want to thank my husband Michael Cranston and our two sons Collin and Dillon, for they have provided a loving, supportive, and stress-free environment for me to work on my book over the years.

Introduction

This book gives a detailed philosophical analysis of eight central figures in Chinese neo-Confucianism from the Song-Ming era (between the eleventh and the seventeenth centuries). It is a sequel to the author's first book *An Introduction to Chinese Philosophy: From Ancient Philosophy to Chinese Buddhism* (Blackwell, 2006), which examines five major philosophical schools in the ancient period as well as four principal schools of Chinese Buddhism. This book continues the analytical introduction to Chinese philosophy given in the first book and focuses on neo-Confucianism.

The book draws comparisons to analytic philosophy in regard to its main issues and concerns. This approach helps to bring neo-Confucianism into the context of contemporary philosophy and to show how issues expressed in distinctively neo-Confucian terminology relate to issues in contemporary philosophy. One of the aims of this comparative approach is to show that even though Chinese philosophers used different terms, narrative strategies, and analytic modes, their concerns were often similar to those of their Western counterparts, for example: What is the nature of reality? Wherein lies the foundation of our moral values? Is human nature fundamentally good or bad? How do human beings connect to the whole universe? What is the foundation of our knowledge of the world and of moral reality? Such an approach will make these issues accessible to Western thinkers by shedding light on their universality through the analytic explication of these texts. This book will enable Western readers who are not familiar with Chinese philosophical terminology or its intellectual history to gain a philosophical appreciation of neo-Confucianism. Furthermore, by consulting both English secondary sources and representative Chinese works on neo-Confucianism, it will facilitate a more active philosophical exchange between Western philosophers working on neo-Confucianism and contemporary Chinese scholars by coming to see the shared concerns as well as the common pursuits laid out in a clear and accessible language.

Neo-Confucianism: Metaphysics, Mind, and Morality, First Edition. JeeLoo Liu.
© 2018 John Wiley & Sons, Inc. Published 2018 by John Wiley & Sons, Inc.

What Is Neo-Confucianism?

"Neo-Confucianism" typically refers to the revival of classical Confucianism developed between eleventh and eighteenth centuries in China, spanning over four dynasties in Chinese history: Song, Yuan, Ming, and Qing dynasties. Neo-Confucianism was a new form of Confucianism that came after the dominance of Daoism and subsequently Buddhism within Chinese intellectual circles. Comparable to what "Modern Philosophy" accomplished in Western philosophy, neo-Confucianism also revitalized classical philosophy and expanded the traditional philosophical discourse, adding new dimensions and attaining new heights. The transformation of Confucianism as a result of the challenge and influence of Daoism and Buddhism was the most remarkable and significant development in the history of Chinese philosophy. Neo-Confucianism invigorated the metaphysical speculation found in classics such as the *Yijing*, and incorporated different concepts and perspectives derived from Daoism and Buddhism into its discourse. Also, partly as a response to the Daoist skeptical attitude toward the possibility of knowledge, neo-Confucianism brought the theory of knowledge asserted in classics such as *The Great Learning* to a much more sophisticated level.

Frank Perkins gives neo-Confucianism an apt summary: Neo-Confucianism "can be broadly characterized as the attempt to integrate a speculative, systematic metaphysics influenced by Buddhism and Daoism into the ethically and socially oriented system of Confucianism" (Perkins 2004, 20–21). Neo-Confucians were fundamentally concerned with the role humans play in the moral reconstruction of the world around them. In their view, humans not only endow the world of nature with meaning but also share moral attributes with natural phenomena. Neo-Confucians' metaphysical views lay the foundation for their moral theories. The goal of this book is to explicate Song-Ming neo-Confucianism in its three major themes (metaphysics, mind, and morality) and to show how they exemplify a coherent underlying concern: the relation between nature and human beings. In their various debates, neo-Confucians touched on the possibility of an innate moral sense and the various means of moral knowledge. In addition, neo-Confucianism contains an intriguing discourse on the possibility and foundation of morality. In neo-Confucians' views, morality takes its root either in the universal goodness of human nature or in the individual's moral reflection and cultivation of the human mind. This debate between the School of Nature and the School of Mind was one of the major themes in neo-Confucianism. Finally, in neo-Confucianism we see a consistent effort not only to redefine a realist worldview that affirms the world as existing independently of human conception, but also to reassert a humanist worldview that places human beings at the center of meaning and values. Both the realist and the humanist commitments were direct responses to the challenges of Daoism and Buddhism, and they delineate the spirit of neo-Confucianism.

Neo-Confucians were generally concerned with establishing a moralistic naturalism, that is, the natural world in which we live demonstrates many good attributes that are worthy of humans' emulation. We may say that they developed a form of moral metaphysics. According to a contemporary scholar on neo-Confucianism, Yong Huang, "what is more unique about neo-Confucianism is its development of moral metaphysics as an ontological articulation of moral values advocated by classical Confucians" (Huang 2014, 195). What distinguishes neo-Confucianism from classical Confucianism is exactly this moral metaphysics. According to neo-Confucians, there is a higher order governing the world, which they call "heavenly principle," and the content of this higher order is also the objective moral principle for human beings. At the same time, neo-Confucians also embraced the Chinese philosophical tradition (founded in the *Yijing*) of positing a basic element of *qi* as the material/physical foundation of the universe. The core thesis in Neo-Confucian metaphysics is view that *qi* is the primary constituent of all things and that there is an inherent order in the operation of *qi*.

With regard to the psychological foundation of human morality, neo-Confucians were predominately in the Mencian camp. Mencius advocates moral internalism—the foundation of human morality lies within the agent's internal psychological makeup. According to Mencius, humans are different from other animals because they are born with moral sentiments. Humans alone are moral creatures. This is what defines the notion "human" (*ren* 人), which in his usage is not a natural kind but a moral category. There are, according to Mencius, four universal moral sentiments in the mankind: (i) the sentiment of commiseration, (ii) the sentiment of shame and disgust, (iii) the sense of reverence and deference, and (iv) the sense of right and wrong. Since humans are endowed with these moral sentiments, morality is a natural extension of what humans have within themselves. Evil is the result of not cultivating one's "moral sprouts." According to him, morality is not the sheer result of social conditioning and is not derived from social contract or rational consensus based on calculated mutual self-interests. On the contrary, human morality is possible only because we humans are moral creatures.

Neo-Confucians identified the internal source of moral agency in humans' moral sense, moral judgment, moral intuition, or moral sentiments. What they shared in common was the view that moral action is an autonomous act springing from an individual's heart. They dismissed Xunzi's teaching that morality is the product of humans' contrived conditioning (*wei* 偽). According to Xunzi, we need to use rules of propriety and rituals to curtail the bad traits in human nature. Morality is the result of human endeavor and social institutions, while evil is simply the result of following inborn human nature without societal restraints. There is no such thing as "innate goodness," though Xunzi does claim that humans have reason and can appeal to the mind's moral cognition to learn good. From a moral externalist's point of view, morality derives from social conditioning for the purpose of peaceful coexistence. The external social environment is responsible for the existence or the lack of our moral sense. According to this view, humans' moral consciousness and sense of morality are taught and learned. Hence, different social backgrounds and cultural rearing could generate incompatible moral views or even create diverse moral standards. In other words, cultural relativism is a natural extension of moral externalism. One characteristic in neo-Confucianism is their unequivocal conviction in the existence of the objective, universal moral standard, which they identify as heavenly principle. To them, the existence of a moral reality is an indisputable fact of nature, and the universality of moral truths is grounded in humans' shared moral sense.

Neo-Confucians based their moral theories on their metaphysical view of the objective moral reality in the world of nature. This worldview originated in the *Yijing*, and the four attributes of heaven and earth (origination, advancement, enrichment, and perseverance) are the four virtues of each cosmic state represented by 64 hexagrams in the *Yijing*. With a sympathetic reading, we may render this perspective of nature as a version of teleology—the world is governed by the principle of life and the overarching telos assumed in this worldview is simply the creation and sustenance of life. From the contemporary viewpoint, we may see that the world of nature operates under the principle of life, as demonstrated by the fact that evolution continues and multiple forms of organism exist to this day. It is the subject matter of natural sciences to investigate which natural phenomena function to sustain life and what causes natural disasters that destroy life. Looking at aspects of the world of nature from a humanistic perspective, on the other hand, we can say that many natural phenomena, such as sunshine and raindrops from heaven and the richness of the soil from earth, are conducive to the continuation of life. Some natural phenomena such as hurricanes do indeed destroy lives; nevertheless, seasons rotate and life continues after destruction. Ancient Confucians found great solace in the continuation of life as they observed in the world of nature, and this natural fact became the foundation for their conviction that the dominant principle in nature is the continual generation and regeneration of life (*shengsheng buxi* 生生不息). Given this conviction, they viewed the world of nature itself as a "beneficent" universe. From this observation of nature, they concluded that there is an ultimate moral mission for human beings: to contribute to the fulfillment of the principle of life.

Neo-Confucian moral theories are best understood as falling within the category of virtue ethics.[1] Virtue ethics is the approach of ethical theories that emphasize the virtues, or moral character, of the moral agent. As a form of normative ethics, virtue ethics gives the precept of what kind of virtues one ought

---

1 As Stephen C. Angle writes in his *Sagehood: The Contemporary Significance of Neo-Confucian Philosophy*, "It is no coincidence that Western virtue ethics speaks to Neo-Confucianism because *Neo-Confucianism is itself a virtue ethic*" (Angle 2009, 51; italics added). He also explicates Wang Yangming as a virtue ethicist (Angle 2010). Yong Huang analyzes the ethical theory of the Cheng brothers as virtue ethics, and further defines this form of virtue ethics as "ontological virtue ethics" (Huang 2003, 453). See also Huang 2014. Angle and Slote (2013) is a collected volume on virtue ethics and Confucianism. Antonio S. Cua, Kwong-loi Shun, and Philip J. Ivanhoe are among the most noted pioneering scholars on neo-Confucian virtue ethics.

to cultivate, or what kind of moral character one ought to develop. It is an agent-centered approach, in contrast to the act-centered approaches such as deontology, which judges the moral worth of an act in terms of its adherence to some specified moral duties, or consequentialism, which prescribes or prohibits moral acts in consideration of their possible consequences. Virtue ethics focuses less on defining rules for moral acts; instead, it stresses more on defining moral personhood. A virtuous act is one performed by virtuous agents. To define virtuous personhood, virtue ethicists have to identify the essential moral traits that anyone ought to cultivate in order to become a moral agent. They have to address the following question in their attempts to define virtue: What are the virtues such that as long as an agent possesses them, he or she is morally good? Their goal is thus to define those moral virtues that they deem to be enduring and causally efficacious in bringing about moral behavior in individuals. The highest moral character that these neo-Confucians all share in their moral image of the world is that of a sage: the ideal moral agent who has a sanguine vision of what one ought to do in all situations and unwavering moral character. Cultivating sagehood is the common moral aim for neo-Confucianism.

However, among virtue ethicists there are still different approaches. Philip J. Ivanhoe distinguishes two types of virtue ethics: virtue ethics of flourishing (VEF) and virtue ethics of sentiments (VES). The former approach "is grounded in a comprehensive and detailed conception of human nature" and conceives the condition of flourishing for an ideal moral agent as the teleological aim of moral cultivation. The latter, on the other hand, considers a moral agent's virtue in terms of social interactions, and places virtue on the basis of certain emotions or sentiments of human beings as part of humans' psychological makeup (Ivanhoe 2013, 29–30). Both approaches begin with a theory of human nature, and the difference could be characterized as one between an ideal versus an empirical conception of human mind. Hence, the latter (VES) is more empirically grounded. It is particularly in the works on VES that we see the alliance between normative ethics and moral psychology. However, neo-Confucian moral philosophy should be regarded as a form of VEF. Neo-Confucianism grounds its conception of ideal moral agent in sagehood, and all neo-Confucians aimed to present their methodology of arriving at sagehood as the aim of moral cultivation.

Terminology

The Notion of Principle (*li* 理)

The most important notion in neo-Confucianism is undoubtedly that of principle (*li* 理). This explains why neo-Confucianism is called "the Studies of Principle" (*lixue* 理學) in Chinese intellectual history. We shall explain first its origin and significance.

The substantial usage of the word *li* is particularly a neo-Confucian earmark, even though it was already employed in Huayan Buddhism to designate ultimate reality. The word was initially used as a verb, which means "to carve jade" (the Chinese character has jade as a radical). A fine jade craftsman must carefully study the lines and grooves of an uncut jade in order to produce a beautiful piece of jade. By extension, *li* as a noun means the veins or detailed markings of a thing, and *li* as a verb means to regulate, to administer, and to manage. In neo-Confucian discourse, the meaning of *li* includes pattern, sequence, logic, order, and norm. The Cheng–Zhu school also established a normative dimension of the concept *li* for they claim that everything in the world ought to meet the standard set by its own principle.

The English translation of the word *li* in the context of neo-Confucianism includes reason, law, organization, order, pattern, coherence, and principle. Of these translations, "principle" has now become a standard usage. As Wing-tsit Chan explains his choice of "principle": "Li is not only principle of organization, but also principle of being, nature, etc. 'Principle' seems to be the best English equivalent for it" (Chan 1967, 368). To see why principle is equivalent to the Chinese notion of *li*, we need to understand how the word is understood in the philosophical context. The word "principle" comes from *principium* in Latin, which was used as the translation for the Greek word *arché*, meaning origin or beginning. In pre-Socratic philosophy, the pursuit of *arché* was the attempt to define the ultimate underlying principle of all things. Thus, "principle" can be said to be the short form for "first principle." Aristotle applied the notion *arché* (principle) to particular things. The principle of a particular thing defines the conditions of possibility for that thing: for a thing to exist, there has to be its principle, and without having its principle, no thing could possibly come into existence. This sense of "principle" comes very close to the neo-Confucian conception of *li*. Hence, we shall adopt this translation as well.

In the neo-Confucian discourse, principle is the unifying principle of the universe, and thus it can be rendered as the cosmic order, the cosmic pattern, "the network of veins" (Graham 1992, 13), or as the neo-Confucians have it: heavenly principle (*tianli* 天理). At the same time, in each particular thing there is its particular principle. Principle in particular things can be understood as the norm of particular things; it stands for the paradigmatic state of the particular thing toward which it should and would develop if aided by humans. Principle is not only the principle of the natural world but also the principle of the human world. As principle of the human world, it includes human's inborn essence (the *li* of human nature), the way to handle affairs (the *li* of affairs), the norm of human relationships (the *li* of humans), and so on.[2] In particular, the unifying principle in nature and the multiple principles in particular things

---

2 In Part II, we will return to the notion of *li* as it applies to the human world.

prescribe the norm of conduct for human beings: We have a moral obligation to interact with nature and to handle particular things in accordance with their natures, so that the world will flourish under our care and particular things will thrive under our treatment. This is a shared neo-Confucian conviction in their pursuit of the ultimate Principle.

According to Sir Martin Rees, "Science advances by discerning patterns and regularities in nature, so that more and more phenomena can be subsumed into general categories and laws" (Rees 2000, 1). Among neo-Confucians, Zhu Xi[3] may have come closest to developing a systematic knowledge of the natural world (Kim 2000).[4] However, even Zhu Xi's notion of particular principle ends up being more a moral norm for human beings than a natural scientific notion. Later scholars in the Cheng–Zhu school did not inherit Zhu Xi's interest in natural knowledge. The opposing school led by Lu Xiangshan and Wang Yangming further turned the investigation inward: to study the principle inside one's mind since mind is principle.

In the history of Chinese philosophy, the two important notions of *dao* and principle (*li*) are often used together or interchangeably. Both designate the ultimate order of the world. Initially, the two concepts were slightly different. *Dao* is universal, while principle (*li*) is particular. According to the *Hanfeizi*, "Dao is the ground for everything and the sanction for all principles of things. The principle (*li*) for a particular thing is what makes up the thing's pattern, while Dao is what completes all things.... The principle is what regulates a thing, thus different things have different principles. Dao comprehensively sanctions all principles of the myriad things" (*The Hanfeizi* 2007, 106). This distinction is sometimes preserved in neo-Confucian discourse on principle, as Zhu Xi claims, "Dao is the unifying name, while principle concerns particular things" (Zhu 2002, 236). According to Wang Fuzhi, "Dao is the common principle (*li*) of heaven and earth, humans and things" (Wang 1967, 1). However, the universal/particular distinction between *dao* and principle is not commonly observed in neo-Confucian discourse, since most neo-Confucians also separate both *dao* into universal *Dao* and particular *daos*, and "principle" into universal principle ("heavenly principle") and particular principles.

A second distinction between *dao* and principle is that *dao* represents the progressive order of nature, while principle represents the finished pattern. *Dao* has a dynamic sense, while principle has the static sense. In Zhang Zai's usage, *dao* refers to the ongoing progression of the transformation of *qi*, while

---

3 Throughout this book, names of neo-Confucians and other historical figures follow the Chinese tradition of placing family names first.
4 As Yung Sik Kim (2000) argues forcefully, Zhu Xi himself "attained a considerable degree of understanding in many scientific and technical subjects and had an exceptional knowledge about the natural world" (Kim 2000, 6).

li refers to the pattern in such transformations.[5] Wang Fuzhi also takes *dao* to represent the dynamic interchange between *yin* and *yang*, and he takes *li* to represent the internal logic of *qi*. In other words, *Dao* produces things, while principle represents their order. A related distinction that can be drawn between *dao* and *li* is that the former has a sense of origination, universality, and comprehensiveness, while the latter simply denotes the essence of particular things. *Dao* is regarded as the contributor of our moral endowments, the fundamental root of humans' ethical norms. It stands for the highest moral precept exemplified in the world of nature. Only "principle" used in the sense of "heavenly principle" has this connotation.

A final plausible distinction between the two concepts is that *dao* has the normative connotation of "what should be the case," whereas *li* generally denotes "what is" or "what is necessarily so," except in the usage by the Cheng–Zhu school. In other words, *dao* is prescriptive, while *li* is descriptive. *Li* is how things naturally are and how *qi* naturally is. All things have their internal principles and all developments of *qi* have their internal logic. But only humans possess *Dao* since the normative dimension pertains to what humans could and ought to do.

Even though we can make the above preliminary distinctions, in most neo-Confucian discourses, *dao* and *li* do not have such a clear divide. The Cheng brothers use the two words almost interchangeably. According to a contemporary scholar Dainian Zhang's analysis, the theory of principle developed by Cheng Yi is truly a continuation of the theory of *Dao* in ancient Chinese philosophy, and his *li* can be seen as an alias of *Dao* (Zhang 1958/2005, 52). Cheng Yi's famous slogan: "Principle is one but the manifestations are many," should be taken to be "*Dao* is one but the manifestations are many" (Zhang 1958/2005, 73).

The concerns of neo-Confucians regarding principle (*li*) can be summarized in the following list of questions:

1) Has the universe always followed the same principles (*li*)? What is the relation between the operation of the world and these principles? Do principles precede existence or are they formed after existence?
2) Are universal principles prescriptive (i.e., they determine the way things are) or merely descriptive (i.e., they are the summary of the way things are)?
3) What is the nature of the ultimate principle of the universe? Are principles natural or moral, or both?
4) What is the content of heavenly principle? Is it the same universal principle that governs all things, or do individual things have individual principles (*li*)?

---

5 See Zhang 1958/2005, 72–3.

5) With what capacities do we know the principles of myriad things or the universal heavenly principle? Do humans have any intellectual intuition (*intellektuelle Anschauung* as Kant calls it), through which we could suddenly perceive the universal cosmic principle? Or should we accumulate knowledge of particular principles in order to understand the universal cosmic principle?

Neo-Confucians share some common assumptions on certain aspects of principle. For one thing, they all believe that there is only one universal principle, though its manifestations are many. Cheng Yi and Zhu Xi, for example, often likened the relation of the One and the Many to the moon and its multiple reflections in rivers or lakes. Zhang Zai also stressed that principle is one but manifestations are many. Secondly, neo-Confucians share the view that this universal principle is inherent in all particular things. Zhang Zai's "Western Inscription" depicts the universe as one big family, in which all things are related to one another as brothers, sisters, or companions. Cheng Yi and Zhu Xi's view is that the principle inherent in each object constitutes the nature of the thing. Lu Xiangshan and Wang Yangming hold the view that the universal principle is inherent in man's mind. Thirdly, neo-Confucians understand the universal principle and the myriad principles to be fundamentally the same, though the myriad things may not completely manifest the inherent principle. Different explanations were offered as to why there are differences in the manifestations of the one Principle; for example, Zhang Zai attributed them to the varying qualities of the constituting *qi*. Finally, neo-Confucians share the view that the highest form of principle is simply heavenly principle or the great ultimate (*taiji*). In this context, principle takes on a moral dimension. According to Zhu Xi, "The great ultimate is simply the principle of the highest good" (Chan 1963, 640). This supreme principle is a principle with moral attributes, such as humanity, righteousness, propriety, and wisdom. Since there is only one all-encompassing principle of the whole universe, the universe itself is endowed with moral attributes. It is a moralistic universe. That the universe has moral attributes seems to be the view shared by Zhou Dunyi, the Cheng brothers, Zhang Zai, Zhu Xi, and Wang Fuzhi.

What kind of cosmic principle could fit the above descriptions? What could be shared by widely different myriad things and yet remain the same? What could be inherent in both natural objects and moral agents alike? The content of principle is not explicitly defined by neo-Confucians. In Part I of this book, we will analyze the various conceptions of principle among neo-Confucians.

Common Assumptions on Principles of Particular Things

Neo-Confucians believe that particular things have particular principles. As Cheng Yi puts it, "As there are things, there must be their specific principles.

One thing necessarily has one principle."⁶ Zhu Xi also says, "There is only one principle. As it is applied to man, however, there is in each individual a particular principle."⁷ Under this view, different things would have different particular principles, even though all particular principles seem to be integrated into one universal principle.

With regard to particular principles in things, we can provide the following analyses:

1) Principle in things is the way things ought to be (the norm of things, the highest standards of things, and the ideal state of things).
2) Principle in things is the way things naturally are (the essence of things).
3) Principle in things is what makes the things what they are (the blueprint, the foundation of their existence).
4) Principle in things is the *raison d'être* (the ultimate purpose) of the particular thing.
5) Principle in things is the law that governs or regulates things.

In Parts I and II, we will see lots of discussions on the concept of particular principle in things.

The Notion of *Qi*—Cosmic Energy

Another essential notion in neo-Confucianism is that of *qi* 氣 (sounding like 'chi')—commonly translated as cosmic energy, material force, vital energy, or even ether in some early translations. In this book, this Chinese word will be used as it is, as no English translation could completely convey its connotation. According to a contemporary intellectual historian Dainian Zhang, "The so-called *qi* in Chinese philosophy is the being before form and matter and what constitutes form and matter. It can be seen as the "primary stuff" [Xunzi's phrase] for form and matter. In today's terminology, *qi* is the original material for all things" (Zhang 1985/2005, 66). Chung-Ying Cheng gives an enigmatic description of *qi* that captures the richness of this concept well:

> [Qi], an ancient term referring to the indeterminate substance which generates and forms any and every individual thing in the cosmos, no doubt has a rich content. It is formless, yet is the base of all forms. It is the source of everything and the ultimate into which formed things will eventually dissolve. It is non-stationary and forever in a state of flux. It might be conceived as the fluid state of becoming which reveals itself in

---

6 This quote comes from Wing-tsit Chan's Chinese article "The Evolution of the Neo-Confucian Concept of *Li* as Principle." See Chan 1964, 139. It originally appears in *Complete Works of the Two Cheng Brothers* (*er-cheng quan-shu*), 11:52.
7 See Chan 1964, 141. It originally appears in *Complete Works of Zhu Xi* (*zhu-zi quan-shu*), 49:1a.

actualization of natural events and natural objects. But it is best conceived as the *indeterminate unlimited material-in-becoming* which, through its intrinsic dynamics of alternation and interpenetration of the *yin-yang* process, generates Five Agencies, and through their union and interaction generate the ten thousand things.

(Cheng 1979, 262–3; italics added)

Even if the above two analyses did not help elucidate what *qi* really is, there is no denial that the notion of *qi* is fundamental to the Chinese worldview. Laymen and experts alike employ this notion in their daily lives, with more or less different understanding of what *qi* is. Chinese herbology has an elaborated system on the constitution of *yin* and *yang* in various plants and roots; Chinese medicine is the study of the distribution of *yin* and *yang* in the human body. Chinese cooking is an art of creating a harmonious balance, a *Taiji*, between foods of *yang* nature and *yin* nature. Chinese martial arts, finally, are manifestations of the individual's internal strength of *yin* and *yang*. In terms of the philosophical notion of *qi*, from the beginning, Chinese ontology is built on the notion of *qi*. *Qi* is taken to be the constituent of all natural phenomena and every concrete thing; *qi* is also associated with life's conditions and the world's state of affairs. However, even though the notion is frequently employed, there has been no systematic analysis of *qi* and its many characteristics. We will explain the historical developments of the notion of *qi* and see how Zhang Zai reconstructed Confucian *qi*-monism in Chapter 2.

In general, neo-Confucians shared the following assumptions on certain aspects of *qi*:

1) The whole universe is composed of *qi*, which has two forms: *yin* and *yang*. These two forms of *qi* work against each other in their perpetual motion.
2) All things contain both *yin* and *yang* to varying degrees. Nothing is purely *yang* or purely *yin*.
3) *Qi* condenses to form material objects. When material objects disintegrate, on the other hand, their concrete *qi* returns to a rarified form.
4) The nature of *qi* can be pure or turbid—in this distinction lies the differences of good and bad, intelligence and lack of it, and so on.
5) Particular things partake *qi* in varying degrees of quality (pure or turbid, lucid or opaque, light or dense, etc.) as well as in different combinations of *yin* and *yang*. Variances among individual things are extensive not only in the manifestation of principle but also in the distribution of *qi*.
6) It is *qi*, not principle, which plays the actual causal role in the physical realm.

However, these neo-Confucians disagree on whether principle is an abstract order or a pattern superimposed onto the physical realm, or principle is simply the inherent order of *qi*'s operations. We will see the different views in Part I of this book.

Chapter Synopsis

This book is divided into three parts. Part I deals with neo-Confucian metaphysics. Part II examines the neo-Confucians' theories of the origin of morality and its foundation in the objective moral reality, whereas Part III delineates their moral methodologies.

Part I. Neo-Confucian Metaphysics: From Cosmology to Ontology

The major common themes in neo-Confucian metaphysics include (i) how the universe began and what the original state of the world might have been; (ii) what the ontological hierarchy of the world is—whether there is an abstract, overarching principle presiding over the development of *qi*; and (iii) what is the relationship between the two essential elements of the universe: principle (*li*) and *qi*. These are the key points that will be discussed in Part I on neo-Confucian metaphysics.

Chapter 1 focuses on Zhou Dunyi's controversial thesis about the initial cosmic state, which he calls *wuji* and *taiji*. The controversy revolves around the question of whether Zhou Dunyi holds the view that there was nothing (*wu*) at the beginning of the cosmos. The first section of this chapter will explain the historical controversies on the interpretation of this work. The second section will introduce the philosophical debate on being (*you*) and nothingness (*wu*) prior to Zhou's times, to see whether his *wuji* notion is related to the notion of *wu*. The final section will give a new interpretation of Zhou Dunyi's notion of *wuji* and further develop his cosmological view.

Chapter 2 introduces Zhang Zai's theory of *qi* as a form of *qi*-naturalism. Zhang Zai constructed a systematic philosophy that builds on the traditional notion of *qi*. He incorporated the notion of *qi* into his metaphysics as well as his ethics. Before Zhang Zai, there had been cosmogony originating with primordial *qi* (*yuanqi*) and ontology with *qi* as the basic constituent of all things primarily in the Daoist tradition. This chapter will trace the theory of *qi* to its Daoist roots, and see how the notion of *qi* was employed both in Daoists' cosmological explanation and in their ontological analysis. It will then introduce the theory of *qi* as developed by Zhang Zai, and examine how he went back to the theory of *qi* in the *Yijing* and used it to develop a neo-Confucian theory of *qi*.

Chapter 3 presents the metaphysical views held by the Cheng brothers as well as Zhu Xi. In contemporary terms, the main focus in Chapter 3 is on the existence of the law of nature, that is, whether the universe is a cosmic accident or is driven by specific eternal laws of nature. The notion of principle (or heavenly principle) was already present in Zhang Zai's theory of *qi*, but it was the Cheng brothers, in particular, Cheng Yi, who expanded on the notion, and their discussion paved the way for the neo-Confucian discourse on the "principle of

Heaven" (*tianli*).⁸ This chapter begins with the explication of the notion of principle (*li*) and its various renditions in English. It then analyzes how the Cheng brothers, and later Zhu Xi, developed an ontological hierarchy that posits nonreductionism of principle. It also investigates the relation between the universal Principle and particular things. The chapter analyzes the metaphysical worldview presented by Cheng Yi and Zhu Xi as a form of "normative realism."

In Chapter 4, we focus on the further development of the philosophy of *qi* under Wang Fuzhi's elaboration. Due to the scarcity of translations (Wing-tsit Chan's *A Sourcebook in Chinese Philosophy* contains only a snippet of Wang's 20-some volumes), Wang Fuzhi is by far the most undeservingly neglected neo-Confucian in the English-speaking world. Wang Fuzhi was a great synthesizer of the theory of *qi* and the theory of principle: his basic view is that principle is inherent in *qi*. This chapter will open with Wang Fuzhi's metaphysics and extend to his views on the human world. For Wang Fuzhi, the realm of heaven and the realm of humans are simply one unified whole. There is no transcendent realm beyond the human world, and it is the same element, *qi*, and the same principle, which permeate the realm of heaven as well as the realm of humans. Hence, his metaphysical view underlies his philosophy of human affairs—in particular, his philosophy of human nature, his moral philosophy, as well as his philosophy of human history. This chapter depicts Wang Fuzhi's philosophy as the philosophy of Principle Inherent in *qi*, since it is the relationship between principle and *qi* that explains everything for him.

Part II. Human Nature, Human Mind, and the Foundation of Human Morality

What is the origin of human morality? What makes morality possible in human society? Are human beings intrinsically moral creatures, or are we conditioned to be moral agents through social and political regulations? Do we have moral "instincts" and natural moral sentiments? Classical Confucianism, represented by Confucius and Mencius, takes the stance that humans are intrinsically good and that morality is the natural development originating from humans' innate goodness. If morality derives from humans' inborn nature, then how do we explain the lack of morality in some human conduct? How do we explain the fact that not everyone became a moral agent?

One of Chinese Buddhism's basic tenets is that the root of suffering as well as the origin of immorality is humans' emotions and desires. Chinese Buddhist philosophers denounce our natural emotions and desires; along with the denunciation, they also renounce natural human relationships such as family, marriage, and kinship. In the wake of the dominance of Chinese Buddhism,

---

8 "Heavenly principle" and "the principle of Heaven" are used interchangeably in this book.

neo-Confucian philosophers were intent on analyzing the relationship between heavenly principle and human emotions/desires.

The main topic of Part II consists in a major debate between the school of nature and the school of mind. The former school is represented by Cheng Yi and Zhu Xi, who claim that human nature exemplifies the universal moral principle. The latter school is represented by Lu Xiangshan and Wang Yangming, who take the human mind to be the actual realization of the universal moral principle. This debate concerns whether the foundation of morality is primarily metaphysical or mental. The first school constructs metaphysics of morality that takes moral attributes to be intrinsic to human existence; the second focuses on moral intuitions and moral knowledge as ways to foster moral agency. The analysis of this rich and longstanding debate will be presented from the fresh perspective of contemporary moral psychology. Construed broadly, moral psychology investigates the connection between humans' moral behavior and their psychological makeup. Neo-Confucians had varying responses to the question of what makes human morality possible, and many of them developed a sophisticated moral psychology, in which they analyzed the relation between morality and the mind's many functions.

Chapter 5 focuses on Zhu Xi's famous slogan: "Human nature is Principle" or "Cosmic principle is exemplified in human nature." It places Zhu Xi's theory of human nature in the context of his moral metaphysics. According to Zhu Xi, the highest form of principle is simply heavenly principle or the supreme ultimate (*Taiji* 太極). Zhu Xi takes the supreme ultimate to be the principle of the highest good. This supreme principle is the principle with moral attributes, such as humanity, righteousness, propriety, and wisdom. There is only one all-encompassing principle of the whole universe, and it is inherent in our very existence. Under this worldview, Zhu Xi advocates the theory of moral essence ("nature" (*xing* 性)). The moral reality lies in our moral essence. This is Zhu Xi's moral realism. This chapter analyzes Zhu Xi's theory as internal moral realism.

Chapter 6 continues the investigation of the universal moral principle realized in the human mind, and turns to the contrasting view presented by Lu Xiangshan and Wang Yangming. Lu Xiangshan advocates the view that the universal principle is inherent in the human mind. Wang Yangming goes further and asserts that the mind is principle itself. This chapter analyses the views of Lu and Wang and shows how they depict a different metaphysics of mind from that of the Cheng–Zhu school. It further explains Wang's famous *one-body* thesis "We are one body with the world" in the context of his metaphysics, which we will compare with contemporary pragmatist metaphysics.

Chapter 7 introduces Wang Fuzhi's revolutionary thesis that treats human nature as developing, rather than as some inborn essence complete at birth. Wang Fuzhi's theory of human nature is grounded in his metaphysics of *qi*: since *qi* is constantly changing, human nature is not simply what one is endowed with at birth, it is also what is developed throughout one's life.

According to Wang Fuzhi, as we continue to interact with the natural environment and human conditions, we are immersed in the ongoing permeations of *qi*. We make decisions and take actions, and our essences are shaped by our experiences in life. As a result, not only our natural qualities but also our moral essence would become more developed and perfected on a daily basis. In other words, we do not have a determinate essence fixed for life. This is his ingenious thesis of daily renewal of human nature. He developed a sophisticated moral psychology to analyze the connection between morality and mind. This chapter analyzes Wang Fuzhi's moral psychology and explains how he establishes the foundation of morality on humans' moral sentiments, natural emotions, desires, volition, and furthermore, reflection.

Part III. The Cultivation of Virtue, Moral Personality, and the Construction of a Moral World

Part III continues from Part II and reconstructs neo-Confucians' moral philosophy in the context of contemporary virtue ethics and developmental psychology. While Part II provides the metaphysical foundation of moral attributes, Part III deals with the implementation of neo-Confucian moral programs. We will be analyzing various neo-Confucians' views on the realization of moral ideals both in the individual and in the world. In this context, we will also examine the various methods of moral knowledge proposed by these neo-Confucian philosophers.

In contemporary research on Confucianism, there is now an emerging direction to consult empirical sciences as a new way to resituate and reassess its ethical teachings. For example, Edward Slingerland (2011b) cites empirical evidence from cognitive science to support the ethical model of virtue ethics; in particular, he argues that Mencius's moral theory anticipates some of the scientific observations about the human mind, and can be a useful resource for "formulating a modern, empirically responsible ethical model" (Slingerland 2011b, 97). Reber and Slingerland (2011) appeals to empirical findings in cognitive science to validate Confucius's pedagogy of internalizing social norms through intensive, lifelong practice. Bongrae Seok (2008) places Mencius's theory of four moral sprouts in the context of recent developments in cognitive science regarding humans' mental faculty as the foundations of morality. Flanagan and Williams (2010) compares and contrasts Mencius's four moral sprouts against Jonathan Haidt's five psychological modules for human morality and culture. By comparing classical Confucian ethical theories against modern scientific assertions about the human mind and human nature, we can give these ancient theories new meanings, thereby to understand why Confucianism has had such a wide-ranging, long-lasting impact on Asian culture. As Donald J. Munro points out, "Ethical principles must be consistent with human nature in order for people to find them compelling and motivating" (Munro 2002, 131). Part III of this book continues this direction to connect issues in neo-Confucianism with contemporary perspectives in psychology and moral philosophy.

More than 2,000 years ago, Hanfeizi already launched an attack on Confucius's moral ideals from the perspective of empirical evidence: "People within the four seas loved his doctrine of humanity and praised his doctrine of righteousness. And yet only 70 people became his devoted pupils. The reason is that few people value humanity and it is difficult to practice righteousness" (*The Hanfeizi*, Chapter 49, translated by Wing-tsit Chan, in Chan 1963, 258). Hanfeizi's point is that the majority of ordinary people would not act the way Confucius implored, and thus the Confucian ethical teaching does not have any empirical validity. In the contemporary ethical discourse, there are also criticisms of virtue ethics using empirical studies in social psychology and cognitive science as evidence. A great challenge to virtue ethics comes from situationism. John Doris in *Lack of Character* (2002) argues that changes in people's behavior are more due to situational factors than their character traits. Doris advocates situationism and argues that moral traits are situationally sensitive.

Doris characterizes virtue ethics in terms of globalism. Globalism is the view that personality is "an evaluatively integrated association of robust traits," traits that can help their possessors maintain stable and consistent behavioral patterns against situational pressures (Doris 2002, 23). Doris thinks that personality or characterological psychology presupposes globalism, and virtue ethicists are typically concerned with this kind of psychology in their emphasis on cultivating virtue. Personality psychology and characterological moral psychology appeal to people's character or personality traits in their explanation of human behavior. Such explanations, however popular among common folks, are empirically unfounded according to Doris. There are no global character traits, which empirical scientists can invoke as the explanatory basis for human's moral behavior. With case studies in social psychology, Doris shows that people routinely behave inconsistently across different situations, and a large contributing factor to their behavior is situational variables, many of which are morally trivial.

According to situationism, lack of good conduct in certain situations is not an indication of character flaws; at the same time, behaving morally in certain situations also does not manifest a superior moral personality. Virtue ethicists place their bet on cultivating robustly enduring virtues in moral agents, when in the end there is no such proof for the consistency or the stability of moral virtues; furthermore, there is no integration of character traits in moral agents. Situations trump character; therefore, virtue ethicists are misguided to seek the cultivation of moral character or robust moral traits. Doris thus recommends that we abandon the vain pursuit of cultivating virtue or moral character in ethical discourse, and turn our attention more toward situational factors. The goal of moral cultivation should be to foster morality-inducing situations, and the focus of one's ethical attention should be on avoiding situations that might induce morally questionable behavior. Since neo-Confucian moral theories fall into the category of virtue ethics, Doris's claim is a direct challenge to neo-Confucianism. Several chapters in Part III will address this challenge and examine how each neo-Confucian philosopher's proposal on cultivating moral virtue could meet the challenge of situationism.

In Chapter 8, we shall reconstruct Zhang Zai's moral philosophy in the context of moral personality development in cognitive science and developmental psychology. This chapter will explicate Zhang Zai's moral program in terms of the sociocognitive model of moral personality development, since the key elements in Zhang Zai's moral program match the key features of the socio-cognitive model. Zhang Zai's moral philosophy is a moral program that depicts moral development as progressive, primarily cognitive, and originating in autonomous volition. Individual agents must be self-regulating in choosing the right goals; they must learn from others through reading, discussion with friends, and emulating the highest moral exemplars—the sages. Their moral development is partly the result of proper social influences (such as schooling and societal rules of propriety), partly the realization of self-governance and self-regulation. This chapter addresses the question whether Zhang Zai's moral program would be threatened by Doris's situationism.

Chapter 9 introduces the virtue ethics of the Cheng brothers. Whereas Zhang Zai's moral philosophy can be analyzed in terms of the social-cognitive model, the moral theory of the Cheng brothers is closer to that of globalism, the claim that there are "robust" moral traits that one can sustain across situations. The Cheng brothers acknowledge that these moral traits need to be cultivated, and the aim of their moral teaching is to define the essential virtues that lay the foundation for a stable moral character. This chapter will investigate whether the Cheng brother's globalist virtue ethics could meet the challenge of moral skepticism about the existence of robust moral character. It will also investigate what the Cheng brothers mean by "true knowledge" in their form of virtue epistemology, and what they set up as the aim of knowledge as well as the satisfaction conditions for knowledge.

Chapter 10 is devoted to Zhu Xi's virtue ethics and analyzes it as a form of ethical rationalism. Zhu Xi highlights sagehood as the common moral goal for all moral agents, and he advocates that to reach sagehood, one must take an intellectual approach to understanding the principle inherent in one's own nature, the principles in the nature of external objects and affairs, and, finally, the universal moral principle represented as the principle of heaven. Zhu Xi's moral epistemology is the path from investigating particular principles to the holistic grasp of the universal moral principle inherent in all our handlings of particular things. To him, the natural states of particular things already contain normative imperatives for our appropriate interactions with particular things. In other words, the descriptive sense of the nature of a particular thing at the same time implies the prescriptive sense of our conduct with respect to this particular kind of things. This chapter analyzes how Zhu Xi combines the descriptive and the normative dimensions in his moral epistemology, thereby deriving *Ought* from *Is*.

Chapter 11 focuses on Wang Yangming's theory of *Liangzhi*, the innate faculty of pure knowing or moral consciousness. This chapter analyzes Wang Yangming's notion of *Liangzhi* as a form of higher-order perception (HOP). A higher-order perception is an "introspective consciousness" or "the inner perception of current states and activities in our own mind" (Armstrong 2004). Wang Yangming's teaching of *Liangzhi* stresses the mind's intuitive seeing right from wrong in one's own thinking. Our knowing right from wrong is a form of moral intuition, which is inherent in us at the start of our moral cultivation. At the same time, it is a form of self-monitoring and self-rectification, as the self is watching the self's every passing idea. This chapter introduces the phrase *moral reflexivism* for Wang Yangming's moral methodology. To Wang Yangming, the most important task is to convince others that they are already born as sages and they do not need to look elsewhere for moral inspiration. He advocates that everyone is endowed with this pure knowing faculty at birth. Only when one has embraced this philosophy can one achieve the moral/spiritual transformation that Wang Yangming aims to bring about in his audience. His moral program is built on the individual's faith and optimism in the self's capability. This chapter also analyzes Wang Yangming's theory of moral knowledge presented in his thesis of the unity of knowledge and action.

Chapter 12 concludes neo-Confucian moral theories with the socioethical program of moral cultivation developed by Wang Fuzhi. The main idea behind this program is that to construct a moral world, we cannot count on the moral agent's isolated moral conscience or moral sentiments. The conscience or moral sentiments have to be integrated into the whole society, so that moral conduct becomes the norm rather than the exception. The social atmosphere and group mentality can have an affective power on the individual's thinking and action. It is therefore crucial to establish a moral world if we want to enhance individual moral agents' moral resolve. This final chapter examines how Wang Fuzhi's theory, based on Mencius's ideas, leads to a realistic proposal for constructing a moral world. At the end, it goes beyond mere philosophical explication to suggest a socioethical program that can be developed out of Wang Fuzhi's ideas.

This final part of the book redefines neo-Confucian moral philosophies as various forms of virtue ethics, using different theoretical models in moral psychology and cognitive science as comparative schemata. When neo-Confucian virtue ethics is expected to be empirically responsible, its ultimate goal of attaining sagehood is placed in the reality of the psychology of ordinary people. Is it too idealistic? Is it portraying a utopian ethical goal that does not reflect human psychology and goes beyond what ordinary people could accomplish in their lifetime? Should ethicists aim to present theories that reflect what people are like (the *Is*) or to present the normative goals that transform people from what they are to what they ought to be (the *Ought*)? Should ethics be based on the ethicist's metaphysical conception of one's relation to the world? Is such a metaphysically oriented neo-Confucian ethics practicable or even credible with our contemporary mentality? These are all the questions that remain to be considered.

The Philosophers[9]

Zhou Dunyi 周敦頤

From miscellaneous sources, we gather the impression that Zhou Dunyi (1017–1073) was highly respected in his times. He founded a school in order to teach Confucianism to the youth, and local people all voluntarily contributed money or labor. He was someone with a high sense of integrity and a great sympathy for all living things. One time a harsh superior wanted to execute a prisoner who did not deserve the death penalty, and Zhou Dunyi argued vehemently for the prisoner's sake. When it was to no avail, Zhou wanted to resign from his post. His selfless decision changed the superior's mind and in the end, the prisoner's life was spared. Zhou Dunyi was also generous in helping others in need, and took it calmly even when there was not enough rice for his wife to cook.[10] Another famous anecdote told that Zhou Dunyi never cut weeds, because in his eyes weeds and grass were all in the same family, equally valuable (Zhou 1975, 352). He even enjoyed the sight of tall and unruly weeds outside the windows of his study, in that it was a sign of vitality (Chen 1990). Zhou Dunyi was known as someone with little material desire. The Cheng brothers said that from him, they learned to pursue the simple pleasures that delighted Confucius as well as his exemplary student Yan Hui (Zhou 1975, 351).[11] One of Zhou Dunyi's philosophical doctrines is "no desire." This doctrine has been likened to the Daoist teaching of the reduction of desire, or the Buddhist teaching of the elimination of desire. Whatever the inspiration was, Zhou Dunyi apparently lived up to his own standard.

---

9 A sorry miss in this book is the discussion on Shao Yong (1011–77), an early neo-Confucian contemporaneous with Zhou Dunyi. His sophisticated philosophy certainly deserves a thorough treatment in any book on neo-Confucianism, but it is beyond the author's current scope of research.
10 This is recorded in the biography of Zhou Dunyi, written by Zhu Xi (Zhou 1975, 400–402).
11 The story of Yan Hui, as recorded in the *Analects*, is that he was totally content in his poverty: while others could complain about not having fancy food to eat, Yan Hui would find sheer delight in the simplest food and the plainest drink.

Zhang Zai 張載

Zhang Zai (1020–1077) studied Buddhism and Daoism when he was young but was not intellectually satisfied with either of them. He later returned to the study of the Confucian classics and found his true calling as a scholar and a teacher. In his 30s, he lectured on the *Yijing* and his distant nephews Cheng Hao and Cheng Yi were in the audience. Thereafter the three of them began a lifelong scholarly exchange of philosophical ideas.

Zhang Zai passed the civic exam when he was already 36, and held various local official posts for 12 years. He had a brief fling with a political career in the imperial court, but did not have much success because he and his brother both openly criticized the policy of the prime minister at the time. He eventually resigned from his position and returned to his hometown Hengqu for retirement. He was thus known as Mr. Hengqu (橫渠). This was the period for his philosophical advancement since he led a reclusive life, and devoted all his energy to thinking, reading, and writing. Others described him as sitting alone in a room the whole day, with many bamboo books by his sides. He kept on reading and thinking, and if he had any thought, he immediately wrote them down. Sometimes he would even wake up in the middle of the night, lit a candle, and continued to work. He composed several commentaries on the classics, most notably was his commentary on the *Yijing*. During this time he also wrote his own philosophical masterpiece, *Correcting Youthful Ignorance* (*Zhengmeng*), which greatly influenced Wang Fuzhi three hundred years later. He died from illness at the age of 57, with no money left for burial. His former students had to rush to his side to take care of the funeral (Huang 1987).

Cheng Hao 程顥 **and Cheng Yi** 程頤

Cheng Hao (1032–1085) and Cheng Yi (1033–1107) were brothers separated by merely one year. Their writings had been collected together from the start as "The Posthumous Work of the Chengs" and many of their conversations or comments were grouped under "recorded conversations of two Cheng masters." Even though their philosophical ideas were similar and their discourses were often recorded without specific reference to the source, one could still discern subtle differences in the two brothers' philosophical interests that had profound impact. From the two Cheng brothers emerged two different directions of neo-Confucian thought. Cheng Hao, alias Mr. Mingdao (明道), influenced the ideas of Lu Xiangshan and Wang Yangming, whose philosophy has been called "the School of Mind" (*xinxue* 心學). Cheng Yi, alias Mr. Yichuan (伊川), on the other hand, was later promoted by Zhu Xi (1130–1200) to become the founder of "the School of Principle" (*lixue* 理學) or "the School of Nature" (*xingxue* 性學). Both of them studied with Zhou Dunyi for one year when they were teenagers, and they were related to Zhang Zai as distant nephews. In their discourses, they made frequent reference to Zhang Zai's ideas and his work; in particular, the latter's "Western Inscription." Both of them corresponded with Zhang Zai on philosophical ideas. The two brothers continued Zhou Dunyi and Zhang Zai's revival of Confucianism, and further enriched the philosophy with many topics and concepts that later became the defining themes of neo-Confucianism. Therefore, we can say that what we now call "Song-Ming Neo-Confucianism" really emerged with them. According to renowned historian Feng Youlan, the real establishment of neo-Confucianism as an organized school really began with the Cheng brothers (Feng 1983, 498).

Under Zhou Dunyi's influence, Cheng Hao aspired to become an intellectual at a young age, and devoted his time to studying the Confucian classics. He passed the civic exam at the age of 26, and had various assignments as the local governor. He was known as a benevolent and fair official, winning the love and respect of the people under his governance. He always had the motto "regarding the people as if they were wounded" by his seat to remind himself to be tender and caring with them. One of Cheng Hao's most notable accomplishments was education of people in the city of Jincheng (晉城). He was assigned the post of magistrate in Jincheng, which was backward and full of illiterate citizens at that time. For hundreds of years, no one in that town had ever succeeded in passing the civic exams to earn an official post. Cheng Hao gathered the most intelligent youths and founded an academy to educate them. He provided them with lodging and food as well as school supplies, and gave them intensive education. In 10 years, hundreds of people passed the civic exams and more than 10 people received governmental positions. After Cheng Hao had left the post, the people of Jincheng still credited him for the transformation of their culture. Even to this day, there are many historical remains associated with Cheng Hao. The city of Jincheng is currently rebuilding Cheng Hao's Mingdao Academy.

Cheng Hao died of an illness at the age of 54, whereas his younger brother by one year Cheng Yi lived to his 70s and spent most of his adult life in teaching. Hence, the latter had a lot more discourse recorded by his students. Unlike his brother Cheng Hao, Cheng Yi turned down many offers for government posts, and even once remarked "I would only consider the offer when I am too starved to even get out of the house one day" (Li 1986, 49). The only post that he would be willing to accept later was to be the mentor to the young emperor. In contrast to Cheng Hao's easy-going and amiable personality, Cheng Yi was allegedly a stern and serious person. Even with the young emperor, he would not relax his austere mannerism. His students regarded him with awe and reverence. Once when two new students went to visit him for the first time, he had a conversation with them and then closed his eyes to meditate. Without knowing whether the interview was over, the two men stood by his sides and did not dare to stir him up. When he eventually opened his eyes a long while later, he found them still standing there and sent them home. They came out to find that the snow outside had already accumulated one foot high. These two students later became famous followers of Cheng Yi and developed their philosophical views under his instruction. This incident became a famous story and there is even a Chinese phrase, "standing in the snow within the Cheng Gate" (*chengmen lixue* 程門立雪), coined after this event to depict a student's utmost respect and earnest attitude toward the teacher (Li 1986, 52).

Zhu Xi 朱熹

If it were not for Zhu Xi (1130–1200), there probably would not have been neo-Confucianism. His contribution to neo-Confucianism was not only his promotion of the philosophical ideas of Zhou Dunyi, Zhang Zai and the Cheng brothers but also the establishment of his own systematic philosophy. His coedited anthology of these early neo-Confucians' writings and remarks, *Reflections on Things at Hand* (*Jinsilu* 近思錄, translated into English by Chan Wing-tsit, see Chan 1967), is an essential primer for anyone wishing to study neo-Confucianism.

Zhu Xi was an astute student since early childhood. When he was four, his father pointed to the sky and taught him "heaven." He immediately asked: "What is it above heaven then?" which impressed his father greatly (Chan 1990, 1). In his youth, Zhu Xi was more interested in Buddhism and Daoism, but gradually came to the realization that the society's religious fascination with searching for the Buddha or with the Daoist pursuit of immortality had led the nation to a tattered state. At the age of 30 he went to see his father's former classmate, a Confucian master Li Tong, and stayed for several months to learn from him. Li Tong's instruction convinced him that Confucianism has a more profound teaching and a sounder social effect. He henceforth abandoned Buddhism and devoted himself to the revival of classic Confucianism.

Zhu Xi passed the prestigious civic exam at the young age of 19, and began a long series of official positions. His main interest was in teaching and writing, however. In 1178, with the emperor's support, he renovated an old and deserted academy named the White Deer Cave (*bailudong*) Academy and turned it into a thriving academy for scholars. He was in charge of the academy and invited guest speakers, enriched its library, and set up a systematic education. The structure of this academy would later become the model for other academies in China in the next seven hundred years. The academy, located in Jiangxi province, China, with a monument for Zhu Xi inside, is now a national cultural treasure. Zhu Xi was also responsible for selecting two chapters from the *Book of Rites* (*Liji*), that is, the "Doctrine of the Mean" and the "Great Learning," to list them together with *the Analects* and *the Mengzi*, as the *Four Books* (*Sishu*). His commentary on the Four Classics became the standard texts for the civic exams in the next few hundreds of years, until the exam system was abolished in 1905. His influence in the Chinese intellectual as well as political history was insurmountable.

In his old age, however, Zhu Xi was caught in a political rivalry between two high officials, and he supported the prime minister who was framed and exiled. In retaliation, the succeeding prime minister accused Zhu Xi of preaching falsehood, and launched a six-year political persecution targeting him and his followers. Some of his students were exiled and some imprisoned. In 1200, Zhu Xi had lost his eyesight in the left eye and the right eye was also almost blind, but he worked even harder to organize his previous writings to complete them before he died. He passed away at the age of 71, and even with the official ban against people attending his funeral, there were still over one thousand attendees.

Lu Xiangshan 陸象山

Lu Xiangshan (1139–1193) was born as Lu Jiuyuan 陸九淵, but was later more generally known as Mr. Xiangshan because he taught at Xiangshan Academy for some time and left a profound influence on the scholars who studied with him. Similar to Zhu Xi, he was also a child prodigy in philosophical thinking. When he was merely three or four, he asked his father: Where do heaven and earth end? His father smiled but did not answer. He pondered on this question to the point of losing sleep and forgetting to eat. In his early teens, when he read the annotation in an ancient book about the meaning of the Chinese word for the universe, *yuzou* (宇宙), which denotes both space and time, he suddenly came to the realization and declared: The universe's affairs are all my own affairs; my own affairs are the affairs of the universe. From this point on, he developed his own philosophical system that took a different direction from that of Cheng Yi and Zhu Xi, known as the Cheng–Zhu school. Three hundred years later, Wang Yangming would be so inspired by his ideas that a rival school of the Cheng–Zhu school emerged: the Lu–Wang school. The former advocated that principle is inherent in human nature, while the latter pronounced that the entire universe is in our mind and principle is in the mind. In Chinese intellectual history, the former is called the School of Nature (*xing xue*) and the latter is called the School of Mind (*xin xue*).

After passing the civic exam at the age of 34, Lu Xiangshan held several governmental positions in addition to teaching at Xiangshan Academy for four years. On his last post, he was well loved and respected by the local people for his benevolent governance and his grand achievement in eliminating theft and robbery. Unfortunately, he contracted some illness and died one year later. For his burial, thousands of people crowded the streets and alleys just to pay their final tribute to him. He did not produce much philosophical writing, and did not care for writing commentary on the classics. His proud statement was: "The Six Classics are merely footnotes to me!" (Lao 1980, 408).

Wang Yangming 王陽明

"Wang Yangming" is the alias of Wang Shouren 王守仁 (1472–1529), who was commonly known as Mr. Yangming on account of the nickname he adopted when he was sent to exile and lived in the Yangming Grotto in Guizhou province for three years. The grotto is now one of China's nationally protected cultural relics.

When Wang Yangming was little, he did not begin to talk until the age of five. But as soon as he talked, he recited a book that his grandfather used to read to him. He came from a scholarly lineage and received excellent education from his grandfather before the age of ten. He went with his father to Beijing when he was 11 and traveled with the latter to many remote regions outside China's boarders. As a young man, he loved riding horses and archery and did not do well with the government's civic exams. In 1499, at the age of 28, he finally passed the exam and earned the qualifications to enter into politics. His political career was turbulent, however. The emperor at the time had a favorite court eunuch, who managed to have the emperor cane and dismiss the senior officials who tried to persuade the emperor to get rid of this eunuch. Wang Yangming saw the injustice in this and presented a remonstrative letter to the emperor. Both the emperor and the eunuch were infuriated by his audacity. As a result, Wang Yangming was publicly caned 40 times at the imperial court, and then sent away to exile in Guizhou, where he resided in his namesake, the Yangming Grotto. The grotto was located in a remote mountain far away from the populace. It was damp and unsuitable for living, and his health deteriorated. The locals took pity on him and volunteered to build a simple wooden house outside the grotto. To amuse himself and also to lift his morale, Wang Yangming nicknamed himself "Yangming," and christened this house "What Uncouthness Cabin" (*helouxuan* 何陋軒) derived from the Analects: "If the gentleman were to reside there, what uncouthness would there be?" (the *Analects* 9:14).

Three years later, after the eunuch was executed as the result of another political clash, Wang Yangming was again called back to the imperial court and offered various positions. His military talents were soon recognized and appreciated by a high official, and he was sent to quell the rebels who were starting a revolution in the South. He captured the ringleader alive, but the officials by the emperor's side suggested that he let the ringleader go, so that the emperor could again capture him to earn the credit for ending the unrest. Wang Yangming thought that this would only lead to unnecessary bloodshed, and decided to give up his political career. He returned home on the false pretense of being ill.

After the next emperor took the throne in 1521, Wang Yangming was again offered governmental positions, but the new emperor found him to be insolent and arrogant. In 1527, he was called upon to quell several other revolts that were getting out of control, and despite his success, he did not gain the emperor's appreciation. The long travels in his military service also ruined his health, so he delivered his resignation and returned home without waiting for the emperor's approval. All his titles were nearly stripped because of this defiant act. Nevertheless, the local people all worshiped him. He died on the way back home, and when his hearse traveled to the province of his home state, soldiers and townsfolk all lined up the roadsides in tears. It was recorded that at his deathbed, an accompanying student asked if he had any last words. His reply was: "The mind is totally luminous and bright. What is the need to say anything more?" (Ching 1987, 2).

Wang Yangming was disillusioned with Zhu Xi's teaching after he jeopardized his health from following the latter's teaching to investigate the principle in external things. He spent day and night trying to study the bamboo trees, and on the seventh day he became seriously ill (Chan 1963, 249). From this experience, he concluded that to seek the "principle of Heaven," we do not need to look outside of our own mind. Inspired by Lu Xiangshan's teaching, he founded the school of mind. He wrote a poem describing his intellectual awakening:

> Everyone has within an unerring compass;
> The root and source of the myriad transformations lies in the mind.
> I laugh when I think that, earlier, I saw things the other way around;
> Following branches and leaves, I searched outside!
> (Ivanhoe 2009, 181. Cited in van Norden 2014)

After neo-Confucianism spread to other parts of Asia, Yangming studies in Japan were equally fervent as Zhu Xi studies were in Korea. According to Robert C. Neville, Wang Yangming's influence in East Asia is roughly comparable to Descartes's influence in the West (Neville 1983, 703).

Wang Fuzhi 王夫之

Wang Fuzhi (1619–1692) (alias "Chuanshan 船山") was the most prolific philosopher in Chinese history. The *Complete Posthumous Works of Chuanshan* (*chuanshan yishu quanji*) includes 21 volumes of his own writings, and this is not even his whole work since some were destroyed or lost during the turmoil of his life. He wrote extensive commentary on the Four Books and the Five Classics, and these commentaries contain his highly sophisticated metaphysics, epistemology, and moral philosophy. He gave detailed analysis of historical trends and events, and developed an innovative philosophy of history. He presented his perspective on Chinese politics and his patriotism in a small book *On Yellow Emperor* (*huang shu*), which inspired many Chinese intellectuals after his times. He also delivered his views on two major Daoist works, the *Daodejing* and the *Zhuangzi*, in several complete commentaries. His aesthetics is represented in his commentary of ancient poems and poems of the Tang dynasty as well as of the Song dynasty. In addition, he was an inspired author of voluminous fine poetry, which also exemplifies his aesthetic view.

Wang Fuzhi was born at the end of the Ming dynasty (1368–1644), in the midst of political upheaval when the royal family of Ming no longer could sustain its political power and national security. His father was a learned scholar, so he grew up in a highly intellectual environment. At the age of seven, Wang Fuzhi had completed reading all 13 classics. When he was 25, some local lord kidnaped his father and demanded his service in exchange for his father's life. Wang maimed himself badly and had others carried him to the bandits. The bandits had no way but to let both the father and the son go. The following year, the Manchus invaded China and established a new dynasty (the Qing dynasty, 1644–1911). The Ming royalties fled to the south and established a new government. Upon reflection on how the previous neo-Confucianism in the Ming dynasty (in particular, Wang Yangming's school of mind that focuses on meditation and thinking) has brought about the dynasty's cultural as well as political downfall, Wang Fuzhi began his writing career to renew what he took to be the true spirit of Confucianism.

The next few years brought constant struggles between the rump Ming government and the new powerful Manchu government. Wang initially participated in the resistance movement along with his father, uncle and two brothers, but all of them died in the battlefield. He then formed numerous resistance troops with fellow idealists, but kept losing his associates through defeats in wars. When he was serving the Ming emperor in the South, he was nearly imprisoned for speaking up against political factionalism. This experience angered him so much that he spit up blood. Wang Fuzhi eventually concluded that it would be a futile task to restore the Ming royalty. In 1661, the last emperor of the Ming dynasty was caught and the Manchus took control over the whole China. Refusing to collaborate and to avoid being constantly solicited by local authorities for his service, Wang Fuzhi escaped to remote mountains and fled from one place to another. He eventually settled down in a hut at the foot of a barren mountain that he named "Chuanshan 船山" (literally "boat mountain," named after a huge boulder in the shape of a boat on this mountain). Wang Fuzhi stayed here for the remainder of his life, and hence took up the alias "Wang Chuanshan." He chose this place because he felt ashamed to be under a foreign rule and yet could not find any way out of this predicament. In his *Memoir of Chuanshan* (*chuanshanji*), he wrote:

> People of the past could choose wherever they wanted to travel and find the best place to settle down. I, on the other hand, cannot find a single inch of the land under heaven to suit my sorrowful mood. … Those who

can look up the sky with no regret, and look down at the ground with no sorrow, should have beautiful landscape for their abodes. For me, however, even if thorny bushes surrounded my lodging and thick frost covered the land, the place I live would still be beyond my share. ... In the morning of springtime or the dusk of fall, I only wanted to seal my windows with mud and close myself in. What is there any point in choosing anywhere else? ... This is why Chuanshan (the Boat Mountain) is my mountain. It has nothing to keep its name spread afar and nothing to be passed down to future generations. When I am old and gone, the Boat Mountain will simply return to its standing as a barren mountain. ... This is where I will spend the rest of life until I die.[12]

Wang Fuzhi died at the age of 74. He devoted more than 40 years to writing and completed more than 100 books, the manuscripts of which were collected and organized by his son 14 years after his death. It was not until 1842 that his complete works were put into print. Some of his works were thus lost forever.

It is no exaggeration to claim that among neo-Confucians, Wang Fuzhi had the most sophisticated system of philosophy. His contribution to Confucianism was that he went back to classical Confucianism to revive its true spirit. His philosophy incorporated the quintessence of the *Yijing* and the other Five Classics as well as the doctrines of the Analects and Mencius. His personal credo was "The Six Classics make it incumbent upon me to break a new path and present a new facet," and he devoted most of his mature life to the reconstruction of these classics. With his reconstruction, he brought the discourse of Confucianism to a new height. In a contemporary scholar Yun Chen's words: "Wang Chuanshan extended human cultivation of the self to human acts of reforming the world; and reintroduced the topics of the nature and culture into the Confucian ontology. Confucianism was truly released from the study of the internal nature and mind. Only at this juncture did the holistic lifeworld (*lebenswelt*), as well as a cultural creation in the broad sense, obtain an ontological legitimacy" (Chen 2002, 225).

This introduction will end with a poem written by Wang Fuzhi, as it depicts well the neo-Confucian spirit in their tumultuous lives:

> Wherein lies our life?
> It is being manipulated by the cruel fate
> into multiple shapes,

---

12 This beautiful prose is in the *Complete Collected Works of Wang Fuzhi*. It was once selected into standard Chinese textbooks for high school students in Taiwan. On a personal note, this short piece was what inspired me to pursue philosophy at the tender age of 15. The complete prose can be found online: http://www.zhchsh.net/a/chuanshanguli/chuanshanzhuanti/2012/0905/8114.html

Even if one puts up all the struggles,
one cannot fight with fate.
Who'd have the extra heart
to be sentimental about it?
After pondering over life hundreds of times,
I decide to just hand it over to the wind
for the creation of the music of heaven.
After all wars are over;
after all chess games are finished,
Who still sets the boundaries?

Let us be the faint trace of smoke,
drifting through the clear blue sky;
Let us be the light wings of butterflies,
fluttering by the silent flowers.
Let us laugh about how thousands of years,
would turn into oblivion in a split second.
Let us be a tiny dove,
or be a giant roc,
in concord with chance.
Looking back at the countryside,
I see the exuberant sea of spring.
Facing toward the human world,
I roam about freely,
Through hardships, through adversity,
I will not change my Way.
　　　　　　　＿＿＿＿ Wang Fu-chih (1619–1692)

Part I

Neo-Confucian Metaphysics:
From Cosmology to Ontology

1

From Nothingness to Infinity: The Origin of Zhou Dunyi's Cosmology

Introduction

Zhou Dunyi (1017–1073 AD) has been generally regarded as the pioneer of neo-Confucianism, even though some scholars argue that what he teaches is not pure Confucianism. Zhou himself absorbed teachings of Daoism and Buddhism to some extent, and he, unlike other neo-Confucianists, did not severely criticize those two schools' doctrines. Some of his philosophical notions can be traced back to either a Daoist or a Buddhist origin. However, the strongest philosophical heritage in Zhou's work is that of the *Book of Changes* (the *Yijing*) and the "Doctrine of the Mean," both constitutive of core Confucianism. Furthermore, the cosmological explanation that Zhou offered would later become the dominant thesis of the Cheng–Zhu school (see Chapter 3). The Cheng brothers (Cheng Hao and Cheng Yi) studied under him for about one year in their teens. Even though the mentorship was short, it left an ineradicable impact on the two brothers' minds that they decided to pursue scholarship instead of politics. Zhu Xi, as the philosophical descendent of the Cheng brothers, would later become the most fervent defender of Zhou Dunyi's philosophy. He argued that Zhou's thought was truly representative of Confucianism. One might say that it was largely through Zhu Xi's exposition and elaboration that Zhou Dunyi's philosophy acquired the status that it had in neo-Confucianism.

There are only two short philosophical texts by Zhou Dunyi: *The Exposition of the Taiji Diagram* 太極圖說[1] and *Penetrating the Book* (of

---

1 Wing-tsit Chan (in the *Sourcebook*) translates this book as "An Explanation of the Diagram of the Great Ultimate"; Derek Bodde (Fung's *History of Chinese Philosophy*) translates it as "Diagram of the Supreme Ultimate Explained"; Joseph. Adler (in de Bary and Bloom 1999) translates it as "Explanation of the Diagram of the Supreme Polarity." Here I choose to keep the term *taiji* since all translations would carry extra connotation.

Neo-Confucianism: Metaphysics, Mind, and Morality, First Edition. JeeLoo Liu.
© 2018 John Wiley & Sons, Inc. Published 2018 by John Wiley & Sons, Inc.

Changes) 通書.² In the former, Zhou explicates the cosmic origin, the cosmic order and the cosmic constitution. He calls the cosmic origin *wuji* (無極) (the controversy surrounding this term will be explained later). The cosmic order is given as a generation process from *Taiji* (the Supreme Ultimate)³ to the cosmic energy *yin* and *yang*, to the five elements (water, fire, wood, metal, and earth), and finally to the formation of the myriad creatures of the world. The cosmic constitution can be reduced to two principles: the principle of male and the principle of female, represented by the cosmic energy of *yang* and the cosmic energy of *yin*, respectively. Zhou Dunyi only offered this brief cosmological narrative in his entire work, but it became a core thesis in neo-Confucianism. Since this cosmological narrative was given in terse phrases without much explanation, it has stirred up widely different interpretations. The key term here is *wuji*, which did not appear in any ancient Confucian text. It was first seen in the *Daodejing*: "He will never deviate from eternal virtue, but returns to the state of the Ultimate of Non-being (*Wuji*)" (Chapter 28; Chan 1963, 154). Many scholars of Chinese intellectual history have worked as historical Sherlock Holmes in their investigation of the speculated origin of Zhou's *Taiji* diagram. The focus was on whether Zhou Dunyi got the *Taiji* diagram from a Daoist's inspiration. Many philosophers have also debated on the connotations of the notion of *wuji*—on whether it is related to Laozi's notion of *wu* 無 (nothingness). Neo-Confucians had a strong distaste for the Daoist's discourse on *wu*. The fundamental tenet of neo-Confucianism is realism: the world as we know it is real and it exists independently of our conceptions and perceptions. The unease neo-Confucians had was on whether Zhou Dunyi's discourse on *wuji* would lead to the Daoist rejection of the robust independent reality of the phenomenal world.

The controversy over the meaning of this notion is even preserved among contemporary English translations of the text. *Wuji* has been translated as "the Ultimateless" (Feng 1983; Derk Bodde's translation), "the Ultimate of Nonbeing" (Chan 1963; Neville 1980), "Non-polar" (Joseph A. Adler's translation, in de Bary *et al.* 1999), and "ultimate void" (R. Wang 2005). All these various translations reflect the difficulty in deciphering Zhou's idea of *wuji*. Without understanding what the term means, however, we cannot possibly understand Zhou Dunyi's cosmology. The first section of this chapter will explain the historical controversies on the interpretation of this concept. The second section

---

2 Wing-tsit Chan translates this book as *Penetrating the Book of Changes*; Derek Bodde translates it as *The Explanatory Text*; Joseph A. Adler translates it as *Penetrating the Classics of Changes*. Here I follow Chan's and Alder's translation.

3 In accordance with traditional usage, when the term *taiji* depicts *the* ultimate cosmic state, it is capitalized in this book. When it is used as an adjective or to refer to the term itself, then it remains small letters. The same applies to other special terms such as *wuji*, *dao*, principle, and so on.

will introduce the philosophical debate on being (*you*) and nothingness (*wu*) prior to Zhou's times, to see whether his *wuji* notion is related to the notion of *wu*. The final section will give a different interpretation of Zhou's notion of *wuji*, and further develops his cosmological view. To serve as the entry to neo-Confucianism, this chapter will trace the historical lineage of the founding ideas of Zhou Dunyi.

Historical Controversies over *Wuji*

The opening line of *The Exposition of the Taiji Diagram* "Wuji er Taiji"[4] has received the most critical examination by later scholars. Its interpretation and philosophical implications can be seen as one of the major topics of neo-Confucianism. Zhu Xi and Lu Xiangshan had a heated debate over what the term *wuji* could mean in this context, and whether Zhou Dunyi, on account of using this term, ultimately deviated from true Confucian teaching. The debate initially began with letter exchanges between Zhu Xi and Lu's older brother Lu Suosan. Lu Suosan argued that the term *wuji* came from Laozi, and it did not appear in any classic Confucian text.[5] He further argued that Zhou Dunyi only mentioned *wuji* in this work, whereas in Zhou's later and more mature work *Penetrating the Book* (of Changes), the notion was never once discussed. This shows either that this opening line was not written by Zhou himself but was interpolated by someone else, or that Zhou had later rejected the cosmic origin theory depicted in this opening line. Lu Xiangshan picked up the argument from where his brother left off and argued that the word *ji* (極) signifies the mean or center (*zhong* 中) and the term *taiji* simply denotes the Supreme Mean. On the other hand, the term *wuji* means "without the mean (center)" or "without Taiji." *Taiji* is the totality of things in the universe; therefore, "without Taiji" designates a cosmic state of nothingness.[6] Lu Xiangshan also argued that the Chinese conjunctive term between the two terms *wuji* and *taiji*, *er* (而), is not merely to be interpreted as a conjunctive relation: "and also"; rather, it is to be seen as depicting a logical or even temporal order: "and then." He thinks that the first line of *the Exposition* should be understood as "Without-Taiji and then Taiji." Lu Xiangshan argues that this idea is clearly derived from Chapter 40 of

---

4 The transitional word "er" here also allows for different interpretations: "and," "and then," "and also," "and yet," and so on. How to choose the exact translation for this word would depend on the interpreter's understanding of the connection between the two concepts *wuji* and *taiji*.
5 This is a mistaken view, since Xunzi uses it in multiple contexts. The term in *Xunzi*'s usage is synonymous with *wuqiong* (無窮) and both mean "endless, boundless." It is true, however, that in Xunzi's usage the term does not seem to have much philosophical import.
6 Lu Xiangshan's letter to Zhu Xi, No. 1, recorded in Huang Zongxi 1975, Volume 4: 111–12.

the *Daodejing*: "All things in the world come from being. And being comes from [nothingness]"[7] (Chan 1963, 160). Lu thought that in this respect Zhou Dunyi's cosmic view ultimately takes from Laozi's cosmogony: Nothingness is the beginning of the universe; Being comes from Nonbeing. Zhu Xi, on the other hand, argued that the term *wuji* simply depicts the nature of the totality of the cosmos, *Taiji*, as being without limitation, and therefore it does not designate a separate cosmic state of nothingness or Nonbeing. Zhu Xi pointed out that in the development of Confucianism, there were many notions that were introduced by later Confucians. Even the term *Taiji* itself did not appear in earliest texts of the *Yijing* but was introduced into the *Yijing* by Confucius.[8] According to Zhu Xi, Zhou Dunyi amended this cosmic philosophy with a new and alien notion *wuji*. Philosophically, there is no evidence that he has violated true Confucianism by the introduction of this notion. Furthermore, the Chinese word "ji 極" simply means "ultimate," not "the mean" as the Lu bothers had claimed. The Chinese word "wu" in this context cannot be understood as a noun designating a particular object. The structure of *wuji* is similar to other Chinese terms such as "*wuqiong* 無窮" (that which cannot be exhausted).[9] All these terms signify the limitation of language; they point to what our words cannot describe. In this kind of terminological structure, the Chinese word "wu" does not stand for "nothingness." Therefore, Zhu Xi argues, Zhou Dunyi's *wuji* should be understood as a depiction of something that is so grand, so ultimate, that we cannot confine it with our descriptions. This state is exactly the state of Taiji, that which is so grand and so supremely ultimate. Therefore, according to Zhu Xi, *wuji* and *taiji* are simply two names of the same state; they stand for two sides of the same coin.[10]

The exchanges between Zhu Xi and the Lu brothers culminated in the famous Goose Lake Debate (*erhu zhihui* 鵝湖之會) in 1175. It evolved into a debate between the two schools on the methodologies of attaining sagehood—Zhu's school emphasized empirical investigation and studying books written by the sages, while Lu's school focused on internal reflection and self-cultivation. The former accused the latter as groundless, while the latter

---

7 Wing-tsit Chan translates *wu* as *nonbeing*, whereas in this chapter we are using *nothingness* to render *wu*.
8 This is Zhu Xi's view. Contemporary scholars have generally placed the authorship of the *Commentary on Yi* in a timeframe much later than that of Confucius.
9 Even though Zhu Xi himself did not give other examples, we can list them here: *wu-liang* (無量) (that which cannot be quantified); *wu-jin* (無盡) (that which cannot be terminated), *wu-bi* (無比) (that which cannot be compared to), *wu-zhi* (無止) (that which cannot be finished), *wu-shang* (無上) (that which cannot be topped); *wu-shu* (無數) (that which cannot be counted; countless), and so on.
10 These arguments were presented in multiple letters Zhu Xi wrote toLu Xiangshan, recorded in Huang Zongxi 1975, Volume 4:112–19.

criticized the former as being scattered and paying too much attention to trivialities. The open debate lasted three days and continued through correspondences. The Goose Lake Debate was a major event in the history of neo-Confucianism, and the trigger for the whole debate was on the interpretation and placement of Zhou Dunyi's idea of *wuji*. We can see why there is a need to further analyze this notion in Zhou's philosophy.

The Exposition of the Taiji Diagram is an accompanying piece of the *Taiji* diagram (see Figure 1.1). Historians also questioned the source of this diagram. The first controversy was stirred up by a Confucian scholar Zhu Zhen 朱震 (ca.1072–1138), born around the time of Zhou's death. Zhu Zhen was an expert on the *Yijing*, and studied Chen Yi's commentary on the *Yijing* in depth. In his preface to his Commentary on the *Yijing* (hanshangyizhuan 漢上易傳), he traced the lineage of Zhou Dunyi's *Taiji* diagram to Chen Tuan 陳摶 (871–989), an enigmatic hermit two hundred years before Zhou's time. Chen Tuan allegedly had a diagram named "The Wuji Diagram" (see Figure 1.2), which again was derived from an earlier diagram contained in the Daoist Canon (*Daozang* 道藏).[11] According to a historian in the Qing dynasty, Huang Zongyan 黃宗炎 (1616–1686), Zhou Dunyi's *Taiji* diagram is almost exactly like Chen Tuan's *wuji* diagram, except that the former's flow chart proceeds from top to bottom, while the latter's flow chart proceeds from bottom to top. Huang Zongyan claims that Chen Tuan's *wuji* diagram is a diagram of the Daoist's method of alchemy.[12] It gives instructions on how to refine one's energy and spirit to cultivate an internal force, and the final stage of attainment is the state of vacuity and emptiness. Huang alleged that Chen Tuan carved this diagram on Mount Hua. He also endorsed Zhu Zhen's explanation of the lineage of this diagram and claimed that Zhou Dunyi received this diagram from Mu Xiu 穆修 (979–1032), whose academic lineage can be traced back to Chen Tuan. He thinks that what Zhou did was to reverse the order and use it to explicate the *Yijing*. In Huang's assessment, Zhou's theory was a confused conglomeration of Daoist alchemy, Laozi's theory and the *Yijing*'s terminology. By using this diagram, Zhou was seriously distorting the original teaching in the *Yijing* (Huang 1995, 1187–92). Huang's harsh criticism was later echoed and further defended by his son Huang Baijia 黃百家 (1643–1709). Mao Qiling 毛奇齡 (1623–1716) argues that not only did Zhou's diagram come from the Daoist, but his philosophical ideas also came from Buddhism. Zhu

---

11 Feng Youlan says that the author of the earlier Daoist diagram in the *Daoist Canon* was unknown, but the diagram could be dated to 712–755 AD (Feng 1983, 438).
12 In the Daoist tradition, there are two kinds of alchemy: external alchemy and internal alchemy. The former aims to refine herbs to find the elixir of life; the latter aims to cultivate one's internal energy to achieve concentrated and balanced force field. Chen Tuan's method is supposedly of the internal kind.

36 | From Nothingness to Infinity: The Origin of Zhou Dunyi's Cosmology

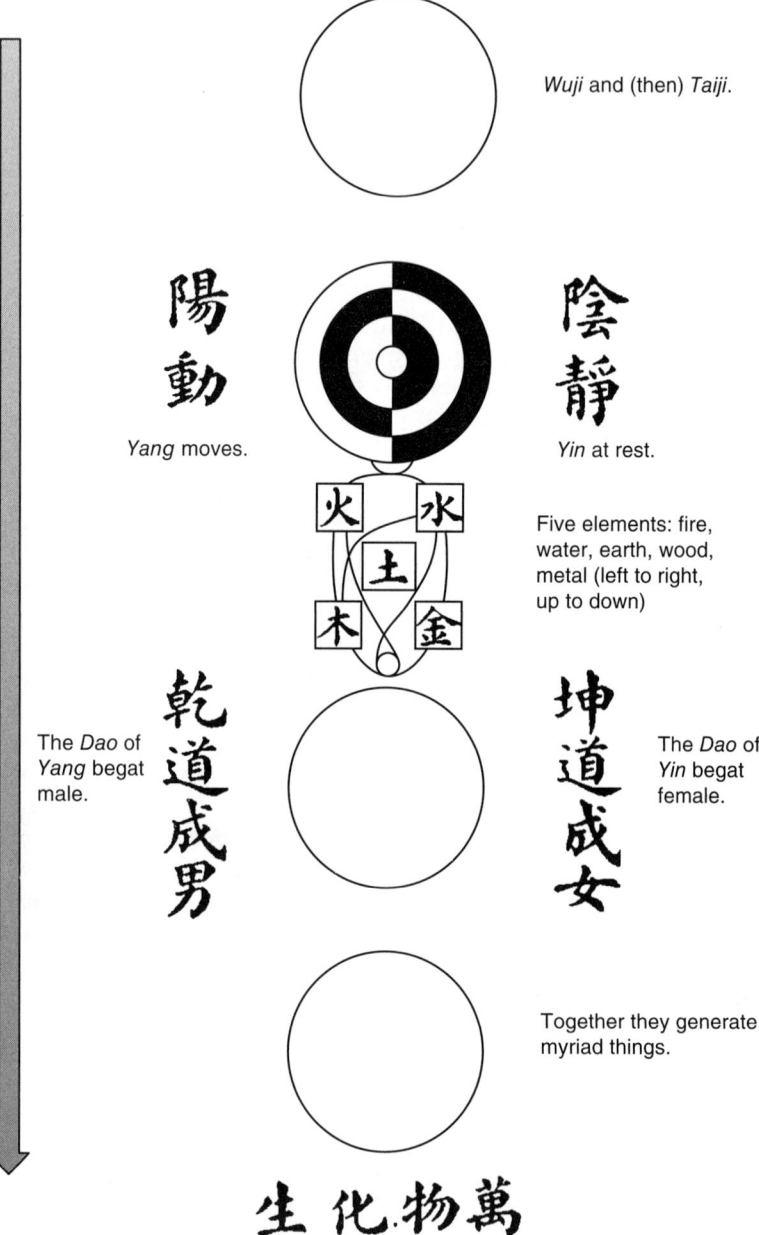

Figure 1.1 Zhou Dunyi's *Taiji* Diagram

Historical Controversies over Wuji

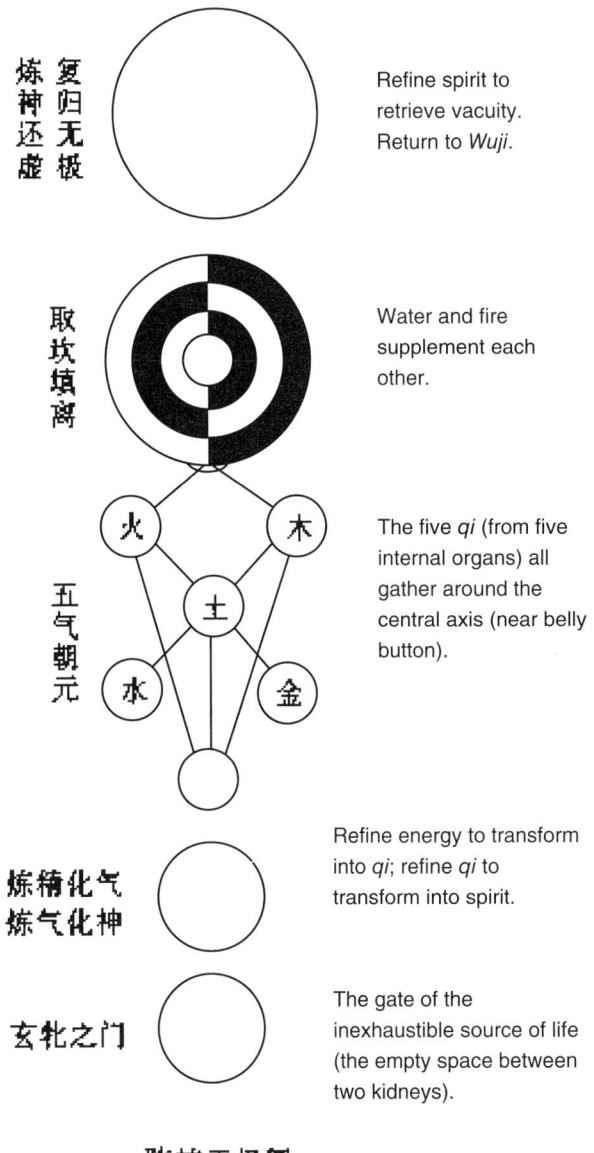

Figure 1.2 Chen Tuan's *Wuji* Diagram

Yizun 朱彝尊 (1629–1709) argues that the origin of *Wuji* diagram could be traced even beyond Chen Tuan, to an early Daoist Heshanggong 河上公.[13] All these historians discredited Zhou Dunyi's Confucian spirit. Through history, it has become a widely held view today that Zhou Dunyi was heavily influenced by the Daoist philosophy, and his notion of *wuji* was chiefly a Daoist idea (Wang 2005; Chen 1990; Lao 1980; Chan 1963, among others).

However, some contemporary scholars began to challenge this view. The most comprehensive analysis and compelling arguments came from Shen Li (2001). According to Li, there was never any historical record of Chen Tuan's carving the *Wuji* diagram on Mount Hua, and no one in history ever recounted seeing this diagram. The first reference of it actually came from Huang Zongyan himself, six hundred years after Zhou's time. It is thus quite a suspicious account (Li 2001, 37). He thinks that the *Wuji* diagram actually came after Zhou Dunyi's *Taiji* diagram and was some later Daoists' concoction based on Zhou's diagram (Li 2001, 54–64). Li further argues that even if Zhou did receive his academic training from Chen Tuan's school (which is already problematic according to Li, because Zhou was only 15 at the time of Mu Xiu's death), this does not mean that Zhou's philosophy must be merely that of his teachers (Li 2001, 16). Yu Guo (2003, 2001, 2000) shares the same view. These two scholars' detailed analyses provide compelling reasons to reject the historical attribution of the source of Zhou's *Taiji* diagram to Chen Tuan. We should therefore not take it for granted that Zhou Dunyi's philosophy is of a Daoist spirit simply because of his usage of the term *wuji* and his *Taiji* diagram.

In the next two sections, we will trace the notions of *wu* and *wuji* to their historical sources to analyze their possible connotations. We will conclude that these two notions, though connected, are not used to express the same philosophical idea. This philosophical analysis will give us an insight on Zhou Dunyi's philosophical interest and his contribution to the new discourse of neo-Confucianism.

Being (*You* 有) and Nothingness (*Wu* 無)

An identifying distinction between Confucianism and Daoism is that the former advocates "being" (*you* 有), while the latter promotes "nothingness" (*wu* 無) as the foundation of all things. There is no consensus among scholars on how to translate the Chinese words *you* and *wu*. A. C. Graham translates

---

13 This is in Zhu Yizun's "Investigation of the lineage of *Taiji* Diagram (*taijitu shoushou kao* 太極圖授受考)." *Heshanggong* is not a true name, but the name of the alleged author of a commentary on the *Daodejing*. We do not know the author's real name or his background. He might be around the Warring States period. He wrote the first commentary on the *Daodejing* and had a legendary reputation as a hermit and a Daoist alchemist.

them as "something" and "nothing" (Graham 1959/1990); Wing-tsit Chan translates them as "being" and "non-being" (Chan 1963, 160), while Ames and Hall translate them as "determinate" (*you*) and "indeterminate" (*wu*) (Laozi 2003, 139). The Chinese word *you* means "to have," but in the context of metaphysics, it signifies existence, Being, or simply beings as referring to the myriad things. This word itself is not the focus of dispute; however, its counterpart, *wu*, is.

The Chinese word *wu* has three written forms, each with its own etymology. *Wu* is the opposite of *you*, and has often been translated as "nonbeing." However, a better rendition of this word is the negation of something; hence, it should be translated as nothing or nothingness. According to a historically revered lexicographer Xu Shen 許慎 (ca.58–ca.147), the etymology of the Chinese word *wu* has three origins and thus the word has three possible meanings: (i) (*wu*亡), gone, (ii) (*wu*無), meaning what seems to be nothing but is actually something, and (iii) (*wu*无), the original void. His analysis shows that, in as early as the Han dynasty, the word *wu* was already ambiguous. A contemporary scholar Pu Pang argues that these three written forms of the Chinese word *wu* (亡, 無, 无) represent three possibilities of the state of nothing (Pang 1995, 271):

The first *wu* (亡) represents "what used to be, no longer is": This first sense of *wu* can be manifested in states such as loss or death. This state of *wu* is the cessation of being, and is thus relative to a particular existence. The state of *wu* is logically posterior to the state of being. This Chinese written form *wu* (亡) should be translated as gone, without, or as the word stem "-less."

The second *wu* (無) represents "what seems to be nothing but is actually something": The second sense of *wu* depicts what is formless, shapeless, invisible, and imperceptible; however, it is not nothing. Pang argues that the written form *wu* 無 and the Chinese word for dance *wu* 舞 have the same origin and are closely related in a historical context: The primitive people danced in religious ceremonies as a tribute to the invisible, unknowable realm and whatever spirits that might grant them good fortune. Therefore, dance (*wu* 舞) is a way to communicate with the invisible something (*wu* 無). This state of *wu* is therefore still something, but it is a transcendental something that goes beyond human perceptions and defies human conceptions. It can further be seen as a something that encompasses all and is the master of everything. In this sense, this notion of *wu* represents being and thus is the opposite of the previous notion of *wu* 亡—the negation of being (Pang 1995, 277–78).

The third *wu* (无) represents "there never has been, nor ever will be": In Pang's analysis, the third word form of *wu* (无)[14] signifies the absolute emptiness and

---

14 In simplified Chinese, the second and the third word forms of *wu* cannot be distinguished, since the third form (无) is used as the simplified form of the second form (無).

nothingness. It is not relative to or dependent on the state of being; rather, it is the primordial state of the world. In Xu Shen's celebrated encyclopedia of Chinese vocabulary (*Shuowen Jiezi* 說文解字), the word *wu* (无) is interchangeable with the word *yuan* (元)[15], which means the origin, the primordial, and the fundamental. Xu Shen further explains: The vacuous and the primordial is *Dao*. The annotation written by Duan Yucai 段玉裁 (1735–1815) remarks that among the Six Classics,[16] the *Yijing* is the only book that employs this word. Pang argues that this word form was especially created, possibly as late as the Warring States Period (approximately 475–221 BCE), to mark a separate notion of *wu* as absolute nothingness (Pang 1995, 281).

The concept of *wu* was first used as a philosophical concept in Laozi's *Daodejing*.[17] In the *Daodejing*, the word *wu* appears over one hundred times. Even though the current text uses the same word form, the notion has different connotations. According to a contemporary intellectual historian Dainian Zhang, "It is in the Laozi that 'being' and 'beingless' [*wu*] first emerge as a philosophical pair. By 'being' the Laozi refers to the concrete existence of heaven, earth, and the myriad things. [*Wu*] in the Laozi has different meanings. It can refer first to the empty part of a given thing; second to the state before or after a particular thing existed; third to the highest origin that transcends all particular things" (Zhang 2002, 151). The first notion of *wu* appears in Chapter 11 of the *Daodejing*: "Thirty strokes are united around the hub to make a wheel. But it is on its [*wu*][18] that the utility of the carriage depends. Clay is molded to form a utensil. But it is on its [*wu*] that the utility of the utensil depends. Doors and windows are cut out to make a room. But it is on its [*wu*] that the utility of the room depends. Therefore, just as we can take advantage of what is (*you*), so can we make use of what is not (*wu*)" (Chapter 11, Chan 1963, 144, with modifications). The word *wu* can be rendered as empty space or simply as emptiness in this context. It is a pragmatic, rather than a metaphysical, notion.

The second usage, as a form of negation of a particular state of affairs, can be found in Laozi's combining *wu* with other items: *wu-ming* 無名 is "nameless," *wu-wei* 無為 is "nonaction," *wu-si* 無私 is "selfless," *wu-zhi* 無知 is "without cunning," *wu-shen* 無身 is "without the body," *wu-zhuang* 無狀 is "without shape,"

---

15 Note the similarity in the word forms.
16 The Six Classics include: the *Yijing*, the *Book of Documents* (*Shujing*), the *Book of Poetry* (*Shijing*), the *Classic of Rites* (*Lijing*), *Spring and Autumn Annals* (*Chunqiu*), and *Record of Music* (*Yueji*). The *Record of Music* is unfortunately lost after the first emperor of China (258–10 BCE) burned books extensively. Hence, the Six Classics was replaced by the designation the Five Classics starting in the Han dynasty.
17 Historically, the *Daodejing* is attributed to Laozi, whose identity is not established. From now on we will follow the Chinese tradition in using Laozi as the alleged author of the *Daodejing* (which is also called the *Laozi* in the Chinese tradition).
18 Chan translates *wu* as "nonbeing," but in this quote and the following we will use the original *wu* to maintain an open interpretation.

wu-wu 無物 is "without object," *wu-yu* 無欲 is "without desire," *wu-suo-gui* 無所歸 is "without a home," *wu-gong* 無功 is "without credit," and so on. The majority of the word *wu* used in the *Daodejing* belongs to this category. It negates whatever item (name, deed, credit, etc.) associated with it in the usage. Later in this chapter we shall see that the troubling term that Zhou Dunyi allegedly derived from Laozi, *wuji*, should be understood as *wu-ji* and be rendered as "without boundary."[19]

The third notion of *wu*, the state of *wu* that precedes all existence, can be seen as a cosmogonic notion depicting the primordial state of the universe. In the explication of the *Daodejing*, we can see that this cosmogonic notion corresponds to the second sense of *wu* analyzed by Pu Pang: it signifies something vague, elusive, formless, shapeless, inaudible, invisible, and naturally, nameless. This undifferentiated something, which existed before heaven and earth, is what Laozi calls *Dao* or "Great."

> Chapter 25: There was something undifferentiated and yet complete, which existed before heaven and earth. Soundless and formless, it depends on nothing and does not change. It operates everywhere and is free from danger. It may be considered the mother of the universe. I do not know its name; I call it "*dao*." If forced to give it a name, I shall call it "Great." Now being great means functioning everywhere. Functioning everywhere means far-reaching. Being far-reaching means returning to the original point.
>
> *(Chan 1963, 152)*

> Chapter 14: We look at it and do not see it; its name is The Invisible. We listen to it and do not hear it; its name is The Inaudible. We touch it and do not find it; its name is The Subtle (formless). These three cannot be further inquired into, and hence merge into one…. Infinite and boundless, it cannot be given any name. It reverts to [the undifferentiated *something*].[20] This is called shape without shape, form without object. It is the Vague and Elusive. Meet it and you will not see its head; follow it and you will not see its back…. From this one may know the primeval beginning [of the universe]. This is called the bond of *Dao*.
>
> *(Chan 1963, 146; parentheses in original but italics added)*

---

19 The full repudiation of the standard translation of "*wuji*" as "the Ultimate of Nonbeing" will be elaborated in the next section.

20 Chan's *Sourcebook* translates the sentence as "It reverts to nothingness" here. However, the original Chinese text does not use *nothingness* (*wu*無), but *something* (*wu*物). See Chapter 25 of the *Daodejing*: "There was something (物) undifferentiated and yet complete, which existed before heaven and earth." (Chan 1963, 172) See also Chapter 51 of the *Daodejing*: "Something (物) gives them physical form" (my translation).

Chapter 21: The thing that is called *Dao* is eluding and vague. Vague and eluding, there is in it the form. Eluding and vague, in it are things. Deep and obscure, in it is the essence. The essence is very real; in it are evidences. From the time of old until now, its name (manifestations) ever remains, by which we may see the beginning of all things. How do I know that the beginning of all things [is] so? Through this (*Dao*)".
(Chan 1963, 150; parentheses in original but italics and square brackets added)

If the primordial cosmic state in the *Daodejing* is depicted as an undifferentiated something, then the word *wu* in the most notoriously nihilistic chapter of the *Daodejing*, "All things in the world come from being (*you*). And being comes from [*wu*]" (Chapter 40; Chan 1963, 160), should not be understood as "absolute emptiness" or "nothingness." In other words, it should not be interpreted as the third sense of *wu* signified by the third word form of *wu* (无) in Pang's analysis. Pang himself argues that Laozi's usage of the word *wu* could not possibly capture this connotation since the notion did not get developed until later in Chinese history (Pang 1995, 282). In Chapter 34, Laozi describes the nature of *Dao* as "flows everywhere," "can go left or right," so *Dao* seems to be something that moves. In other words, Laozi's *Dao* is not nonbeing or absolute nothingness; it is rather something that cannot be defined, categorized, perceived, or described. This is what the *Daodejing* calls "the mother of the universe" (Chapter 52; Chan 1963, 164).

This philosophical concept of *wu* became the major theme in the philosophical developments during the Wei and Jin dynasties (220–420). Two leading philosophers, He Yan 何晏 (ca.193–249) and Wang Bi 王弼 (226–249), further developed Laozi's notion of *wu* and established *wu* as the ontological basis of all existence. According to a revered intellectual historian Yongtong Tang (1893–1964), the focus of Wei-Jin philosophy was no longer cosmogony or cosmology, but ontology. The philosophical pursuit at the time went beyond speculating on the origin of the universe, and started investigating the substance or the fundamental essence of all things (Tang 2001, 43–44).[21] He Yan's "Treatise on *Dao*"[22] says, "Being, in coming into being, is produced by [*wu*].... Because of it[23] darkness becomes black and plainness becomes white. Because of it the carpenter's square draws a square and the compass draws a circle. The compass and square obtain forms but [*Dao*] has no form. Black and white obtain names but [*Dao*] has no name" (Chan 1963, 324). Even though the

---

21 Tang's analysis on *Wei-Jin* philosophy has become the received view among contemporary scholars.
22 The whole treatise is lost. What we have is only a short segment recorded in Zhang Zhan's annotation of the *Liezi*, an ancient Daoist text.
23 Wing-tsit Chan's translation here uses "because of," so he probably took this to be a logical relation rather than a causal one.

"production" relationship between being and *wu* is obscure, it is clearly no longer a relationship of cosmogonic generation speculated in the *Daodejing*. He Yan's "Treatise on Wuwei" states, "All things in the world has *wu* as its foundation.... *Yin* and *yang* depend on it to transform life; all things depend on it to form concrete shapes.... Therefore, the function of *wu* is without titles, but it is highly valuable."[24] His "Treatise on the Nameless"[25] may give us a clue as to how this *wu* could be the foundation of being:

> No matter how far apart things are, things of the same kind respond to one another, and no mater how near they are, things of different kinds do not violate each other. It is like the *yang* in the *yin* or the *yin* in the *yang*. Each attracts and responds to its own kind.
>
> *(Chan 1963, 325)*

Here he seems to be developing Laozi's principle of complementarities: the opposites complement and complete each other. In other words, without nonexistence, there cannot be existence, just as without empty space, there could not be any chamber, carriage, vessel, wheels, and so on. The concept of *wu* in He Yan's usage seems to be a conceptual construct, to serve as the counterpart of existence (being)—it has to be posited to make existence possible. The word *wu* here can be rendered as nonbeing, as the opposite of being.

Unlike He Yan, who did not leave substantial work behind, Wang Bi produced copious work in his brief lifetime (he died at the age of 24). His *Commentary on Laozi's Daodejing* (*Laozi Daodejing zhu* 老子道德經注) and *A Brief Exposition of the Essence of Laozi's Teachings* (*Laozi zhilue* 老子指略) brought Laozi's notion of *wu* to a new dimension. Wang Bi writes, "All being originated from nonbeing (wu). The time before physical forms and names appeared was the beginning of the myriad things" (Chapter 1; Chan 1963, 321). This remark can be given either a cosmogonic or an ontological reading: Was he talking about the primordial state of the whole universe or the original state of particular things? In the *Daodejing*, the concept of *wu* was used to depict the time before anything was formed and named. In this commentary remark, on the other hand, Wang Bi seems to be dealing with the original ontological state of nonbeing of each particular thing. In the same chapter, Wang Bi continues to say, "All things in the world emerged from subtlety to completion; everything starts with nonbeing (*wu*) and then comes into being" (my translation, Wang Bi 1980, 1). He interprets Laozi's "undifferentiated something" (Chapter 25) from an epistemic point of view: "It (*Dao*) is that which we cannot know, but it completes everything. That is why it is called undifferentiated and yet complete.

---

24 This short treatise is partially recorded in the *History of Jin* (*Jinshu* 晉書), Volume 43.
25 Same as "the Treatise on *Dao*," this piece is recorded in Zhang Zhan's annotation of the *Liezi*, Chapter *Tianrui* 天瑞.

We do not *know* its origin, and that is why we say it precedes heaven and earth" (Wang Bi 1980, 63; emphasis added). The cosmogonic sense of *wu*'s preceding being in the *Daodejing* is greatly reduced in this commentary. Yongtong Tang interprets Wang Bi's notion of *Dao* as an a-temporal state: Laozi depicts *Dao* as "preceding heaven and earth," while in Wang Bi's commentary *Dao* is neither before nor after heaven and earth (Tang 2001, 137).

For Laozi's Chapter 38 on virtue (*de*), Wang Bi added the following comment: "Although it is valuable to have *nonbeing* [*wu*] as its function, nevertheless there cannot be substance without *nonbeing*" (Chan 1963, 323; emphasis added). According to Wing-tsit Chan, this is the first time in the history of Chinese philosophy that the notions of substance (*ti* 體) and function (*yong* 用) were used together.[26] This set of notions "were to become key concepts in Chinese Buddhism and Neo-Confucianism" (Chan 1963, 323). From Wang Bi's introduction of the relation between substance and function, we can also see his interest in the ultimate nature of things. He takes this ultimate nature, the substance, of all things as *Nonbeing*. How can "nonbeing" serve as the ontological foundation for being? Starting with examples of vessel, container, carriage (the first usage of the word *wu* in the *Daodejing*), where the nature of these things depends essentially on the nonbeing in their internal sphere, we can see also that without the nonbeing (emptiness) outside of each thing's boundary, the thing could not be that thing. Spatially, nonbeing defines the boundaries of particular things. Diachronically, each existing thing has its pre-existing state and its post-existence state. Both of these states are states of its "nonbeing." Therefore, without either spatial or temporal nonbeing outside of each being, no particular thing could be what it is, or could ever come into existence. Nonbeing is thus the ontological foundation for each particular being. However, this nonbeing is not necessarily nothingness since it is not necessarily the nonbeing of the universe and the myriad things. The sense of *wu* employed by Wang Bi is *wu* in the relative sense—the nonbeing is relative to being while at the same time it is what makes particular beings possible.

From the *nonbeing* essential for individual things, Wang Bi further introduced an all encompassing *Nonbeing* as the foundation of all things (the third sense of *wu* in Pang's analysis): "The ten thousand things have ten thousand different forms but in the final analysis they are one. How did they become one? Because of Nonbeing [*wu*]" (Chapter 42; Chan 1963, 323). If we understand the "nonbeing" here as the "negation of (ten thousand different) forms," then we can see how the myriad things can merge into one, and this one seems to be the totality of *qi*: "Although things exist in ten thousand different forms, their material forces (*qi*) are blended as one" (Chan 1963, 323). Nonbeing is without forms, without shapes and without names (designators). As Wang Bi remarks, "The formless and nameless is the master of all things" (Chapter 14;

---

26 The pair of concepts will be discussed more in details in Chapter 4 of this book.

Wang Bi 1980, 32). This sense of *nonbeing* could be close to how Hegel describes "nonbeing": it is the absence of all determination. Any determination restricts the existent thing and renders it partially complete. In *A Brief Exposition of the Essence of Laozi's Teachings*, Wang Bi gives a fuller explanation:

> If the temperature is tepid, then it cannot at the same time be cool; if the sound is one pitch, then it cannot be another pitch. Forms must necessarily divide; pitch must necessarily belong to its own category.... Name necessarily introduces distinction; title necessarily depends on some basis. When distinctions are made, it cannot encompass all; when there is further basis, it cannot be exhaustive".
> (*Wang Bi 1980, 195–96*)

Name is used to "define the other" (Wang Bi 1980, 197). If we give *Dao* a name, then it has an other, outside of it, opposing it. Therefore, *Dao* must necessarily be without names. Title is used to rank things into a hierarchical structure, and it requires some basis for judgment. *Dao* is the basis of everything; it requires no further basis. Hence, it cannot be given a title. In this way, the nameless, untitled *Dao* is the ontological foundation of all things. Wang Bi's *Dao* is nameless, shapeless, formless—total absence of determination, it is *wu*—the absolute Nonbeing. This Nonbeing is not just an "undifferentiated something" like the *Daodejing's Dao*; rather, it is nonbeing in the absolute sense since it is the negation of all existence as well as the substance of all things. As Yongtong Tang explains, "This wu is substance wu, not wu in the relative sense of being (*you*) and nonbeing (*wu*)" (Tang 2001, 45). Wang Bi's theory of *wu* has evolved into a version of meontology—the philosophical study of *Nonbeing* or absolute *nothingness*.[27]

What does it mean to have nonbeing as substance? Substance means the original nature of things. Tang's analysis is that Wang Bi's theory of nonbeing as substance is close to Buddhism's claim of emptiness as the true nature of things (Tang 2001, 47). For Wang Bi, substance is not a thing; it does not exist in space or time, but is beyond space and time. Tang argues that Wang Bi's quest was not about what things are made of, and is thus not a scientific endeavor (Tang 2001, 136).

Since Yontong Tang's analysis of *wu* as an ontological foundation rather than as a cosmogonic state is widely accepted, it is now a consensus among scholars that Wei-Jin Philosophy is fundamentally a philosophy of *wu* (here properly translated as nonbeing) as substance (Tang 2001; Kang 2003; Hong 2008).

---

27 "Meontology" is derived from the Greek word "me"—*non* and "on"—*being*. According to Bret W. Davis, "'First Philosophy' in the Western tradition is ontology, which asks the question of 'being qua being'.... In place of ontology, first philosophy in the East is more often a 'meontology': a philosophy of nonbeing or nothingness." See his *Stanford Encyclopedia* entry on the Kyoto School (http://plato.stanford.edu/entries/kyoto-school/#WesBeiVsEasNotOntVsMeo).

Wang Bi's contribution to the development of this notion is indisputable. He and He Yan are considered as the representatives of the School of Nonbeing. However, the teaching of nonbeing (*wu*) began as a metaphysical speculation, and ended as a philosophy of life. What Wang Bi did was not just to turn the *Daodejing*'s cosmological speculation on the state of nothingness into an ontological analysis of the ultimate nature (or substance) of all exiting things, but also to elaborate on the ethical application of the notion of non-discrimination, non-determination—his notion of nonbeing. According to Wang Bi, the whole *Daodejing* could be summarized in one sentence—"elevating the essential and eliminating the frivolous" (Wang Bi 1980, 198). What is essential begins with the mental state of simplicity and sincerity:

> Warding off evil lies in preserving people's sincerity, not in the sharp detection of their evil; ceasing extravagance lies in removing luxury items, not in publishing more laws. The way to curtail robbery is to reduce desires, not to be imposing harsher punishments…. Start planning before any early signs (of trouble) appear, take action before everything began…. This is why [Laozi] manifests the simple and the unadorned while abandoning sageliness and wisdom. He reduces selfish desires and spurns cunning and craftiness. These are all what is called elevating the essential and eliminating the frivolous.[28]
>
> (Wang Bi 1980, 198)

Wang Bi made it clear that his speculative philosophy is meant to cure social ills. However, the shift from an ontological confirmation of the state of nonbeing to an ethical advocacy of negation of discernment and distinction had serious social ramifications. Situated amid political turmoil and vicious persecution of the times, Wei-Jin intellectuals were seeking ways out of their precarious predicament. The doctrine of nonbeing and negation gave them an excuse to abandon social bounds and conventional values. A famous slogan among them was "forsake titles and norms to go with nature" (Kang 2003, 209). Legend has it that seven Wei-Jin intellectuals were close friends and often gathered in a bamboo forest to drink and recite poetry all night. They were known as "the Gang of Seven in the Bamboo Forest."[29] Even though these intellectuals had deep philosophical insights and their goal was to pursue spiritual refinement in the midst of political perils, many others merely imitated their conduct without adopting any philosophical position. The doctrine of nonbeing led to the downfall of

---

28 The main idea for this long passage comes from Chapters 19 and 57 of Laozi's *Daodejing*. See Chan 1963, 149, 166–67.

29 The seven intellectuals were Ji Kang, Ruan Ji, Xiang Xiu, Liu Ling, Ruan Xian, Wang Rong, and San Tao. The location of the bamboo forest is in dispute, but the orthodox view is that it was near Ji Kang's residence. Ji Kang was later framed by his political enemy and executed in 263 at the age of 40.

social mores of the times. In response, some philosophers began to advocate the value of being ("*you*"), and they were known as the School of Being.

Two leaders of the School of Being were Pei Wei (267–300) and Guo Xiang (252–312). Even though Pei Wei supposedly wrote two treatises on this topic, today we have only one short piece by Pei Wei, entitled *Veneration of Being (Chongyoulun* 崇有論*)*.[30] Pei Wei was concerned with his contemporary intellectuals' deviation from social norms and the decline of morals, and he thought that the doctrine of nonbeing was the culprit for the social decline and ethical downfall of the times. He thought that those who indulged in the discourse of nonbeing used it as an excuse to spurn etiquette and decorum, disregard order of seniority and hierarchy of ranking. He criticized them for depravity to the point of "going naked in public, losing any sense of propriety in their speech and conduct" (collected in Gu 1980, 376). Therefore, he advocated the return to the Confucian teaching of being. The first step is to refute the doctrine of nonbeing. Pei Wei writes:

> The absolute Nonbeing cannot possibly resort to anything to generate something. Therefore, the beginning existence has to be self-generating. Since self-generation has to rely on being as substance, without prior being it is insufficient to generate any new existence. Anything that comes into existence must already have its own being; hence, nonbeing is simply the absence, or the loss, of being. [It does not exist on its own.]
> *(in Gu 1980, 377)*

Since this passage is obscure in meaning, we can reformulate Pei Wei's argument as follows:

If there were absolute Nonbeing, it could not possibly resort to anything to generate something.
If (1), then the beginning existence had to be self-generating.
Self-generation must rely on being as substance.
Therefore, anything that comes into existence must already has its own being.
Therefore, there could never have been absolute nothingness.

Pei Wei further argues that only things that exist can be of service to things that exist; therefore, nonbeing has nothing to do with the generation of existent things.

---

30 Various historical records ascribed two treatises on this topic to Pei Wei; one of which is "Veneration of Being," while the other one is "Valuing Nonbeing." It is in dispute among contemporary scholars whether Pei really did write the second treatise. See Kang 2003, 212. However, in "Veneration of Being," Pei Wei also presents an aspect of nonbeing that should be valued: nonbeing can be applied to preserve being, as for example, the reduction of desires can benefit one's health, and the cessation of extravagance can bring one back to moderation (in Gu 1980, 376). It is likely that Pei did write a separate article on *how to* value nonbeing.

In contemporary terminology, we might say that Pei Wei is against having any absence in the entire causal chain of generation. Only things that exist can affect or produce other things. As he puts it, "Whatever that can aid and complete an existing thing must also exist" (Gu 1980, 387). Nothing (no-thing) can emerge out of nothingness. Being is primary and nonbeing is secondary; no things could subsist independently of the existence of the phenomenal world.

In this treatise, Pei Wei's ontological speculation is primarily motivated by his pragmatic concern for the ethical implication of one's ontological conviction. For him, it is essential to venerate being:

> Once one devalues the existence of myriad things, one would disregard objects' different forms, which leads to the abandonment of social regulations. Once one abandons social regulations, one would neglect ethical norms. If one neglects ethical norms, then one would also forgo rites and rituals. Once a society loses its rites and regulations, there is no way to keep it in check.... Therefore, a leader must be careful with what is taught.
> *(Gu 1980, 375)*

In other words, it was primarily to revert the social trend of neglecting social regulations and ethical norms that Pei Wei advocated the thesis of being.

Guo Xiang's philosophical ideas are preserved only in his Commentary on the *Zhuangzi*.[31] Unlike Pei Wei, whose ontology of being was primarily driven by his pragmatic concern for the social ramifications of the doctrine of nonbeing, Guo Xiang had a keener interest in the speculative cosmogony of being. He thinks that being cannot come from nonbeing, both because nonbeing itself cannot produce anything and because being itself has to be self-generated. According to him, "Since nonbeing is nonbeing, it cannot produce being. Before being itself is produced, it cannot produce other beings. Then by whom are things produced? They spontaneously produce themselves, that is all" (Chan 1963, 328). Guo Xiang calls the self-generation of things "spontaneous transformation" (*duhua* 獨化). By "spontaneous," he means "without external factor or outside force." The world is self-sufficient and complete on its own. It does not depend on any external force. In other words, there is no Creator and no creation ex nihilo. As Guo Xiang puts it resolutely:

---

31 In *History of Jin* (*Jinshu*), it is recorded that Xiang Xiu (approx. 227–72, one of the *Gang of Seven in the Bamboo Forest*) first composed his commentary on Zhuangzi, which became the basis for Guo Xiang's commentary. But there were two different accounts of Guo Xiang's contribution: one says that Guo Xiang elaborated on Xiang Xiu's commentary and expanded it with more chapters; the other says that Guo Xiang plagiarized Xiang Xiu's ideas and claimed to be his own. Contemporary scholars do not share consensus on whether Guo Xiang plagiarized or how great his contribution was. See Kang 2003, 226–35 for a detailed account of this controversy. Here we shall take "Guo Xiang" simply as "the author of the *Commentary on the Zhuangzi*," with the understanding that the reference could include both Xiang Xiu and Guo Xiang.

But let us ask whether there is a Creator or not. If not, how can he create things? If there is, he is incapable of materializing all the forms. Therefore, before we can talk about creation, we must understand the fact that all forms materialize by themselves. If we go through the entire realm of existence, we shall see that there is nothing ... that does not transform itself behind the phenomenal world. Hence everything creates itself without the direction of any Creator. Since things create themselves, they are unconditioned. This is the norm of the universe.
(Chan 1963, 330–31)

The implication of this self-transformation view is that the world (something, not necessarily the world as we have it) has always existed. To unpack this dense passage, we can summarize Guo Xiang"s argument as follows:

If being cannot come from nonbeing, then it must come from being.
If being comes from being, then being is self-produced.
If being is self-produced, then it must be present from eternity.
Therefore, there is, and there has always been, being.

Guo Xiang further argues that there always will be being too: "Not only is it impossible for nonbeing to be changed into being. It is also impossible for being to become nonbeing. Therefore, although being as a substance undergoes infinite changes and transformations, it cannot in any instance become nonbeing" (Chan 1963, 335). He did not offer any explanation for what this ever-present, all-encompassing Being could be. He did, however, indicate that it could not be *qi* and could not be *Dao*:

What came into existence before there were things? If I say *yin* and *yang* came first, then since *yin* and *yang* are themselves entities, what came before them? Suppose I say Nature came first. But Nature is only things' being themselves. Suppose I say perfect *Dao* came first. But perfect [*Dao*] is perfect nonbeing. Since it is nonbeing, how can it come before anything else? Then what came before it? There must be another thing, and so on ad infinitum.
(Chan 1963, 335)

His conclusion is thus that the self-transformation of things is the only plausible explanation for how things came about.

For Guo Xiang, the ethical application of the doctrine of being is the obtainment of tranquility and felicity, which comes as a result of one's following the principle of things. He states, "The perfect man is not besieged by calamities, not because he escapes from them but because he advances the principles of things and goes forward and naturally comes into union with good fortune"

(Chan 1963, 328). Guo Xiang fully embraces the philosophy of life advocated by Zhuangzi, and yet he is not anti-Confucian. On the contrary, he shows how Zhuangzi's view is compatible with Confucian ethics. As he says, "A gentleman who profoundly penetrates all things and is in harmony with their transformations will be contented with whatever time may bring. He follows the course of Nature in whatever situation he may be" (Chan 1963, 331). The joy and harmony Guo depicts here is very close to "the delight of Confucius and Yan Hui" on which Zhou Dunyi frequently commented. We should see that even though the doctrine of nonbeing is derived from Daoist's discourse on *wu*, Daoism as expounded by the *Daodejing* and the *Zhuangzi* is not necessarily the doctrine of nonbeing developed by the school of nonbeing in the Wei-Jin era. As we will see, Zhou Dunyi would also find valuable philosophical ideas in the *Daodejing* when he developed his own cosmology.

What the school of being affirms is the reality of the phenomenal world. The notion of being is not about some abstract, absolute Being separate from all particular beings, but about the existence of all things—"the multiple beings" (*qunyou* 群有). Being (*you*) is simply the totality of the existence of myriad things. In contemporary philosophical demarcation, the doctrine of being can be seen as a version of objective realism—realism of ordinary objects and natural phenomena. Both Pei Wei and Guo Xiang believe in the presence of order in the phenomenal world. Pei Wei is committed to a rudimentary form of contemporary natural kind theory. He believes that the categorization of things follows some inherent principle of individuation—things of different kinds have different characteristics. "Things are divided into different kinds in accordance with their distinct natures" (cited in Gu 1980, 374). Guo Xiang, on the other hand, can be attributed a *no error* theory: There is no error in nature; things in nature follow natural laws and everything is in its right place. As he puts it, "The principles of things are from the very start correct. None can escape from them. Therefore a person is never born by mistake, and what he is born with is never an error" (Chan 1963, 332).[32] Because the doctrine of being affirms the commonsense world, it further upholds the value of human conventions, systems, and activities. What humans accomplish in this world is real and can amount to something; hence, one should not deny this world to pursue some transcendental ideals. This philosophy very much aligns with the this-worldly orientation of Confucianism,[33] in contrast to the other-worldly pursuit of Daoism or Buddhism.

To sum up, the debate on Being and Nonbeing in Wei-Jin philosophy was primarily a dispute in two dimensions: the ontological foundation of the

---

32 Wing-tsit Chan thinks that this is clearly a form of determinism and fatalism. "Fate is not merely something beyond human control or understanding; it is necessary truth." (Chan 1963, 332–33) This interpretation is problematic, however.
33 Confucianism is committed to one reality—our world. It does not posit a transcendental realm or a noumenon hidden behind this experiential world.

phenomenal world and the ethical application of the ontology. It was not a pursuit of the cosmogonic origin or cosmological foundation of the phenomenal world as it was manifested in the *Daodejing*. The reason why we have taken such a long detour to introduce the philosophical background of the issues surrounding the two notions, *you* and *wu* (being and nothingness or nonbeing), is to explain why Zhou Dunyi's notion of *wuji* (無極) would raise such an uproar among philosophers of his times and intellectual historians. If his idea of *wuji* indeed came from the Daoist tradition, in particular, associated with the school of nonbeing, then his whole philosophy would be utterly distasteful to his contemporary neo-Confucians who aimed to restore social morals from the corruption of the school of nonbeing.

What Zhou Dunyi accomplished, as the pioneer of neo-Confucianism, was to bring back the speculation of the cosmological origin of the phenomenal world, and established a new form of ethics based on his metaphysical view. We will see that Zhou's ethical proclivity is clearly opposite of the spirit of the school of nonbeing. Instead of focusing on the concept of *wu* (either in the sense of nothingness or nonbeing), Zhou employed the term "wuji," which should be rendered as "wu-ji," namely, "without boundary." Hence, we shall translate it as the boundless or infinity. Zhou Dunyi's emphasis on the state of *wuji* is a totally separate concern from the notion of *wu* for the school of nonbeing.

The Boundless (*Wuji*) and the Supreme Ultimate (*Taiji*)

Previously we have explained that the term *wuji* in the *Daodejing* should be understood as the negation of *ji* 極. According to the classic *Shuowen Jiezi* by Xu Shen, the word *ji* means the main supporting beam of a building. Duan Yucai's annotation explains that whatever that is extremely tall and extremely far away is called *ji*. The word is nowadays used as utmost, extreme, or ultimate. Therefore, the term *wuji* should be translated as without the ultimate boundaries or "infinite," "boundless." The standard translation "the ultimate nonbeing" (Chan 1963; Neville 1980) or "Ultimate of Nonbeing" (Zhang 2002) has actually reversed the Chinese word order, and renders it as *jiwu*—the ultimate *wu*. However, even within the Daoist tradition, Wang Bi's interpretation of Laozi's *wuji* (Chapter 28) is simply "inexhaustible" (*wuqiong* 無窮) (Wang Bi 1980, 74), and this shows clearly that he did not identify *wuji* with *wu* itself. We will now discuss how Zhou's notion of *wuji* is developed in a different context from the notion of *wu* in the Daoist and Wei-Jin philosophy.

A contemporary scholar Yi Jiang has correctly associated the notion of infinity with *wuji*. He says, "Ancient Chinese philosophers mainly discussed infinity in terms of *wuji* (boundless) and *wuqiong* (endless)" (Jiang 2008, 568).

His interpretation of Zhou Dunyi's opening line of *the Exposition* is that the boundless leads to the extremity of boundary. "It is not that there is another thing, the boundless"; rather, the boundless is nothing other than *taiji*, the extremity of boundary (Jiang 2008, 568). This interpretation endorses Zhu Xi's view that *wuji* and *taiji* are simply two sides of the same coin. How do we understand this connection in contemporary terms?

Finite things are determined and hence limited: they must have boundaries set in space and in time. On the other hand, *Taiji* (the supreme ultimate) is indeterminate, unlimited, and hence boundless (*wuji*). From Zhou Dunyi's text itself, it is not clear whether "the boundless" depicts the way *Taiji* is or designates a state existing prior to the state of *Taiji*. *The Exposition* begins with "*Wuji* and (then) *Taiji*" and later states "*Taiji* is originally *wuji*." We can have two equally credible cosmogonic interpretations:

1) There was initially the state of the boundless (*Wuji*), which emerged into a state of a supremely massive *Taiji*. *Taiji* is originally the boundless.
2) The state of *Taiji* is both supremely massive and boundless (*wuji*).

To settle on a correct interpretation, we need to examine the nature of *Taiji* itself to see whether it could be boundless at the same time.

To begin with, if something exists in time, then there must be a time before its existence and most likely a time after its existence. Both the pre-existing and the post-existing states of the thing is its nonbeing. We can call this particular nonbeing a local non-existence. Local non-existence could be rampant in the world of being. For the whole universe to emerge into existence, on the other hand, there has to be a state that has no existence of any particular thing anywhere—there has to be a global non-existence or we can call it absolute nothingness. If we go with interpretation (1) above, then there was a time when *Taiji* was nonexistent—the whole world was not always existent. In this case, to say that the initial state was the boundless would be the same as saying that it was absolute nothingness. It is understandable why so many scholars throughout history have taken Zhou Dunyi's cosmogony to be posting the state of nonbeing or nothingness as the initial cosmic state.

However, if we take a close look at Zhou's description, then we can see that there was a definite stage for the emergence of particular things, but there was never a depiction of the generation of *Taiji* itself. "The two forms of *qi* (*yin* and *yang*) intermingled, and the myriad things were born" (Zhou 1975, 14). Particular life forms are generated by the movement and transformation of *qi*, but *Taiji* is not generated by *qi*—quite the opposite. *Taiji* generates *yang* and *yin* through its movement and stillness; *yin* and *yang* further generates the five basic elements (metal, wood, water, fire, and earth) for concrete things. Heaven and earth had a beginning, and there was a time when myriad concrete things began to form. If we call concrete things "something," "the determinate," "beings," then there was a time when there was nothing rather than something, and the world was indefinite rather than determined. Nevertheless, this does not mean that there was a time when *Taiji* did not exist. Zhou's whole *Exposition* is about how *Taiji* generates the myriad things through the separate functions of *yin* and *yang*. It never depicts how *Taiji* was generated in the first place. In the *Yijing*, *Taiji* is posited as the primordial state—it has always existed. We could safely assume that Zhou Dunyi's view of *Taiji* is the same as that in the *Yijing*, the source of his philosophical ideas.

If *Taiji* itself did not come into being from nonbeing while the myriad things do, then *Taiji* is divided into two stages: the pre-myriad-things *Taiji* and the *Taiji* with myriad things. What could the pre-myriad-things *Taiji* be like? This may be why Zhou Dunyi brought in the notion of *wuji*. *Taiji* was initially boundless because its existence was beyond both space and time. The space–time framework came into existence after the myriad things were formed and divided—their spatiality marks space because they were separated, and their changes mark time because they come into existence, go through change, and go out of existence. The pre-myriad-things *Taiji* itself could not be identified with the space–time framework itself, as there was no space or time to begin with. There was nothing inside it or outside it; hence, it was without boundaries. It can properly be called "the Boundless."[34]

How do we understand Zhou Dunyi's notion of *Taiji*—whether *Taiji* was before the emergence of the myriad things or filled with the myriad things? What is the nature of *Taiji*? Zhu Xi thought that *Taiji* was simply a cosmic order, the principle (*li*), but is this really Zhou's view? From Zhou Dunyi's own explanation of the cosmogonic process, we should see that *Taiji* is not an abstract order or the pattern of *qi*, since he depicts *Taiji* as having motion and rest—its motion generates *yang* and its rest generates *yin*. Lai Chen, a leading contemporary scholar on neo-Confucianism, argues that Zhou Dunyi's cosmology is a form of *qi*-monism (Chen 2005, 40). Yu Guo (2003, 2001) also argues that for Zhou Dunyi, *Taiji* was initially just one *qi*, which then separated into *yang* and *yin* through motion and rest. Guo cites comments by Zhou Dunyi's contemporary, Liu Mu 劉牧 (1011–1064) and Shao Yong 邵雍 (1011–1077), to show that it was a common view among neo-Confucians in Northern Song dynasty to regard *Taiji* as one *qi*—before *yin* and *yang* are divided. According to Liu Mu, "Yi has *Taiji*, which generates the two modes (*liangyi* 兩儀). *Taiji* is simply one *qi*. Before heaven and earth are divided, the primordial *qi* is intermingled as One. Once the one *qi* is divided, it is called the two modes" (Liu 1995, 1). According to Shao Yong, "Taiji is one, as it becomes

---

34 A parallel conception of the boundless can be developed out of the Western philosophical notion of *nothingness*. As Roy Sorensen explains, "A concrete entity has a position in space or time.... Sine they have locations, they have boundaries with their environment. (The only exception would be an entity that take up all space and time)" ("Nothingness," *Stanford Encyclopedia of Philosophy*, parentheses in original).

differentiated, the two modes (*yin* and *yang*) appear." He also says, "*Qi* is one. When the one *qi* is divided, *yin* and *yang* are distinguished" (Guo 2001, 3). From these two quotes, it is clear that for Zhou Dunyi, *Taiji* could very well be identified with the one undifferentiated *qi*. Since this seems to be a widely endorsed view in Zhou's time,[35] his comment on "Wuji and then Taiji" may be expressing the evolution of *qi* as coming from boundlessness (*Wuji*) to supremely ultimate (*Taiji*).

If "Wuji and then Taiji" is to be interpreted as a statement on cosmogonic development, then how do we unpack Zhou Dunyi's cosmology? Lai Chen gives a good analysis: "*Taiji* is the primordial undifferentiated state of chaos, while *Wuji* depicts this formless and disordered state of infinity before the universe was formed. As a primeval matter itself, *Taiji* was initially formless and boundless, and this is what is meant by 'Wuji and then Taiji'" (Chen 2005, 39). This "primeval matter" referred to here is simply the primordial *qi*, before *qi* was separated into *yin* and *yang*. Zhou Dunyi's cosmology is simply an explanation of the development of *qi*—a process of division from being one homogeneous state to having two modes of *yin* and *yang*, and finally to the generation of multiplicity.

For our contemporary elucidation, it is possible to associate *qi* with the outdated notion of ether, but a more promising approach is to associate *Taiji* with the space–time framework. According to Roy Sorensen, "Historians of science wonder whether the ether that was loudly pushed out the front door of physics is quietly returning through the back door under the guise of 'space.' Quantum field theory provides especially fertile area for such speculation. Particles are created with the help of energy present in 'vacuums.' To say that vacuums have energy and energy is convertible into mass, is to deny that vacuums are empty. Many physicists revel in the discovery that vacuums are far from empty" (Sorensen 2009, Section 10). Understood in this light, Zhou Dunyi's notion of *taiji* is much more intelligible and plausible.

We can now give a contemporary reinterpretation of Zhou Dunyi's view of *Taiji*. We can also understand why he introduced the notion *wuji* into his cosmological explanation of the universe. The Chinese term for the universe is "yuzou" (宇宙), which literally means space and time: "the four directions (front, back, left, and right) plus the two dimensions (up and down) is called 'yu'; from the ancient and the past to the present and the coming is called 'zou.'"[36] Before heaven and earth were separated and concrete things were

---

35 The view did not originate in Northern Song dynasty neo-Confucians. It was a prevalent view in Han dynasty, before Wei-Jin philosophy shifted the interest from cosmology to ontology.
36 This analysis originally came from Wenzi, allegedly a disciple of Laozi and a contemporary of Confucius. It was recorded in Duan's annotations to Xu Shen's *Shuowenjiezi*, and is now an established analysis of the term.

formed, the space–time framework itself could be infinitely expansive while at the same time infinitely minute—"its extensiveness is such that nothing could be outside of it; its minuteness is such that nothing could be inside of it."[37] The space–time framework itself "depends on what it frames,"[38] hence, it was without limits and without boundaries when there were no concrete things in space and time. In other words, before any concrete object appeared, space–time would simply have no bounds since there would be nothing external to it either. Hence, it should be called "the Boundless (*Wuji*)." After heaven and earth were separated and the universe formed, there emerged an infinitely massive space–time framework, which Zhou Dunyi calls the Supreme Ultimate (*Taiji*). We can understand why Zhou Dunyi would say that *Wuji* and then *Taiji*; *Taiji* was initially *Wuji*. The cosmological development of *Taiji* is the expansion of matter within a supremely massive space–time framework. Since *Taiji* is identified with *qi* itself, it is not a passive space–time framework as a mere container for concrete things; rather, it is matter and energy conjoined with the framework. In Zhou's depiction, *Taiji* has motion and rest; hence, it is not a vacuum, or at least not an empty vacuum, because it is filled with energy. Zhou's view may be different from Newton's conception of space as "an external, homogenous, three-dimensional container of infinite extent," but it seems to be compatible with Newton's conjecture about what existed before concrete things came around: "the world was empty of objects for an infinite period prior to creation" (see Sorensen 2009, Section 4).

We shall now go back to the question that haunted scholars for hundreds of years: Does Zhou Dunyi's "Wuji and then Taiji" commit him to a version of creation ex nihilo? Even though we have separated the notion of *wuji* from the notion of *wu*, does the state of primordial chaos still end up being a state of nothingness? Sze-kwang Lao argues that since *Wuji* is a separate state from *Taiji*, Zhou's view is positing *wuji* as the substance of everything and hence, it does imply "being comes from nothingness" (Lao 1980, 114). Even though Shen Li rejected tracing the source of Zhou's *Taiji* diagram to the Daoist *Wuji* diagram, he nonetheless argues, "As long as one acknowledges that there is a beginning to heaven and earth, to *yin* and *yang*, one can only trace the origin back to nothingness. Being emerges out of nothingness can be said to be an inevitable conclusion" (Li 2001, 49). However, even when contemporary scholars still embrace the creation ex nihilo interpretation of Zhou Dunyi's cosmology, they do not necessarily treat the initial state to be the later Daoist conception of nonbeing or absolute nothingness.

---

37 The original Chinese sentence is: *qida wuwai* (其大無外); *qixiao qunei* (其小無內). It was first employed in the *Guanzi* (compiled during 475–221 BCE approximately) as a description of *Dao*.
38 This is Roy Sorensen's description of Einstein's conception of space. See Sorensen 2009.

Robert C. Neville, for example, takes Zhou's view to be a version of creation ex nihilo, but he explains this process as one in which determinate world emerges out of the state of indeterminacy. Thus, creation is a "decisive process eliminating alternatives" (Neville 1980, 22). Tongdong Bai also argues that there is a sense of nothingness (*wu*), which signifies "the ultimate potentiality that is not fixed and can be led to a myriad of actualities" (Bai 2008, 347).[39] If we accept this understanding of "nothingness," then the "nihilo" from which all things are generated is neither absolute nothingness nor void. It is rather a state of indeterminacy, full of potentiality and possibilities. This would be a reasonable way to understand Zhou Dunyi's boundless amorphous *qi*: as the primordial matter, it is seething with energy. This explains why the myriad things could eventually emerge out of this primordial *qi*. How does something come out of nothingness?—It is because there was always something in nothingness. Under this understanding, Zhou's *Wuji* is not absolute nothingness or complete void. At the same time, since *Taiji* is the totality of *qi*, *Taiji* is not the same as void even before *qi* is divided into *yin* and *yang*. It has no forms, shapes, boundaries, determinacy, and yet it is not empty. This analysis of the connection between *Wuji* and *Taiji* supports the first reading of Zhou Dunyi's cosmology: There was initially the state of the Boundless (*Wuji*), which emerged into a state of a supremely massive *Taiji*. *Taiji* was originally the Boundless.

A stronger, but equally plausible, interpretation of the ontological status of Zhou Dunyi's *Taiji* is to identify it with Being itself. If *Taiji* is the unified and undifferentiated *qi* and *qi* is the constitutive principle of all things, then *Taiji* is responsible for all beings. *Taiji* can thus be interpreted as Being, which must also be both eternal and infinite. According to Gi-Ming Shien's analysis of the nature of Being,

> Being itself transcends both time and space, since it endures for eternity and is the source of all things. We cannot even imagine that Being or the One has either beginning or end....Being also transcends space and is quantitatively infinite. It is unlimited by anything and is boundless. In this sense it is infinite. These two attributes, eternity and infinite, represent supreme existence and are the summit of absolute perfection. Thus, Being can be the source of all things.
>
> *(Shien 1951, 22)*

---

[39] Bai's article is on Laozi. He argues that when Laozi says "*Dao* generated the 'One,'" Laozi's *Dao* is to be identified with this sense of *wu*.

Even though here Shien is analyzing the abstract notion of Being, the analysis fits Zhou's notion of *Taiji* perfectly. Zhou's *Taiji* also transcends space and time, and by associating it with the notion *wuji*, Zhou depicts it as infinite and boundless. Pure Being as such is "unlimited in its nature." According to Shien, "Regarded from the standpoint of its lack of limitation, it is completely independent, that is, absolute. 'Absolute' means that it is relative to nothing and is self-sufficient" (Shien 1951, 23). In Zhou Dunyi's depiction, *Taiji*, the supreme ultimate, is the absolute self-sufficient and self-contained perfection. Exactly because it is relative to nothing else, it is identical with the Boundless (*Wuji*). Zhou's *Taiji* is simply Being itself; hence it is both supremely massive and boundless (*wuji*).

Whether there is a state of *Wuji* before *Taiji* or *Taiji* is simply *wuji* (boundless) at the same time, there is no hint whatsoever in Zhou Dunyi's cosmology of the Daoist rendition of being comes out of pure nothingness.

From the boundless amorphous *qi* to the supremely ultimate space–time framework, there had to be further changes to bring about concrete things. The first change is the state of motion and rest of this amorphous *qi*. Through motion *Taiji* generates *yang*; through resting it generates *yin*.[40] The two modes of *qi* are thereby distinguished. This is a revolutionary move in the cosmological thinking of Confucianism. As Robin Wang explains, "While no one has solved the problem of how the universe could be produced by the supreme ultimate, Zhou Dunyi's contribution is to identify directly and clearly *yin yang* with ... movement and rest as critical to the generation of the universe" (Wang 2005, 316). Zhou Dunyi further elaborated on the *Yijing*'s cosmogonic picture and added the five elements widely discussed by Confucians in Han dynasty (206 BCE–220 CE): water, fire, earth, wood, and metal. We could see this stage as a turn toward qualitative rather than quantitative change.[41] *Qi* as a pure form of energy constitutes elements of matter. The next stage is the separation of male and female, which is the basis for almost all organic life forms.[42] The basic elements in conjunction with the principles of male and female produce (or constitute) the myriad concrete things.

---

40 "Generate" is the literal rendition of the text. It could be plausibly argued, however, that the motion of *qi* itself is simply *yang* while the resting state is simply *yin*. The identification of *yang* with movement and *yin* with rest is exactly Robin Wang's (2005) interpretation of Zhou's contribution.

41 Yu Guo (2003) explains that the ancient Chinese cosmological thinking involves qualitative change rather than quantitative change.

42 Some organic entities carry out asexual reproduction, as in the case of amoeba. However, in most cases, it seems that reproduction is possible only with both male and female elements.

We can draw a flowchart of Zhou Dunyi's cosmogonic view:

Primordial Infinite Chaos (undifferentiated and unbounded *qi*)
↓↓
Supreme Ultimate
(spacetime framework)
↓↓
Yin and yang
(rest and movement)
↓↓
Five elements (water, fire, earth, wood, metal)
↓↓
Male and female
↓↓
The myriad things

Based on this view of the origin of the universe, Zhou Dunyi developed his ethical view, which is directly related to the affirmation of the reality of the phenomenal world. His *Penetrating the Book* (of Changes) begins with the pronouncement of the attribute of authenticity (*cheng*) as pertaining to the principle of male and to the sage: "Great is the primordial principle of male (*qianyuan* 乾元)! It is in virtue of which that the myriad things emerged, and it is the source of authenticity. The way of the principle of male generates and transforms everything, such that everything obtains its correct nature and destiny. Authenticity is established in this world and it is perfectly good" (Zhou 1975, 116). Here he is not only affirming the realness of the myriad things but also acknowledging the "integrity"[43] of their existence—their natures and destinies are fixed. The heavenly attribute of authenticity further becomes the foundation for human morals: "Sagehood is nothing but authenticity. Authenticity is the basis of the Five Constant Virtues (humaneness, righteousness,

---

43 The "integrity of existing things" is a phrase borrowed from Neville. However, Neville uses this phrase in the context of the creation theory. See Neville 1980, 24. In Zhou Dunyi's view, the integrity of existing things comes from the creative force of *qi* itself. Zhang Zai claims that this regulative principle is inherent in the nature of *qi* itself, while Zhu Xi would later identify the cosmic principle (*li*) as what is responsible for the integrity of existing things.

propriety, wisdom and faithfulness) and the fountainhead for all human conduct" (Zhou 1975, 123). From this we can clearly see that Zhou Dunyi's cosmological view does not lead to the denial of the reality of the world as we see it, or the ethical values that we humans establish in our society.

Conclusion

Zhou Dunyi's "Wuji and then Taiji" is a statement of cosmogony, not a statement of ontology. It is not related to the dispute between the doctrine of *wu* and the doctrine of *you* in Wei-Jin philosophy, and it does not lead to the rejection of social norms and ethical standards. His *Exposition of Taiji Diagram*— exactly because of the controversy surrounding it—led to a lively debate on the cosmogonic origin of the universe. He may have been inspired by Chen Tuan's alchemic methodology,[44] but there is no evidence that he was ever a descendent of Chen's school or that his *Taiji* diagram was modeled after Chen's *Wuji* diagram. His speculation of the origin of the universe is compatible with the cosmogonic view in the *Daodejing*, but it is very different from the ontology of nonbeing developed in Wei-Jin philosophy. Neo-Confucianists' vehement rejection of the doctrine of *wu* was prompted by their repulsion of the ethical implications of this ontological doctrine. Even if the *Daodejing*'s theory itself encourages the denouncement of social norms and ethical standards, Zhou Dunyi's cosmogonic speculation does not lead to such a conclusion. To restore the true spirit of Zhou's philosophy, it is essential to disassociate it from the doctrine of *wu* in Wei-Jin philosophy. In this light, we may see how Zhou Dunyi's philosophical ideas opened a new path for the development of neo-Confucianism. As Youlan Feng puts it in his historical assessment of Zhou: "The earliest of the neo-Confucianists were chiefly interested in cosmology. The first cosmological philosopher is [Zhou Dunyi]" (Feng 1966, 269). This cosmological turn may be Zhou's greatest contribution to neo-Confucianism. In the next chapter, we will see that the theory of *qi*'s original state and its development would be fully expounded by Zhang Zai (1020–1078).

---

44 There is one place in Zhou's *Complete Works* where he mentioned Chen Tuan by his style name Mr. *Xiyi* 希夷先生: "It is only after reading the alchemic aphorism that I believed in *Xiyi*, for he has understood the subtle signs of the creation and transformation of *yin* and *yang*" (Zhou 1975, 345). This poem was one of the three poems written after Zhou visited a Daoist monastery in *Fongdu* (today's Chongqing, China), and the title referred to the "engraving on the stone" in this monastery. It is possible that Zhou did see Chen Tuan's alchemic aphorism that later Daoists put alongside the *Wuji* Diagram, while the diagram itself was later concocted by later Daoists.

Primary Sources

Zhou, Dunyi 周敦頤1975. *The Complete Work of Master Zhou* 周子全書. Taipei: Guanxueshe Chubanshe.

Selection in English*

Chan, Wing-tsit (ed.) 1963. *A Sourcebook in Chinese Philosophy*. Princeton University Press. Chapter 28.

---

* Primary sources are in Chinese, while the selections are in English.

2

The Basic Constituent of Things: Zhang Zai's Monist Theory of *Qi*

Introduction

Zhang Zai (1020–1077) constructed a systematic philosophy built on the traditional notion of *qi*. He incorporated the notion of *qi* into his metaphysics as well as his ethics. Before Zhang Zai, there had been primarily in the Daoist tradition cosmogony originating with primordial *qi* (*yuanqi*) as well as ontology with *qi* as the basic constituent of all things.[1] The notion of *qi* or primordial *qi* was commonly used as early as in the pre-Qin philosophy, but there was no unified theory of *qi*, and different philosophers used the notion of primordial *qi* to depict different stages in the development of the universe.[2] Zhang Zai renewed and systematized the philosophy of *qi* in the *Yijing* tradition and made it an integral part of neo-Confucianism. He has been rightly called "the epitomizer of the theory of *qi*" (Cheng 1986; Zhang 1958/2005). In his theory of *qi*, we will see how he categorized the various notions relating to *qi*, and how he resolved some of the difficult questions that former *qi*-theorists had not been able to address.

In term of cosmogony, the notion of *qi* was developed primarily by the Daoists at first. Laozi and Zhuangzi both appeal to the transformation of *qi* in their cosmological explanation. Later Daoists, and a few Confucians such as Dong Zhongshu (179–104 BCE), used the term "primordial *qi* (*yuanqi* 元氣)" to designate the state before the universe was formed. Daoist metaphysics is fundamentally built on the notion of *qi*. This chapter will trace the theory of *qi* to its Daoist roots, and see how the notion of *qi* was employed both in their cosmological explanation and in their ontological analysis. It will then

---

1 Some Confucians also embraced the worldview of primordial *qi*, such as Dong Zhongshu (179–104 BCE) in Han dynasty (206 BCE–220 CE), and Liu Zongyuan (773–819 CE) in Tang dynasty (618–907 CE). However, their interest was not mainly in cosmogony.
2 For example, the *Huainanzi* takes primordial *qi* to be the state of *qi* before the formation of heaven and earth (see below for detailed discussion), while Liu Zongyuan takes primordial *qi* to be what pervades in the middle between heaven and earth (Liu 1979, 442).

Neo-Confucianism: Metaphysics, Mind, and Morality, First Edition. JeeLoo Liu.
© 2018 John Wiley & Sons, Inc. Published 2018 by John Wiley & Sons, Inc.

introduce the theory of *qi* as developed by Zhang Zai, and examine how he went back to the theory of *qi* in the *Yijing* and reinvented the theory of *qi* in neo-Confucianism.

The Concept of Primordial *Qi* (*Yuanqi*)[3]

The term "primordial *qi*" (*yuanqi*) was first seen in a pre-Qin Daoist text the *Heguanzi*[4]: "Heaven and earth are composed of primordial *qi*, while the myriad things rely on heaven and earth [for their existence]" (the *Heguanzi*, Chapter 11, 255). The word *yuan* (元) has many connotations, but in conjunction with *qi* as in *yuanqi*, it means primordial, elemental, originating, and single.[5] In the *Yijing*, *yuan* is included in the four cardinal virtues of the optimal states of *yin* and *yang*: origination (*yuan* 元), fecundity (*heng* 亨), succor (*li* 利), and perseverance (*zhen* 貞). Han dynasty philosopher Dong Zhongshu defines *yuan* as the foundation of everything.[6] In ancient texts, "primordial *qi*" typically designates the state of *qi* before the formation of heaven and earth. This state is often referred to as "chaos" (*hundun* 混沌), a nebulous state of infinite space and formless *qi* that preceded the existence of the ordered cosmos. Since it is without the separation of heaven and earth, without any distinction of objects and things, it is a unified, singular One. This cosmological singularity is called the primordial *qi*.

The theory of primordial *qi* provides a cosmogonic depiction of the initial state of the universe. In the *Heguanzi*, Chapter 5, for example, it is depicted: "From singularity (or One) comes *qi*; from *qi* comes the inkling of vitality" (The *Heguanzi* 2004, 71). A commentator Lu Dian (1042–1102) explicates this claim: "Singularity (One) is the beginning of primordial *qi*" (The *Heguanzi* 2004, 71). The Heguanzi, Chapter 10, gives other descriptions of this state such as "the exalted grandeur" (*taihong* 泰鴻), or "the exalted singularity" (*taiyi* 泰一). According to the *Heguanzi*, there exists a constancy of "the great homogeneity" (*datong* 大同) in this state (The *Heguanzi* 2004, 222). This initial state of the universe before the formation of heavenly bodies described in the *Heguanzi* is thus a massive, homogenous *qi*, but it is not a completely chaotic state.

The *Zhuangzi* is another pre-Qin philosophy work that embraces the theory of primordial *qi*. In the *Zhuangzi*, the initial state of the universe is depicted as a state of "chaos" (*hundun*).[7] This primeval state of chaos is the formless

---

3 Part of this section is based on Liu 2015.
4 See Yi 2003, 58 and Cheng 1986, 6. The authorship of the *Heguanzi* is unknown, and the dating (the Warring States period) is not without controversy.
5 In Xu Shen's authoritative encyclopedia of Chinese vocabulary (*Shuowen Jiezi*), *yuan* is simply given as "the beginning" (*shi* 始).
6 Cited in Zhang 1958/2005, 57. Zhang thinks that what Dong Zhongshu meant by *yuan* is simply *Taiji*.
7 The term "chaos" in cosmogony refers to the earliest condition of the universe, before the ordered cosmos was formed.

indiscernible state of *qi*, which fills up the whole space and is identifiable with space itself, since nothing could be external to it. In the *Zhuangzi*, this initial state is called either "the supreme singularity" (*taiyi* 太一) or "the grand singularity" (*dayi* 大一), as it is so grand that nothing could be outside of it. In this primeval state of chaos, there was no separation of heaven and earth and no concrete objects. In this sense, it is a "void"—empty of things. In time, however, *qi* congregates to form concrete things. As a result, the universe is divided into particulars and thereby losing its "oneness." The whole universe is simply the result of the transformation of *qi*, which begins with chaos: "the initial state of indiscernible, imperceptible chaos transforms into *qi*, *qi* transforms into shape and form, shape and form transform into life" (The *Zhuangzi* 1961, Chapter 18, 612). In the *Zhuangzi*'s cosmogony, there is no need for a transcendent Creator, since this process of transformation is the natural flow of *qi* itself.

It was in the *Huainanzi*, a Daoist text with miscellaneous topics written around the second century BCE,[8] that the Daoist cosmogony based on the notion of primordial *qi* received the fullest exposition for the first time. The *Huainanzi*'s notion of *Dao* appears to be a depiction of primordial *qi*: "[*Dao*] covers heaven and supports earth. It is the extent of the four quarters of the universe and the dimensions of the eight points of the firmament. There is no limit to its height and its depth is unfathomable" (Chapter 1; Chan 1963, 305). The *Huainanzi*'s notion of *wu* (nothingness) depicts a formless, soundless, intangible, unbounded something (Chapter 2), which is "the ancestor of the myriad things" (Chapter 1). In the *Huainanzi*'s analysis, when *qi* first emerged, it is undifferentiated and homogeneous. It is only later that primordial *qi* is split into *yin* and *yang*. This began the formation of heaven and earth. Finally, life began to emerge and things developed into different categories. In this narrative, the world of concrete things initially emerged out of primordial *qi*, not absolute nothing.

However, in the *Huainanzi* there also emerged a competing worldview, according to which primordial *qi* was not the initial state. As told by the *Huainanzi* :

> Before heaven and earth took shape, there was only formless chaos. This primeval state was thus called "the great beginning" (*taizhao* 太昭). *Dao* originated in this state of vast void (*xukuo* 虛廓) and the vast void produced the universe (of space and time *yuzou* 宇宙). The universe generated *qi*. *Qi* is extended in space—that which was clear and light drifted up to become heaven, and that which was heavy and turbid solidified to form earth.
>
> (*The Huainanzi*, Chapter 3, modification of Chan's translation, Chan 1963, 307)

---

8 The *Huainanzi* is allegedly a joint production of intellectual hangers-on hosted by Liu An (179–122 BCE), the prince of Huainan, who supervised and may have contributed to the whole production as well.

In this description, before the universe began and before there was time or space, there was only a formless void. It appears that in this cosmogonic picture, this void precedes primordial *qi*. The *Huainanzi* does not explain how the universe was formed out of this void, nor does it explain how the universe generated *qi*.

In another chapter, the *Huainanzi* provides an account of the development of the universe by explicating the "seven stages" thesis first introduced in *the Zhuangzi*.[9] The *Zhuangzi* has the following account:, "There was a beginning. There was what had been before there was a beginning. There was what had been before what had been before there was a beginning. There was something. There was nothing. There was what had been before there was nothing. There was what had been before what had been before there was nothing" (*The Zhuangzi* 1961, Chapter 2, 79). According to the *Huainanzi*, these seven cosmogonic stages can be interpreted as follows:[10]

1) There was a beginning: There was simply boundless disorder when buds and sprouts were bursting, but shapes and forms had not yet materialized. Life was about to emerge but things had not developed into different kinds and categories.
2) There was what had been before there was a beginning: Before the beginning, *qi* had already manifested the movements of ascending and descending. *Yin* and *yang* intermingled and interacted spontaneously. *Yin* and *yang* roamed freely to fill up the whole universe. This was a time of abundant and vibrant potentiality, but no sign of things yet.
3) There was what had been before what had been before there was a beginning: Heaven and earth had not yet been separated; the whole realm was void and desolate. It can be seen as an indistinct state between something and nothingness. Once *qi* was activated, it pervaded the whole deep, dark abyss.
4) There was something: The myriad things appeared in great abundance. Plants bourgeoned and flourished luxuriantly; insects swarmed and teemed with vitality. There are now tangible, measurable, and enumerable concrete things.
5) There was nothing: When one looks, one cannot see it; when one listens, one cannot hear it. One tries to touch it in vain and one reaches for it

---

9 In the *Zhuangzi*, this passage may have been satirical in nature. However, in the *Huainanzi*, this passage is taken as a serious cosmogonic speculation.
10 The following quote is loosely translated from the *Huainanzi*, Chapter 2, in consultation with Wing-tsit Chan's translation in *A Source Book in Chinese Philosophy* and John S. Major *et al.* (trans.) *The Huainanzi* (2010).

without success. Immense and expansive, it cannot be measured with any instrument, and its brilliance cannot be grasped or conceived.[11]
6) There was what had been before there was nothing: This stage encloses heaven and earth and molds the myriad things, and it penetrates the undifferentiated abyss. It is so vast that nothing could be outside of it; at the same time, it is so minute that nothing could be inside it. It is absolutely without bounds or boundaries, and it generates the root of something and nothing.
7) There was what had been before what had been before there was nothing: At this stage heaven and earth have not yet formed, *yin* and *yang* have not yet been differentiated, four seasons have not yet been separated, and the myriad things have not yet been generated. All is tranquil, peaceful, quiet, and translucent. It is absolutely formless.

We may analyze the seven stages as falling into two retrospective narratives: (3) to (1) depicts the formation of the universe, while (7) to (4) depicts the emergence of concrete things. Stage 1 is the beginning of the world as we have it. Stage 2 is the state of *qi* that has manifested the two modes *yin* and *yang*. Stage 3 depicts the dark, desolate abyss. Stage 7 to Stage 4 seems to be depicting the same cosmogonic process in terms of the emergence of concrete things. There are two possible ways to read the two narratives. We could see Stage 7 as identical with Stage 3, or slightly prior to it; we could see Stage 6 as matching Stage 2, or prior to it. Stages 5 and 4 could be depicting the transition from nothing to something in Stage 1, or it could identify two coexisting states of something and nothingness. There is no established rendition of the order of these seven stages. Here we shall keep both possible readings and arrange them into the following simplified chart:[12]

#7
There was what had been before what had been before there was nothing.

There was no movement and no division of heaven and earth or the four seasons. All is tranquil, peaceful, quiet, and pure.

#3
There was what had been before what had been before there was a beginning.

Heaven and earth had not yet been separated; the whole realm was void and desolate.

---

11 The original text uses *guanyao* (光耀), which literally means "brilliance." However, the *Huainanzi* uses *guanyao* in the same paragraph to refer to an imaginary character in *the Zhuangzi*, Chapter 22. In that allegory, Guanyao was the interlocutor of another imaginary character "Nonbeing" (*wuyou* 無有). The commentary of *the Zhuangzi* says that this character stands for *intelligence*, as the function of intelligence is to illuminate and inspect; hence the name "Brilliance" (*guangyao*).
12 This arrangement is slightly different from that of Hu Shi, who has the order of 7, 3, 6, 2, 1, 4, and 5. See Hu 1931, 26–28.

#6 There was what had been before there was nothing.	Heaven and earth have been separated, and *qi* is undifferentiated and homogeneous. *Qi* encompasses the whole universe.
#2 There was what had been before there was a beginning	*Qi* has already been divided into *yin* and *yang* and there is movement of *qi*. There is no sign of concrete things yet.
#5 There was nothing.	There was nothing visible, audible, tangible, accessible, or conceivable.
#1 There was a beginning.	The emergence of life: Things are budding and sprouting, but have not yet developed into shapes and categories.
#4 There was something.	Concrete things are formed: There are tangible, measurable and enumerable concrete things.

This cosmogonic narrative is not a fully developed theory and many questions remain unresolved: how did homogeneous primordial *qi* become divided into *yin* and *yang*? How did the motionless initial state of *qi* develop movements of ascent and descent? How were heaven and earth brought apart? How did something pop out from the void or nothingness? How were concrete things categorized and how did life emerge? These questions would have to wait until Zhang Zai developed his theory of *qi* to have some answers.

A noted astronomer in Han dynasty, Zhang Heng (78–139 CE), incorporated the theory of primordial *qi* into his scientific explanation of the origination of the universe.[13] His representative work in astronomy, *Spiritual Constitution of the Universe* (*Lingxian* 靈憲, Needham's translation), is considered one of the highest achievements in the history of Chinese astronomy. Apparently influenced by the *Huainanzi*, Zhang Heng depicted the emergence of something from nothing as the development of primordial *qi*. He named the primordial matter "the Great Element (*Taisu* 太素)," and before the Great Element emerged, there was an expansive dark formless abyss called "the Grand Obscurity (*Mingxing* 溟涬)." The Grand Obscurity may have existed since time immemorial. Inside it there was emptiness (*xu*) and outside of it, there was only nothingness (*wu*). It was a deep, dark abyss—a complete lightless void. In the second stage, something came out of nothingness and the primordial

---

13 According to Joseph Needham, Zhang Heng was "not only the inventor of the first seismograph in any civilization but [also] the first to apply motive power to the rotation of astronomical instruments" (Needham 1994, 22).

matter, the Great Element, began to germinate. At this stage, *qi* merged into one and there was no differentiation of *qi's* quality. All were intermingled and homogeneous. Zhang Heng saw this stage as what was meant by Laozi's remark "There was something undifferentiated and yet complete, which existed before heaven and earth" (the *Daodejing*, Chapter 25). He called this stage "Grand Chaos (*Panghong* 龐鴻)," and claimed that it also lasted for an indefinitely long period of time. Finally, the undifferentiated primordial *qi* was divided, and *qi* developed variations of qualities such as its force and its purity. Heaven and earth were separated, and in between, the myriad things began to take shape and form categories. Zhang Heng called this stage "the Great Incipience" (*Taiyuan* 太元).

In Zhang Heng's cosmogony, there are three stages in the development of the universe. He seems to take the three stages as the natural development of *Dao*, and calls them "the root of *Dao*," "the core of *Dao*," and "the actuality of *Dao*," respectively.

The Grand Obscurity (*Mingxing*)	There was only a dark abyss, a lightless void. There was absolutely nothing.
The Grand Chaos (*Panghong*)	The Great Element (*Taisu*) emerged out of nothingness; heaven and earth have not yet been formed. Primordial *qi* is undifferentiated and fused.
The Great Incipience (*Taiyuan*)	*Qi* is divided into *yin* and *yang*, endowed with various qualities. Heaven and earth are separated, and the myriad things began to take shape and form categories.

Zhang Heng's cosmogony is a simplified version, reducing the seven stages in the *Huainanzi* into three stages. Both of them took the appearance of heaven and earth to be a later development and both understood the primordial cosmic state to be a desolate, quiet, dark abyss. It is not clear on either picture when and how primordial *qi* originated. For the *Huainanzi*, the initial formless, undifferentiated state could be what is meant by "primordial *qi*." For Zhang Heng, there was only a dark abyss at the beginning. Not only were there no form and no light, there was no primordial *qi* either. Primordial *qi* emerged out of this pure nothingness, and was initially homogenous and undifferentiated.

Whether or not primordial *qi* is taken to be the initial state, on both accounts it is responsible for the generation of myriad things. To begin with, primordial *qi* splits into *yin* and *yang* with their different attributes. *Yin* with its heaviness formed earth; *yang* with its lightness formed heaven. The myriad things are constituted out of *yin* and *yang* with different degrees of their varying attributes. This is clearly a picture of the emergence of something out of nothingness, and this something is initially a homogeneous primordial *qi*. There is no creation theory, and no divine intervention. The universe naturally evolved out of nothingness, and this evolution results from the way the world is—we can call it *Dao*. This account became the core of the Daoist cosmogony.

In the Daoist cosmogony, two major problems remain unresolved:

The problem of generation: How could primordial *qi* emerge out of total abyss, complete void? Basically, this is the question of how something could come out of nothing.

The problem of division: How could the one undifferentiated primordial *qi* develop the two modes of *yin* and *yang*? If there was homogeneity in the initial state of *qi*, how did diversity and division come about?

Both of these questions are difficult to answer, and Daoist philosophers did not attempt to explain how the generation and division came about when the initial state was a dark empty abyss. We shall see how Zhang Zai abandoned the Daoist's postulations of absolute void and homogeneous primordial *qi* in his reconstructed *qi*-cosmology.

Another major development of the Daoist philosophy of *qi* is to appeal to the notion of *qi* to provide the ontological explanation of the constitution of all things: all things are made of *qi*. For instance, *the Zhuangzi* says: "If we look at the myriad things from their commonality, then we can see that all things are one" (Chapter 5. 190). *The Zhuangzi* views the production of life in particular things as the transformation of *qi*. Life is simply "the amalgamation of *qi*"; death is simply "the dissolution of *qi*." Hence, "what penetrates everything in the world is only this one *qi*" (Chapter 22, 733).

The *Huainanzi* also appeals to the different attributes of *yin* and *yang* to explain the variances among particular things. The attribute of *yang* is light and its movement takes the form of ascent; the attribute of *yin* is heavy and it moves downward. The light and rising *qi* congregates to form heaven, while the heavy and descending *qi* solidifies to form earth. According to the *Huainanzi*, "Creatures with feathers fly in the sky; hence they belong to the category of *yang*. Creatures with shells and scales hibernate underground; hence, they belong to the category of *yin*" (The *Huainanzi* 1990, Chapter 3, 108). Granted, this categorization is at most a crude classification of *yin* creatures and *yang* creatures and cannot be viewed as a scientific taxonomy. However, the classification of all things into either *yin* nature or *yang* nature later became the dominant taxonomy in Chinese herbal medicine.

Wang Chong (27–97), a philosopher in the late Han dynasty, was committed to providing a rational, naturalistic explanation to how events in the human world are related to natural phenomena. His *Disquisitions* (*Lunheng* 論衡)[14] set out to dispute the correlation theories held by Han Confucians such as Dong

---

14 This translation comes from *Encyclopedia Britannica*.

Zongshu as well as popular folk superstitions about supernatural phenomena. He argues that heaven and earth are part of nature, and they do not have any will to punish or reward human deeds. He traces the theory of primordial *qi* to the *Yijing*, and accepts the view that primordial *qi* is the state of *qi* before *qi* was divided into *yin* and *yang*. Since heaven and earth are developed out of *yang* and *yin*, primordial *qi* must have existed before the formation of heaven and earth (Wang Chong 1990, 661–2). However, Wang Chong also thinks that infants are born with primordial *qi* inside their bodies. Hence, primordial *qi* for him is not only a cosmologically prior state of the universe's existence but also an ontologically prior state of the existence of particular things. Wang Chong developed the theory of primordial *qi* as a naturalized worldview, according to which primordial *qi* is the constituent of all things. This is the view that Zhang Zai later inherited and further developed.

We shall now turn to Zhang Zai to see how he continued the lineage of the theory of *qi* while making major revisions in the main theses to revert its Daoist association back to a Confucian view.

The Initial Cosmic State: The Supreme Vacuity (*Taixu* 太虛)

Zhang Zai embraced *Qi*-monism, but he did not adopt the term "primordial *Qi*" and did not inherit the theory of primordial *qi* in the Daoist tradition. On the contrary, Zhang Zai's main contribution to neo-Confucianism is exactly his reconstruction of *Qi*-monism in the spirit of Confucianism. The main difference between the Daoist cosmology and the Confucian cosmology, as we have seen in the previous chapter, is exactly on whether the world originated in nothingness or something. Zhang Zai's theory of *qi* traces back to the *Yijing*. The *Yijing* regards the origin of the universe as the Supreme Ultimate (*Taiji*), and uses the interaction between *yin* and *yang* to explain the emergence of myriad things. According to a contemporary scholar Yishan Cheng (1986), the *Yijing*'s cosmogony and the Daoist cosmogony were competing views since the pre-Qin era, and there are obvious correspondence and opposition between the two views. A major difference is that for the *Yijing*, *Dao* is not a pre-cosmos substance as it is in the *Daodejing*, but the order of the constant interchange between *yin* and *yang* (Cheng 1986, 27). We will see how Zhang Zai's reconstruction of *Qi*-monism takes the *Yijing* tradition rather than the Daoist tradition.

On Zhang Zai's view, there was never a time or any cosmic state in which there was absolute nothingness or an undifferentiated primordial *qi*. He rejects both the *Huainanzi*'s cosmogonic hypothesis of an initially undifferentiated primordial *qi* and Zhang Heng's speculation that Being initially came from a dark void. His theory of *qi* differs from previous Daoists' cosmology in three main aspects:

1) *Qi* exists from the beginning of the universe. Since *qi* is something, there was never absolute nothingness or void.
2) *Qi* is in constant movement and transformation from time immemorial; hence, there was never a static state of motionlessness or quietude.
3) *Qi* is inherently orderly and the cosmic principle (*li*) is inherent in *qi*. There was never a state of pre-cosmos chaos (*hundun*).

Zhang Zai refers to the initial cosmic state as "the supreme vacuity" (*taixu*).[15] The term *taixue* initially came from *the Zhuangzi*, and in that context, it means either the realm of impenetrability or the vast space in the sky. It then became a common term in Daoist texts. The *Huainanzi* explains that *qi* is generated by a vast void (*xukuo* 虛廓), thus the void is a state before the emergence of *qi*. Daoists commonly embrace the view that the emergence of *qi* is a step away from the initial vacuity. Zhang Zai, however, takes the supreme vacuity and the presence of *qi* to be simultaneous from the start.[16]

Even though it is indisputable that Zhang Zai takes the supreme vacuity to coincide with the existence of *qi*, contemporary scholars on Zhang Zai disagree on the whether they are identical states. The relation between the supreme vacuity and *qi* can be said to be the central issue among Zhang Zai scholars. On one view, the supreme vacuity is simply the formless state of *qi* (Zhang 1996; Chen 2005; Yang 2005, 2008; Wang 2009); on the other view, the supreme vacuity is the substance of *qi* and thus is different from *qi* itself (Mou 1999; Ding 2002, 2000).[17] If we examine Zhang Zai's usage carefully, we can see that both explanations are well supported by textual evidence. Zhang Zai uses an analogy to explain the relation between *qi* and the supreme vacuity: "The condensation and dispersion of *qi* in the supreme vacuity is analogous to the solidification and dissolution of ice in water" (Zhang 2006, 8). From this analogy, we can see that in Zhang Zai's usage, "the supreme vacuity" and *qi* are

---

15 This is Wing-tsit Chan's translation.
16 Zhang Zai's view may have been inspired by another source. According to Yishan Cheng (1986), in the second half of the Han dynasty, there were two competing views: one is the standard Daoist view that "vacuity generates *qi*"; the other is the view that *qi* is inherent in the vacuity. The ancient encyclopedia of Chinese medicine, *Huangdi Neijing* 黃帝內經, for example, gives the description that *qi* is widely spread throughout the supreme vacuity. A lost but newly excavated Daoist text, *the Origin of Dao* (*Daoyuan* 道原) also expresses the view that as a primordial state, the supreme vacuity contained some subtle, refined vital *qi* (*jingqi* 精氣). See Cheng 1986, 30–3.
17 Wang Fuzhi also took Zhang Zai to be advocating the separation of substance and function with the terminology of the supreme vacuity. We will see his modification of Zhang Zai's view in Chapter 4.

not different things, though they are different states of the same thing.[18] Zhang Zai calls the supreme vacuity "the substance (*ti* 體) of *qi*,"[19] as water is the substance of ice. Substance remains unchanged through its various transformations, and the transformed state nonetheless has the same substance. Whether it is formless *qi* or coalesced *qi*, it is the same stuff (substance). The supreme vacuity depicts a particular state of *qi*—when *qi* is not condensed into solid forms. As things, the supreme vacuity and *qi* are one and not two; as states, the supreme vacuity and *qi* are two and not one.

In sum, in Zhang Zai's cosmology, the universe began in the state of the supreme vacuity, and the supreme vacuity is nothing but the state of *qi* without any concrete shapes and forms. Under this view, the whole universe is simply the transformation of *qi* alone. Zhang Zai's metaphysics can be rightly called *qi*-monism.

Vacuity Versus Vacuum

In Zhang Zai's usage, the word "vacuity" (*xu* 虛) does not mean void or emptiness; rather, it is rendered a different meaning, namely, "not solid" or "unfilled." Zhang Zai claims that the supreme vacuity contains *qi* and since *qi* is real, the supreme vacuity is not an absolute void. According to Zhang Zai, "The kind of realness of ultimate vacuity is such that it is replete (*shi* 實) but not solid (*gu* 固)… Replete but not solid, hence it disperses from the One" (Zhang 2006, 64). With this new interpretation of the word "vacuity," Zhang Zai uses "the supreme vacuity" to refer to the state of *qi* before concrete forms arise. He claims that the supreme vacuity is the original state of *qi*: "The supreme vacuity has no form. It is the original state (*benti* 本體)[20] of *qi*. Its condensation and dispersion are simply external forms of change" (Zhang 2006, 7). The supreme vacuity is also the ultimate state of *qi*, to which all temporarily solidified concrete things would eventually disintegrate and return. Things with forms have provisional existence; things without forms last forever. According to Zhang Zai, "Gold and metal will sometimes rot; mountains will someday crumble. All things with forms are destructible. Only the supreme vacuity [being formless] does not vacillate, and this is why it has the utmost realness" (Zhang 2006, 325). *Qi* permeates the whole universe, or we should say that space is simply the expansion of *qi*. Before concrete things are formed, the

---

18 Haicheng Wang (2009) argues that this analogy also shows that in Zhang Zai's view, the supreme vacuity and *qi* are of the same nature and not heterogeneous (89).
19 The word *ti* has been translated as *original state*, *fundamental state* or *essence*, in addition to *substance*.
20 The term is often translated as "substance." We will have a detailed account of this term in Chapter 4.

universe is called "the supreme vacuity." With *qi*'s movement, *qi* condenses into concrete things and in time, it will again disperse back into vacuity. In other words, concrete things are located in vacuity. The state of vacuity becomes supreme when there are no concrete things.

We have seen earlier that in the Daoist cosmogony, there is an unsolved problem of how primordial *qi* could have emerged out of total void. Zhang Zai rejects the hypothesis that absolute void or nothingness could have been the initial state. He says: "When one knows that the supreme vacuity is simply *qi* itself, one sees that there cannot be nothingness (*wu*)" (Zhang 2006, 8). Taking up the separation of "boundlessness" (*wuji*) and "nothingness" (*wu*) implicit in Zhou Dunyi's philosophy, Zhang Zai made explicit refutation of the nothingness thesis in the Daoist cosmology and the emptiness thesis in the Buddhist worldview:

> If one argues that vacuity can generate *qi*, then since vacuity is infinite while *qi* is finite, one is committed to the division and segregation between substance and function. Such a view falls into the camp of Laozi's naturalist thesis of "being emerges out of nothingness," and fails to recognize that being intermingled with non-being is the [universe's] constant state. If one argues that myriad phenomena are merely concrete things perceived in the supreme vacuity, then one is committed to the disconnect between concrete things and vacuity … and falls into the Buddhist view that the phenomenal world is simply the result of our visual impairment.
>
> *(Zhang 2006, 8)*

According to Zhang Zai, what the *Yijing* teaches is different from the previous two views because there is no dichotomy of being and nothingness in this worldview. He argues that being is always mixed with non-being, and the difference between the two is simply the congregation or dispersion of *qi*: "When [*qi*] gathers, how can we not call it existing (being)? At the same time, when it disperses, how can we jump to the conclusion that there is nothing?" (Zhang 2006, 182). In this quote, he rejects applying the distinction of "being" and "nothingness" to the presence and absence of concrete things in *qi*. In other words, *qi* is something even when it does not constitute things. In contemporary scholar Lai Chen's explanation, "the supreme vacuity" originally refers to space itself, but in Zhang Zai's conception of space, "there is no absolute void because space is filled with an imperceptible thin *qi*" (Chen 2005, 47). Zhang Zai would claim that there was never a pure vacuum, because he thinks that in the initial state, "the supreme vacuity was already seething with *qi*, which incessantly moves upward and downward" (Zhang 2006, 8). It is obvious from the depiction here that Zhang Zai took *qi* to have real physical existence (since it has movements). *Qi* is something and has always been in existence since time immemorial; hence, there was never a state of nothing. This initial state was vacuous simply because there were no concrete forms. In Zhang Zai's conception, vacuity is no more than formlessness. *Qi* carries energy with it; hence, even before concrete things are amalgamated, the state of *qi* (the supreme vacuity) is still seething with energy and not a complete vacuum.

Zhang Zai's conception of vacuity or emptiness may have been derived from that of Liu Yuxi 劉禹錫 (772–842), a contemporary of Liu Zongyuan 柳宗元 (773–819) in the Tang dynasty. Liu Zongyuan wrote a short piece *Discourse on Heaven* (*Tianshuo* 天說), in which he advocates a naturalized view of heaven and earth. Heaven and earth cannot reward the good or punish the bad, according to Liu, because they are simply part of nature. They cannot assign punishment or reward, just as fruits and plants cannot do so (Liu Zongyuan 1979, 443). In response, Liu Yuxi composed three *Treatises on Heaven* (*Tianlun* 天論). In the second treatise, Liu Yuxi explains the meaning of "emptiness" (*kong* 空):

> When we talk about formlessness, don't we mean emptiness? However, emptiness is simply the state when forms are inaudible and intangible. As substance, it does not obstruct concrete objects; as function, its resource is always being. It must rely on concrete things to manifest itself.... I firmly proclaim: what our eyes can see are the crude forms, while what our minds can perceive are the subtle forms. How could there really be any formlessness between heaven and earth? What the ancients called "formlessness" is simply what does not have constant forms and must rely on concrete things to be manifested.
> *(The Second Treatise on Tian, collected in Liu Zongyuan 1979, 448)*

The *Huainanzi* calls the formless state "the void," while Zhang Zai as well as Liu Yuxi calls the state of vacuity "formlessness." On the surface, they seem to be saying the same thing. To see how the two views differ, we need to compare the two notions void and formlessness. Naturally, absolute vacuum would be formless, but formlessness is not necessarily a vacuum. Take air for example. Air is formless, but it is not nothing, and the space filled with air is not an absolute void. Daoists take the initial formless state to be a vacuum, and they regard this vacuum to be the same as nothingness. Zhang Zai, in the Confucian tradition, takes the initial formless state to be the expansive and mobile *qi*, with two opposing forces constituting its movement. Since *qi* is a physical entity, the supreme vacuity is not a vacuum. It is formless simply in the sense that there is no concrete matter with any definite shape and form. Daoists cannot explain how primordial *qi* emerged out of a desolate void, while Zhang Zai's theory does not have that problem. He could explain the emergence of something out of nothing (no-thing; i.e., no concrete things) as the natural development of *qi*. *Qi* changes from a thin, vacuous state into a state filled with concrete things; concrete things will all eventually dissolve into nothingness and *qi* is then back to the state of the supreme vacuity. In other words, Zhang Zai's cosmology can be seen as a cyclical development of *qi*. Under this view, the world has always existed—be it empty of or filled with concrete things. There was never, and never will there be, absolute nothingness.

The Supreme Equilibrium (*Taihe* 太和) and the Supreme Ultimate (*Taiji*)

Zhang Zai's second contribution to the development of *qi*-philosophy is his attempt to explain the generation of myriad things by the movements of *yin* and *yang*. The crux of his explanation is the notion of polarity. We have seen that Daoist philosophers, whether it is the authors of the *Zhuangzi*, of the *Huainanzi*, or Zhang Heng, all presumed that the original state of *qi* is a homogeneous, undifferentiated primordial *qi*. Furthermore, the notion *One* takes a preeminent place in their philosophy. One problem for the Daoist cosmogony is the problem of division: How did the one *qi* split into two modes of *yin* and *yang*; how did the One multiply into the many? Zhang Zai views the nature of *qi* differently: "*Qi* always has *yin* and *yang*" (Zhang 2006, 219). He rejects the view that *qi* was initially undifferentiated, and then split into two forces.[21] In Zhang Zai's understanding, *yin* and *yang* are "one thing but two aspects" (*yiwu liangti*—物兩體); in other words, *qi* is the unification of two opposites. This unification is ultimately in a balanced state, which Zhang Zai calls "the supreme equilibrium" (*taihe*).[22] Even with the polarity of two opposites *yin* and *yang*, the totality of *qi* is always in equilibrium with the intermingling of *yin* and *yang*.

The notion of the supreme equilibrium, along with the supreme vacuity, is Zhang Zai's highest designation of the ultimate cosmic state. While "the supreme vacuity" depicts the stuff of the universe—formless *qi*, "the supreme equilibrium" depicts the constant state of the universe—harmonious interaction between *yin* and *yang*. Zhang Zai views the universe as imbued with a "pre-established harmony" (not in Leibniz's sense), which governs the continuing development of the universe. Zhang Zai says that the supreme equilibrium is also the so-called *Dao* (Zhang 2006, 7), and *Dao*, according to the *Yijing*, is simply "once *yin* and once *yang*" (Zhang 2006, 187). Hence, "the supreme vacuity," "the supreme equilibrium," and *Dao* are three designations of the existence of *qi*: the initial *qi* exists in a formless, harmonious state, which contains the interaction and interchange between two opposite forces *yin* and *yang*. All production and change are the result of *yin* and *yang* colliding against each other.

---

21 Whether *yin* and *yang* are two separate *qi* or two modes of one *qi* is not a resolved issue.
22 This term in Zhang Zai's usage has typically been translated as "the supreme harmony." Here "equilibrium" is chosen to express the idea that *yin* and *yang* are always well balanced in their distribution and interaction.

Because such collision is constantly in a harmonious equilibrium, neither *yin* nor *yang* will ever be depleted, and consequently, the world will never go extinct.

Zhang Zai further defines "the supreme ultimate" (*Taiji*) as the one thing with polarity (Zhang 2006, 235); in other words, the supreme ultimate is the totality of *qi* and the unification of *yin* and *yang*. The supreme ultimate is both the One and two—this understanding is different from the *Daodejing*'s claim: "*Dao* generates the One; the One generates two, two generates three and three generates the myriad things" (Chapter 42). In the *Daodejing*'s assessment, opposites destroy the One. The *Daodejing* places great value on the One,[23] while Zhang Zai argues that One and two are equally important, as without the One, there could not be two and without two, the One could not be manifested. Movement is possible exactly because there exists opposition. He gave the examples of "two opposites" as hollowness and fullness, motion and rest, integration and disintegration, purity and turbidity (Zhang 2006, 233). We can see from these examples that opposites in Zhang Zai's conception are not merely the result of conceptual distinctions as they are in the *Daodejing*'s examples: beautiful and ugly, good and evil, difficult and easy, long and short, and so on. Zhang Zai has in mind movements and states of *qi* when he discusses "one thing with polarity"—*qi*, as a mobile physical entity, necessarily has opposite directions of movement and various states of aggregation.

We can now see that for Zhang Zai, opposition is necessary for production. He takes the opposing natures of *yin* and *yang* to be what brings about *qi*'s movement. He says, "The *qi* of the supreme vacuity is simply *yin* and *yang* combined as one thing, but *yin* and *yang* are separated as two simply on account of the two states: advancement (*jian* 健) and yielding (*shun* 順). *Yang* is that which advances and *yin* is that which constantly yields" (Zhang 2006, 231). Because of their nature, *yin* and *yang* must continually interact and interchange. Zhang Zai explains the generation of natural phenomena and myriad things by appeal to the movements of *yin* and *yang*:

> *Qi* permeates the extensive supreme vacuity, it moves upward and downward incessantly.... *Yang*'s clarity makes it rise up; *yin*'s turbidity brings it earthward.... Their interaction and their aggregation produced wind and rain, frost and snow. Whether it is the fluid configurations of myriad things or the solid mass of mountains and valleys, everything down to the dregs of wine or the ashes of fire is all governed by the movement of *qi*.
>
> (Zhang 2006, 8, 224)

---

23 For example, Chapter 39 of the *Daodejing* says, "Of old those that obtained the One: Heaven obtained the One and became clear. Earth obtained the One and became tranquil. The spiritual beings obtained the One and became divine. The valley obtained the One and became full. The myriad things obtained the One and lived and grew. Kings and barons obtained the One and became rulers of the empire. What made them so is the One" (Chan 1963, 159).

In other words, opposition produces change. Change generates diversity. So here we have a crude picture of the ontology with *qi* as the basic constituent of the myriad things. We shall now turn to this issue.

Qi as the Constituent of Material and Immaterial Things

For Zhang Zai, *qi* is real and *qi* is the essence of concrete forms. The coalescence and dispersion of *qi* underlie the phenomena of life and death.[24] *Qi* consolidates into concrete things; concrete things disintegrate back to the vacuous *qi*. Zhang Zai calls the supreme vacuity the substance (*ti* 體) of *qi*, and the concrete things the function (*yong* 用) of *qi*.[25] Forms and the formless are simply various stages of the transformation of *qi*.

Qi philosophers before Zhang Zai embraced the thesis that the emergence of concrete things is the result of the congregation of *qi*, but they never fully developed or defended it. To better understand the *Qi*-generation thesis, we may compare it to a contemporary astronomical view in contrast: the nebular hypothesis. The nebular hypothesis was originally proposed by Immanuel Kant and later modified by Pierre-Simon Laplace. The basic idea of this hypothesis is that planets in the solar system were formed by the condensation of hot gaseous nebula. In Kant's understanding, gases contain particles that have gravitational attractions among one another. The attraction brings rapid movements and eventually the nebula consolidates into planets. Gas is the kind of substance "possessing molecular mobility and the property of indefinite expansion, as opposed to a solid or liquid."[26] *Qi*-generation thesis could be compared to the nebular hypothesis because *qi* and gas possess some properties in common: high mobility, indefinite expandability and a vaporous nature. The *qi*-generation hypothesis and the nebular hypothesis share the same narrative that solid forms are the result of the mobility and consequent condensation of an insubstantial, vapor-like substance. This comparison should help us better appreciate the *qi*-generation thesis in *qi*-monism.

Zhang Zai explicates the production of concrete forms in relation to light: "When *qi* congregates, light can shine on it to generate forms; when *qi* is dispersed, light cannot apply to it [since light will penetrates through thin *qi*] and there would be no forms" (Zhang 2006, 8, 182). This explanation seems to point

---

24 According to a contemporary scholar, Wing-cheuk Chan, Zhang Zai treats the primordial *qi* (*yuanqi*) as the "ontological ground" of the whole cosmos (Chan 2011, 95).
25 We will have a more detailed discussion on the issue of substance and function (*ti* and *yong*) in Chapter 4.
26 This definition comes from dictionary.com. On Merriam-Webster, "gas" is defined as "a fluid (as air) that has neither independent shape nor volume but tends to expand indefinitely."

out that light defines form. In contemporary understanding, we know that light enables vision. Zhang Zai may not have thought about the connection between light and perception, but he did use perceptibility as the criterion for concrete forms. Zhang Zai replaces the dichotomy between being and nonbeing with the distinction between visible (light) and invisible (darkness). He claims that this distinction is exactly what was intended in the *Yijing*: "[In the *Yijing*] the sages observed the whole universe. They only acknowledged knowing the cause for the separation between darkness and light, but they did not say they knew what sets being and nonbeing apart" (Zhang 2006, 8, 182). With this distinction, Zhang Zai redirected an ontological pursuit for ultimate reality, such as the Daoists' preoccupation with nothingness and the Buddhists' fascination with nirvana, into an epistemic pursuit. What is the reality that humans could perceive and know became a central issue in neo-Confucianism.

Zhang Zai's *qi*-monism cannot be categorized into the materialist camp, because *qi* is not purely matter. The tradition of Chinese philosophy does not subscribe to the dichotomy between matter and spirit or the material and the immaterial. *Qi* is both the constituent of material things and the essence of immaterial things. Under Zhang Zai's development, the realm of *qi* covers the mechanistic, the organic, and the spiritual dimensions of existence. Zhang Zai explains the production of everything in terms of *qi*: animate things are created by *qi*'s congregating and dispersing, and plants are produced by *qi*'s rising and falling (Zhang 2006, 19). Zhang Zai thinks that spirits and ghosts are simply different functions of *qi*: when *qi* integrates into concrete things, it is called the heaven's "magnificent transformation" (*shenhua* 神化); when the *qi* that constitutes a living thing has dispersed and merged with the vacuous *qi*, it is called the return of the realm of ghosts. Life and death of a living thing is not segregated into distinct realms; rather, they only represent different formations of the *qi*'s constitution. This is why Zhang Zai says, "The words 'ghost' and 'spirit' only signify the passage of coming and going or the process of expansion and condensation" (Zhang 2006, 16). An individual's existence may be transient, but the stuff that makes up the individual—*qi*—is nonetheless indestructible. Therefore, while the world can go from exuberance into emptiness, *qi* itself is ever-present and will never be annihilated.

A Necessitarian Theory of Principle (*Li*) in *Qi*

Another major contribution that Zhang Zai made to the discourse of neo-Confucianism was his introduction of the idea of cosmic necessity or cosmic principle. He conceives of *qi* as an orderly *qi* with an inherent cosmic principle (*li*). "With the *qi* between heaven and earth, there may be hundreds and thousands of various developments, and yet there is a principle that it follows without any aberration" (Zhang 2006, 7). To him, the emergence of the universe and myriad phenomena is necessitated by a cosmic principle (*li*): "The supreme vacuity cannot be without *qi*; *qi* cannot but coalesce to form myriad things and myriad things cannot but disintegrate back to the supreme vacuity. All these developments follow the order of necessity and it is simply what could not have been otherwise" (Zhang 2006, 7). In this statement, we see that Zhang Zai is committed to some form of cosmogonic determinism. The "cannot be" should be analyzed as a physical necessity: it is the law of *qi* that *qi* constantly consolidates and then disperses. The physical necessity constitutes the law of nature. Zhang Zai attributes all changes in the universe to the operations of *yin* and *yang*. Since *yin* and *yang* perpetually work against each other, *qi* necessarily comes together to form material objects, while material objects necessarily disintegrate into vacuous *qi* itself. This necessary tendency of *qi* is the cosmic principle (*li*). Zhang Zai explains, "Although *qi* in the universe integrates and disintegrates, and attracts and repulses in a hundred ways, nevertheless the principle (*li*) according to which it operates has an order and is unerring.... The supreme vacuity of necessity consists of *qi*. *Qi* of necessity integrates to become the myriad things. Things of necessity disintegrate and return to the supreme vacuity. Appearance and disappearance following this cycle are all a matter of necessity" (Chan 1963, 685; with slight modifications).

In contemporary philosophical jargon, we can say that Zhang Zai's view belongs to the camp of the Necessitarian Theory of Laws of Nature. According to Norman Swartz,

> Within metaphysics, there are two competing theories of Laws of Nature. On one account, the Regularity Theory, Laws of Nature are statements of the uniformities or regularities in the world; they are mere descriptions of the way the world is. On the other account, the Necessitarian Theory, Laws of Nature are the "principles" which govern the natural phenomena of the world. That is, the natural world "obeys" the Laws of Nature".[27]
>
> (Swartz 2009)

On the Necessitarian account, laws of nature "govern" the world, while on the Regularity theorist's account, "laws of nature do no more or less than correctly describe the world" (Swartz 2009). Zhang Zai's view belongs to the Necessitarian camp since he regards principle (*li*) as that which governs the development of *qi* as well as regulates *qi*'s movement, and *qi*'s movement is responsible for the development of all states of affairs and all particular things.

The Necessitarian Theory of Laws of Nature can be further divided into two camps: those who believe that the world of nature necessarily obey some law,

---

27 Swartz, Norman 2009. "Laws of Nature." *Internet Encyclopedia of Philosophy* (http://www.iep.utm.edu/lawofnat/).

and those who believe that the physical necessity "inheres in the very woof and warp (the stuff and structure) of the universe" (Swartz 2009, parentheses in original). To better understand the distinction, we shall call the former view "the externalist" view of nomological necessity and the latter "the internalist" view of nomological necessity. This division is well reflected in the debate among neo-Confucians. Zhang Zai's principle (*li*) exemplifies the internalist's conception of the nomological necessity of the world. The nomological necessity is derived from the stuff of the universe, that is, *qi*, as well as from the structure of the universe, that is, *Taiji*. In the next chapter, we will analyze the externalist view of nomological necessity represented in the theory of Zhu Xi.

We can summarize what Zhang Zai considers as the nomological necessity inherent in *qi*:

1) *Qi* necessarily follows the order of "once *yin* once *yang*"; in other words, the rotation and exchange of *yin* and *yang* is inevitable. This pattern of the perpetual exchange between *yin* and *yang* is what the *Yijing* has depicted as *Dao*.
2) *Qi* necessarily moves unceasingly. The movements of *qi* include ascending, descending, expanding, and condensing. The state of *qi* is never stagnant; hence, the universe is forever developing.
3) *Qi* necessarily coalesces and disperses. When *qi* coalesces, it forms concrete things. Concrete things do not last forever and eventually they disintegrate into formless *qi* again. The emergence of particular things is a cosmic necessity, but so is their eventual dissolution.
4) *Qi* necessarily contains the polarity of *yin* and *yang*. Without *yin*, there could not be *yang*; without *yang*, there could not be *yin*. The coexistence and compresence of *yin* and *yang* in all particular things is a nomological necessity of particular existence.

In Zhang Zai's view, none of the earlier formulations of the nature of *qi*, and consequently the constitution of concrete things, is an accidental truth. The world is governed by a pervasive order; it did not originate in chaos (*hundun*), nor does it proceed in random. To answer the question: Why is the world orderly rather than chaotic, Zhang Zai can appeal to the physical nature of *qi*. The order in the universe is not a "cosmic coincidence,"[28] since everything is regulated by the principle that is inherent in the stuff that makes up the world. Everything is the way it is because there are laws of nature epitomized as the principle (*li*) of *qi*. If *qi* simply is this way, then there is no need to ask why it is so. The "why" question becomes superfluous. The metaphysical speculation on the cosmic order is further developed in neo-Confucianism as the issue of principle (*li*). We will turn to that issue in the next chapter.

---

28 Swartz's phrase. See Swartz 2009.

At the end, we can summarize Zhang Zai's notion of *qi* as follows:

1) *Qi* is continuous and gapless; it fills up the whole space (vacuity).
2) *Qi* is self-sufficient.
3) *Qi* is permanent and inexhaustible.
4) *Qi* is self-moving and self-propelling.[29]
5) *Qi* has an internal order; it is thus self-regulating.

Conclusion: Theory of *Qi* and Beyond

The notion of *qi* underlies Chinese philosophy and many other aspects of Chinese culture such as Chinese medicine and martial arts. However, it has always been seen as a mysterious, all-encompassing umbrella concept that defies analysis and frustrates understanding. At the end of this chapter on Zhang Zai's theory of *qi*, we can consider how to relate the concept of *qi* to modern physics.

The importance of the notion of *qi* in Chinese philosophy is tantamount to the notion of atom in Western tradition. However, *qi* is a different kind of matter from atoms. As the constituent of things, *qi* is different from atoms in that it is a "continuous, fluid and diffuse material existence," in which there is no empty space or vacuum (Yi 2003, 59). In Yishan Cheng's study of the ancient Chinese theory of primordial *qi*, he summarizes the main difference between the Western naïve materialism and the theory of primordial *qi* as a form of naturalized materialism: "Western naïve materialism begins with matter of fixed shapes to look for *the one* in the many natural phenomena. It concludes that all things are made of indivisible particle-like units of matter. The theory of primordial *qi*, on the other hand, begins with the matter that is before forms and shapes, and defines *the one* in many as the formless matter. Its conclusion is that material things result from transformations of some continuous matter" (Cheng 1986, 1). Since atoms are discontinuous, there is space within and without concrete things. On the other hand, in the philosophy of *qi*, there is no separation between space and matter. *Qi* is continuous and gapless and it fills up the whole space—the extent of space itself is exactly the extent of the propagation of *qi*. This view is shared by later *qi*-philosophers under Zhang Zai's influence. For example, Zhang Zai's successor Wang Fuzhi (1619–1692) says: "*Yin* and *yang* fill up the supreme vacuity. Other than *yin* and *yang* there is nothing and there is no gap" (Wang 1967, 10). Wang Fuzhi's contemporary and close friend Fang Yizhi (1621–1671) also says,

---

29 According to a contemporary Zhang Zai scholar, Lihua Yang, *qi* in Zhang Zai's philosophy cannot be viewed as some passive "material cause" because *qi* itself contains an essential mobility (Yang 2005).

"There is no gap in *qi*; everything is transferrable and corresponding" (*Notes on the Principles of Things* [*Wuli Xiaozhi*] in Cheng 1986, 22). *Qi* is seen as a continuous matter; thus, the worldview based on *qi*-ontology is different from the materialistic worldview based on atom-ontology.

Nowadays it is believed that normal matter (concrete things) makes up less than 5% of the universe. The rest of the universe is made up of "dark matter" and "dark energy"—and dark energy fills up to 70% of the universe.[30] Both notions of dark matter and dark energy are as enigmatic as *qi* is. Currently, cosmologists still do not have any confirmed theory about the formation of the universe or its constitution. The fact that normal matter constitutes only less than 5% of the universe shows us that materialistic postulates—be it atoms, particles, or strings—cannot fully capture the universe's existence. The theory of *qi* may find a place in future sciences.

Some contemporary scholars (Yi 2003; He 1997) have compared *qi* to quantum field, and they suggest that the transformation of *qi* from the continuous vacuous state to discrete concrete things can be reinterpreted as the transition from quantum field to particles in contemporary physics. To support his view, Zuoxiu He further argues that the theory of primordial *qi* is the origination of the contemporary quantum field theory. He traces the quantum field theory to Einstein, Einstein to Leibniz, and Leibniz to the theory of primordial *qi* (He 1997). It is beyond the scope of this book to investigate the historical connections between the concept of primordial *qi* and the idea of quantum field. However, it is true that Leibniz was highly interested in Chinese philosophy and was especially taken in by Chinese theory of *qi*. Leibniz compared *qi* to ether,[31] which, in Leibniz's time, was believed to be a continuous substance that fills up space. Leibniz separates matter into two kinds: those that are solid (or impenetrable), rigid and indivisible (such as atoms), and those that are penetrable, fluid and infinitely divisible (such as ether).[32] He suggests that fluidity is the more basic condition and it belongs to "prime matter" only.[33] In Leibniz's description, primary matter is a "continuous mass filling the world,"

---

30 The information about dark energy comes from NASA's astrophysics page (http://science.nasa.gov/astrophysics/focus-areas/what-is-dark-energy/).
31 *Qi* is sometimes translated as "ether," as in, for example Tang 1956, McMorran 1975, and Graham 1958.
32 Gottfried Wilhelm Leibniz 1896. *New Essays on Human Understanding*. New York: The Macmillan Books. Book II. Chapter 4 (of Solidity), Section 3.
33 Leibniz says, "I think that perfect fluidity is appropriate only to *prime matter* (i.e. matter in the abstract), considered as an original quality like motionlessness. But it does not fit *secondary matter* – i.e. matter as it actually occurs, invested with its derivative qualities – for I believe that no mass is ultimately rarefied and that there is some degree of bonding everywhere." (Leibniz 1896, 223) Gottfried Wilhelm Leibniz 1896. *New Essays concerning Human Understanding*. New York: The Macmillan Books. Book II. Chapter 23 (of Our Complex Ideas of Substances), Section 23.

"from which all things are produced through motion, and into which they are resolved through rest." In this primary matter there is no diversity, mere homogeneity" (Leibniz 1896, 637). If there are two kinds of matter, then perhaps *qi* is this other kind of matter characterized by fluidity and continuity.

Wing-cheuk Chan also compares Zhang Zai's theory of *qi* to Leibniz. He argues that the notion of primordial *qi* (*yuanqi*) should be compared to Leibniz's notion of primitive force; furthermore, *yang* corresponds to Leibniz's active primitive force while *yin* corresponds to his passive primitive force (Chan 2011, 96). The primitive force consists of both the active and the passive force, just as *qi* is the unity of both *yang* and *yin*. There cannot be the one without the two, as Zhang Zai indicates in the quote that the supreme ultimate (*Taiji*) is "one thing with two aspects" (Zhang 2006, 48). Chan also points out the similarity between Zhang Zai's notion of supreme equilibrium (which he translates as supreme harmony) and Leibniz's concept of harmonica universalis (Chan 2000, 220). Both concepts depict the universe as possessing a constant, natural state of harmony, which is "nothing but the identity in difference" or the "synthesis without mutual destruction" (Chan 2000, 220). However, we should also note the differences between the two philosophies. For Leibniz, the pre-established harmony in the world is guaranteed by God; for Zhang Zai, on the other hand, the pre-established harmony is simply a state of *qi*, a state of nature itself.

Zhang Zai's notion of supreme vacuity has also been compared to Descartes's conception of space (He 1997). There is good reason for making this comparison. Descartes repudiated the notion of absolute void or vacuum: "With respect to vacuum, in the philosophical sense of the term, that is, a space in which there is no substance, it is evident that such does not exist, ... since there is extension in it there is necessarily also substance" (Descartes 1644/2004, 47). Descartes's conception of an empty space is similar to what Zhang Zai says of the supreme vacuity: "in truth, by the term vacuum in its common use, we do not mean a place or space in which there is absolutely nothing, but only a place in which there is none of those things we presume ought to be there.... [It] is in the same sense that we say space is void when it contains nothing sensible, although it contains created and self-subsisting matter" (Descartes 1644/2004, 47). In other words, what Descartes means by an empty space is simply the space without perceptible objects. We can see that it is similar to Zhang Zai's terminology of "vacuity," which is simply vacuous of things with concrete forms, but not an absolute void.

Zhang Zai's contribution of neo-Confucianism is his systematization of the theory of *qi*. His *qi* philosophy was later elaborated and fully developed by Wang Fuzhi, and the school of *qi* theory became one of the three major branches in neo-Confucianism—the Cheng–Zhu school, the Lu–Wang school and the school of the philosophy of *qi* (*Qixue* 氣學). Furthermore, Zhang Zai's introduction of the notion principle (*li*) and his Necessitarian view of laws of nature was further developed by his student Cheng Yi and later in the Southern Song dynasty, by the great synthesizer of neo-Confucianism, Zhu Xi. We shall turn to this topic in the next chapter.

Primary Source

Zhang Zai 張載 2006. *The Complete Work of Zhang Zai (*張載集*)*. Beijing, China: Zhonghua shuju.

Selection in English

Chan, Wing-tsit (ed.) 1963. *A Sourcebook in Chinese Philosophy*. Princeton University Press. Chapter 30.

3

Cheng–Zhu School's Normative Realism: The Principle of the Universe

Introduction

The key issue in this chapter is about the existence of laws of nature, that is, about whether the universe is a "cosmic accident" or is "driven by specific, eternal laws of nature."[1] This exploration reflects a shared human puzzlement. "Science has long been based on the notion that law and order rule the universe," but with the advent of new chaos theory, the question of the existence of cosmic law and order was in question: "Chaos raises some fundamental questions about the universe: Since order can generate chaos as well as pattern, what is the role of natural law? Is it chaos, not order, which rules the universe? And where do nature's complex patterns come from, if not from simple laws?"[2] In Chapter 2, we have seen that there are two camps with regard to the normativity of laws of nature: Regularists and Necessitarians. Regularists think that laws of nature are nothing but regularities observed in nature. It is a contingent fact that the world is the way it is. Necessitarians, on the other hand, think that there is a way the world must be. Zhang Zai belongs to the Necessitarian camp. His notion of principle (*li*) represents the physical necessity of the world. In this chapter, we will see the further development of the Necessitarian notion of principle (*li*) in the philosophy of the Cheng brother (in particular, Cheng Yi) and Zhu Xi, identified as the Cheng–Zhu school.

According to a contemporary scholar Yong Huang, it was due to the Cheng brothers, Cheng Hao (1032–1085) and Cheng Yi (1033–1107), that in neo-Confucianism we see "the development of a sophisticated Confucian moral metaphysics." Therefore, they can be truly regarded as "the founder of Neo-Confucianism" (Huang 2014, 14). In Huang's understanding, the Cheng brothers' moral metaphysics "centered on the most fundamental idea of *li*" (Huang 2014, 14).

1 Norman Swartz, "Laws of Nature," in *Internet Encyclopedia of Philosophy*, (http://www.iep.utm.edu/lawofnat/).
2 Ian Stewart, "Does chaos rule the cosmos?" In *Discover Magazine*, November 1992. (http://discovermagazine.com/1992/nov/doeschaosrulethe147).

Neo-Confucianism: Metaphysics, Mind, and Morality, First Edition. JeeLoo Liu.
© 2018 John Wiley & Sons, Inc. Published 2018 by John Wiley & Sons, Inc.

The neo-Confucian metaphysics of *li* was already present in Zhang Zai's theory of *qi*, but it was the Cheng brothers, in particular, Cheng Yi, who expanded on the role and significance of *li*. Their discourse on *li* paved the way for the neo-Confucian discourse on the "principle of Heaven" (*tian li*). In this chapter, we will give a detailed analysis of their notion of *li*, which we will keep the common translation of "principle" as explained in the "Introduction" of this book.

Zhu Xi's (1130–1200) "chief contributions to Chinese philosophy," in an apt description by Donald Lach: "were clearer distinctions on moral issues, the coordination of the moral teachings of his predecessors, and—more than any of his predecessors—the gathering of data for a partly metaphysical and partly cosmological foundation for his moral philosophy" (Lach 1945, 449). This "partly metaphysical and partly cosmological foundation" is *li*—"principle." In Zhu Xi's metaphysics, principle is also the most important notion, which he relates to the ultimate reality—*Taiji*.

This chapter begins with the explication of the notion of principle (*li*) understood by the Cheng brothers. It then analyzes how the Cheng brothers, and later Zhu Xi (1130–1200), developed ontological hierarchy that posits nonreductionism of principle. It also investigates the relation between the universal principle and particular things. The chapter construes the metaphysical worldview presented by the Cheng brothers and Zhu Xi as a form of normative realism— the view that certain normative principles are fact-based and certain normative truths are objective truths about the world rather than merely human constructions or projections. Under normative realism, statements about these normative truths have truth conditions independent of human opinions and not restricted to human verifiability. Even though the Cheng brothers as well as Zhu Xi had not thought about the status of principle in these terms, their commitment to the realness and objectivity of principle does support this new construal.

Cheng Hao's Conception of Principle (*Li*): The Principle of Heaven

The two brothers shared many views in common with the notion of principle; however, the notion was further developed from Cheng Hao to Cheng Yi. Cheng Hao's usage of principle encompasses both the universal and the particular dimensions—there is one principle unifying all things and there are myriad particular principles for each kind of particular things. The universal principle is identified with *Dao* or heavenly principle. Particular principles are identified as the paradigm or the archetype of each kind of things, and Cheng Hao calls it the "nature" or "essence" (*xing* 性) of things.

Cheng Hao can be credited for introducing the notion of heavenly principle into the discourse of neo-Confucianism. By Cheng Hao's own account, he came by the notion of heavenly principle on his own and not from anyone before him.[3] By conjoining the notion of principle with the notion of heaven, Cheng Hao gave the notion of principle a moral dimension that makes it comparable to the concept of *Dao*. Cheng Hao and Cheng Yi both use heavenly principle interchangeably with *Dao*. According to Cheng Hao, "There is *Dao* and there is principle. It is what governs both Heaven and the human world and there is no difference between the two" (Chengs 1981, 20). Cheng Yi also says "Principle is nothing but the *dao* of Heaven" (Chengs 1981, 290). From this point on, the neo-Confucian conception of heavenly principle became equivalent to the notion of *Dao* in classical Confucianism.

Another important feature of Cheng Hao's notion of principle is the unification of the descriptive dimension of how things are, with the prescriptive dimension of how one ought to treat things in accordance with the thing's nature. For Cheng Hao, the primary significance of principle does not lie in its regulative function for the operation of *qi*, as Zhang Zai saw it, but in adding a normative dimension to human affairs—both in interpersonal relationships and in humans' interaction with the world. The nature of things is not determined by human stipulation, not by artificial taxonomy, and does not alter along with scientific paradigm shifts. It is a fact about the world as it is, and truths about the nature of things hold whether or not humans obtain knowledge of these truths. The nature of a particular thing is called its "principle" in the sense of being its epitome, its norm, or simply the way it ought to be under the ideal condition. Each kind of things has its principle; hence, there are as many particular principles as there are kinds of things. It falls on humans, the facilitator of heavenly principle, to ensure the fulfillment of particular things' principles. As Cheng Hao puts it, "One must treat each thing in accordance with its nature" (Chengs 1981, 125).

To Cheng Hao, normativity is a fact of nature: there are certain rules or regulations on the way things are, and the same rules command human compliance in our treatment of things. The prescriptive force is not based on a consequentialist thinking about what would happen to us if we did not comply. Rather, the normativity is mandated by our very existence in the world[4]: As human beings, we ought to treat particular things in accordance with their principles. The particular principles or the norms of each kind of things are to be discovered,

---

3 Cheng Hao says, "Although my learning came from others, the two words 'heavenly principle' came from my own understanding" (Chengs 1981, 424).
4 Following the traditional teaching of classical Confucianism, neo-Confucians took our nature to be a sacred attribute of our being humans. This teaching is especially manifested in the quote from the *Doctrine of the Mean*: "What Heaven mandates is called [human] nature. To follow our [Heavenly mandated] nature is called '*Dao*'" (Chan 1963, 98, with ample modifications). The description "Heaven's mandate" does not have any religious connotation; it merely underscores the universality and indubitability of our having these moral attributes. We will delve into the issue of human nature in Part II of this book.

not created or stipulated. They are part of the fabric of the world. Prior to human investigation and scientific taxonomy, the world is already organized, structured, and regulated by principles. The existence of norms is real and human-independent. This is why we call such a view normative realism. The unification of the factual and the normative dimensions was established through Cheng Hao's employment of the Chinese word *li* (理), which has both connotations in Chinese. Zhu Xi would later develop this theory in full.

We can summarize the connotations of "principle" in Cheng Hao's (1981) following remarks:

Principle consists in polarity—"All the things in the world must have opposites. Nothing can stand alone. This is what is naturally so, not something arranged" (p. 121).

Principle of particular things is simply the norm of each kind of things—"Once there is a kind of things, there must be its norm. Everything in the world has its principle" (p. 123).

Principle lies in each thing's nature—"Heaven produces things of different lengths and different sizes. One must treat each thing in accordance with its nature. Heavenly principle is such, so, how could anyone violate it?" (p. 125).

Cheng Yi's Conception of Principle (*Li*): Principle is one but its manifestations are many

Cheng Yi embraced his brother's normative realism, and further enriched the conception of principle with many interesting discourses. The most important thesis he introduced is "Principle is one but its manifestations are many (*li* yi *wan shu* 理一萬殊)".[5] This slogan later became a key theme in neo-Confucianism. The thesis is important because it lays out a worldview of organization, cohesiveness, and above all, unification. The world we perceive appears to be myriad in things and diverse in nature; however, everything is governed by one principle alone. What is this principle? How could this one principle be the grounding as well as the law for all phenomena? Presumably, if we could perceive this principle, then we would be able to unlock the mystery of the world. Where do we start to get to know the principle? The epistemology of principle became the focus of the neo-Confucian discourse.

There are several existing interpretations of the thesis "Principle is one but its manifestations are many," and they are all supported by textual evidence in Cheng Yi's remarks.

---

5 This phrase is different from Cheng Yi's other phrase which is often conflated with it: "Principle is one, but each one's due is different (*li yi fen shu* 理一分殊)." See below.

(1) It means "*qi* has many different distributions which are all regulated by the same pattern of the ultimate reversal between *yin* and *yang*."

According to Cheng Yi, "Scattered as particular principles, principles have myriad differences, but unified in *Dao*, these different principles are all in accord. This is why the *Yijing* says, 'Change (*yi* 易) has the Supreme Ultimate (*Taiji*), which generates the two norms (*liangyi* 兩儀).' The Supreme Ultimate is simply *Dao*, and the two norms are *yin* and *yang*. *Yin* and *yang* is one *Dao*. The Supreme Ultimate is boundless (*wuji*)" (Chengs 1981, 667). In this quote, Cheng Yi identifies the Supreme Ultimate with *Dao* itself, and he explains the relation between principles and *Dao* as "many to one." *Dao* regulates the operation of *qi*, which constitutes the myriad things. Since *qi* is scattered in particular things, the distribution of *yin* and *yang* in things differs one from another. Ultimately, however, all things must obey the pattern of *qi*'s operation—*Dao*, also called "the order of heaven" (Chengs 1981, 274) and "the principle of heaven" (Chengs 1981, 30). Cheng Yi further gives a more exact account of this one principle: it is *qi*'s yielding and extending, moving to and fro (Chengs 1981, 167) and *qi*'s aggregation and dispersion (Chengs 1981, 931). This sense of "principle (*li*)" is the same as Zhang Zai's notion of principle. "Principle" (*li*) in this usage can be rendered as "pattern" or more specifically, the pattern of *qi*'s operation. This is the most commonly adopted interpretation both historically and among contemporary scholars.

(2) It signifies the part/whole relationship in the holistic organization of the world.

According to Cheng Yi, "The principle of one thing is exactly the principle of all things, just as one day's progression is exactly the whole year's progression" (Chengs 1981, 13). James Behuniak Jr. argues that principle in East Asian Buddhism should be analyzed as "wholeness," and this wholeness "is something that happens, and it is capable of happening on multiple levels without obstruction" (Behuniak 2009, 36). This analysis fits the analogy of day and year in Cheng Yi's remark.[6] Under this analysis, everything is part of the whole progression of the universe, which itself has an inherent order and principle. Since everything fits the overall principle, the development of each thing must also have its own principle. The Chinese word *li* in this usage can be rendered as "coherence," "law," or "order." The development of things in nature follow a certain order, as for example, "if a sand island suddenly appeared in the ocean, it would then have plants and trees, since they come into being when there is earth. When there are plants and trees, birds and beasts will then come into being of themselves" (Chengs 1981, 199). This comment is remarkably close to being a claim about natural evolution. Following a natural order, things come into existence and this is why each thing's principle coheres with the overall

---

6 An interesting similarity is that Behuniak appeals to the "Day" analogy in Plato's *Parmenides* in his explication of the notion *Li*, while Cheng Yi also used "day and year" as his analogy.

principle in nature. In this context, we can see why Willard Peterson argues that in the teachings of Cheng Yi, the word *li* should be translated as "coherence," by which he means "the quality or characteristic of sticking together" (Peterson 1986, 14). He thinks that Cheng Yi's "one principle with multiple manifestations" is a thesis about the unitary coherence of all things. This sense of principle was later further developed by Zhu Xi.

(3) It denotes the many stages in *Dao*'s life-generating process.

In some contexts, Cheng Yi clearly identifies principle with *Dao*, which is the life-generating operation of heaven and earth (Chengs 1981, 4, 290, 1225, 1253). Focusing on this usage, Yong Huang argues that principle in the Cheng brothers' conception is not a thing, but an activity—it is the "life-giving activity" (*sheng* 生) (Huang 2007, 195–6); in particular, it is the "life-giving activity of the vital *qi*" (Huang 2007, 199). Since this life-giving activity of *qi* is responsible for the generation of all things, it is inherent in each particular thing. Huang explains, "Thus understood, we can easily see why each of the ten thousand things possesses the *li* completely: everything has its life-giving activity and there is indeed no life-giving activity over and above the life-giving activities of the ten thousand things, as there is no thing over and above the ten thousand things" (Huang 2007, 199). From studying each particular thing, we can understand that the progression of the whole universe is nothing but *qi*'s life-generating activity propelling everything forward. *Li* in this context can be seen as a shorthand for *tian-li* (heavenly principle) and thus interchangeable with *Dao*.

(4) It refers to the *raison d'être* for each thing in the overall existence of the world.

On some occasions, Cheng Yi specifically defines particular principle as "what makes it so" (*suoyiran* 所以然) for a particular thing. We may say that principles for particular things are their *raison d'être*—the reason for each particular thing's existence, or "the conditions of being"—the essential conditions for a thing's existence. A. C. Graham focuses on this usage in his analysis of the concept of principle in the Cheng brothers' usage. He quotes from Cheng Yi: "To exhaust the principles of things is to study exhaustively *why they are as they are* ([*suoyiran*]). The height of heaven and thickness of earth, the appearance and disappearance of the spirits, must have *reasons* ([*suoyiran*])" (Chengs 1981, 157; cited in Graham 1992, 8; italics in original). Graham argues that the reason for each thing's existence is normative rather than descriptive in the Cheng brothers' conception. He says: "It will be noted that in most of these quotations the *li* accounts not for the properties of a thing but for the task it *must* perform to occupy its place in the natural order" (Graham 1992, 18; italics added). Principles for particular things are subsumed under one all-encompassing principle, since they prescribe how each thing must function to fit into the overall scheme of things. Each thing has the way it is and the way it ought to be, and we must deal with it in accordance with its principle. Hence, the descriptive principle of each thing's nature entails the prescriptive principle of human conduct. This leads to the next sense of *principle*.

(5) It depicts the various dues demanded from us in our overall treatment of things.

Cheng Yi expresses this ethical precept as "Principle is one but things have different dues (*li yi fen shu* 理一分殊)." This phrase has frequently been misinterpreted and conflated with "Principle is one but its manifestations are many (*li yi wan shu* 理一萬殊)." It is the same idea behind both phrases. However, in the ethical context, Cheng Yi was addressing a student's question about Zhang Zai's moral precept in his "Western Inscription": whether the goal is the same as the Mohist's precept of universal love. Cheng Yi's explanation is that each one's due[7] is different, so we should not treat all people with no discernment whatsoever (Chengs 1981, 1201–3). "Principle" in this context should be rendered as "ethical norm" or "normative principle." Wing-tsit Chan focuses on this aspect of the notion of *li* in Cheng Yi's philosophy. He thinks that Cheng Yi's interest was primarily ethical and the goal was "to understand principle as a way of self-cultivation" (Chan 1978, 107). He also noted the mistake in the traditional translation of *"fen"* as "distinction," and explained that the word means "duty, share, endowment" instead (Chan 1978, 106).

The analysis given here shows that Cheng Yi's notion of principle is multifarious and not necessarily a single notion. However, these connotations of principle are not in competition with one another, as they are interrelated in the Cheng brother's overall worldview. Their worldview differs from that of Zhang Zai, their uncle, in one major respect: to them, principle is not merely the principle *of qi*; rather, it is the principle *for qi*. In other words, to the Cheng brothers, normative facts are not reducible to facts of nature or facts of *qi*. Normative principles constitute the normative realm, which is integral to the part and parcel of the world. Their worldview incorporates an "ontological hierarchy" between principle and *qi*, which Zhu Xi later took pains to explicate and defend.

An Ontological Hierarchy of the Cheng Brothers: Non-Reductionism of Principle

Even though the Cheng brothers greatly admired Zhang Zai and the ethical paradigm that Zhang Zai introduced in his "Western Inscription", they did not completely accept Zhang Zai's metaphysics. One major departure from Zhang Zai's philosophy was their separating the metaphysical layer of principle from

---

7 The Chinese word is *fen*, in the fourth tone. The same word also has a first tone reading, in which case it means "divide" or "apart." This is why there has been such a widespread conflation with the other phrase. Once we see the phrase in its context, its meaning becomes clear. A supporting evidence for our reading here is another comment made by Cheng Yi: "The principles of all things are already self-sufficient, and yet one often cannot fulfill one's due (*fen*) in the interactions between the emperor and the subject or between a father and a son" (Chengs 1981, 1267). In this quote, the word *fen* is clearly used as *due* or *obligation*.

the physical layer of *qi*. In this respect, the two Cheng brothers share the same view. Cheng Hao and Cheng Yi both reject Zhang Zai's treatment of the supreme vacuity as the ultimate substance. According to Cheng Yi, Zhang Zai "treats *Dao* as a grand vacuity, but vacuity is in relation to concreteness, and cannot be what transcends forms" (Chengs 1981, 1174). Cheng Hao made the same criticism (Chengs 1981, 118). Both of them think that *qi* belongs to the lower layer of the world that consists of concrete forms, while Principle or *Dao* belongs to the higher, permanent, enduring realm, which must also "transcend forms." Therefore, Principle and *Dao* cannot be identified with *yin* and *yang*'s operation or the order of *qi*. In other words, they reject Zhang Zai's *qi*-monism.

The Cheng brothers introduced a different worldview, according to which the heavenly order that we call *Dao* or principle is not merely an operation of *qi* and is not derived from the realm of *qi*. They posit an ontological layer of *Dao* or Principle over and above the layer of *qi*. According to Cheng Yi, "In the quote from the *Yijing*, 'Once *yin* and once *yang* is the so-called *Dao*,' *Dao* is not simply [the transition between] *yin* and *yang*; it is that which makes [*yin* and *yang* alternate] as once *yin* and once *yang*" (Chengs 1981, 67). Saying that *Dao* is what makes *yin* and *yang* alternate, Cheng Yi has separated *Dao* from what makes up the physical world—*qi*. He calls the realm of *Dao* "metaphysical" (*xingershang* 形而上)—literally, transcending form. *Yin* and *yang* are different modes of *qi*, and *qi* is in the material realm of forms (*xingerxia* 形而下) (Chengs 1981, 162). *Dao* and the material world are thus separated. For Cheng Yi, the separation between the realm of principles and the realm of *qi* is not temporal but ontological. The realm of principles is empty because there are no concrete things; however, the principles of concrete things are already there in the latent form. Between principles and their concrete manifestations, there is no temporal difference: "The time before the principles are manifested does not come first and the time after the principles are manifested does not come later" (Chengs 1981, 153). Cheng Yi's discourse on principle clearly reflects not a cosmogonic concern as in Zhang Zai, but an ontological one.

The basis of the Cheng brothers' layered worldview is the famous slogan in the *Yijing*: "What transcends forms is called *Dao*; what is with forms is called concrete thing" (*Xici*). In this quote, "what transcends forms" means what is abstract and imperceptible, while "what is with forms" means things with concrete shapes and forms. We can see that this hierarchical worldview was already implicated in the *Yijing*. In a contemporary scholar Lai Chen's interpretation, the former is the intelligible realm, graspable only with reason, while the latter is the sensible realm, perceptible by senses (Chen 2005, 62). A. C. Graham argues that what distinguishes the principles, which are above form, from the things and activities below form, "is not generality but permanence" (Graham 1992, 13). That is to say, things with concrete forms must eventually perish, but the abstract thing, being abstract, is indestructible. Combining these two reasonable interpretations, we can say that the Cheng brothers think that our world belongs to the sensible realm, which is filled with myriad concrete objects. However, among these myriad concrete objects, there is nonetheless something universal and everlasting, which is *Dao*. This *Dao* is what governs the universe and regulates everything. It is the highest normative principle— and the Cheng brothers identify it with heavenly principle.

According to Cheng Yi, heavenly principle is self-sufficient and self-complete: "Heavenly principle is just one principle. How could it ever be depleted? .... How could we ever talk about adding to it or taking away from it? Heavenly principle in itself is self-complete and in which all principles are contained" (Chengs 1981, 31). According to a noted historian of Chinese philosophy Youlan Feng, "Principle subsists eternally, without undergoing either addition or diminution. There it is, irrespective of whether men know it or not" (Feng 1983, 503). In other words, Feng attributes a form of eternalism to Cheng Yi's notion of *Principle*. The presence of the one Principle (heavenly principle) and the many particular principles belongs to the eternal realm and not confined to the experiential realm of human beings. Feng sees Cheng Yi as taking the realm of Principle to be a transcendent realm that is "independently subsisting apart from actual things" (Feng 1983, 507). This interpretation seems to fit the text.

Cheng Yi depicts the realm of Principle as "empty, vast and formless, and yet it nonetheless contains abundant images (*xiang* 象) of myriad things" (Chengs 1981, 153). The "images" here can be interpreted as the blueprints of concrete things, and for Cheng Yi, they are the particular principles of concrete things. Cheng Yi explains:

> The construction of [concrete things] is derived from the image. The image is preserved in the diagram [of the *Yijing*] but the diagram is not necessarily earlier than the [concrete things]. The sages were able to construct the [concrete things] because they knew the image without having to see the diagram.... It may be objected that there can be no natural image since the [caldron] was made by man. The answer is that certainly it is man-made, but the fact that things can be made edible by cooking, and that its use depends on a certain form and construction, is not man-made but natural".
>
> *(Chengs 1981, 957; translated by A. C. Graham, in Graham 1992, 20)*

In this comment, Cheng Yi presents an interesting hypothesis: For each kind of things, there is a certain "form and construction" for its coming into being. This predetermined form and construction remains latent before concrete things are actually invented or produced. Under this hypothesis, the whole is already complete in its initial form. Each thing's coming into existence is not a process in which being emerges out of nonbeing; rather, it is a process from latency to manifestation, from the thing's having mere "conditions of being" to its actual form and construction. In the next chapter, we will see how Wang Fuzhi rejects this very hypothesis of *the world in completion.*

From this discussion, we can see that for the Cheng brothers, in addition to the eternal Principle, there are also eternal particular principles for particular things. We have explained that principles in particular things should be interpreted as "the norm" or "the normative state," and their existence is objectively real as a natural "fact." To the Cheng brothers, this normative reality imposes an epistemic as well as an ethical obligation on us: We ought to know the principle of each thing in order to act appropriately in accordance with the thing's nature. According to Cheng Yi, "There is a principle for each and every thing. One must exhaustively investigate the principles of things" (Chengs 1981, 188). To know why things are the way they are (*suoyiran*) is essential to our leading a moral life, because our dealing with things involves our attitudes and actions. The same applies to human relationships. According to Cheng Yi, "Everything must have its norm. For a father, it is paternal love; for a son, it is filial piety. For an emperor, it is humaneness and for a subject, it is reverence" (Chengs 1981, in Cheng's Commentary on the *Yijing*, 968). In other words, there is a normative requirement for each role that one plays in the human society. A principle is not only how a thing ought to be but also how one ought to act with regard to the thing. To "investigate principles" in things is to understand how one ought be behave with respect to the object or thing at hand. This is how the Cheng brothers established the direction in neo-Confucianism to connect ethics and epistemology with metaphysics. This marriage between ethics and metaphysics is further enhanced in the philosophy of Zhu Xi.

Zhu Xi's Notion of Principle as a Holistic Order of the World

Zhu Xi sometimes takes "principle" to signify "order." When being asked whether principle is in *qi*, he replies, "There is order in the complicated interfusion of the *yin* and the *yang* and of the Five Agents. Principle is there" (Chan 1963, 635). But he also takes principle to be inherent in one's nature. In Zhu Xi's terminology, *dao*, "principle," and "nature" refer to the same thing, but with different scopes. According to Zhu Xi, "The term [*dao*] is used with reference to a universal order, whereas the term nature (*xing*) is used with reference to an individual self.... The [particular *dao*] is the principle inherent in things, whereas nature is the principle inherent in the self. But the principle in all things is also the principle inherent in the self" (Chan 1963, 616). From this quote, we see that the cosmic order is called *dao*, while each individual thing partakes this cosmic order. This cosmic order exemplified in each particular thing is its "nature." Zhu Xi thinks that each existence contains both a physical form and an essential nature. Using human beings as an example, Zhu Xi says, "In speaking of man's body, the breath he takes in is the *qi* of *yin* and *yang*. His body, the flesh and blood, is constituted by the Five Agents. His nature is the principle" (Zhu 1986, 94:3131). What makes up an individual is the combination of *qi* (cosmic force), matter (the Five Agents), and principle. Since cosmic principle is order, Zhu Xi finds order in all things.

We could perhaps interpret the cosmic order in Zhu Xi's view as a holistic web of entities, each occupying its proper position in the web and each fulfilling its proper function. All particular things are related to one another in this cosmic web, exemplifying the whole cosmic order. Each particular thing's nature is simply the way it should be in this cosmic web. Joseph Needham explains:

> Things behaved in particular ways not necessarily because of prior actions or impulsions of other things, but because their position in the ever-moving cyclical universe was such that they were endowed with intrinsic natures which made that behavior inevitable for them. If they did not behave in those particular ways they would lose their relational positions in the whole (which made them what they were), and turn into something other than themselves. They were thus parts in existential dependence upon the whole world-organism.
> *(Cited in Alder 1981, 291)*

Since there is a grand scheme of things in the whole universe and everything is "well placed" in this grand scheme, our knowledge of this cosmic order can only be obtained by our understanding the principle inherent in each particular thing. According to Zhu Xi, "To investigate principle to the utmost means to seek to know the reason for which things and affairs are as they are and the reason according to which they should be" (Chan 1963, 611). In other words, to have knowledge of a particular thing is to see its placement in the whole web and to understand its proper function within this web. We can say that Zhu Xi's epistemology is based on his ontological assumptions. In Chapter 10, we will return to Zhu Xi's moral epistemology.

Zhu Xi's Notion of the Supreme Ultimate and Its Instantiation in Particular Things

In Wing-tsit Chan's assessment, even though the idea of One principle with multiple manifestations originates in Cheng Yi, the doctrine was not fully developed until Zhu Xi (Chan 1963, 639). For Zhu Xi, particular principles and the one universal Principle are related as individual nodes and the whole network in an ontological distribution. The totality of all the particular principles, according to Zhu Xi, is simply called "the supreme ultimate (*taiji*)": "The supreme ultimate is nothing but the principles of the myriad things. In terms of heaven and earth, there is the supreme ultimate in heaven and earth; in terms of the myriad things, there are principles within each of the myriad things" (Zhu 1986, I:1; Zhu 2002, 14:113). His notion of the supreme ultimate is thus different from that of Zhang Zai as we saw in Chapter 2. For Zhang Zai, the supreme ultimate is the totality of *qi*'s various manifestations and constitutions; for Zhu Xi, the supreme ultimate is the totality of principles.

However, Zhu Xi has different interpretations of the notion of the supreme ultimate. On the one hand, he deems the supreme ultimate to be the totality of the universe—including not just the present things but also all that is past and future. According to Zhu Xi, "The coherence of all the ten thousand things in heaven-and-earth, taken together, is the supreme ultimate. The supreme ultimate originally did not have this name; it is just an appellation" (cited in Peterson 1986, 17). On the other hand, he also takes the supreme ultimate to be the totality of principles: "The supreme ultimate is nothing other than principle" (49:8b, Chan 1963, 638). Wing-tsit Chan analyzes the relationship between the myriad things and supreme ultimate in Zhu Xi's philosophy as that of part-whole: The supreme ultimate is the "sum-total" of all particular principles. "In other words, the universe is a macrocosm while everything is a microcosm" (Chan 1978, 110). The apparent ambiguity can be resolved once we see that for Zhu Xi, a thing and its principle are one and the same. The difference between principle and thing is simply that the former is latent while the latter is manifest. The universe already contains the totality of all principles and all things. It is only relative to human society that some principles are manifested in particular things. The supreme ultimate is the collection of all principles, latent and manifest alike. In this respect, Zhu Xi's notion of the supreme ultimate continues Cheng Yi's idea that the world already *exists in completion* independently of human history. It is only relative to human perspectives confined in their particular timeframes that things become real and present. Even before humans invented cars and airplanes, for example, the principles for those things are already included in the supreme ultimate. These principles need material objects and human inventions to be brought to the world of concrete things; nevertheless, they exist independently of their physical instantiations. Therefore, Zhu Xi seems to be committed to *eternalism* as well.

Another important clarification that Zhu Xi makes of Cheng Yi's idea of One principle with multiple manifestations is that principles are for each kind of particular things. In other words, principles belong to the genus and not to tokens of particulars. Lai Chen analyzes Zhu Xi's notion of particular principle as "the essence and rules of things" (Chen 2005, 127). However, if a particular principle is simply the existing state of a particular thing, then there is no "rule" to be spoken of since *to be is to be the norm*. Zhu Xi identifies particular principle with the "nature (*xing*)" of particular thing, and calls it "how things ought to be (*dangran* 當然)" (Zhu 2002, 14:196). Here his notion of principle also takes up a normative dimension as that of the Cheng brothers.

Zhu Xi also assigns value to principle. He explains that as how things ought to be, principles are all "good" (Zhu 2002, 14:196), and "the supreme good" is simply "the ultimate state of all things' being what they ought to be" (Zhu 2002, 14:446). From his comment here about "the ultimate state of all things," we can deduce that each particular thing on its own might not exemplify the principle of its kind: some things are simply less than good for its kind. Hence, effort is required to fulfill its principle, and such efforts can only come from human beings since things themselves do not have volition or goals. In this way, Zhu Xi's metaphysics of the taxonomy of things is infused with an ethical demand: human beings must realize the particular principles in things. The world of nature and the world of human ethics are inextricably merged into one in Zhu Xi's worldview. The world with concrete things is our "field of action": we act upon external objects so that they may satisfy their ultimate norm—their principles. On our part, such a moral precept defines our own principle: by our nature, we ought to act in the way to achieve particular things' principles. As we will explore Zhu Xi's theory of human nature in Chapter 5, for Zhu Xi, the way we are and the way we ought to be are also essentially intertwined.

Zhu Xi's Analysis of the Relationship between Principle and *Qi*

Zhu Xi's conception of principle is further refined than those of the Cheng brothers. According to a contemporary scholar Chung-Ying Cheng's analysis, Zhu Xi's notion of principle refers to the "well-placedness" of the whole cosmos. According to Cheng, "Li … refers to the intelligibility and rationality of things in the world. It can be further explained as the well-placedness of things in the world. It is therefore a term implying external patterning and internal organization and obviously should be understood as presupposing an organic unity of reality" (Cheng 1979, 262). Under this interpretation, the one Principle is the overall pattern of the universe. It signifies the global coherence of the way things are interrelated. The particular principles of individual things, on the other hand, must also exemplify a local coherence. Both global coherence (the one Principle) and various forms of local coherence (particular principles) are realized in the world through the function of *qi*.

Zhu Xi takes principle and *qi* to be separate categories, even though he frequently emphasizes the inseparability of the two. To Zhu Xi, principle is not just the principle derived from *qi*'s operation; it holds its own ontological ground. Contemporary scholars struggle with whether to label his view as dualism, in that he was ambivalent in calling principle and *qi* as one or two things.[8] Zhu Xi was also ambivalent about whether principle precedes *qi* or is separable from *qi*. Insofar as Zhu Xi treats principle as irreducible to the functions of *qi*, his view can be seen as a form of dualism. However, he repeatedly declared that principle could not exist outside of *qi*. According to Zhu Xi, "principle is not a separate entity" (Zhu 1986, I:3; Chan 1963, 634); it has "no form or concrete existence" (*xingti* 形體) (Zhu 1986, I:1); it is what is "above form" (*xingershang*) (Zhu 1986, I:3). Furthermore, principle could not exist independently of *qi*: "Without this *qi*, this principle would have no place to hook onto" (ibid. I:3). In all these remarks, we see that Zhu Xi did not want to treat principle and *qi* as separate substances. Principle in his understanding is not a concrete substance independent of *qi*; hence, his view is not a form of *substance dualism*.

However, even though Zhu Xi denies that principle is a separate substance, at times he also presents it as a distinct entity. A controversial and widely quoted comment comes from Zhu Xi's correspondence with an acquaintance, in which he clearly separated principle and *qi* as "two entities":

> What are called principle and [*qi*] are certainly two different entities. But considered from the standpoint of things, the two entities are merged one with the other and cannot be separated with each other in a different place. However, this does not destroy the fact that the two entities are each an entity in itself. When considered from the standpoint of principle, before things existed, their principles of being had already existed. Only their principles existed, however, but not yet the things themselves.
> *("A Reply to Liu Shuwen", Zhu 2002, 46:2147; Chan 1963, 637)*

Furthermore, Zhu Xi also explicitly states that if we must discuss which has priority, then we say principle comes before *qi*: "Fundamentally principle and [*qi*] cannot be spoken of as prior or posterior. *But if we must trace their origin, we are obliged to say that principle is prior*" (Zhu 1986, I:3, Chan 1963, 634, emphasis added). Obviously, if x is prior to y, then $x \neq y$. Therefore, Zhu Xi does view principle and *qi* as distinct *categories*, if not distinct "substances."

One way to unify all these seemingly contradictory discussions on the relationship between principle and *qi* is to incorporate contemporary metaphysical notions of supervenience and determination.[9] "Supervenience" is generally defined as the dependence, as well as determination, relation between two sets of properties. One set of properties is termed the supervening properties, while the other set is called the supervened base properties. If property

---

8 For instance, Wing-tsit Chan calls Zhu Xi's view "seemingly dualistic" (Chan 1963, 590) while Lai Chen interprets it as a form of "objective idealism" (Chen 2005, 128).
9 For a more detailed discussion on the notion of *supervenience* in Neo-Confucian metaphysics, see Liu 2005.

A supervenes on property B, then A is the supervening property while B is the base property. Base properties determine the supervening properties in the sense that anything that has property B will necessarily have property A, or any two things identical in their base properties will also have the same supervening properties. The determination relationship is asymmetrical: the base property B determines the distribution of the supervening property A but not vice versa. These notions were initially introduced in the context of naturalized ethics and aesthetics to explicate the relationship between some abstract properties (such as "being good," "being beautiful," etc.) and their underlying physical or natural properties (such as "having done so-and-so," or "having such-and-such composition," etc.). The idea of supervenience is to ground the abstract properties in question on relevant physical/natural properties, in the sense that any two things idential in their physical attributes must also share the same abstract properties. The notions later became a dominant analysis in philosophy of mind for many years, and mental properties are said to supervene on neurophysical properties of the brain. In philosophy of mind, the intense interest in the notion of supervenience sprang from the desire to defend a form of physicalism, such that the mental is completely (or partially, depending on the theory one holds) determined by what goes on inside the individual's brain,[10] while at the same time, the mental could find a place in the purely physical world through its grounding in base physical properties.

Furthermore, the causal relevance of higher-level supervening properties has always been a major concern for the ontologists who hold a hierarchical or layered worldview. It is believed that if the mental supervenes on the physical, then we can conceive of the causal role of mental properties as a form of "supervening causation." In other words, we can still have "mental causation"— our beliefs and desires do cause our actions via the mediation of the neurophysiological activities within our bodies. Another appeal of the notion of supervenience is that it further preserves a unified phyiscalist worldview. If the abstract properties in question—be they ethical properties, aesthetic properties, or mental properties—do supervene on the underlying physical properties, then they do not constitute a self-subsisting ontologial realm or a distinct layer of existence. There is nothing—no substance and no property—over and above the physical realm. In other words, there is no dualism if superveninece holds between the two set of properties.[11]

---

10 If one holds that the mental is completely determined by the neurophysiological properties of the brain, then one defends individualism or mental (content) internalism. On the other hand, if one holds that the mental is also partially determined by what goes on in the physical and/or the sociolinguistic environments, then one would be defending physical externalism and social externalism.

11 In philosophy of mind, there is dispute whether supervenience is compatible with property dualism, but it is indisputable that supervenience is incompatible with substance dualism.

If we apply the terminology of supervenience to the relation between principle and *qi*, we could treat *x*'s having or exemplifying principle as one set of properties, and *x*'s being constituted by *qi* as the other set of properties. We now have a definition of the supervenience of principle (*li*) on *qi* as follows:

> Li-Qi Supervenience: Things identical in the make-up of *qi* will share the same principle (*li*).[12]

Zhang Zai's theory of the relationship between principle and *qi* can be analyzed as "supervenience"—principle supervenes on *qi* and is thereby determined by the operation of *qi*. As we saw in Chapter 2, Zhang Zai attributes all changes in the universe to the operations of *yin* and *yang*. Since *yin* and *yang* perpetually work against each other, *qi* necessarily comes together to form material objects while material objects necessarily disintegrate into vacuous *qi* itself. This necessary tendency of *qi* is principle, and Zhang Zai expresses the necessity as how *qi* must be. After the development of *qi* advances to a certain stage, its further development must take a certain direction. This necessary tendency is formed after the actual instantiation of *qi*. If principle is simply the post-developmental pattern of *qi*, then it is determined by *qi*; it does not determine *qi*. Once the operation of *yin* and *yang* has advanced to a certain stage, the principle is necessarily there. Even though we do not need to reduce cosmic principle to a purely physical or material level, it is nonetheless nothing over and above the physical level. Therefore, the notion of necessity here is the physical necessity of the way our world is.[13] Since principle could not be different in any other way once *qi* has manifested a certain pattern, any two things identical in their constitutions of *qi* must be identical in their principle. Therefore, under Zhang Zai's theory, principle supervenes on *qi*.

On the other hand, Zhu Xi's theory of the relationship between principle and *qi* is not "supervenience." In Zhu Xi's interpretation, principle depends on *qi* for its manifestation, yet it is not determined by *qi*. Zhu Xi understands "principle" to be the order for the operation of *qi* as well as for the production of the whole universe. This cosmic order (principle) has nowhere to be instantiated except on the level of *qi* and physical form (concrete things). However, Zhu Xi's principle is not determined at the physical level of *qi*. Therefore, under his view, principle does not supervene on *qi*.

---

12 There are many other formulations of the basic notion of *supervenience*. This analysis comes from Jaegwon Kim, who further defines "supervenience" as "Necessarily, for any property F in A, if any objects x has F, then there exists a property G in B such that x has G, and necessarily anything having G has F" (Kim 1984, 260).
13 It is not metaphysical necessity; in other words, we are not considering *possible worlds* here, since this conception was foreign to neo-Confucianism.

At the same time, determination works in reverse for Zhu Xi—he holds that principle determines qi's realization and operation. This determination is also asymmetrical: principle is the determinant while qi is the determined, but not vice versa. Determination is a two-place relationship, and thus if x determines y, then x is not identical to y. This explains why Zhu Xi would claim that principle and qi are two "entities." The determinant (principle) naturally could not subsist without the determined (Qi), since without the determined, there would be no determinant. The determined (Qi) needs the determinant (principle) for it to be determined, since without the determinant, the determined would not be determined. The determinant and the determined are logically inseparable, but the determinant must be logically prior to the determined, since it is what determines the latter. This analysis can clarify Zhu Xi's confusing comments on the inseparability between principle and qi and the priority of principle.

However, here we encounter a grave difficulty in Zhu Xi's theory of principle: it plays no role in the actual production of the myriad things. Both Zhang Zai and Zhu Xi acknowledge that qi and qi alone is responsible for the production of things. If, under Zhang Zai's view, principle supervenes on qi in the sense that it is determined by qi,[14] then it can derive causal relevance through its necessary connection with qi, since qi is the one that does the real work to produce all things in the universe. Principle in Zhu Xi's interpretation, on the other hand, superimposes order onto qi, and yet it is causally impotent in itself. As Zhu himself acknowledges, "Qi is capable of consolidating and producing things, but Li (principle) has no feeling and will, no calculation, no creation and production.... Li is only a world of purity and openness, traceless and *it is incapable of creating and thing-making*" (cited in Cheng 2002, 108, emphasis added). In this way, Zhu's principle becomes a "metaphysical dangler." If it is a metaphysical dangler, then it is not necessarily a part of the physical world. In Zhu Xi's view, principle is eternal in that principle would have existed even if the physical world had never come into existence, and it would continue to exist well after the physical world has ceased to exist. Between Zhu's principle (li) and qi, there is an unbridgeable gap. This view is definitely incompatible with physicalism. If, given the closure principle of the physical, all causation is done at the physical level, then the mere positing principle above the realm of qi has already made principle (li) causally inert. If principle plays no causal role in our physical world, then it cannot be said to "govern" the physical world. Ultimately, Zhu Xi's theory fails to give a coherent explanation of the causal role of principle, or its determining power over the operation of qi.

---

14 According to Jaegwon Kim, when one set of properties supervenes on another set of properties, "the relation between two families of properties is that the supervenient properties are in some sense *determined by*, or *dependent on*, the properties on which they supervene." See Kim 1984, 260.

Conclusion

The Cheng–Zhu school constructed a unique interpretation of the role of principle in the universe—it is permanent, complete, and independent of human conception. The material world in which we situate cannot exist without principle—it could not even have come into existence without principle. Heavenly principle and its myriad manifestations in particular things define the norms for the world's existence. Humans' role is to grasp the principles in particular things and work to ensure that each thing fits its norm. In their worldview, nature precedes human effort while human effort completes nature's order. Principle sets the norm, and yet it is causally impotent in ensuring the realization of the norm. Here we seem to have a picture of divided world: the eternal realm of principles and the fluctuating realm of material things constituted by *qi*. Human beings would have to be the medium to connect the two realms. Human beings do not create or invent the norms, but they are needed to perceive the norms in particular things and to assist in the realization of these norms in the material world. This is clearly a worldview that combines ethics with metaphysics.

Primary Sources

Chengs, Hao and Yi 1981. *Collected Works of the Two Cheng Brothers (Erchengji)*. Four volumes. Beijing: Zhonghua Shuju Chubanshe.
Zhu Xi 1986. *The Classified Dialogues of Zhu Xi (Zhuzi Yulei)*. Eight volumes. Beijing: Zhonghua Shuju Chubanshe.
Zhu Xi 2002. *The Complete Work of Zhu Xi (Zhuzi Quanshu)*. 27 volumes. Shanghai: Guji Chubanshe.

Selections in English

Chan, Wing-tsit (ed.) 1963. *A Sourcebook in Chinese Philosophy*. Princeton University Press. Chapters 31, 32, 34.
Chan, Wing-tsit (trans.) 1967. *Reflections on Things At Hand: The Neo-Confucian Anthology*. New York: Columbia University Press.
Bruce, Joseph Percy 1922 (trans.). *The Philosophy of Human Nature*, by Chu Hsi, Translated from the Chinese (Classic Reprint). London: Forgotten Books, 2013.
Gardner, Daniel K. 1990 (trans.). *Learning to Be a Sage: Selections from the Conversation of Mater Chu, Arranged Topically*. Berkeley, CA: University of California Press.

4
Wang Fuzhi's Theory of Principle Inherent in *Qi**

Introduction

This chapter concludes the first part on neo-Confucian metaphysics with Wang Fuzhi's theory. We have seen in the previous chapter that Zhu Xi's dichotomy of principle and *qi* renders principle causally inert and ontologically irrelevant. Wang Fuzhi endorsed Zhang Zai's *qi*-monism, and gave the role of principle in *qi* a clearer exposition than Zhang Zai ever did. He also inherited the Cheng–Zhu school's notion of heavenly principle, and fully developed his own moral metaphysics based on the *Yijing*. Under Wang Fuzhi's construal, principle is not only the principle inherent in *qi*'s operation but also the moral reality of the human world. He was a committed moral realist just as the Cheng brothers and Zhu Xi were. In combining both Zhang Zai's naturalistic *qi*-monism with the Cheng–Zhu school's moralistic heavenly principle, Wang Fuzhi can be said to be a true synthesizer of Song-Ming neo-Confucianism.

For Wang Fuzhi, the realm of heaven (*tian*) and the realm of humans are simply one unified whole. There is no transcendent realm beyond the human world, and it is the same element (*Qi*) and the same Principle (*li*) that permeate the realm of heaven and the realm of humans. Hence, his metaphysical view underlies his philosophy of human affairs, in particular, his philosophy of human nature, his moral philosophy, as well as his philosophy of human history. The title of this chapter depicts Wang Fuzhi's philosophy as the philosophy of principle inherent in *qi*, since it is really this relation between principle and *qi* that explains everything for him.

---

* Part of this chapter is a revised version of the author's previous comprehensive paper on Wang Fuzhi. See Liu 2010.

Neo-Confucianism: Metaphysics, Mind, and Morality, First Edition. JeeLoo Liu.
© 2018 John Wiley & Sons, Inc. Published 2018 by John Wiley & Sons, Inc.

Wang Fuzhi's Moral Metaphysics—Principle Inherent in *Qi*

Beginning with an authoritative historian Youlan Feng, contemporary Chinese scholars have often interpreted Wang Fuzhi's monism as a form of materialism, in particular, naïve materialism (*pusu weiwulun* 樸素唯物論).[1] This label highlights a core concept in his philosophy: *qi*. Wang Fuzhi was a great systematizer of the philosophy of *qi*. *Qi* is a real substance of the world, and *qi* constitutes concrete objects. In this respect, it is understandable that scholars take him to be advocating a form of materialism. However, this interpretation greatly misrepresents Wang Fuzhi's metaphysics. As a contemporary Chinese scholar Shouzheng Yan points out, Wang Fuzhi's monism should not be seen as materialism, because the nature of *qi* is not the same as the materialist's notion of "matter," which is traditionally seen to be inanimate, inert and has to be supplemented with energy in order to form living things. *Qi*, on the other hand, contains energy within and is thus self-propelling. *Qi* is the source of life, but it also underlies the realm of death.[2] Furthermore, materialism in contemporary usage is identified with physicalism, the view that everything in the universe is governed by physical laws and can ultimately be explicable in physical terms. Wang Fuzhi's theory certainly does not allow for such a reductionist implication. His monistic worldview includes a moral dimension that cannot be reduced to the physical realm, and in his understanding, *qi*, with its internal logic and law, is responsible for both the material and the spiritual realms. It is therefore best to abandon the term "materialism" in depicting his philosophy.

Wang Fuzhi derived his metaphysical view primarily from the *Yijing*, and he was also heavily influenced by Zhang Zai's philosophy, which, according to him, is nothing but the study of the *Yijing* (Wang 1967, 4). Six hundred years prior to Wang Fuzhi, Zhang Zai had developed a new philosophy of *qi*. In Chapter 2, we have seen how Zhang Zai constructed a systematic philosophy that expanded on the traditional notion of *qi*. In Zhang Zai's view, *qi* is responsible for the production of myriad things. The coalescence and the dispersion of *qi* underlie the phenomena of life and death. *Qi* solidifies into concrete things; concrete things disintegrate back to the vacuous *qi*. *Qi* is real, not

---

[1] Another common and more apt label among contemporary Chinese scholars for Wang's metaphysics is realism (Xiao and Xu 2002; Chen 2002; Zhang 2004, among others).

[2] According to Yan, "The living and the dead are simply various forms of *qi* itself. Hence, the nature of *qi* is both material and spiritual.... There is no duality of mind and body in Chinese thought" (Yan 2000, 9). Another scholar Zhaoxu Zeng also criticizes previous scholars for attributing materialism to Wang Fuzhi, accusing them of "not understanding that *qi* for Wang Fuzhi includes not just the material world, but also spirit and mind" (Zeng 1983, 212).

empty; *qi* is authentic (*cheng* 誠),[3] not vacuous. Wang Fuzhi took up Zhang Zai's notion of *qi* and further developed the theory of *qi* into a philosophical system that covers metaphysics, ethics, and philosophy of history.

Wang Fuzhi wrote a detailed commentary on Zhang Zai's *Correcting Youthful Ignorance* (*Zhengmeng* 正蒙), in which he elaborated on Zhang Zai's metaphysical view and especially the latter's philosophical terminology. Wang Fuzhi clearly defines "the great ultimate (*taiji*)" as the totality of the universe, and he stresses that the great ultimate consists of nothing but *yin* and *yang*. In his ontology, *qi* is the sole constituent of all things, and *qi* alone is responsible for the commonality as well as the differences among particular things. According to Wang Fuzhi:

> *Yin* and *yang* exhaust the totality of the great ultimate. Whatever lies between the two realms of heaven and earth—be it concrete form or abstract image, spirit or energy, clear or turbid—is all made up of *yin* and *yang*. From natural phenomena such as snow and wind, water and fire, mountains and lakes, to tiny creatures such as larvae or sprouts, everything is the combination of *yin* and *yang*. From that which has a material form to that which has not yet been formed, and even to the beginning state of the formless, harmonious whole, which is called the great equilibrium (*taihe* 太和), it is all just the permeation of *yin* and yang. However, each thing is distinctly its own. The nature, quality, and efficacy of things cannot be unified as the same.
>
> *(Wang 1980, 478)*

Wang Fuzhi adopts Zhang Zai's view that *qi* condenses into solid forms and concrete things, while concrete things again disintegrate back to formless *qi*. Form and formlessness are simply various stages of the manifestations of *qi*. He also endorses Zhang Zai's depiction of the initial cosmic state, a formless *qi*. Zhang Zai calls it the great vacuity (*taixu*), but this description could easily lead to a Buddhist reading of emptiness or a Daoist reading of nothingness— both of which highly objectionable to a Confucian. With the terminology of "the great vacuity" (*taixu*), Wang Fuzhi emphasizes that *qi* exists from the beginning of the universe and is in constant movement and transformation. The great vacuity contains *qi*; hence, it is not nothingness and cannot be identified with the void. According to Wang, "What humans perceive as the great vacuity is simply *qi* itself, not void. The great vacuity contains *qi* and *qi*

---

3 This Chinese word *cheng* has standardly been translated as "sincerity"; however, in the context of metaphysics, the rendition does not make sense. The notion of *cheng* is one of the most important notions in the *Doctrine of the Mean*, and scholars have written abundant analyses on what it means and how to translate it. Here we shall just render it as "authenticity" with the caveat that no English word could fully capture the rich and diverse connotations of the Chinese word as used in the *Doctrine of the Mean*.

permeates the great vacuity. There is no so-called 'nothingness'" (Wang 1967, 13). For his own cosmology, he seems to prefer Zhang Zai's other term, the great equilibrium (*taihe*), which Zhang Zai identifies with *Dao*. With this notion, Wang Fuzhi explains it as the utmost harmony between *yin* and *yang*. Even though *yin* and *yang* have different natures and tendencies, their interaction achieves a perfect equilibrium and there is never any imbalance or obstruction. He often used the great equilibrium in conjunction with another concept derived from the *Yijing*: dense mist (*yinyun* 氤氲), describing it as "the original state of the intermingling of the great equilibrium, which necessarily contains the logic as well as the tendency to oscillate mutually" (Wang 1967, 1). This remark shows that Wang Fuzhi takes the original state of the universe to be a dynamic state that contains a perfectly balanced internal order in the integration of *yin* and *yang*. In its original state, the universe is not yet divided into myriad things, and yet *qi* is perpetually moving and transforming harmoniously. According to Wang Fuzhi, "The great vacuity is self-moving. Movement propels further movement; it is neither stagnant nor static" (Wang 1977b, 183). The nature of *qi* is simply the movement and integration of both *yin* and *yang*, and there is an internal order within such a movement. This internal order of *qi*'s operation is simply principle (*li*).

Under Wang Fuzhi's interpretation, *qi* is not a blind force, working under the regulation of some independent superimposing principle. Rather, *qi* is itself regulated, with its own internal order that he identifies as "principle" (*li*). Wang Fuzhi calls *qi* a "principled" *qi* in the sense that *qi* is intrinsically regulated. What characterizes Wang Fuzhi's philosophy is exactly this thesis: Principle is inherent in *qi*. Principle is simply the principle of *qi*; it is the order inherent in *qi* itself. Against Zhu Xi's postulating principle in a transcendent realm and rendering it eternal, Wang Fuzhi reinvigorated Zhang Zai's philosophy of principled *qi*. He rejects Zhu Xi's separating principle and *qi* into distinct ontological categories. In the previous chapter, we have seen that even though Zhu Xi often emphasized the coexistence and physical inseparability of principle and *qi*, he did consider them as logically and metaphysically distinct. Wang Fuzhi maintains that Zhu Xi was mistaken. He argues that principle is not independent of or separable from *qi*: "only when there is *qi* could there be principle" (Wang 1977a, 31:13). Furthermore, he points out that Zhu Xi's view renders principle an isolated dangling entity, while "outside of *qi*, there cannot be any dangling, isolated principle" (Wang 1974a, 10:660). Wang continues, "Principle is simply the principle of *qi*. The way *qi* ought to be is principle itself. Principle is not prior and material force is not posterior" (Wang 1974a, 10:660). In other words, principle is simply the order inherent in *qi* itself. Therefore, principle does not have any transcendent status; it is also not logically prior to *qi*.

Wang Fuzhi built upon Zhang Zai's naturalistic philosophy of *qi* and assigned value to *qi*. For Wang, *qi* is not merely manifested in the physical realm but also in the abstract and moral realm. There is good in *qi*'s development. Lai Chen, a distinguished contemporary scholar of neo-Confucian philosophy, refers to Wang's theory as the "doctrine of the goodness of *qi*" (*qi shan lun* 氣善論) (Chen 2004). He quotes the following passage by Wang: "[The *Yijing* says,] '*Yi* has the Great Ultimate (*Taiji*), whence generates the Two Modes (*lianyi*).' The Two Modes are nothing but *qi*, only when it is good (*shan* 善) can it become the mode. Therefore the six *yang* in Qian [hexagram] and the six *yin* in Kun [hexagram] all contain the four virtues of origination, fecundity, succor, and perseverance (*yuan heng li zhen* 元亨利貞)" (Chen 2004, 167). From this passage, we can see that the goodness of *qi* lies not just in having an internal logic (*li*) but also in having the virtues associated with creation. This moralized *qi* is the foundation of Wang Fuzhi's moral metaphysics.

Wang Fuzhi's moral metaphysics is derived from the traditional Confucian view established in the *Yijing*. According to Junyi Tang, a leading Confucian of the twentieth century, the conviction in the moral attributes in the world of nature has been a shared view among Confucians of all times. In Tang's view, "Chinese traditional thought, from the *Commentary on the Book of Changes* down to the Confucianists of the Han, and even the Song and Ming ... is convinced that the universe is filled with moral values, sometimes expressed in terms of originating growth, prosperous development, advantages, and correct firmness, and sometimes in terms of human-heartedness [humaneness], righteousness, decorum, and wisdom" (Tang 1956, 127). However, the traditional view emphasizes the principle of the generation of life manifested in nature, in particular, in the functions of heaven and earth. Wang Fuzhi associates this principle of life with *qi* itself, thereby elevating *qi* to a new ontological status. His *qi* is self-sufficient, self-propelling, self-regulating, and above all, good.

This moralistic attribution to natural phenomena or to *qi* itself is of course problematic from a contemporary naturalist point of view. In contrast to the perspective of a contemporary scientific-minded person, what Confucians in general and Wang Fuzhi in particular expressed is a different appreciation of the way the world operates: the world is "beneficent" in the sense that everything works in harmony, in equilibrium, in perfect unity that facilitates life and progression. The world itself is great—hence the designations of the great ultimate and the great equilibrium. Without an omnipotent and omnibenevolent God, the Confucian worldview affirms nature's providing all living things a life-conducive environment. If the world ever comes to total destruction, then it would be the fault of human beings.

The Unification of Substance and Function

Even though Wang Fuzhi inherited Zhang Zai's *qi*-monism, he did take issue with Zhang Zai. In Zhang Zai's view, *qi* itself is the substance (*ti* 體)—the fundamental state—of the universe. When it consolidates, it forms material objects; when it disintegrates, it is simply a massive formless *qi*, which he calls the great vacuity (*taixu*). Thus, *qi* remains for Zhang Zai an abstract entity divided into two mode of existence: its substance (*ti* 體) and its function (*yong* 用). Material objects are the manifestations of *qi*; they are *qi*'s function. The great vacuity, on the other hand, is the substance of *qi*. The substance is invisible and formless, whereas the functions are manifest and concrete. Contrary to Zhang Zai, Wang Fuzhi does not posit a separate fundamental state (*ti*) independent of its function (*yong*). He pushes Zhang Zai's monism one step further to argue that the universe is *one* not just in its constitutive elements but also in its ontological order. On Wang Fuzhi's view, it is wrong to assume that there is another state of *qi* that is separate from, and logically prior to, the existence of material objects. Just as Zhu Xi was wrong to treat principle as substance and *qi* as function, so was Zhang Zai wrong to treat *qi* as having a substance state and a function state. Wang Fuzhi thinks that there is no substance standing behind our experiential world. The reality is nothing but *qi* and its function manifested in concrete things. He frequently remarked on the unification of substance and function. This thesis would later become the central thesis of a renowned New-Confucian of the twentieth century, Xiong Shili (1885–1968).[4]

The significance of the issue of whether substance and function are separate or unified is that it reflects whether one is committed to a hierarchical ontology.[5] In the Western philosophical tradition, the term "substance" stands for the fundamental grounding of reality. As Howard Robinson explains, "The philosophical term 'substance' corresponds to the Greek *ousia*, which means 'being,' transmitted via the Latin *substantia*, which means 'something that stands under or grounds things.' According to the generic sense, therefore, the substances in a given philosophical system are those things which, according to that system, are *the foundational or fundamental entities of reality*" (Robinson 2014, emphasis added). In other words, substance in this traditional usage means the primary stuff that constitutes the world. As foundational entities, substances are supposedly "ontologically basic"; as fundamental entities, substances are supposed to have permanent existence that is self-subsisting. "Ontological basicness" and "permanence" are the two criteria for substance in its generic concept. Whatever that is called the function of substance, on the other hand, would only have impermanent, dependent existence.

---

4 "New-Confucian" is separate from "Neo-Confucian": the former refers to Confucians of the twentieth century, while the latter refers to Confucians between the 11th and the 19th centuries. The name Xiong Shili is put in the traditional Chinese style, with family name preceding the given name.
5 A contemporary scholar Chung-ying Cheng in his analysis of the notions of *ti* and *yong* argues that the notion *ti* (substance) already implicates its function. (Cheng 2002, 152) Hence, the two terms serve as counterparts of each other, and one cannot talk about *substance* without including the notion of *function*.

To see whether the Chinese philosophical issue of *ti* and *yong* is akin to the Western philosophical issue of substance and function, we can briefly compare the two concepts. According to the authoritative ancient Chinese lexicographer Xu Shen, the Chinese word "*ti* 體" originally means human body, which includes 12 bodily parts, such as head, arms, legs, and so on. Extended meanings of *ti* include "the totality of a thing" and "the form of material existence," both applicable in this context. *Ti* can be used in conjunction with the word *ben* (本), which means "original," and form the concept relevant in this philosophical discourse: *benti* (本體). *Benti* means "the original state of things," "the principal part of things," or "thing-in-itself." *Benti* is commonly translated as "substance" and it is an appropriate rendition. *Yong* (用) has been standardly translated as "function," which is also an apt translation as it is the counterpart of the term "substance."

However, the issue of the relation between substance and function in the Chinese tradition is not reflected in the Western tradition, or at least not with the same terminology. In the Western tradition since Aristotle, the category of substance belongs to particular things and not to the kind of stuff. Substances are viewed as particulars that endure in space and time, upon which we establish individuation and identity conditions. Aristotle took primary substances to be individual objects, which are subjects of predication (and never as predication of something else). Descartes separated material substance and mental substance in his treatment of the mind-body problem. In his usage, a substance is an enduring entity with certain attributes, such as *thinking* for mental substance and *being extended* for material substance. Locke took substance to be an unknowable *bare substratum* underneath an individual object's perceptible qualities. Hume rejected the existence of substance on the same understanding of "substance" as some enduring imperceptible thing that can be the subject of change and the ground for re-identification. He further argued that since substance is not perceivable, we do not have any idea of it. Kant, following Hume, took the concept of substance to be a subjective imposition of the mind on the world.[6] In this context of substance as enduring particulars, the notion of function applies to the function of particular things as well. It is typically used in the Aristotelian sense: To ask what a particular thing's function is, is to inquire about its natural purpose or its teleological end. Each thing has its function, which is what it does best by nature. A thing's function can thus be seen as the defining feature, or the essence, of the thing. The function can belong to the particular thing either by design or by nature, and yet it presumably serves a purpose. For example, the function of eyes is sight, while the function of ears is hearing. From a teleological point of view, a thing's function is what it performs

---

6 Leibniz's notion of *substance* is perhaps more about the *stuff*: he took *monads*, the simple, indivisible and non-extended units of all material things, to be substances. There are an infinite number of substances as there are infinitely many monads.

in relation to the whole system. The relation between a thing's substance and its function is the issue about what a thing does essentially.

In the Chinese tradition, on the other hand, the relationship between substance and function represents a different philosophical concern. A scholar on the *Yijing* in the Tang dynasty, Cui Jing (dates unknown), gives the following explanation of these two concepts:

> Everything in the world has its form and its mater. Within its form and matter there is both the substance and the function. The substance is its form and matter, while the function is the wonderful operation of its form and matter. If heaven and earth have the world as substance, then the function is the origination and generation of the myriad things. If animals have their bodies as substance, then their spirit and intellect are the functions. If plants have the branches as substance, then the vitality is the function.
> *(Cited in Zhang 1958/2005, 38)*

This explanation can represent the standard conception of the relationship between substance and function in Chinese philosophy. "Substance (*ti*)" and "function (*yong*)" apply to particular things as well as to the universe as a whole. For each thing, the substance is the thing's basic condition, while the function is the further development or the manifestation of the substance. In this sense, substance and function are both part of the whole process. Chung-Ying Cheng sees the unity of substance and function as the quintessential thesis of Chinese philosophy, which he argues, would prevents the dichotomy commonly posited in Western philosophical tradition:

> Throughout the history of Chinese philosophy, the principle of substance and function in unity is well maintained and cherished. This explains why in the history of Chinese philosophy there is the absence of the fundamental dualism of mind and body à la Descartes, or the fundamental dualism of reality and appearance à la Plato, or the fundamental dualism of knowledge or understanding of objects and rational intuition of things-in-themselves à la Kant
> *(Cheng 2002, 156)*

Even though both Zhang Zai and Wang Fuzhi would embrace the unity of substance and function in the above sense, their views are nonetheless different. Zhang Zai uses substance (ti) to mean the fundamental state or the intrinsic state of *qi*. He talks about the transformation of *qi* from the state of formless vacuity to the state of integration and disintegration of concrete things. The former is the fundamental state of *qi*; the latter is the operation of *qi* in action. In Wang Fuzhi's conception, on the other hand, substance (*ti*) is taken in a collective sense, as the ultimate underlying principle, or we can say, ultimate reality, of all things. In association with the word substance (*ti*), the word "*yong*" does not signify the teleological function of any particular thing, but the manifested representations of the substance; in other words, the appearances of ultimate reality. The issue of substance and function in Wang Fuzhi's philosophy would be tantamount to the issue of reality and appearances, one and the many, or noumenon and phenomena in Western philosophy. To claim the unity of substance and function, as Wang Fuzhi did, is to say that ultimate reality is not separate from the appearances in our phenomenal world. "The unification of substance and function" has the further connotation that the world we experience is nothing but the manifestation of ultimate reality. Accordingly, there is no gap between our experiential world and the way the world truly is.

In Zhang Zai's conception, *qi* in the state of the great vacuity meets the two criteria for substance: ontological basicness and permanence. Hence, we can translate Zhang Zai's "*ti*" as "substance" and can call the great vacuity a substance. Zhang Zai thinks that *qi* in the state of concrete things is the function of the great vacuity. Zhang Zai thus separates *qi* into two states: the great vacuity as substance and concrete things as function. What Wang Fuzhi wants to challenge, is this rigid division between substance and function. On his view, substance and function are interchangeable. *Qi* is both substance and function; the great vacuity and the realm of concrete objects stand on the same ontological level and can serve as each other's "substance." According to Wang,

> When we talk about the substance and the function, we cannot separate the two. With such a fundamental state as substance, there must be such a function; with such a function, there must be such a fundamental state. When we talk about the substance, the function is already contained; when we talk about function, the substance must already reside within.
> *(Wang 1974a, 7:473)*

In other words, the pre-object state of *qi* (the great vacuity) and the post-object state of *qi* (the world we live in) are simply interchangeable states of *qi*. Without the former, the latter could not come to be, and this relationship is what Zhang Zai's ontological picture presents. However, without the latter, the former also could not exist, and this is what Wang Fuzhi wants to establish. In elevating the world of concrete things, which he calls "*qi* 器,"[7] to the same level as that of the great vacuity, Wang Fuzhi expresses a commitment to the reality of the experiential world. His metaphysics can be compared to contemporary commonsense realism: the world we experience along with all particular things is the only reality there is. There is no prior state empty of objects that lay as the foundation of the experiential world. Therefore, his "unification of substance and function" is not a trivial terminological dispute against Zhang Zai. Rather,

---

7 Though sounding the same in Mandarin, this word *qi* (器) is totally different from the word *qi* (氣) that signifies the basic constituent of the world. This word means vessel, container, or object, and so on.

it reconfirms the classical Confucian commitment, exemplified in the *Analects*, the *Mengzi*, and the *Yijing*, to our world as the only reality.

Principle as the Necessary Law of the World

Following Zhang Zai, Wang Fuzhi also embraces the Necessitarian theory of principle in *qi* and he too takes up the internalist position—Principle is the inherent order of the distribution and the development of *qi*. He describes this internal order as what *qi* "necessarily is"; in other words, *qi* cannot fail to deviate from this law. According to him, the law of *qi* is simply "once *yin* and once *yang* (*yi yin yi yang* 一陰一陽)," which is what the *Yijing* has defined as "*dao*." Wang Fuzhi takes the principle of *qi* to be the constant reversal between *yin* and *yang*. The development of *qi* consists in the perpetual movement of *yin* and *yang*. The two forms of *qi* constantly interact with each other; while one expands, the other withdraws. However, expansion can never reach the point of exhaustion, and withdrawal cannot become extinction. By elaborating on the *Yijing*'s statement "Once *yin* and once *yang* is called '*Dao*,'" Wang Fuzhi suggests that the over-development of *yin* or *yang* always leads to its regression. Hence, there is a pattern of once *yin* and once *yang*, so too is there the principle of the impossibility of either lone *yin* (*du yin* 獨陰) or lone *yang* (*du yang* 獨陽). Everything contains both *yin* and *yang* in various distributions. This manifested regularity is what *qi* necessarily demonstrates, and according to Wang Fuzhi, it is because this is *qi*'s intrinsic state: "Qi originally possesses an internal order" (Wang 1974a, 10:666). *Qi* is in perpetual motion; *yin* and *yang* constantly work against each other. According to Wang Fuzhi, "If one rises, the other falls. They constantly seek out each other: *yin* must go to *yang* and *yang* must go to *yin*" (Wang 1967, 37). The flow of *yin* and *yang* is constantly dynamic, but the totality of *qi* is fixed in the supreme ultimate (*taiji*). As a result, as one form of *qi* expands, the other must be condensed. A balance between *yin* and *yang* in a given object or even in the whole cosmic state could be temporarily reached. However, owing to the dynamic nature of *qi*, it is impossible to maintain this balance forever. The cyclical condensation and expansion of the two forms of *qi* is inevitable. Wang Fuzhi thinks that this inevitable alternation and the necessary reversal is principle itself. In this sense he calls "principle" "what is necessarily so."

Under Wang Fuzhi's Necessitarian theory, some states of affairs are physically impossible. The "once *yin* and once *yang*" rule applies both diachronically and synchronically, both globally and locally. Diachronically, it would be impossible to have permanent persistence of any state of affairs—the interchange between *yin* and *yang* takes place incessantly and thus states of affairs necessarily change to their opposites. Wang Fuzhi employs this cyclical view of order and chaos in his philosophy of history. In human history, we have seen how the most prosperous dynasty eventually degenerated into chaos, while the most ferocious tyranny in history never lasted forever. The "once *yin* and once *yang*" principle dictates the human world as much as it does the world of nature. The eventual termination of any state of affairs seems to be simply the way things are and there is no fatalist implication in Wang Fuzhi's view.

Synchronically, each state of affairs of the world would necessarily contain opposites, though the opposites would maintain equilibrium on a global level. Locally, what the principle prescribes is that there would be nothing consisting of sole *yang* or lone *yin*—everything must contain both *yin* and *yang*, though the distributions of *yin* and *yang* are naturally different in particular things. A demonstration of this principle is best seen in human beings—each male has traits of *yin* while each female also has traits of *yang* in varying degrees. The *yin–yang* equilibrium principle is also manifest in Chinese medicine. Elements of *yin* and elements of *yang* are found in natural herbs and plants, and by taking Chinese medicine extracted from these natural herbs, one could enhance the *yang* or the *yin* that is deficient in one's body. *Yin–yang* co-constitution is essential to the very existence of all things. Hence, once *yin* and once *yang* is also the governing principle for the existence of concrete things.

In Wang Fuzhi's explanation, the nomological determination is an upward determination from the composition of *yin* and *yang* to the macro-phenomena including objects and states of affairs. Everything is constituted by *qi* and every state of affairs is a state of the arrangement of *yin* and *yang*. The principle inherent in *qi* is thus also the principle for everything. The implication of this philosophy is that human action and human agency are cast into the swirling world of *qi*. We can decide on the best course of action to take in a given situation, but what our actions can achieve depends heavily on things around us: the past conditions and the concurrent happenings in the local environment as well as in the larger environment. How others conduct themselves and what others do in the given situation could have a great impact on the consequences of our actions. Cause and effect can never be viewed merely as a linear progression from one event to the next. Rather, they should be viewed as each action or each event's contribution to the distribution of *yin* and *yang* in the world. Our best effort could enhance the insufficient *yang* or suppress the overpowering *yin* in our environment, but others' actions could counteract our efforts. Ultimately, there will be plenty of undesirable developments that individuals cannot overturn since the world follows the principle inherent in *qi*. Wang Fuzhi calls such limitations of life one's "fate (*ming* 命)." As we have explained in the biography of Wang Fuzhi in the Introduction of this book, he had a firsthand experience of this irreversible fate in his life.

The Unification of *Dao* and Concrete Things (*Qi* 器)

Wang Fuzhi did not simply replace the classical Confucian notion of *Dao* with the neo-Confucian notion of principle or heavenly principle. The notion of *Dao* also plays a significant role in his metaphysics. In Wang Fuzhi's usage, *dao* and principle (*li*) are slightly different concepts though they sometimes overlap. One way to distinguish the two concepts is to say that *dao* represents the dynamic progressive order of the movement of *qi*, while *li* represents the finished order or the internal logic of *qi*.[8] In his exposition of *dao*, for example, Wang Fuzhi embraces the thesis expressed in the *Yijing*: "Once *yin* and once *yang* is called '*Dao*.'" According to Francois Jullien's analysis, the "one-one" could mean either that *yin* and *yang* are inseparable, or that *yin* and *yang* succeed each other with no interruption. On this reading, the phrase means that *yin* and *yang* are interdependent and/or mutually alternating (Jullien 1993, 247). If the concept of *dao* denotes both sets of relations, then it signifies not only the distributional internal order (*li*) in *qi* but also the dynamic order of the exchange between *yin* and *yang*.

A more important distinction between the two concepts in Wang Fuzhi's usage is that *dao* has the normative connotation of "what ought to be the case," whereas *li* seems to denote "what is" or "what is necessarily so." In other words, *dao* is prescriptive while *li* is descriptive. *Li* is how things naturally are and how *qi* naturally is.[9] All things have their internal principles and all developments of *qi* have their internal order. But *dao* is uniquely assigned to human beings. What Wang Fuzhi means by "what ought to be the case" is not an ontological necessity or physical necessity, but a normative necessity. *Dao* prescribes the norms of human conduct. According to Wang:

> Today I can sum it up in one sentence: Objects themselves simply do not have *dao*. When we discuss the *dao* of cattle's cultivating the land or the *dao* of riding horses, we are only speaking of the *dao* of how humans use things. So in a way things and objects do have *dao*—it is only the *ized dao* of humans' interaction with things or treatment of objects. Therefore, *dao* pertains only to human beings.
>
> *(Wang 1974a, 2:70)*

In this passage, Wang Fuzhi clearly spells out what Zhu Xi has implicated in his theory of particular principles in things: Only humans have the ability to make moral judgments and to aim to do the right thing. Zhu Xi takes particular

---

8 However, this distinction does not apply in all cases. In some contexts, the two concepts seem to be synonymous and the two terms are interchangeable in these contexts. In some other contexts, the word *dao* includes the meaning of *li*, but not vice versa.

9 As we will see later, this notion of *principle* refers to principle in things. Wang Fuzhi has another notion of *principle* that is the principle in human nature. In that usage, the notion of *principle* and *dao* are interchangeable.

principles to be in the nature (*xing* 性) of particular things, but Wang Fuzhi wants to make it clear that only humans can fulfill particular things' natures. Therefore, in his view, we should not identify particular principle with nature. Zhu Xi's normative realism places norms in external things, and this metaphysical conviction led to his adopting an investigative intellectualist approach to morality: One ought to investigate principles in particular things in order to know one's own moral essence (*xing* 性) and to know how to properly deal with things. To underscore the fact that normative principles are only for human beings and realizable by human beings, Wang Fuzhi uses *dao* instead of *li* in this context. He says, "Objects all have their nature, but we cannot say that they have *dao*. *Dao* is what distinguishes men and objects, what separates human beings from beasts" (Wang 1967, 79). In particular things, the particularized *dao*—the *dao* in various things and objects—signifies the particular moral duties humans have toward that kind of thing. This is where Wang Fuzhi introduces his theory of the relationship between *dao* and concrete existence (*qi* 器)—his famous doctrine of *dao–qi* unification.

The emphasis on material objects and concrete existence is an important aspect of Wang Fuzhi's metaphysics. "Concrete existence" (*qi* 器) is a notion derived from the *Yijing*, which posits *dao* as meta-physical (what is above physical form [*xingershang* 形而上]) and concrete existence as physical (what has physical form [*xingerxia* 形而下]). In Chapter 2, we have seen that the Cheng–Zhu school puts *Dao* on a transcendent level, treating it as over and above concrete existence. Youlan Feng depicts Cheng Yi's metaphysics as positing a transcendent realm that is "independently subsisting apart from actual things" (Feng 1983, 507). *Dao* prescribes the way concrete things ought to be; it has an *a priori* content and an everlasting value. Zhu Xi also views heavenly principle to be above physical form, and considers what is with physical form to be "dregs and sediment" (渣滓), the most turbid and low existence (Zhu 1986, 5:25). Wang Fuzhi's theory is revolutionary in his rejection of the division between the two realms, and his emphasis on the value of things with physical forms (concrete things 器). What is "beyond physical form" includes our concepts, thoughts, values, morals, and above all, principles of things—none of which needs to be posited in a separate transcendent realm. Furthermore, the world is nothing but the realm of concrete things. Wang Fuzhi regards *dao* as an *a posteriori*, post-instantiation norm for concrete things. *Dao* is realized in concrete things; without a particular kind of concrete things, there cannot be the *dao* of that kind. He would thus be against Cheng Yi and Zhu Xi's *eternalism* of principle. He argues that *Dao* does not predetermine the world; rather, it is developed as the world evolves: "What exists in this world is nothing but concrete things. *Dao* is simply the *dao* of concrete things; concrete things may not be called the concrete things of *Dao*" (Wang 1977b, 5:25).[10] The realm of

---

10 The Chinese text reads, "天下唯器而已矣。道者器之道, 器者不可謂之道之器也。"

Dao and the realm of concrete existence are unified as one. This is his thesis of the unification of *Dao* and concrete existence (*daoqiheli* 道器合一).

Wang Fuzhi holds the same view with regard to principle: "*Li* can only be sought by following events, but *li* cannot be pre-established to limit the happening of events" (Wang 1972, 7:4001).[11] Principle is to be derived from the universal pattern or order in concrete things, and it only exists to the extent that concrete things exist. He thinks that the mistake of Daoism and Buddhism lies in their presupposing the nature of *Dao* or Principle, and uses it to deny the realness of material objects and their functions. He argues that to understand the principles in particular things, we must begin with a close examination of concrete things themselves. We cannot start with an absolute principle that supersedes our experiential world, and overrides all changing phenomena. Change is real, and our impermanent world is the only reality there is. The concrete world takes primacy over the abstract Universal—be it *Dao* or Principle.

Wang Fuzhi's thesis marked a clear empirical turn, in that if *Dao* is nothing but the *a posteriori*, post-instantiation norm for concrete things, then metaphysics,[12] the study of *Dao* or "what is beyond physical form" (*xingershang*), should no longer be the study of some transcendent realm of abstract principles. Rather, metaphysics should begin with science, or at least it must be grounded in empirical studies of concrete things. To do metaphysics, one can no longer rely simply on pure speculation as Cheng Yi did, or mere reflection of the mind as Wang Yangming did. One must also devote to the understanding of how each kind of thing functions and coheres with one another. In a sense, Wang Fuzhi was continuing the direction that Zhu Xi had started but did not fully develop: the investigation of things can lead to the comprehension of the supreme ultimate. Since our world is the only reality there is, the best approach to investigating reality is simply to understand concrete things in our world. This empirical turn later became the dominant positivism (實證學) in the Qing dynasty championed by philosophers Dai Zhen (1724–1777), and others.

To dispel the misconception that there are still two realms belonging to the transcendent and the phenomenal, Wang Fuzhi explains that what is above physical form is not "without form or formless" (*wuxing* 無形); rather, it emerges after physical forms have manifested themselves (Wang 1974a, 5:1028).

---

11 I wish to thank Kam-por Yu for suggesting that I add this quote for further discussion: "有即事以求理, 無立理以限事." This quote comes from Wang Fuzhi's *Supplementary to An Extensive Discussion on Master Zuo's Commentary on the Annuals of Spring and Autumn* 續春秋左氏傳博議. 1669. It is collected in *The Complete Collection of the Posthumous Works of Chuanshan* 船山遺書全集. Vol. 7.

12 "Metaphysics" is translated into Chinese as *xingershangxue*—the study of what is beyond physical form.

We call them "above form" simply because they are not confined to the existing forms. He analyzes the differences between "beyond physical forms" and "having physical forms" as the difference between how things ought to be, and the actualized objects:

> What is called "beyond physical forms" is what has not taken form, where there is implicitly an inviolable heavenly rule…. When shapes are formed and become visible, what those forms can be used for in order to fulfill their natural capacities … are still hidden in the forms and not visible. This is called "what is beyond physical forms." What is called "having physical forms" is what can be seen and followed after concrete things are formed. The *dao* that is beyond physical forms is obscure. Only after forms are set can what each thing is supposed to be and what function it is supposed to have become determined. This is why what is beyond physical form cannot be separated from form.
> (Wang 1980, 568)

In his examples of what "has physical forms," Wang includes both concrete objects (such as carriages or containers) and actual relationships (such as those between fathers and sons, between the ruler and the ministers). He further explains: "There is no *dao* of the father before there is a son; there is no *dao* of the elder brother before there is a younger brother. There are many *daos* that could exist but are not yet existent. Therefore, it is indeed true that without a concrete thing, there cannot be its *dao*" (Wang 1967, 5:25). In his worldview, as the world evolves and as human society progresses, more and more things will emerge and more and more *dao* will be realized. The *dao* of each thing does not exist before the thing is invented or a relationship developed; it is simply that there is a way each thing ought to be and that is its *dao*. *Dao* as particularized is not a mysterious order "beyond physical forms"; it is simply what is already contained in each object and each human affair. Under Wang Fuzhi's depiction, the world of concrete things is a world *in creation*, not a world *in completion*. The world as we experience it, the physical realm, is what Wang Fuzhi takes to be the only existence. He was a committed commonsense realist through and through.

Wang Fuzhi highlights humans' contribution to the creation of *daos*: the *daos* of various things do not pre-exist before the human world has come up with the concrete things or relationships. The many particular *daos* come to exist only after such particular things have been invented by humans, or such particular interpersonal relationships have evolved in human societies. However, by unifying *dao* with concrete things, Wang Fuzhi also makes the point that for each thing that has ever come to existence, there is a certain way it ought to be. Particular *daos* have to wait for human invention of the particular things, but they are not arbitrarily stipulated by humans. In this respect, he also preserved the Cheng–Zhu school's normative realism.

The Role of Humans in the World of Nature

Wang Fuzhi not only elaborated on Zhang Zai's theory of the principle of *qi* but also expanded on the Cheng brothers' notion of heavenly principle. In Wang Fuzhi's usage of heavenly principle, principle has both the naturalistic connotation (the way the world is) and the normative connotation (indicating objective, universal moral principle). It is what combines the moral or the good with what is natural.

Wang Fuzhi posits a realist sense of heavenly principle, which is independent of humans' conception: "Humans must follow the principle of heaven as the principle, while heaven does not employ the principle of humans as its principle" (Wang 1977b, 225). There is a way the world is, which is not prescribed by the human world. What Wang Fuzhi means by "heaven" is neither a personified, mysterious being, nor a transcendent ontological category. He distinguishes "heaven-as-heaven" (*tianzhitian* 天之天) and "heaven-as-human" (*renzhitian* 人之天), and reasserts an objective, realistic status for heaven-as-it-is. Heaven is not what humans define or create, and it is not ontologically reducible to the human mind or consciousness. Heaven-as-heaven can be viewed as the world as it is, while heaven-as-human can be interpreted as the world as humans know it. The former is not completely exhaustible by human understanding, and human conceptions often present partial aspects of heaven-as-it-is. For example, the sun and the moon operate in their own order, but for men they represent light and darkness and they bring about day and light. Human conceptions add a different dimension—often accompanied by value assignments—to the way the world is.

In our epistemic quest to finding out the truth about the world, there are naturally restrictions as to what humans can uncover. According to Wang Fuzhi:

> The logic and the circumstances of heaven are not what human affairs can completely cover. With the vastness of heaven and earth, the changes of wind and thunder, the operation of the sun and the moon, or the fluidity of lakes and the durability of mountains, there must be what humans do not know and cannot participate in negotiating.
> *(Wang 1980, 617)*

Such limitations, however, are not permanently fixed. In time, with the progression of human history and the expansion of human knowledge, "what used to be heaven-as-heaven is now heaven-as-human; what will be heaven-as-human in the future is still just heaven-as-heaven for now" (Wang 1974b, 132). Human endeavors partake in the formation, creation, and understanding of the world; hence, what lies outside of the human world is progressively transformed into part of the human world in time. In other words, Wang Fuzhi acknowledges the limitation of human knowledge and human accomplishments, but he does not think that it poses an insurmountable obstacle between heaven and men. His notion of heaven is simply the totality of the natural world, and in his view, human knowledge approximates the truth of this totality, and human accomplishments help to complete heaven's creation. In this sense, the progressive creation of *qi* is not only a function of naturalized *qi* but also the function of human beings. It is nature and culture—heaven and human beings, which collaboratively construct this dynamic universe. Without human contribution, the world cannot be complete. As Wang says, "There are originally no bounds to the transformation and the virtues of heaven and earth. They are only manifested through humans" (Wang 1974a, 5:312).

It is in the context of heaven-as-human that Wang introduced a second sense of principle (*li*), by assigning it the seven virtues associated with *yin*, *yang*, and the five elements:[13]

> What is referred to as *li* has two senses: one is the existing order and pattern of the myriad things in nature; the other is the ultimate principle of the virtues of perseverance (*jian* 健), accord (*shun* 順), humaneness (*ren* 仁), rightness (*yi* 義), propriety (li 禮), wisdom (*zhi* 智), and faithfulness (*xin* 信). It is what heaven endows in men and what humans receive as their nature.
>
> *(Wang 1974a, 5:324)*

This passage shows that Wang Fuzhi intentionally separates the principle that is the natural order of things, and the principle that is the ultimate moral completion in the human world. We can say that the former represents what *is* while the latter represents what *ought to be*. According to Lai Chen, the former is "the principle of things" (*wu li* 物理), and the latter is "the principle of human nature" (*xing li* 性理) (Chen 2004, 107). By using this notion of principle in connection with the notion of heavenly principle, Wang endeavors to connect the world of nature and the human world, and he places morality in the center of reality.

In Wang Fuzhi's moral metaphysics, not only is *qi* ascribed a value of good but also is principle elevated to the level of *Dao* and associated with the connotation of the moral prescription of *Dao*. His worldview presents a harmonious ordered universe, with the creation of life as the principle in nature, and the sustenance or invention of concrete existence as the mandate for human beings. The world is not predetermined according to any eternal abstract form. In his view, the world is continuing to evolve, to change, and to progress to a much richer landscape in virtue of human contribution and human endeavors.

---

13 When *principle* represents not just what things are, but also what things ought to be, it is synonymous with *dao*.

Conclusion

In this chapter, we have seen how Wang Fuzhi both inherited and improved on his predecessors' theories. Based on his meticulous reading of classical Confucian texts (in particular, the *Yijing* and the Four Books) as well as his own thinking, he drew various insights from several neo-Confucians of the Song dynasty. His greatest inspiration came from Zhang Zai, whose *qi*-monism laid the core of Wang Fuzhi's metaphysical view. However, he rejects Zhang Zai's dichotomy between the great vacuity as substance and the concrete things as function. He is committed to our experiential world—or, in his terminology, the world of concrete existence (*qi* 器)—which he holds to be the only reality there is. His thesis of the unification of *Dao* and concrete existence continues the Cheng–Zhu school's normative realism, but places the source of normative principles (or *Dao*) internally within the human world. He underlines the role of humans in the creation and transformation of the world of nature. Human agency is thereby given a crucial place in the naturalistic world of *qi*.

In conclusion, Wang Fuzhi has constructed a sophisticated metaphysical system that unifies the two ontological categories, principle and *qi*, separated by Zhu Xi. In Zhu Xi's ontological picture, *qi* is a blind physical force that requires the regulation of principle. Wang Fuzhi's *qi*-monism, on the other hand, is a form of principled *qi*-monism—principle is internal to *qi* as *qi* is necessarily self-regulating. Zhu Xi takes principle to be the ontological, or at least the logical, foundation of *qi*—principle is what makes *qi* possible. Wang Fuzhi, on the other hand, takes *qi* to be the ontological foundation of principle—*qi* is what establishes and completes principle. His philosophy of principle inherent in *qi* serves as the foundation for his philosophy of human nature and human mind. We will come back to Wang Fuzhi in Chapter 7, where we will explicate his theory of human nature.

Primary Sources

Wang Fuzhi 王夫之 1972. *The Complete Collection of the Posthumous Works of Chuanshan* 船山遺書全集. Vols. 1–22. Taipei, Taiwan: Chinese Chuanshan Association & Liberty Press 中國船山學會與自由出版社.

——1967. *Commentary on Zhang Zai's "Rectifying the Youth"* 張子正蒙注, 1685–1690. Taipei, Taiwan: Shijie shuju.

——1974a. *Discourse on Reading the Great Collection of Commentaries on the Four Books* 讀四書大全說, 1665. Taipei, Taiwan: Heluo tushu chubanshe.

—— 1974b. *Extensive Commentary on the Book of Odes* 詩廣傳, 1683. Taipei, Taiwan: Heluo tushu chubanshe.

——. 1977a (1673–1677). *A Textual Annotation on the Book of Rites* 禮記章句. Taipei: Guangwen shuju.

———. 1977b (1655). *Supplementary Commentary on the Book of Changes* 周易外傳 Taipei: Heluo tushu chubanshe.

———. 1980 (1685). *Textual Commentary on the Book of Changes* 周易內傳. Collected in *Chuanshan's Commentary to the Book of Changes* 船山易傳. Taipei: Xiaxueshe.

———. 1996. *A Contemporary Interpretation of the Meaning of the Four Books (Sishu xunyi* 四書訓義*)*, 1679. Reprinted in *The Complete Books of Chuanshan (Chuanshan quanshu)*. China: Yuelu shushe, Vols. 7–8.

Selection in English

Chan, Wing-tsit (ed.) 1963. *A Sourcebook in Chinese Philosophy*. Princeton University Press. Chapter 36.

Part II

Human Nature, Human Mind, and the Foundation of Human Morality

5

Zhu Xi's Internal Moral Realism: Human Nature Is Principle

Introduction

Neo-Confucians typically treat human nature (*xing* 性) as that which heaven confers on man; in other words, it is what we are endowed with. Humans and other creatures derive their nature from heavenly principle. It is the same heavenly principle that is shared by humans and other creatures. What makes humans different from other creatures lies in the endowment of *qi*. The purity or impurity of *qi* in each being is responsible for the good or evil in different lives. On the basis of this general consensus among neo-Confucians, Zhu Xi further asserts that moral principle is real and is inherent in human nature. This internalization of moral principle can be described as what Kai Marchal (2013a) calls "moral inwardness," which means that the moral principle itself "transcends any social structure and is unrelated to particular actions and situations" (Marchal 2013b, 192). For Zhu Xi, the moral principle we humans must embrace as absolutely and objectively true is already internal to us—it is within our nature endowed by heaven. Zhu Xi's famous slogan, "Heavenly principle is in our nature," defines his realistic commitment to both the moral principle itself and to our capacity to realize this moral principle. This is his version of moral realism that combines the objective with the intersubjective, and both of which are internalized in the agent's inborn constitution—the agent's moral selfhood. As Kai Marchal puts it, "for Zhu, morality is identical … with the sphere of the inner self" (Marchal 2013b, 199). In this chapter, we will take a close look at this form of "internal moral realism" in Zhu Xi's philosophy.

What Is Human Nature (*Xing*)?

In Kwong-loi Shun's classic analysis of the usage of the Chinese word *xing* (which we translate as "nature" in line with the standard practice) in early Chinese texts, he points out that *xing* was derived from the word *sheng* (生)

Neo-Confucianism: Metaphysics, Mind, and Morality, First Edition. JeeLoo Liu.
© 2018 John Wiley & Sons, Inc. Published 2018 by John Wiley & Sons, Inc.

(life, growth), and it initially signifies "the direction of life process" (Shun 1997, 1–2). In the usage by Mencius, the key classical Confucian philosopher whose theory of human nature defines the theme in neo-Confucianism, *xing* picks up a moral dimension. Mencius takes *xing* to be a species' natural tendencies, and he vehemently defends the view that humans have inherent moral tendencies. In Shun's words, to say that *x*'s have certain characteristic tendencies as their *xing*, is to say that these tendencies are "part of the constitution of x's" (Shun 1997, 8). In this sense, the word "*xing*" is appropriately translated as "nature."

Even though the definition of human nature is the principal project in neo-Confucians' moral philosophy, this issue may not be a pertinent topic for contemporary ethicists or psychologists because it is fundamentally a metaphysical issue. Neo-Confucians' general concern is the metaphysical, rather than the empirical, foundation of human morality, and they embrace the moral metaphysics advocated in classical Confucian texts such as the *Yijing*, the *Mengzi* (Mencius), and the *Doctrine of the Mean*, in particular. Classical Confucianism's moral metaphysics connects human existence to some contingent *a priori* grounding—heaven's endowment. Neo-Confucians, without exception, all embraced this view. In their eyes, we are moral creatures not by way of social conditioning; we are made this way *by our nature*. Of course, such a view should be empirically testable and even falsifiable; however, to neo-Confucians, this metaphysical fact about human nature is their *first principle*—taken for granted, indisputable, and objectively true. Zhu Xi, in particular, held the defense and elaboration of this metaphysical conviction about human nature to be his primary philosophical and pedagogical concern.

Zhu Xi's view of our moral nature is based on his metaphysics about the world's constitution. According to him, everything is made up of *qi*, which is further regulated by principle. To produce anything, the operation of *qi* has to be functional and the constitution of *qi* must reach minimum equilibrium—it must contain both *yin* and *yang* and the combination cannot be self-destructive. The *Yijing*'s famous slogan, "Once *yin* and once *yang* is called '*dao*,'" is interpreted as a regulative principle of the flow of *qi*. What it depicts is the fact that everything has a balanced interplay between *yin* and *yang* and neither can be lost if the thing is to exist. Zhu Xi phrases this as the claim that "everything contains a supreme ultimate (*taiji*) within itself" (Zhu 2002, 14:184).

If everything contains a supreme ultimate within itself, then how do we explain the differences between humans and beasts, between sentient beings and inanimate objects? Zhu Xi attributes the differences to the distribution of *qi*. *Qi* constitutes the physical aspects of all creatures, and some creatures do not have the sharp senses that others do; some creatures lack the keen intelligence that humans possess. A creature's physical constitution can pose a limitation to what it could possibly achieve; for instance, some animals simply cannot reason and some do not have linguistic capacities. Zhu Xi explains these physical restrictions with the example of ants. Even though ants are part of nature and share with human beings a common order, they are so tiny that they cannot possibly manifest any structure other than the division of power and labor (Zhu 2002, 14:185).

When a student asked whether our heavenly endowed nature has varying degrees of completeness, Zhu Xi gave an analogy of the brilliance of the sun and the moon:

> [Our heavenly endowed nature] does not have degrees of sufficiency or deficiency. It is like the brilliance of the sun and the moon, which can be fully seen if shone in the open space, but which could be invisible when shone under the roof of a hut. Those who are dull in intelligence or dreggy in their mind are constituted by turbid *qi* and this is why their nature is obstructed as if they were under the roof of a hut. Nevertheless, any human with obstructed nature is in principle salvageable. As for beasts, on the other hand, even though they also are endowed with a nature, there is no way for them to clear away the obstruction [of their physical constitution (*qi*)].
>
> *(Zhu 2002, 14:185)*

From this reply, we can see that Zhu Xi takes humans to be distinct from other creatures in terms of their physical constitution, which then is responsible for the differences in their mental constitutions. However, even though humans and nonhuman creatures have different endowments in accordance with the limitations of their physical structures, they are nonetheless all endowed with a distinct principle. Particular principles define the nature and functions for each kind of things. Zhu Xi gives another metaphor of a ladle of water to explain the sameness and differences in particular principles of things:

> Humans and beasts are both endowed with a principle, and in this respect, they are no different from one another. However, man and beast have different natural qualities and capacities. Metaphorically, it is like ladling out the same river water. If you use a spoon, you can get a spoonful; if you use a bowl, then you get a bowlful, and so on and so forth. Each accords with its own measurement and capacities, and consequently its principle varies.
>
> *(Zhu 2002, 14:185)*

This explanation again shows that the qualitative differences in creatures' mental capacities result from the physical differences in their constitution.

We can see in Zhu Xi's many discussions that he is ambivalent on whether human nature is the same or distinct from other creatures' nature. On the one hand, he wants to assert that everything in the world takes a partition of the supreme ultimate; on the other hand, he does not want to deny the uniqueness of human nature. However, this apparent incoherence could be resolved once we understand what Zhu Xi means by the word "nature" (*xing*).

To begin with, Zhu Xi identifies a thing's particular principle with its function, such as in this example: "a boat can only travel on water while a cart can only travel on land" (Zhu 2002, 14:189). Based on its particular structure, each thing has its specific operation and usability. We can extend the functional analysis of a thing's nature to human nature as well: To say that we have a certain nature, is to say that we are endowed with particular function to fulfill the role of human beings as defined by the principle of human beings. When it comes to the principle of men exemplified in human nature, however, principle takes up a normative sense of *what we ought to do*. According to Zhu Xi, "'Heaven's Mandate is the so-called nature.' Mandate, is like an official communiqué; nature, is the duties that one ought to do, such as a registrar's keeping records of expenses and a sentry's keeping watch over the surrounding" (Zhu 2002, 14:192). In other words, human nature is what we should arrive at, so it represents our normative aim and our end state. Indeed, Zhu Xi did say that human nature is what we are endowed with, but this only means that we are born with a normative duty as human beings. Zhu Xi's view of nature is thus the fusion of what *is* and what *ought to be*: a thing's nature is its function which it ought to fulfill in order to meet its name; a person's nature is the normative duty which he or she ought to carry out in order to be deemed human. Since humans and other creatures have different functions and normative duties, they have different principles and hence cannot be attributed the same nature. However, in the sense that they all have their respective principles and normative roles, they are all endowed with the same heavenly principle. We may put Zhu Xi's view in a contemporary way: everything under the sun has its proper role in the entire cosmic plan.

According to Zhu Xi, "Human nature is simply the four cardinal virtues: humaneness, righteousness, propriety and wisdom" (Zhu 2002, 14:192). In this passage and elsewhere, Zhu Xi defines the content of human nature as the four cardinal virtues, rather than the four moral sprouts that Mencius famously advocated as the root or sprout of the four cardinal virtues: the heart of commiseration, the sense of shame and disgust, the sense of reverence and deference, and the sense of right and wrong. When Mencius proclaims the goodness of human nature, he is referring to our natural moral sentiments, or as Kwon-loi Shun calls them, our "emotional dispositions in the direction of the ethical ideal" (Shun 1997, 14). When Zhu Xi professes to take up Mencius's view of human nature, however, he has modified the view to be about our normative aims. In other words, for Mencius, human nature consists in our natural moralistic sentiments[1]; for Zhu Xi, human nature consists in our moral assignments as members of the human species. In this respect, Zhu Xi has turned the

---

1 According to Kwon-loi Shun, Mencius regards *xing* "as constituted by, or at least as having as a central component, the development of the ethical predispositions of the heart" (Shun 1997, 10). By "the heart," Shun means the four moral sentiments that Mencius refers to as the *four moral sprouts*.

descriptive sense of human *xing* (nature) in Mencius's usage into the prescriptive sense. Zhu Xi's understanding of human nature can still be traced back to Mencius, however. In the *Mengzi*, the word "*xing*" is sometimes used as a verb as well. According to Kong-loi Shun, the verbal use of the word "*xing*" in the *Mengzi* "has to do with making certain things truly part of oneself" (Shun 1997, 9). This usage points to the effort one takes to *own* one's given nature. Mencius praises the morally superior people because they can "naturize" (*xing* as a verb) their natural tendencies. Here we see that even in the *Mengzi*, the notion of human nature already signifies a norm for human thinking and conduct. Such a normative aim—to own one's nature, or to be true to one's nature—defines our moral qualifications, without which we are not qualified as "humans."

In the Mencian tradition, humans are separate from other beasts not just in the biological taxonomy (or in their *qi* constitutions) but also in the moral taxonomy. "Human beings" form a moral kind, and what defines the criterion of this moral kind is exactly "human nature." As Kwon-loi Shun points out, the notion of man (*ren* 人) in the *Mengzi* denotes not a biological kind but a normative kind characterized by humans' capabilities of culture:

> What distinguishes [man (*ren*)] as a species is not their biological constitution, but their capacity of certain cultural accomplishments; for example, the text describes one who denies social distinctions (3B:9) or fails to make use of one's capacities (6A:8) as one who is, or has become close to, a lower animal. So, in the *Mengzi* as in other early texts, [man] is viewed as a species distinguished from lower animals by the capacity of cultural accomplishments such as forming social distinctions and abiding by norms governing such distinctions."
>
> *(Shun 1997, 12)*

If "human" designates a normative kind, then what is called "human nature" is not our inborn state, but the norm that governs human species as a cultural or moral kind. Building on Mencius's view of a normative kind, Zhu Xi declares the normative sense of "nature" unequivocally: "The nature [of everything] is principle; it is the principle of what should be (*dangran zhi li* 當然之理). In this sense, there is nothing in the nature that is not good" (Zhu 2002, 14:196). What he claims here is that a particular thing's nature is what the thing ought to become. Human nature is good, not in the sense that we are guaranteed to be free from wrongdoing, but in the sense that we all *ought to be* good. As defined in the *Doctrine of the Mean*, which Zhu Xi endorses, this ought-to-ness comes from heaven's mandate; in other words, it is our inborn obligation or our assigned role in the universe. While the origin of this normative regulation of ought-to-ness is objective and external to us, it is at the same time inherent in our very existence. The standard of right and wrong is embedded in our nature, but it is not invented or constructed by us. Zhu Xi's moral realism is committed to the reality of moral principle, and yet he defines it internally within human nature. Hence, it can be called internal moral realism.

The Root of Good and Evil

To neo-Confucians, the problem of evil poses a real threat to Mencius's optimism on human nature and it has to be confronted. Zhu Xi took this challenge seriously. Zhu Xi fully embraced Mencius's view on human nature, but he also criticized it as missing an important aspect: the constitutions of *qi*. According to Kwon-loi Shun, "Zhu Xi endorsed the Cheng brothers' distinction between two ways of viewing the nature—original nature (本然之性) and material nature (氣質之性)—regarding the former as perfectly good and the latter as having the potential to be not good" (Shun 2010, 178). Shun calls the distinction "two ways of viewing the nature," but they are actually two natures derived from different sources—principle and *qi*. The Chengs brothers' idea of the two natures came from Zhang Zai. Zhang Zai suggests that we have both the heavenly endowed nature and the *qi*-constituted nature.[2] The former is what Mencius talks about as the moral essence shared by all people; the latter is responsible for the moral discrepancies that we observe in people. The Cheng brothers commented that (for Mencius) to have a discourse on nature (*xing*) without mentioning *qi* is not offering a complete account. They think that Zhang Zai's idea of the *qi*-constituted nature completes the picture. The different compositions of *qi* from person to person explain why some people are naturally kinder or wiser than others, or why some have weak will and lacking moral resolve. In other words, good and evil among us are partly the result of our innate physical as well as psychological dispositions.[3] All these philosophers explain the presence of human evil in terms of our varying inborn *qi* constitutions. This emphasis on the *qi* aspects of our existence attributes the root of good and evil to the way we are when we were born. If human morality is not purely the result of social conditioning, then neither is human immorality. According to Zhu Xi:

> Mencius' discourse is all about the goodness of human nature. When it comes to the not-so-good part, Mencius attributes the cause to one's being led astray. So it is like at the beginning everyone is purely good and it is only later that one becomes not so good. But this view is neglecting

---

2 The suggestion of "two natures" did not originate with Zhang Zai, but it is a complicated issue and goes beyond the scope of this book. A detailed discussion on Zhang Zai's notion will be given in Chapter 8.
3 Here a caveat is warranted: Shun points out that "Confucian thinkers do not draw a sharp distinction between what we would describe as the psychological and physical aspects of the person, and thus to speak of the psychological is already to frame our discussion in a way that goes beyond the way they would themselves present their views" (Shun 2010, 177).

the *qi* aspect in the exposition of human nature, and it is thus inadequate. It is only after Master Cheng put forth the aspect of *qi*-disposition (*qizhi* 氣質) to supplement Mencius' theory, that we now have a complete discourse on human nature.

(*Zhu 2002, 14:193*)

In this passage, Zhu Xi argues that when one talks about human nature, one cannot dispense with the physical and psychological dispositions of each individual. These dispositions make up what Zhang Zai had called "the *qi*-constituted nature (*qi zhi zhi xing* 氣質之性)." Zhu Xi gives an analogy to explicate Zhang Zai's idea of the two natures: "The nature that is endowed by heaven must be embedded in the physical constitution of the thing. It is analogous to a ladle of water: without the container, the water would have no place to settle" (Zhu 2002, 14:195). In this analogy, Zhu Xi treats the two natures as the container versus the contained: our moral essence needs to be realized in our concrete makeup such as our temperaments, intelligence or other personality traits. Since *qi* is the actual constituent of all beings, the various constitutions of *qi* are responsible for our moral differences as well as our other differences in capacities, intelligence, physical structure, and so on. Just as ladles have different sizes and capacities to contain various amount of water, so too would our different concrete *qi* constitutions sustain our moral essence in varying degrees.

Mencius was of course aware of the problem of evil, but he attributed the causes to outside influences (6A:6), forced circumstances (6A:2), underdevelopment of one's inborn moral sprouts (6A:6), one's lack of reflection (6A:6), one's taking up bad behaviors repeatedly until one's originally good nature is maimed (6A:8), one's failure to retrieve one's lost mind (6A:10) (6A:11), and one's self-abandonment (2A:6). The main difference between Mencius's explanation of the root of human immorality and that of these neo-Confucians is that while Mencius looks for external influences or later human efforts, they attribute it to our inborn differences. Even if the *qi*-constituted nature is not derived from the universal good principle—is not the "Mandate of Heaven," it is nonetheless what we inherit at birth. In other words, it is partly beyond our control.

On Cheng Hao's definition of "nature" (*xing*) as "what is inborn," Zhu Xi comments:

> What is imparted by Heaven to all things is called "mandate." What is received by them from Heaven is called nature. ... Man's nature and mandate exist before physical form, while *qi* exists after physical form. What exists before physical form is the one principle harmonious and undifferentiated, and it is invariably good. What exists after physical form, however, is confused and mixed, and good and evil are thereby differentiated."

(*Modification of Chan 1963, 597*)

In this remark, we see that Zhu Xi separates the *a priori* and the *a posteriori* aspects of our mental and moral makeup. The *a priori* aspect is what he calls "nature," and it is purely good. On the *a posterior* level, however, we are not morally equal. According to Zhu Xi, "All humans have good nature, and yet some people are born good while some are born bad. This difference is due to their various constitutions of *qi*" (Zhu 2002, 14:198). Some people are born with a higher proclivity to becoming bad. For instance, some people are prone to anger and violence, while some people tend to be weak-willed and indecisive. These are our personality flaws, and we are born with them. This is why even though all humans have the same endowment of heavenly principle, each person's potential of becoming a full-fledge moral agent has varying degrees of success. Therefore, Zhu Xi's answer to the existence of human evil is simply that it is a natural fact of our mental makeup. Mencius's view follows from that of Confucius: "By nature men are initially alike. It is through habituation (*xi* 習) that they become wide apart" (*the Analects* 17:2). Both of them attribute the root of human evil to external influences and later human effort. By adding inborn differences between good and evil into humans' nature, Zhu Xi has actually deviated from the traditional Confucian teaching of universal goodness in human nature.

If our *qi* constitution is the reason why some of us are more likely to become bad people, then is there anything we could do to transform our given state? In this context, we turn to Zhu Xi's moral psychology.

Zhu Xi's Moral Psychology of Emotion

Of our *qi*-constituted nature, Zhu Xi focuses on our feelings and emotions (*qing* 情). He embraces Zhang Zai's doctrine that mind encompasses both nature and emotions (*xin tong xing qing* 心統性情). According to Zhu Xi, "The nature is simply the principle of the mind, while feelings and emotions are simply the manifestations of the nature. … Zhang Zai's doctrine of mind encompasses both nature and emotions is excellent" (Zhu 2002, 14:227). In Zhu Xi's moral psychology, human mind is fully responsible for our morality as well as our moral failure, and he thinks that the mind can sometimes be "not good" (*bu shan* 不善) (Zhu 2002, 14:228). However, if our mind encompasses both nature and emotions while our nature is purely good, then the part that could lead our mind to deviate from good must be our feelings and emotions.

Zhu Xi has a guarded view against human feelings and emotions. Even the four moral sprouts, the moral sentiments involving commiseration, righteousness, propriety, and wisdom, which Mencius praised as the proof of the goodness of human nature, are not totally unproblematic, since they could also lead to wrongful acts. According to Zhu Xi, "In human mind, if one has too much commiseration, then one could become indulgent and weak. If one has too much sense of shame and disgust, then one could end up feeling morally incensed towards the wrong things" (Zhu Xi 2002, 14:193). In other words, our emotions, even when they are the so-called moral sentiments as the four moral sprouts, could deviate from the norm and incite us to commit moral ills.

Zhu Xi separates our heart/mind into two dimensions: one is in accord with *Dao* and is called "the heart of *dao*" (*dao xin* 道心); the other is characterized as "the heart of men" (*ren xin* 人心). This distinction originates in the classic *Book of Documents* (*Shangshu* 尚書), "The heart of men is precarious (*wei* 危) and the heart of *dao* is subtle (*wei* 微)," Zhu Xi identifies the heart of *dao* as the mind's cognitive apprehension of principle, and he locates the heart of men at the level of human emotion and desire. However, he repeatedly emphasizes his one-mind theory: the division between the two hearts is merely based on the mind's intentional object; it does not mean that we literally have a divided mind. He says, "The mind has intelligent awareness. When *what it apprehends* is principle itself, it is called 'the heart of *dao*'. When *what it apprehends* is desire, then it is called the 'heart of men'" (Zhu 1986, 4:1487; emphasis added). This comment shows that the distinction is merely based on the intentional object of one's "intelligent awareness." In response to a student's question about this division, Zhu Xi explains, "There is only this one mind. When the mind's perception follows the desire of the senses, then it is the heart of men; when the mind's perception follows the path of moral righteousness and principle, then it is the heart of *dao*" (Zhu 2002, 16:2663). In his assessment, the difference between the supreme moral agents—the sages—and ordinary people simply lies in the fact that the sages maintain only the heart of *dao*, while ordinary people are often ruled by their passions and desires. Even though the heart of men is not purely evil, it is easily tempted to go astray; hence, it has a "precarious" status. In other words, our emotions and desires are not to be given free rein, as they cannot be trusted.

To Zhu Xi, "evil" results from the imbalance of emotions. As biological and moral beings, we have our natural emotions and innate moral sentiments. "If our feelings and emotions are all expressed with due measure and degree (*zhongjie* 中節), then they are good; if they miss the appropriate measure and degree (*bu zhongjie* 不中節), then they become evil" (Zhu 2002, 14:363). The Chinese phrase *zhongjie* here literally means "in agreement with ritual propriety," "following the right pitch (in music)," "seasonal harmony," or "having the right measurement," and so on. In other words, there is an external, objective standard for whether something is *zhongjie*. How to define the objective standard for the appropriate measure and degree of our natural emotions and desires is of course not an easy task. Zhu Xi's answer is to appeal to the mindset of the sages. Their emotions and conduct would always have "appropriate measure and degree." Hence, how the sage would feel and react in the given situation becomes the external standard for all of us. We therefore need to learn from the sages.

Zhu Xi links desire with emotion and gives the metaphor of water to explain their relations: "Desire is generated by feeling and emotion. Human mind is like water, and human nature is the water at rest, while emotion is the water in flow. Desire, on the other hand, is like the ripples and waves of water, which can be good and can be bad" (Zhu 2002, 14:229). Even though Zhu Xi does acknowledge that some desires can be good, such as a moral agent's desire to achieve humaneness, in general he argues that human desire and heavenly principle are incompatible: "In one's heart, if heavenly principle is preserved, then human desire will disappear; if human desire wins over, then heavenly principle is extinguished. There has never been a mixture of heavenly principle and human desire in the same heart" (Zhu 2002, 14:388). There is thus a constant battle in one's heart between good and evil, between heavenly principle and human desire. "If one of them advances, then the other retreats; and vice versa. There is no way to stay neutral and not make any advancement or retreat" (Zhu 2002, 14:389). The danger of being led astray by one's desire is the reason why one cannot do it alone; one needs to study and learn. "Before one learns, one's heart is filled with human desire. After one starts learning, then heavenly principle naturally gets exposed and human desire gradually diminishes. This is of course good. However, there will be layer after layer of obstructions that need to be removed. Even after one has removed the major desires, one still needs to scrutinize one's deeper, subtler desires" (Zhu 2002, 14:389). Ultimately, the goal of learning is "to completely remove human desire so as to return to the precept of heavenly principle" (Zhu 2002, 14:390). The more one learns about right and wrong, truth and morality, the less desire one will have. Without the distraction of desire, one will naturally turn to the correct path. In other words, moral attainment must rely on the censorship of desire through learning from the sages.

However, if evil derives from the mind's emotional manifestations and material desire, then human mind is not a sufficient grounding for human morality. As Philip J. Ivanhoe points out, under Zhu Xi's theory of human nature, we are not guaranteed moral success and we cannot fully trust human mind's capacity in fulfilling our moral predispositions:

> Given that our original, pure natures remain mired in *qi*, no matter how hard or how long we work at self-cultivation, we never can fully escape the limitations of *renxin* [human mind]. As a result, our ethical status remains in a "precarious" state, and we are "prone to error." These aspects of Zhu's philosophy led him to view the human heart-mind with a significant level of distrust and to look to the heart-mind of the Way [*Dao*] as his absolute standard and guide.
>
> *(Ivanhoe 2009, 39)*

We can conclude that even though Zhu Xi confirms the goodness of human nature, he is not optimistic about the individual's attainment of moral goodness. We have a purely good moral essence, but this *a priori* moral grounding is stuck in the *a posteriori qi* constitutions, which are manifested in our personality, temperament, emotion, and desire. The *qi*-constituted nature prevents the heavenly endowed moral essence from being completely realized in the individual's mind. To combat moral impurity or moral failure resulting from our *qi* constitutions, we need to appeal to the mind for its effort in self-cultivation.

The Role of Human Mind (*Xin*) in Moral Cultivation

The preceding discussion shows us that for Zhu Xi, our inborn nature is not what makes our moral accomplishment possible. In other words, our good nature is causally insufficient for our morality. Even if we have an innate moral essence that defines what we are and what we ought to be, once born, our *qi* dispositions immediately dominate our daily conduct. To retrieve the moral status granted us by our nature, we need to put in efforts to rectify our emotion and desire if they deviate from heavenly principle inherent in our nature. In Chapter 3, we have examined Zhu Xi's division of principle and *qi*, and noted that his principle is causally detached from the operations of *qi*. Here in the discourse of human nature, we also see the causal inefficacy of the good nature. When someone asked Zhu Xi: "If our heavenly endowed nature is all good, then why is it that our *qi*-constituted nature could be not good?" Zhu Xi's answer is that even though principle itself is all good, different people have various dispositions such that "*qi* is powerful and principle is weak, thus principle cannot rule over qi" (Zhu 2002, 14:200). From this we see that for Zhu Xi, the principle inherent in human nature cannot ground our morality. Even if it itself is good, it is not responsible for our goodness.

Earlier in Zhu Xi's analogy of "nature" with "job descriptions," we already see that to him, human nature is a given, but it is causally inefficacious in carrying out the normative duties in itself. Just as the registrar's duty of record-keeping by itself cannot make the registrar keep those expense records, human nature by itself is not what makes us carry out the normative duties associated with being humans. What turns human nature into an actualized state of human existence is human mind. Whereas Zhu Xi uses the analogy of an official's duty for human nature, he uses the analogy of an official for human mind (Zhu 2002, 14:192). This shows that Zhu Xi takes "mind" to be where our agency resides. Without human mind, human nature by itself is insufficient for our moral realization. He says, "If there were no mind, where do we place [human] nature? There must be a mind to administer the nature, to make it functional" (Zhu 2002, 14:192). This quote clearly shows that in Zhu Xi's theory of human nature, nature is a passive given state, while mind is the active agency. For our moral realization, human nature can be seen as the ontological grounding, but it is really human mind that has the causal efficacy. As Zhu Xi states empathically, everything is the mind's doing:

> In the *Doctrine of the Mean*, when it talks about "Heaven's mandate is the so-called nature," it means the mind. "To follow our nature is the so-called '*dao*'" also means the mind. "Cultivating *dao* is the so-called teaching" refers to the mind as well.... As for achieving knowledge (*zhi zhi* 致知), it is the mind's achieving knowledge; investigation of things (*ge wu* 格物) is also the mind's doing. To have self-discipline (*ke ji* 克己), is the mind's having the disciplinary power.
> *(Zhu 2002, 14:362)*

However, we have also explained that the mind encompasses both human nature and humans' affective states that include emotions and desires. If the former is causally ineffective and the latter is the root of evil, then there has to be some other function of the mind that is responsible for human morality. Zhu Xi identifies it with volition (*zhi* 志). Volition, as he sees it, is "the commander-in-chief of the mind" and it sets the direction of one's thinking (Zhu 2002, 14:358). Volition and desire are both intentional—they are about objects or events in the external world, but volition differs from desire in that desire is passively triggered by external objects, while volition is the mind's taking the initiative to set out to do something.

According to Zhu Xi, "To firm up one's volition to do good, one must be like the thirsty or hungry people's wanting to eat and drink. If one ever takes it idly, then one's volition cannot be set" (Zhu 2002, 14:282). In other words, there has to be eagerness, earnestness, and directness in one's resolve to be good. This intent must always be preserved, and Zhu Xi calls it "not losing one's original heart/mind" (*bu shi benxin* 不失本心) or "retrieving one's lost heart/mind" (*qiu fangxin* 求放心) (Zhu 2002, 14:282). The determination and direction come from the individual's effort, and thus moral fulfillment is not universally guaranteed by our given nature.

Zhu Xi argues that the sages are simply "those who have done what human beings ought to do" (Zhu 2002, 14:280). In other words, the sages are the people who fulfill humans' moral status and realize their nature. Since to be a sage is simply to be a human being in the paradigmatic sense, everyone should have the volition to learn from the sages, and further to have "achieving sagehood" as his or her responsibility. Moral accomplishment begins with this first step: to set the mind on the right direction toward sagehood. And yet, it cannot be achieved without one's constant check on one's emotion and desire to the point of eliminating human desire. Zhu Xi's slogan "completely remove human desire so as to return to the precept of Heavenly principle" has often been criticized as instigating the overly moralizing and constrictive culture in Song–Ming societies.

In Chapter 7, we shall see how Wang Fuzhi severely attacked the denouncement and suppression of human desire in Song-Ming neo-Confucianism.

Conclusion

In this chapter, we see that Zhu Xi believes in the natural endowment of humans' moral essence. This is a metaphysical conviction of the reality of human morality. As he sees it, there is a deductive connection between the way the world is and the way we are: "The moral qualities of Heaven and Earth are four: origination, advancement, enrichment and perseverance. ... Therefore, in the mind of man there are also four moral qualities—humaneness, righteousness, propriety and wisdom" (modification of Chan's translation, Chan 1963, 594). Zhu Xi embraces classical Confucian moral metaphysics wholeheartedly and develops his theory of human nature on this basis, which we have defined as internal moral realism.

Under Zhu Xi's internal moral realism, moral facts are independent of human opinions, and moral truths are regarded as truths of nature. Human beings occupy a specific normative role in the universe, and humans' normative duties are defined as their nature. Ultimately, however, even though Zhu Xi advocates humans' possessing a moral essence and argues that there is an objective moral principle inherent in our existence, his faith in humans' moral success is placed in individual effort rather than in this *a priori* moral nature. His disparaging attitude on human emotion and desire turns his moral psychology into an anti-sentimentalist pronouncement.

In Chapter 10, we will examine Zhu Xi's detailed program for moral cultivation.

Primary Sources

Zhu Xi 1986. *The Classified Dialogues of Zhu Xi (Zhuzi Yulei)*. 8 volumes. Beijing: Zhonghua Shuju Chubanshe.
Zhu Xi 2002. *The Complete Work of Zhu Xi (Zhuzi Quanshu)*. 27 volumes. Shanghai: Guji Chubanshe.

Selections in English

Chan, Wing-tsit (trans.) 1963. *A Sourcebook in Chinese Philosophy*. Princeton, NJ: Princeton University Press. 4th printing, Chapter 34.
—— 1967. *Reflections on Things at Hand* (compiled by Zhu Xi). New York: Columbia University Press.

Bruce, Joseph Percy (trans.). 1922 *The Philosophy of Human Nature*, by Chu Hsi, Translated from the Chinese (Classic Reprint). London: Forgotten Books, 2013.
Gardner, Daniel K. (trans.). 1990 *Learning to Be a Sage: Selections from the Conversation of Mater Chu, Arranged Topically*. Berkeley, CA: University of California Press.

6

Lu Xiangshan and Wang Yangming's Doctrine of Mind Is Principle

Introduction

Lu Xiangshan and Wang Yangming are standardly grouped as the Lu–Wang school, distinct from Cheng Yi and Zhu Xi's Cheng–Zhu school. Whereas the Cheng–Zhu school advocates the nature is principle, Lu Xiangshan and Wang Yangming profess "the mind is principle." As a metaphysical claim, the thesis "the mind is principle" can easily be interpreted as the statement that human mind is the ultimate reality and thus gives people the association of Berkeley's idealism. As Philip J. Ivanhoe points out, "it is not uncommon to find modern scholars claiming that Lu's idealism denies the existence of a mind-independent world" (Ivanhoe 2009, 34). In the classic *A Sourcebook in Chinese Philosophy*, Wing-tsit Chan also identifies Wang Yangming's view as "dynamic idealism," and criticizes it as "entirely subjective," confusing reality with value (Chan 1963, 655). However, as Ivanhoe correctly explicates, Lu's claim "does not in any way entail a denial of the mind-independent existence of the world, and he surely never doubted or questioned the existence of the material world" (Ivanhoe 2009, 34). With the agreement that idealism is the wrong interpretation of Lu–Wang's "the mind is principle," this chapter will introduce a different analysis of Lu Xiangshan and Wang Yangming's view as a form of humanistic moral realism and pragmatist metaphysics.

As explained in the Introduction of this book, the debate between the Cheng–Zhu school and the Lu–Wang school centered on their claims on whether principle lies in human nature or in human mind. The former has been called "the school of nature" (*xingxue* 性學), while the latter has been called "the school of mind" (*xinxue* 心學). Scholars have focused on nature versus mind in this debate, but the nature of the controversy has not been made clear. In this chapter, we take the difference between Zhu Xi's "human nature is principle" and Lu–Wang's "the mind is principle" to be primarily a disagreement on the origin of human morality. For Zhu Xi, morality is transcendent and independent of human conceptions; for Lu Xiangshan and Wang

Neo-Confucianism: Metaphysics, Mind, and Morality, First Edition. JeeLoo Liu.
© 2018 John Wiley & Sons, Inc. Published 2018 by John Wiley & Sons, Inc.

Yangming, on the other hand, morality is privileged to the human mind. Using a pragmatist metaphysical description, we may also say, in this kind of worldview, "morality is a human phenomenon, something that emerges from human life in a human world, instead of being anything pre-existent 'in itself' or handed down to us from above, as it were" (Pihlström 2005, 33). Whereas Zhu Xi implores us to "investigate the principles of things" as these principles stand outside of us, Lu Xiangshan and Wang Yangming advocate seeking or establishing the principles from within one's own mind. In other words, what Lu Xiangshan and Wang Yangming assert is that morality is not pre-established for us through some heavenly mandate. One's commitment to becoming a sage determines one's set of values, and one's self-set values incline one to seek principles in some particular ways. The particular moral commitments of each and every moral agent (we are, after all, all sages, according to Wang Yangming) constitute a public moral reality defined by our joint sentiments and concerns. This is the moral reality that we humans share in common. Moral facts are established by us, and are immediately perceivable by us. In order to establish moral objectivism in this sense, Lu Xiangshan and Wang Yangming have to be able to prove that we do have shared intersubjectivity in our moral senses, moral sentiments, and moral judgments. In this chapter, we shall see how objectivity cashes out in human intersubjectivity for these two philosophers.

The Mind Is Principle and Principle Is in the Mind

Lu Xiangshan's famous slogan "The mind is principle (*xin ji li* 心即理)" (11:5b–6a) has been subjected to various interpretations, especially on the relationship between mind and principle. Wing-tsit Chan calls Lu's view "idealism" (Chan 1963, 573), while Lai Chen disagrees with this explanation and argues that Lu Xiangshan does not regard the principles of heaven and earth as generated by the human mind (Chen 2005, 151–2). Zongsan Mou thinks that this thesis expresses the Kantian notion of autonomy: the will sets the moral laws for the self to follow (Mou 1979, 10–11). Philip J. Ivanhoe sees a Hegelian spirit behind Lu's endeavor: to find a unity of the world that "not only explains but justifies a universal scheme subsuming both the social and political order and the individual" (Ivanhoe 2010, 254). These diverse interpretations demonstrate the difficulty in understanding Lu Xiangshan's real intent when he announced that the mind "is" (*ji* 即) principle.

The Chinese word *ji* (即), though standardly translated as "is", also means "being close by" or "inseparable." Neither of these literal renditions of the word could give us a clear indication on the correct understanding of the connection between the mind and principle. From textual analysis, however, we can see that the thesis "the mind is (*ji*) principle" expresses inseparability, rather than identification, between the mind and the principle. Lu says, "The mind is one and principle is one. The mind and principle can never be separated into two" (1:3b–4a, Chan 1963, 574). In claiming the mind is principle, Lu Xiangshan is not saying that the law of the universe is the mind's construction and thus depends on the mind for its existence. According to Lu Xiangshan, "There is of course concrete principle in the universe" (14:1a, Chan 1963, 579); furthermore, "Principle exists in the universe from the very beginning" (2:9a–b, Chan 1963, 578). In other words, when he asserts that the universe is my mind; my mind is the universe (Lu 1981, 483), he is not denying the mind-independent existence of the universe or its principle.

Embracing Mencius's thesis of the four moral sprouts, Lu proclaims that the senses of commiseration, righteousness, propriety, and wisdom, among other moral virtues, are the principles in our mind. Lu says, "Seriousness is this principle. Righteousness is also this principle. What is internal is this principle. What is external is also this principle.... Therefore Mencius said, 'All things are already complete in oneself'" (1:3b–4a, Chan 1963, 574). From this statement, we can see that the word "principle" (*li*) in Lu's conception is different from that of Zhu Xi and Zhang Zai, who refer to both principle in mind and principle in *qi*. Lu Xiangshan's notion of principle does not refer to the pattern of the universe (in Zhu Xi's sense) or the order of *qi*'s operation (in Zhang Zai's sense). The notion *principle* in Lu Xiangshan's discourse has a normative sense and signifies only moral principles. In other words, Lu Xiangshan's thesis "the mind is principle" is simply claiming that the moral principle governing the universe is already contained in the human mind. Furthermore, he claims that the presence of moral principles in the human mind is universal: our mind is "what Heaven has endowed in us. All men have this mind, and all minds are endowed with this principle" (11:5b–6a, Chan 1963, 579). Lu Xiangshan has a particular concern—what matters in his philosophy is only what relates to human conduct and human morality.

Inspired by Lu Xiangshan's view, Wang Yangming developed an influential neo-Confucian school of the mind, parallel to the development of the school of human nature advocated primarily by Zhu Xi. Building on Lu's conception of moral principles contained in the mind, Wang Yangming advocated that all affairs and all principles are in the mind. His concern went beyond Lu's moral pursuit and evolved into a subjectivist view of reality as a whole. According to Wang Yangming, "The principles of things are not outside one's heart-mind. If one looks outside the heart-mind and seeks the principle of things, one will find no principles" (Ivanhoe's translation; Ivanhoe 2009, 110). When his friend questioned him on the seemingly mind-independent existence of flowering trees in the deep mountains of Nan Zhen, he replied:

> Before you looked at these flowers, both the flowers and your mind were in a state of quietude. However, when you came and looked upon these

flowers, their colors suddenly became vivid. From this, we know that the flowers are not outside your mind.
(Wang 1994, 234, modification of Ivanhoe's translation, see Ivanhoe 2009, 109)

This quote gives the impression of Berkeleian idealism. However, it would also be a misconstrual to read Wang Yangming's comment here as an idealist declaration. Wang Yangming is not denying that flowers in the deep mountains exist prior to human perception; rather, he is claiming that their attributes are made vivid by perception—we endow objects with their properties, since it is on the basis of perceptions that objects acquire perceivable properties. Rather than claiming "to be is to be perceived," Wang Yangming is saying that "to have properties is to be perceived." The existence of each object is indeed not dependent on the mind, however, properties of the object are, since they are defined or even formed in relation to human senses. For example, what is visible is what human eyes could see; what is audible is what human ears could detect. Wang Yangming puts color in this category of perception-based properties. This categorization is comparable to that of John Locke. Locke separates properties into primary qualities and secondary qualities, and color belongs to the group of secondary qualities. Primary qualities are supposed to be truly in the object themselves, while secondary qualities are the joint collaboration of the object and the mind. To Wang Yangming, on the other hand, all properties would belong to the second category, since he claims that no things and states of affairs are outside the mind.

To Wang Yangming, human mind grounds reality in the sense that without human mind, the world would cease to have its categories and distinctions. According to him:

> What fulfills the realm between heaven and earth is simply human mind's spiritual lucidity (*lingming* 靈明). Without this spiritual lucidity, human beings are nothing but their bodily confinements. My spiritual lucidity is the master of heaven and earth, ghosts and spirits. Without my spiritual lucidity, heaven would have none to observe its height; without my spiritual lucidity, earth would have none to detect its depth. Without my spiritual lucidity, even ghosts and spirits would have no effects of felicity or misfortune, calamity or auspiciousness.
> (Wang 1994, 272)

This comment defines the world's nature and categorization in terms of the subjective perceiver's perception and conceptions. According to Ivanhoe, Wang Yangming's "the mind is principle" thesis is the assertion that the mind "is itself the principle that structures, orders, and gives meaning to the phenomena of the world" (Ivanhoe 2009, 112). If we render "*li*" as "pattern" in this context, we can also explicate Wang Yangming's view as proclaiming "patterns in the mind." Principle is in the human mind, because human mind is what gives pattern or structure to the world. The naked world outside of human perception and intellectualization has no meaning, not just *to us*, but *tout court*.

Wang Yangming's metaphysics is not akin to the Consciousness-Only school's idealism that reduces all existence to the mind's cognition. To him, the world truthfully and objectively exists outside the mind; it is only the categorizations and functions of the myriad things that are mind-dependent. According to him, "For heaven, earth, ghosts, spirits as well as the myriad things, apart from my spiritual lucidity there wouldn't be anything; at the same time, without them there also wouldn't be my spiritual lucidity. In this way, [the world and I] have one *qi* penetrating both. How could one be separated from the other?" (Wang 1994, 272). In other words, there exists mutual grounding and interdependence between the world and the mind. Both the world and the mind are constituted by *qi*; *qi* is real, hence, the world and the subject are both real. According to David W. Tien, "Contrary to many modern interpretations of Wang's metaphysics, Wang was not an adherent of a Berkeleian ontological idealism, which claims that the physical exists only as an appearance to or an expression of heart/mind.... In the terms of Neo-Confucian philosophy, Wang Yangming is a *li-qi* realist who holds to the existence of a world external to the heart/mind, that *li* exists in the external world, and that there is *qi* that is external to the heart/mind" (Tien 2010, 299). Since both the world and the perceiving subject are real, the world itself is not mind-dependent even if the nature and the categorization of all things are mind-dependent.

Borrowing from a famous assertion by a contemporary philosopher Hilary Putnam, we may explain Wang Yangming's view as the claim that "the mind and the world jointly make up the mind and the world."[1] Putnam's further clarification of his own position is even more applicable to Wang Yangming's metaphysics: "the universe makes up the universe—with minds—collectively—playing a special role in the making up" (Putnam1981, p. xi). Under this light, Wang Yangming's worldview is still a form of realism. It is not contrary to commonsense realism since he would not deny that commonsense objects such as trees and flowers truly exist outside the mind. It stands opposed to any form of metaphysical realism, however, in that Wang Yangming would reject the existence of any transcendent realm (such as Zhu Xi's principle) that is completely inaccessible to human experience. For both Lu Xiangshan and Wang Yangming, outside of human experience, there is no reality to speak of as our mind (our perception and conception) contributes to the structure of the world.

---

1 This comment comes from Putnam's *Reason, Truth and History* (Putnam 1981, xi). Putnam calls his view "internal realism" or "pragmatic realism."

Humanistic Moral Realism

In contemporary terms, we may say that what Lu Xiangshan and Wang Yangming established is a form of moral realism. Moral realism is a theory about the ontological and epistemic status of moral facts and moral properties. Moral realism, first and foremost, makes an ontological commitment to such properties and facts. In its generic form, moral realism shares two basic claims of generic realism[2]: (1) existence: there are moral facts and moral properties; (2) independence: moral truths are true independently of anyone's beliefs, moral convictions, conceptions, or perspectives.

Lu Xiangshan and Wang Yangming are both committed to moral realism, and their moral realism further incorporates moral universalism and moral objectivism. Moral universalism is the view that moral principles apply universally to individuals situated in similar contexts, and standards of right and wrong, good and evil, are not relative to individual or cultural evaluations. Moral objectivism, though closely associated with moral universalism, makes the specific claim that there is objectivity in moral truths: a moral belief or moral assertion is not made true by individual endorsement or even universal consensus. Objectivity is opinion-independent, since truth is not dependent on any individual's opinion or moral perspective. Furthermore, this notion of objectivity is not reducible to mere intersubjectivity, because it is not solely based on communal consensus, however universal such consensus is. Even if there is a group of rational cognizers with an ideal process of deliberation, they do not, and cannot, decide or dictate moral truths. They can at most be called "ideal observers" of moral facts, which are facts about the world. In other words, under moral objectivism, moral facts are not established or constructed by human beings, though they are discoverable and assertible by ideal cognizers of these moral facts.

According to Sayer-McCord, "Truth-conditions are 'subjectivist' if they make essential reference to an individual; 'intersubjectivist' if they make essential reference to the capacities, conventions, or practices of groups of people; and 'objectivist' if they need make no reference at all to people, their capacities, practices, or their conventions" (Sayer-McCord 1988, 14). By this criterion, Lu–Wang's conviction in the existence of heavenly principle qualifies as "objectivist." According to Lu Xiangshan, "This principle exists throughout the universe. Whether or not human beings understand or follow it never has added to or diminished it in any way" (Second Letter to Zhu Xi, Ivanhoe's translation. See Ivanhoe 2009, 61–2). This comment clearly shows that for Lu Xiangshan, even

---

2 According to Alexander Miller (2010), *generic realism* is the thesis that *a, b, c,* and so on, exist, and the fact that they exist and have properties such as *F-ness, G-ness,* and *H-ness* is (apart from mundane empirical dependencies of the sort sometimes encountered in everyday life) independent of anyone's beliefs, linguistic practices, conceptual schemes, and so on.

though principle is in the mind, it is not invented or stipulated by the mind. The existence of principle is an objective fact of our moral reality, and individual opinions cannot determine its content or nature. Objectivity in Lu–Wang's moral realism is opinion-independent, since truth is not dependent on any individual's opinion or moral perspective.

However, Lu Xiangshan and Wang Yangming's moral realism is also committed to the human perspective on moral truths. Their thesis "the mind is principle" or "principle is in the mind" elevates human's moral conception to an *a priori* level. It is not just through contingent consensus that our shared moral landscape has its objective value; rather, we share the same moral landscape exactly because our mind has this innate special access to objective moral truths—heavenly principle or *Dao*. Objectivity is indeed not dependent on mere intersubjectivity, and yet some intersubjective moral conceptions are truth-tracking, exactly because they are derived from humans' inborn moral consciousness. Moral principle is in human mind; hence, humans are equipped with an inborn moral perception that can immediately and correctly perceive moral truths. In other words, humans' intersubjective moral perception can guarantee objective moral truths, on their view, because they believe in human mind's magical capacity of having immediate access to objective moral truths. What the Lu–Wang school advocates is not that human mind can collectively *determine* moral truths, but that human mind can individually *perceive* moral truths. The objectivity of moral truths lies not in our shared opinions but in our shared capacity of moral perception. If what we have in our mind is moral perception, then what is perceived is not dependent on or determined by our mind. The object of our moral perception is heavenly principle, and heavenly principle is part of the fabric of the world. At the same time, even if no one else has ever existed, an individual person can still be confident in his or her correctly perceived moral truths,[3] because each one of us is endowed with this capacity. On this view, objectivism, intersubjectivism, and subjectivism are oddly merged into one.

Even if the Lu–Wang's view smacks closely of intersubjectivism or subjectivism, it is nonetheless definitively moral realism.[4] David Wong (1986) provides the following analysis of the possible claims of moral realism, which can serve as a helpful contrast with Lu–Wang's moral realism:

1) There are moral facts that obtain independently of human cognitive capacities and conceptual schemes.
2) There are moral facts that obtain independently of our ability to recognize them as obtaining.

---

3 Later in this chapter, we will also explain how errors are possible on their view.
4 As Sayer-McCord says, "Realism is not solely the prerogative of objectivist" (Sayer-McCord 1988, 16).

3) A moral statement is true or false independently of our ability to recognize it as true or false.
4) A moral statement is true or false in virtue of its correspondence with the world (or roughly, it is true or false in virtue of its structure, referential relations between parts of its structure and parts of the world, and the nature of the world) (Wong 1986, 95).

Lu Xiangshan and Wang Yangming would probably reject claim #1: to them moral facts do not obtain independently of human mind. Even if individual persons may have cognitive failures in their grasp of moral truths, there cannot be moral truth that is completely independent of humans' conceptual schemes. Good and bad are human concepts, and they ultimately relate to various states of the human world. As Lai Chen explicates Wang Yangming's "the mind is principle" this way: human mind provides the world with structure and organization, "enabling things to exhibit a moral order" (Chen 1991, 32). For both Lu Xiangshan and Wang Yangming, moral reality is human reality.

On the other hand, Lu Xiangshan and Wang Yangming would have no problem with claim #2, since they do acknowledge possible errors and insufficiency in our ability to recognize moral facts. For the same reason, they would also accept claim #3, which pertains to the opinion-independent status of moral truths. However, they would probably reject claim #4, since the very notion of correspondence already posits a subject/object dichotomy, which is not acceptable to them. If the moral world is made up jointly by the world and human mind, then we cannot possibly investigate the truth of this moral world outside of human mind.

In Lu Xiangshan's conception, moral objectivity is built on humans' "actual forms of life" (Ivanhoe's translation; Ivanhoe 2009, 51), since outside of human existence, there is no morality, no value, and hence no moral objectivity. As Lu Xiangshan clearly states it: "Where principle resides is absolutely not outside of human beings" (Lu 1981, 379). One might wonder, if we humans contribute to the making of our moral reality, is this moral reality still objective in the sense that the external world is? According to both Lu Xiangshan and Wang Yangming, however, moral reality is at the core of the external world. Everything in the world requires our proper treatment, and our understanding of their principles comes primarily from our inner reflection. In our daily encounter with the external world, hence, we are already embedded in the moral reality of all the principles. The collective principles for all states of affairs constitute *Dao*—the highest moral truth of the world. According to Lu Xiangshan, "The *Dao* is the [collection of] publicly shared principles that have existed through the world for tens of thousands of generations and what human beings together rely and draw upon" ("Explaining *the Analects*," Ivanhoe's translation. Ivanhoe 2009, 82). In other words, *Dao* and principles are not our constructions. They serve as the objective foundation of our moral truths.

Lu Xiangshan's view is clearly a form of moral objectivism—moral facts are sharable facts; they have objective truth values and their validity does not subject to individual opinions. Nevertheless, he would agree with Hilary Putnam on the claim that moral truths cannot be divorced from human concerns, and such concerns are universal. According to Putnam, "The fundamental reason that I myself stick to the idea that there are right and wrong moral judgments and better and worse moral outlooks ... is simply that that is the way that we—and I include myself in this 'we'—talk and think, and also the way that we are going to go on talking and thinking" (Putnam 1992, 135). This attitude is similarly expressed in Lu Xiangshan's remark:

> The universe is my mind and my mind is the universe. Sages appeared tens of thousands of generation ago. They shared this mind; they shared this principle. Sages will appear tens of thousands of generations to come. They will share this mind; they will share this principle. Over the four seas sages appear. They share this mind; they share this principle.
> *(22:5a, Chan 1963, 580)*

Furthermore, for Lu Xiangshan, the universality of objective moral truths depends on the universality of internal moral understanding:

> There is only one mind. My mind, my friend's mind, the mind of the sages thousands of years go, and the minds of sages thousands of years to come, are all the same.
> *(35:10a–b, Chan 1963, 585)*

Since Lu Xiangshan declares that the principle of the universe is nothing but the moral principle in human mind, we should take his metaphysical claim to be an assertion about "ethical reality," or, borrowing Sami Pihlström's phrase, "our moral 'image' of the world" (Pihlström 2005, 10). Ethical reality is not, of course, just about individual conduct or interpersonal relationships. Under Lu's "the mind is principle" thesis, the way we interact with the world and the ways in which we handle external objects are already embedded in our ethical system. In other words, our conceptualizations of the world and its myriad things reflect our valuations and ways of coping with the world. Principles of things are simply moral principles in human mind. Consequently, we may see reality *per se* as simply a "reality of values"; reality *is* our ethical reality. If we take "ethics" to be "a matter of viewing the world in a certain way, of having a certain kind of attitude to the world and to one's life" (Pihlström 2005, 11), then ethics is simply a precondition to our existence. As human beings, with our individual self-images, our cultural dispositions, and our humanistic concerns, we are essentially and inevitably ethical creatures. We necessarily react to the world's things and events in certain ways; we do not merely passively receive and respond.

Our engagement with the world reflects our values and choices. For Lu Xiangshan, our commitment to treating the world and its objects in accordance with principle is nothing but our commitment to a moral reality—the normative principles are inherent in the objects themselves, and we are morally required to observe these principles. At the same time, any human being is equipped with the moral perception to recognize the same set of normative principles. Human beings belong to the same moral kind, and we necessarily share the same ethical commitments and moral insights.

In Lu's understanding, the objective principles of things are simply the way things ought to be treated or handled by human beings. In this way, our moral knowledge is already part and parcel of our factual knowledge of the world. We can understand this view to be a form of pragmatism: objects exist in the world in their interrelations with human affairs; to understand their principles is to know how to handle things and utilize them in the proper way. This explains why Lu makes this claim: "The universe's affairs are one's own affairs. One's own affairs are the universe's affairs" (Ivanhoe 2009, 90). For Lu, this objectivity also lies in subjectivity, since to know how to properly deal with things, one ought to first secure one's innate moral principle: "The human mind is most intelligent and principle is most clear. All people have this mind and all minds contain this principle in full" (22:5a, Chan 1963, 580).

Furthermore, the subjectivity is at the same time intersubjectivity, since under the right conditions, everyone will share the same perception and judgment. What he means by "the right conditions" is our clear insights without the distractions of material desires:

> Moral principles inherent in the human mind are endowed by Heaven and cannot be wiped out. Those who are beclouded by material desires so as to pervert principles and violate righteousness, do so because they do not think, that is all. If they can truly examine themselves and think, their sense of right and wrong and their choice between right and wrong will have the qualities of quiet alertness, clear-cut intelligence, and firm conviction.
> *(32:4a, Chan 1963, 580)*

In other words, there is no intractable hierarchy in our moral perception, and ordinary people's moral perception is just as good as those of sages are. One does not need to be trained to master moral principles—all one needs is to open one's mind's eyes: "Moral principles are nothing but those moral principles right before our eyes. Even when our understanding reaches the level of sages, they are nothing but moral principles right before our eyes" (34:1a; Chan 1963, 580). The description "right before our eyes" shows that Lu Xiangshan has in mind a perceptual mode of moral knowledge. Lu Xiangshan claims that such moral knowledge is innate in us: "Principle is endowed in me by Heaven, not drilled into me from outside" (Chan 1963, 574).

We are born with the moral knowledge of the principle; therefore, to know the principle, one needs to focus on the mind, not on the external realm. Lu Xiangshan turns the pursuit of moral truth inward. One needs to discover from within one's mind what one would intuitively judge as good or evil. Wang Yangming would later develop Lu's view into a complete theory of our innate knowing (*Liangzhi* 良知).

How is it possible that all sages would share the same moral judgments, or that they would all perceive right and wrong in the same way? Furthermore, if we are relying on our own mind to make moral judgments, then how do we objectively verify the truth of our judgments? To Wang Yangming, Lu Xiangshan's moral universalism was highly inspiring, and he tried to establish an *a priori* psychological foundation for Lu's conviction in the universality of our moral thinking. Taking up Lu Xiangshan's doctrine of the *universal I*, Wang Yangming also asserted the universality of the subject's inborn mental lucidity. His subject *I* is a universal *I* that all sages and ordinary people share in common. We have explained that for both Lu Xiangshan and Wang Yangming, intersubjectivity is further grounded in objectivity—heavenly principle or *Dao*. There is objective truth to the universal moral principle, which is not *defined* by human consensus but is *reflected* in human intersubjectivity. Wang Yangming explains that human intersubjectivity itself has objective value, because it is grounded in our innate moral capacity. For Wang Yangming, morality is a direct, intuitive response of the agent to the things outside of us. Moral knowledge is a form of moral perception, with the objective moral reality as its perceivable object. Equipped with the same moral sense, which Wang Yangming calls *Liangzhi* 良知,[5] all of us can perceive the same moral truths.

According to Lai Chen, when Wang Yangming presents the thesis that outside of the mind there is no principle, he is primarily stating that "outside of human mind there is no good (*shan* 善)," and the good for Wang Yangming does not refer to happiness or satisfaction, nor to the normativity of external behavior. Instead, the good designates "the moral agent's moral motivation and moral consciousness" (Chen 1991, 30–1). In other words, the good comes from the subject's mental states rather than her behavior's conformity to external norms. Wang Yangming's commitment to moral realism does not rule out the contribution of human beings in the construction of this moral reality. Moral reality is reality of the human world, and it is defined by our universal valuation of the moral intent. As Wang Yangming puts it, "The supreme good (*zhishan* 至善) is nothing but the mind's being as pure as the ultimate heavenly principle" (Wang 1994, 8).

Wang Yangming's pursuit of heavenly principle, as it is for Lu Xiangshan, is fundamentally a form of moral inquiry. According to Sami Pihlström, moral

---

5 See Chapter 11 for a fuller explication of this notion in Wang Yangming's moral philosophy.

inquiry is different from scientific inquiry, in that "while in any normal inquiry the right answers to the questions asked are in some sense supposed to lie 'out there,' waiting for being discovered by the inquirers (us), this is not the case with moral questions or 'moral inquiry' " (Pihlström 2005, 29). Moral inquiry cannot be divorced from the inquirer him-or-her-self since "moral inquiry ... is an investigation of one's own life," and "there usually are no pre-given answers to the questions that arise in the course of such an investigation prior to the actions that constitute one's living of that life itself" (Pihlström 2005, 29). In other words, when it comes to moral reality, what we are asserting or investigating is none other than the reality for us and defined by what is good for the human world.

In summary, the humanist sense of moral realism in both Lu Xiangshan and Wang Yangming's philosophy is manifested in their assertion of "the mind is principle." Moral reality is not outside of the human world, and moral truth cannot be wholly independent of the human mind. Their view is similar to Putnam's particular form of moral realism—pragmatic moral realism. In Pihlström's explication, under this view:

> Moral values, or whatever one is ethically (personally) committed to, can be thought of as "real" within the human world, ... but because of the distinctive character of this ethical dimension of reality, no metaphysically-realist "independence" need or even can be invoked here. The pragmatic moral realist can hold that moral values and duties are personally real, objective to some extent (that is, not subjective or "relative" in any easy way), though of course not objective in the sense in which sticks and stones and electrons are "objective."
> *(Pihlström 2005, 32)*

From this pragmatist's turn, we will now construct Lu Xiangshan and Wang Yangming's metaphysics as a form of pragmatist metaphysics.

Pragmatist Metaphysics

We have explained that Lu Xiangshan opened a new path of moral inquiry from that of the dominant Cheng–Zhu school. Because of their respective worldviews and philosophical concerns, Lu Xiangshan focused on internal inspection while Zhu Xi emphasized external investigation. The former is to seek truth from within one's mind; the latter is to seek truth from studying the world and its objects. Unlike Zhu Xi, Lu Xiangshan advocated searching within oneself rather than examining external realm or investigating principles of particular things. The disagreement between Zhu Xi and Lu Xiangshan on the purpose of study and the primary goal of learning culminated in the notorious Goose Lake Debate in 1175.⁶ Zhu Xi criticized Lu's methodology as idle and insubstantial, while Lu Xiangshan charged Zhu's methodology as trivial and aimless (34:24a–b, Chan 1963, 583). Zhu Xi wrote, "Lu taught people only the doctrine of 'honoring the moral nature.' Therefore, those who have studied under him are mostly scholars who put their beliefs into practice. But he neglected to follow the path of study and inquiry" (34:4b-5a, Chan 1963, 582). In rebuttal, Lu Xiangshan wrote: "If one does not know how to honor one's moral nature, how can he talk about following the path of study and inquiry?" (Chan 1963, 582). He composed a poem at Goose Lake, in which he laid down this derogative comparison between Zhu's methodology and his own: "Easy and simple spiritual practice, in the end, proves great and long lasting. Fragmented and disconnected endeavors leave one drifting and bobbing aimlessly. You want to know how to rise from the lower to the higher realms. First you must—this very moment—distinguish true from false" (Ivanhoe's translation; Ivanhoe 2009, 96).

To see the different orientation of Lu Xiangshan's metaphysics from that of Zhu Xi, we appeal to the contemporary theory of pragmatist metaphysics. Under this interpretation, Lu Xiangshan's emphasis on the close connections between things' existence and our handling of things becomes much more intelligible. Pragmatist metaphysics is the view that "metaphysical issues ought to be approached pragmatically," and by this claim, its advocates mean that we should settle metaphysical issues by considering them "through our human practices of coping with the world we live in" (Pihlström 2009, 2). According to Sami Pihlström, a contemporary defender of pragmatist metaphysics, the problem of understanding human existence is "the most profound problem in pragmatist metaphysics" (Pihlström 2009, 14). Reality is nothing but human reality, and since human existence is inevitably imbued with values and normativity, human reality is grounded on humans' valuational perspectives and ethical concerns. Pihlström argues:

> Consider a stone lying deep on the bottom of an ocean. It is hardly valuable for us in any plausible sense. Yet, the very possibility of identifying a stone as a stone (and not, say, as a collection of molecules) implies a whole system of value commitments. A comprehensive conception of humanly relevant values, of "human flourishing"—to borrow Putnam's (1981) Aristotelian way of speaking—must be in place in order to find it relevant to distinguish stones from nonstones and to find it relevant to place such entities in spatiotemporally described contexts (e.g., an ocean, its bottom, etc.).
> *(Pihlström 2009, 146)*

---

6 See Ching 1974 and Huang 1987 for detailed explanation.

From this perspective, we should see that metaphysics, epistemology, and ethics are intertwined human pursuits in the effort to understand reality. As Pihlström puts it, "When inquiring into metaphysical, epistemological, or ethical (or any other) problems, we are engaged in the same fundamental project of understanding our human life in the human world." Above all, Pihlström claims, "the metaphysics-ethics entanglement ... is the key to pragmatist metaphysics" (Pihlström 2009, viii). Ethics is the grounding for metaphysics, not the other way around. Since we, as value-laden creatures, "are always, at least implicitly, making ethical choices, engaging in moral valuations, formulating our categorization of reality from perspectives or standpoints always already laden with ethical ideals and assumptions," then, "shouldn't we maintain that reality is, for us, inevitably value-laden?" (Pihlström 2009, 91).

From the perspective of pragmatist metaphysics, we can now understand Lu Xiangshan and Wang Yangming' emphasis on the subject I as well as subjectivity in their metaphysics. Pragmatist metaphysicians view reality as "a fusion of the self and the world: there is no world as such, 'in itself,' independently of our subjective, perspectival contributions; nor is our subjectivity, or the self, anything as such, independently of the world in which it is not simply found as an object but within which it is habitually and engagingly embedded" (Pihlström 2009, 13). In other words, the world has meaning because we are engaged with it; our existence only makes sense in the context of our engagement with the world.

According to Lu Xiangshan, "Fundamentally there is nothing wanting in you. There is no need to seek elsewhere. All depends on your establishing yourself in life" (34:10b; Chan 1963, 582). Wisdom lies in knowing oneself. One should learn in order to apply wisdom to life; one should learn for the sake of improving oneself. If we know about the details of things in the world without knowing how to deal with them, then such knowledge is vacuous and meaningless, not just to us, but in absolute terms, since knowledge about the world boils down to knowledge about our treatment of things in the world.

According to pragmatist metaphysics, there is no "world-in-itself": "The world ... is dependent on us, or structured by us, though not causally, empirically, or factually, but formally or transcendentally" (Pihlström 2009, 89). Pihlström explains the world's dependence on us as our imposing on the world "its form(s), under which it is, or may become, a possible object of our inquiries and other engagements" (Pihlström 2009, 89). If we understand principle (*li*) in Lu–Wang's usage as the "forms" we impose on the world, then their statement of "principle is in the mind" makes perfect sense. We give the world its form and we render things intelligible—making them conform to the principles with which we organize the world's existence. We cannot understand reality as something that stands outside of us, waiting for us to investigate. As Pihlström puts it, "Our study of such possibilities for categorization is metaphysical; yet, the (metaphysical) possibilities thus investigated are not 'out there' independently of us" (Pihlström 2009, 91). In Lu–Wang's terminology, we say that principle is not out there in the world; principle is within us. The slogan "the mind is principle" simply means that principle is inseparable from our mind; principle is in the mind.

From the perspective of pragmatist metaphysics, we can also see why Wang Yangming would claim that principles of things are simply how we can properly deal with things. The world is incorporated into our intentionality (*yi* 意). According to Wang Yangming, "The master of the body is the mind (*xin* 心). The mind's activation turns into intentionality (*yi* 意). Intentionality is grounded in one's innate knowing (*zhi* 知), and where intentionality locates is the thing (*wu* 物)" (Wang 1994, 15). In this enigmatic remark on the connection between mind, intentionality, innate knowledge, and thing, Wang takes external things to be our outward-directed intentional acts. He explains, if we set our mind to serving our parents, then serving the parents is a thing. If we set our mind to be benevolent to the people, then being benevolent to the people is a thing. As Wang puts it, "With such intentionality comes such a thing; without such intentionality there is no such thing. Isn't a thing simply the application of intentionality?" (Wang 1994, 117). In other words, the field of our intention constitutes the field of our action, and our world is nothing but our field of action. Our world does not exist outside of our action. This may be Wang Yangming's version of pragmatic metaphysics.

According to neo-Confucians in general, we classify reality such that particular things are grouped into various kinds and each kind has its own principle. For Lu Xiangshan and Wang Yangming in particular, however, things are categorized *by us* and *for us*. This attitude reflects a pragmatist inclination: the division of kinds is not "ready-made"; rather, it is done in accordance with humans' ethical concerns and pragmatic needs. As Ivanhoe puts it, "Instead of presenting a form of panpsychism, such teachings rightly are seen as efforts to bring people back to the importance of engaging with and reflecting upon the *actual phenomena* they encounter in their day-to-day lives. Rather than assaulting the ontological status of material things, such passages call us to pay attention to how we understand and respond to the various phenomena of the world" (Ivanhoe 2009, 109; italics in original). Our understanding and our responses to the world is the only reality that matters to us. The reality is nothing but a humanly *structured* (not constructed) reality.

Conclusion

Both Lu Xiangshan and Wang Yangming treat the subject *I* as the universal *I*; hence, subjectivity to them is tantamount to objectivity. What determines the world's structure and categorization is not individual human beings' particular interests or experiences; rather, the world's principle reflects the universal concern of humanity. Moral objectivity is grounded in our shared human concerns. Unlike for Zhu Xi, under Lu–Wang's view there is no transcendent system of moral rules or heavenly principle. Individuals and things in the world are both elements of the whole system of existence. The world's principle is set in the man–world interactions.

For Lu Xiangshan and Wang Yangming, ethics and metaphysics are inextricably entangled. The entanglement of ethics and metaphysics in their philosophy is manifested in their taking the unity of fact and value for granted. Principles of things—those that we can objectively investigate—are embedded in the contexts of our experiences and practices. To study the way the world is cannot be detached from the pursuit of the way we ought to interact with the world. In this way, we may say that ethical issues are essentially involved in our epistemology and our metaphysics. This is again a theme in pragmatist metaphysics: "when we are saying that ethical facts are needed to make metaphysical truths true, we are already employing a metaphysical concept, the one of truthmaking, which may not be pragmatically specifiable independently of ethical considerations because of its entanglement with human experience and practice" (Pihlström 2009, 104). The world in which we live is the world with which we interact. Our intellectual pursuit of the truth of the world cannot be divorced from our ethical pursuit of the right way to interact with the world. To succeed in our ethical pursuit, however, we cannot look outward for answers. The answers must lie in our own mind. Hence, the mind *is* principle.

On his own philosophical system, Putnam writes in jest, "If I dared to be a metaphysician, I think I would create a system in which there were nothing but obligations. What would be the metaphysically ultimate, in the picture I would create, would be what we *ought to* do (ought to say, ought to think). In my fantasy of myself as a metaphysical super-hero, all 'facts' would dissolve into 'values.'" However, Putnam readily acknowledges, "I am not, alas! so daring as this" (Putnam 1990, 115, italics in original). In this chapter, we have seen that Lu Xiangshan and Wang Yangming have indeed been so "daring" in establishing exactly such a metaphysical view that turns facts of the world into our obligations toward them. Pihlström argues that pragmatist metaphysics ought to be a form of metaphysics "with an ethical grounding." At the same time, "[t]hat grounding is metaphysical, too, because ethics is metaphysics of the humanly structured reality, and vice versa, with every value realized in facts and every fact laden with values (Pihlström 2009, 116). This hope for the future of pragmatist metaphysics can be applied to Lu Xiangshan and Wang Yangming's thesis "the mind is principle." We may see Lu Xiangshan as a path-setter, turning an outward-looking investigative attitude of knowledge into an inward-reflective, self-aware pursuit of those action-guiding principles for our interactions with the world. This direction was embraced by Wang Yangming as the correct path to gaining knowledge of the world. Lu–Wang's metaphysics, under this light, is not a confused worldview that mixes value with reality, nor is it subjectivism or idealism. Rather, it is metaphysics with an ethical grounding in its purest form.

Primary Sources

Lu, Xiangshan 1981. *The Complete Work of Lu Xiangshan*. Taipei, Taiwan: Liren Shuju.
Wang, Yangming 1975. *The Compete Works of Wang Yangming*. Taipei, Taiwan: Zhengzhong shuju.
Wang, Yangming 1994. *The Records of Wang Yangming's Teachings* (*Chuanxilu* 傳習錄). Taipei, Taiwan: Taiwan Shangwu Yinshuguan.

Selections in English

Chan, Wing-tsit (ed.) 1963. *A Sourcebook in Chinese Philosophy*. Princeton University Press. Chapters 33, 35.
Ivanhoe, Philip J. 2009. *Readings from the Lu-Wang School of Neo-Confucianism*. Indianapolis, IN: Hackett Publishing Company.

7

Wang Fuzhi's Theory of Daily Renewal of Human Nature and His Moral Psychology

Introduction

Like other neo-Confucians, Wang Fuzhi's philosophy of human nature is also fundamentally a Mencian view: human nature is good. Mencius identified the four moral sprouts (*si duan* 四端) as what is contained within human nature. The connotation of "*duan* 端" is that it is the beginning state and requires development. Wang Fuzhi takes a step further to define human nature (*xing* 性) as the emerging, developing state of human existence. In other words, Wang Fuzhi takes what we call *xing* to be human's moral and intellectual potential. He says, "What is derived from heaven and in accordance with *Dao*, what is contained within the physical forms and *qi*, which *makes it possible to know all and to do all*—this is what we call *xing*" (Wang 1967, 16; emphasis added). This comment shows that he takes human nature to be a state of our existence that is full of potential. It is not simply what is given and determined at birth.

We have seen in Chapter 5 that Zhu Xi treats human nature as that which heaven confers on human beings. We are all endowed with our moral essence, which is complete at birth, but could be obstructed by the *a posteriori* constitutions of our *qi*-endowment. This view could be categorized to be in the camp of "essence precedes existence" by Jean-Paul Sartre's distinction. According to Sartre, we find such a view everywhere: "Man possesses a human nature; this 'human nature,' which is the concept of that which is human, is found in all men, which means that each man is a particular example of a universal concept—man" (Sartre 2007, 22). Sartre himself promotes his version of existentialism, according to which "existence precedes essence": "man first exists: he materializes the world, encounters himself, and only afterward defines himself....He will not be anything until later, and then he will be what he makes of himself" (Sartre 2007, 22). In this chapter, we will see how Wang Fuzhi's theory of human nature manifests this existentialist spirit. Wang's theory of the daily renewal of human nature captures the sense of indeterminacy at birth as well as the continual progression in a person's existence. This is not

Neo-Confucianism: Metaphysics, Mind, and Morality, First Edition. JeeLoo Liu.
© 2018 John Wiley & Sons, Inc. Published 2018 by John Wiley & Sons, Inc.

to say, however, that Wang denies that we have innate moral traits. He too believes that we have a moral essence, and that human beings are intrinsically moral creatures. We shall thus analyze how he could defend his theory of the daily renewal of human nature in this background assumption of the goodness of human nature.

The Daily Renewal and Daily Completion of Human Essence

According to the Cheng–Zhu school, humans and other creatures derive their natures from heavenly principle. It is the same heavenly principle that makes possible the nature of different creatures. Therefore, humans and other creatures share the same nature. What makes humans different from other creatures lies in the varied endowments of *qi*. The purity or impurity of *qi* in each being is responsible for the good or the bad in different lives. Wang Fuzhi, however, rejected the theory that the nature of humans and of other creatures is the same. He argues that each creature's nature is determined by the stuff from which a life is formed. Humans and animals are made of different *qi*, and thus, they must have different natures. According to him:

> Humans have their *qi*, and that is how they have their nature. Dogs and cattle also have their *qi* and their nature. The coalesced *qi* of humans is good (*shan* 善); therefore, their nature is good. The *qi* that constitutes dogs and cattle does not have this good quality, and thus their nature cannot be said to be good.
>
> (*Wang 1974a, 10:662*)

The nature of vegetation includes growth and decay; the nature of animals includes perception and motion. The nature of human beings, on the other hand, includes moral proclivity. Humans are born as moral creatures because humans are constituted by the combination of *qi* that is "good." We have introduced Wang's theory of the goodness of *qi* in Chapter 4, and now we can see how it applies to human nature. Wang Fuzhi explains that fundamental differences between humans and other creatures lie in the alternation (*bian* 變) and conjoining (*he* 合) of *yin* and *yang*. This presence of goodness in humans is the result of the natural distribution of *qi*: "When there are both alternation and conjoining, not all can be good" (Wang 1974a, 10:660). In other words, the distribution of *qi* in individual creatures varies as the result of *yin*'s and *yang*'s movements or compositions, and the demarcation between humans and other animals is a natural fact. There are certain natural mental qualities and physical attributes that are rooted in the constitution of *qi*. Even with individual variations, each species has its natural potential as well as limitations due to their *qi* constitution.

We can call Wang Fuzhi's view "natural constitutionism." Under Wang's natural constitutionism, humans and other animals are separated in kind because the former are capable of being good while the latter are not. By extension of his natural constitutionism, human morality has its biological or physiological foundation. Humans have a moral essence that separates them from other animals. Animal moral psychologist Frans de Waal would naturally disagree with Wang Fuzhi on this point. However, Wang Fuzhi's view may not be as disparaging on animal morality as it appears to be. According to him, "The *dao* of heaven does not leave animals out, while the *dao* of humans only pertains to human beings" (Wang 1974c: Inner Chapter, 5). That is to say, even if other animals may have the biological makeup of moral sentiments such as empathy, which de Waal singles out as clearly manifested in animal behavior, it is only humans who can devise explicit moral principles (the *dao* of humans), cultivate moral virtues and intentionally aspire to become moral agents. Morality relies on conscious effort, and only humans are capable of putting in conscious effort to cultivate it. As Mencius has informed us with his terminology: having the moral sentiments is merely the "sprout" or the "beginning" (*duan* 端) of moral virtues. Other animals may have the spout as de Waal and other animal psychologists have observed; only human beings, however, are capable of bringing the sprout into fruition.

What is the content of human nature if human nature is derived from *qi*? To Wang Fuzhi, human nature is simply the principle (*li*) endowed in the constitution of *qi*. Humans' physical constitution is nothing but the congregation of *qi*, while principle is the order of *qi*, which is necessarily contained in the congregation of *qi*. Hence, human beings are necessarily endowed with principle. Principle is inherent in human nature according to Wang Fuzhi: "Human nature is simply principle. Principle regulates *qi* and it is simply the principle of *qi*. How could there be any external principle that enters into *qi* and prevails within?" (Wang 1974a, 10:684). Hence, principle must be internal to *qi*. In speaking of the principle of *qi* when the principle is identified with human nature, Wang Fuzhi adds a moral dimension to the connotation of principle. It is thus probably more appropriate to translate Wang Fuzhi's notion of *xing* as "moral essence" rather than simply as "nature."

However, since human nature is constituted by *qi* and *qi* is constantly changing, human nature cannot be a fixed state. Wang Fuzhi thus created his most ingenious doctrine of "the daily renewal and daily completion of human essence." He claims that nature is not simply what one is endowed with at birth; it is also what is developed throughout one's life: "What heaven endows in men is uninterrupted *qi*. If *qi* is uninterrupted, then principle must also be uninterrupted. Therefore, as long as life continues, one's nature gets daily renewal" (Wang 1974a, 10:685). To him, daily renewal is at the same time a progression toward perfection: "Human essence (*xing* 性) is the principle of life (*sheng li* 生理); as one grows daily, it gets daily completion." He further asks, if human nature is a natural fact, then "how could it be that what heaven commands (*ming* 命) in men is only what is given at birth?" (Wang 1975, 3:55). Contemporary scholars Jiefu Xiao and Sumin Xu explain that what Wang Fuzhi meant by "heaven's command" (*tian ming* 天命) is simply the natural process of the transformation of *qi* (Xiao and Xu 2002, 295). Hence, Wang's view should not be interpreted as declaring some kind of divine command. As we continue to interact with the natural environment and to receive the permeation of *qi*, our natural qualities and our moral essence are developed and perfected on a daily basis. The renewal and perfection of our nature, however, depend on our personal effort in life. We may have a certain natural intelligence, which does not restrict our intellect since the more we learn, the smarter we become. We may be born with certain natural talents, but our natural talents will not materialize into real capacities if we do not cultivate them. Only at the moment of our death do we stop progressing and improving. In other words, our nature is only complete at the end of our existence.

Wang Fuzhi takes it to be our intrinsic moral obligation to improve ourselves on a daily basis. According to him, "Heaven daily commands humans; humans daily receive commands from heaven. That is why we say human nature is life itself. It is daily generated and daily completed" (Wang 1975, 3:55). What heaven endows in humans at birth is called [heaven's] "command" (*ming* 命) because at the beginning of one's birth, one has no control over what is given. Everything comes from heaven and all is pure and pristine. After birth, one gains control over one's life and can take or utilize what is given. Wang Fuzhi maintains that what one takes and utilizes is due to one's repeated practice or habituation (*xi* 習) in life, and with one's repeated practice, the pure nature becomes adulterated. However, he also calls the affected and impure nature "heaven's command": "What one takes and what one utilizes is none other but *yin*, *yang* and the five elements. It is all from heaven's command. So how could we not also call them our endowments?" (Wang 1975, 3:56). In other words, we are expected to (commanded to) develop our endowed nature at birth into our completed nature. What we do in life becomes part of our essence, and our thoughts and deeds bring about our maturation. Hence, not only is heaven daily renewing our endowment, but we are also in charge of daily renewing and daily completing our own essence. This is what Wang means by the daily renewal and daily completion of human essence.

According to a contemporary scholar Bing Zhou, Wang Fuzhi's doctrine of the "daily renewal and daily completion of human essence" can be further analyzed into two theses: "the daily renewed nature" refers to the *a priori* nature; "the daily completed nature" refers to the *a posteriori* nature (Zhou 2006, 171). Wang Fuzhi indeed distinguishes the *a priori* nature and the *a posteriori* nature, and includes both in human essence (*xing*): "The *a priori* (*xiantian* 先天) nature is what heaven accomplishes; the *a posteriori* (*houtian* 後天) nature is what repeated practice (*xi* 習) accomplishes" (Wang 1974a, 8:570). We can say that what he means by the *a priori* nature is the fundamental principle of *qi*, which he has defined as human's moral essence such as humaneness, righteousness, propriety, and wisdom. What he means by the *a posteriori* nature, on the other hand, is what individuals end up having as their essence. The moral essence is innate in us; the individual essence is what we accomplish through our lifelong repeated practice and habituation of various thoughts and deeds. With the former, *essence precedes existence*; with the latter, we should say, *existence completes essence*. This view liberates human beings from the sense of predetermination to seek fulfillment of their potential and to define their own essence.

The inclusion of both the *a priori* nature and the *a posteriori* nature into human "essence" shows that for Wang Fuzhi, there is no sharp division between nature and nurture. At any moment of our lives, we can change our nature for the better or for the worse. Since Wang Fuzhi thinks that human nature is developed and altered on a daily basis, he does not take evil to be external to human nature either. Individuals are thus responsible for their being good or bad; their *a priori* nature does not determine the way they are. This view clearly opposes the purely *a priori* status of human nature that was at the center of the debates between Mencius, Gaozi, and Xunzi on whether human nature is good, bad, or neither. It seems moreover to explicate Confucius's remark: "Humans are close to one another by nature. They diverge from one another only through habituation (*xi* 習)" (The *Analects* 17:2).

In summary, according to Wang Fuzhi, our moral sentiments constitute our moral essence (*xing* 性). These four moral sentiments can develop into four virtues: humaneness, righteousness, propriety, and wisdom. They are also the foundation for morality. Hence, what makes morality possible comes from our very existence. Morality is internal to us, and it is a natural development of human essence. This view of human nature leads to Wang's moral psychology: the development of moral sentiments.

Wang Fuzhi's Moral Psychology—Functions of the Mind

Wang Fuzhi's moral psychology is also built upon Mencius's theory of the human mind, which delineates several important notions of humans' innate moral as well as nonmoral capacities. Wang Fuzhi further defines and develops each of these notions, and constructs a more complete theory to explain the possibility and the root of human morality.

Wang Fuzhi's theory of the human mind is closely related to his theory of human nature. The human mind is what realizes the objective moral principle (*Dao*) contained within human nature. In other words, our own effort is required for our moral completion, and effort largely consists in various mental functions. According to him:

> Human nature is contained within the human mind and becomes activated when the mind interacts with things.... Speaking from one direction, we say that only heaven contains *Dao* and *Dao* is realized in human nature. Thus, human nature is what enables us to know *Dao*. Speaking from the opposite direction, however, we say that maximizing the mind's functions is the way to bring human nature to completion, to unify human nature with *Dao*, and to follow *Dao* to serve heaven.
>
> *(Wang 1967, 16)*

Since "maximizing the mind's functions" is the way to complete human nature and to unify human nature with the objective moral principle, we need to understand what functions the human mind possesses. With Zhang Zai's thesis "the mind encompasses both nature and emotions," which Zhu Xi embraced wholeheartedly, Wang Fuzhi emphasizes that nature (*xing* 性) (our moral sentiments) and emotion (*qing* 情) must be distinguished carefully since the two have different origins and serve different functions. He separates the sentiments that enable us to be moral creatures from the rest of our biological existence. He says that this moral essence has an objective foundation in the external moral reality—our nature is simply heavenly principle manifested in humans (Wang 1967, 79–81).

Wang Fuzhi's theory of the human mind includes six key functions of the mind: natural emotions, moral sentiments, desires, talents, volition, and reflection. We shall now explain them one by one.

Natural Emotion (*qing* 情)

Wang Fuzhi identifies seven basic prototypes of emotions: joy, anger, sorrow, happiness, love, aversion, and craving. This division of human emotions originated in the classic *Book of Rites* (*Liji*): "What are human emotions? They are joy, anger, sorrow, happiness, love, aversion, and craving. These seven emotions are *what one is capable of having without prior learning*" (9:22; emphasis added). In other words, these emotions are intrinsic to our biological nature and we naturally have them without being taught or having cultivated them. They are our natural emotions. The *Book of Rites* further explains that humans' greatest desire lies in food and sex, while humans' greatest aversion aims toward death and extreme poverty (9:22). This explanation highlights the fact that our basic desire and aversion are built on our survival instincts. According to the *Book of Rites*, when the ancient sages instituted rites and rituals, their aim was exactly to find the right means to regulate human emotions. This topology of human emotion has since become the standard division of emotions in Chinese vocabulary—"the seven emotions" (*qi qing* 七情).

Wang Fuzhi thinks that emotion is the link between moral essence (*xing* 性) and desire (*yu* 欲): "Emotion is directed by moral essence above, and it directs desire below" (Wang 1974b, 23). In Wang Fuzhi's evaluation, emotion itself is neither moral nor immoral: it is simply how human heart naturally responds to people and things. A mother's love for her baby, for example, is an emotion, not a moral sentiment. Emotions are biologically based and are generally shared by humans and other animals.

Wang Fuzhi maintains that human emotion arises from contacts with external objects. The human mind does not contain any emotion until it has contact with external objects. Emotion must be triggered by the outside world: "It exists when it is discernible; it does not exist when it is not discernible. This is called 'emotion.' Emotion is at the intersection between the mind and objects" (Wang 1974a, 8:573). In other words, emotion is a passively reactive mental state. It is not a self-generated state and has to have its object of arousal. This view corresponds to the view held in contemporary philosophy of emotions, according to which "emotions are reactions we passively undergo" (Deonna and Teroni 2012, 1). According to Julien A. Deonna and Fabrice Teroni, if emotions are reactions, then this "raises the question as to what they are reactions to" (Deonna and Teroni 2012, 3). In contemporary terms, Wang Fuzhi is claiming that our emotions have an intentional structure—they are always emotions about something or someone. For example, we are happy about something or angry with someone; we are sad about some states of affairs and we have craving for some objects. The thing that arouses our emotion becomes the intentional object of this emotion. Since emotion is within us and yet has its intentional object outside our mind, Wang Fuzhi claims that it is "neither strictly within us nor outside of us" (Wang 1974a, 10:675).

To Wang Fuzhi, natural emotions are not cognitive or deliberate, and they are not necessarily rational either. They are the mind's spontaneous reactions toward external things or objects. They need to be checked by the mind's other cognitive functions, so that the expression of emotion is appropriate and reasonable. Emotion is like the mind's young child, which left to its own could become uninhibited and disruptive. However, emotion is not like wild weed that need to be suppressed or eliminated either. Wang Fuzhi rejects the Chinese Buddhist's renouncing human emotions. He takes human emotion to be a brute fact of our biological existence. We all have these emotions, and thus we all ought to learn to harmonize them.

Even though natural emotions are not what make us moral creatures, Wang Fuzhi takes them to be essential to our moral cultivation. He gives a paradoxical claim: "If humans did not have emotions, they would not become evil; however, they would not be able to be good either" (Wang 1974a, 10:678). If we did not have any emotion, we should be ideal rational beings who make decisions based on considerations of the best means to an end alone. However, for Wang Fuzhi, it would not be a moral life if the agents were completely devoid of emotions.

He thinks that human emotions are both the foundation for morality, and the source of immorality. His moral philosophy builds heavily on the role these natural emotions play in our moral lives. Later in this chapter, we will see how moral sentiments and natural emotions should combine to acquire motivational efficacy in producing moral behavior.

Innate Moral Sentiments (*siduan* 四端)

Following Mencius, Wang Fuzhi maintains that human beings naturally have the moral sentiments of compassion, shame and disgust, reverence and deference, and the discernment of right and wrong. Whereas natural emotions would not be present when there were no external objects to stir them up, our moral sentiments are inherent in us whether or not we encounter any context that would lead to the manifestation of these sentiments. As Wang Fuzhi puts it, "Moral sentiments have self-essence (*zizhi* 自質) whereas emotions do not" (Wang 1974a, 10:674). We can even call these moral sentiments our "moral instincts." They are what we spontaneously feel in various given contexts. Even though they are not part of our biological nature as natural emotions are, they are not socially constructed either. Along with other neo-Confucians, Wang Fuzhi also claims that our moral sentiments are part of our moral essence, our moral nature.

According to an influential early twentieth-century social psychologist William McDougall, a sentiment is "an organized system of emotional disposition centered about the idea of some object" (McDougall 2001, 115). Three principal sentiments in his analysis are love, hate, and respect. What he calls "love" is a general pro-attitude that shows "the fundamental tendency to seek the object and to find pleasure in its presence," while "hate" is demonstrated by "the tendency to avoid the object and to be pained by its presence." Respect differs from the above two sentiments, in that it involves "the dispositions of positive and negative self-feelings," and "shame is one of its strongest emotions" (McDougall 2001, 116). McDougall thinks that sentiments are developmental and not innate: "the organization of the sentiments in the developing mind is determined by the course of experience; that is to say, the sentiment is a growth in the structure of the mind that is not natively given in the inherited constitution" (McDougall 2001, 116). Wang Fuzhi's view of our moral sentiments would clearly be at odds with McDougall's definition of "sentiment." However, they share the same view on the value of sentiments in the moral life. According to McDougall, "our judgments of value and of merit are rooted in our sentiments; and our moral principles have the same source, for they are formed by our judgments of moral value" (McDougall 2001, 116). Wang Fuzhi's notion of moral sentiment also includes a cognitive and evaluative sense: moral sentiments are always accompanied by the judgment of right and wrong, and should be distinguished from emotion, which is passive, reactive, and spontaneous. Our sense of compassion, for example, is triggered by our judgment of who deserves our compassion. Even if our ability to have these moral sentiments is part of our inborn nature, the intentional content of our sentiments is determined by our cognitive assessment of the right and wrong object.

In contemporary metaethics, moral sentiments are often categorized as a form of "emotion" or what Hume calls "passion," which supposedly rules reason. However, Wang Fuzhi makes a clear declaration that the two should be separated. According to him, "Emotion comes from the mind, but it is not the moral essence (*xing*) in the mind" (Wang 1974a, 8:573). He calls moral sentiments "the heart of *dao* (*dioxin* 道心)," and emotions "the heart of humans (*renxin* 人心)" (Wang 1974a, 10:674). He thinks that the difference between the two is that moral sentiments are purely good and "can never be spoiled," but emotions "need to be restrained" (Wang 1974a, 10:673). In other words, whereas we can completely rely on our moral sentiments, we cannot trust our emotions. Wang Fuzhi emphasizes that natural emotions and moral sentiments are different kinds of mental states. Even if some of them, for example, the sense of commiseration and the emotion of love, or the sense of disgust and the emotion of anger, may be phenomenologically similar or psychologically affiliated, the sentiment must not be confused with the emotion:

> When one sees a little child about to fall into a well and feels something inside, is it simply sorrow? Is it simply love? When one loathes theft, is one simply feeling angry? It is especially obvious that the sense of reverence and the sense of rightness are not to be confused with the seven modes of emotions. Scholars must not conflate the sentiment of compassion (*ren* 仁) with the emotion of love (*ai* 愛).
>
> *(Wang 1974a, 10:674)*

In this quote, Wang Fuzhi clearly indicates that there is something more to moral sentiments than our emotional responses. An explanation for the difference between emotion and sentiment is that the former is closely associated with spontaneous bodily state, while the latter represents a mental attitude or disposition that has both a cognitive element and an evaluative sense. Emotion "typically manifests itself to us through bodily agitations or disturbances" (Deonna and Teroni 2012, 1), such as the shortness of breathes with anger or the racing heartbeat with falling in love.[1] Moral sentiments, on the other hand, are not necessarily accompanied by any felt physiological alteration. Our sense of commiseration may be triggered by an empathetic contagion, which is indeed a physical reaction, albeit unconsciously. Our sense of shame and disgust may also be associated with either a physical reaction of blushing or a

---

1 In Ronald de Sousa's summary of the philosophy of emotions, he also points out that "emotions typically involve more pervasive bodily manifestations than other conscious states" (de Sousa 2014).

natural emotion of anger. Nevertheless, they are more active than reactive, more cognitive than emotive. Our sense of reverence or our sense of right and wrong, furthermore, typically involves a cognitive attitude and implicit or explicit moral judgments. The "something more" to moral sentiments is exactly our cognitive and evaluative judgment of the situation. To deem moral sentiments as a form of emotion would be overlooking the cognitive as well as the evaluative aspect of moral sentiments.

Some may deny that such a distinction between sentiment and emotion exists, in that the latter could also involve a cognitive and evaluative judgment. The cognitivist theories in contemporary philosophy of emotions, for example, identify emotions with judgments. Under such views, emotions are depicted "as sets of beliefs and desires, affect-laden judgments, and as complexes of beliefs, desires, and feelings" (de Sousa 2014). However, these judgment-like emotions would be what Wang Fuzhi here defines as sentiments. His conception of emotion does not involve belief or judgment. If I feel happy, I am naturally happy, not in virtue of some prior judgment that this is supposed to be a happy moment. Other emotions have similar naturalness and spontaneity. Wang Fuzhi uses such metaphors as "rapids" or "winds" to depict emotion's free rein, without predetermined direction or guidance (Wang 1974a, 10:678). Moral sentiments, on the other hand, always involve a cognitive awareness of the situation in question as well as an evaluative attitude toward the appropriate response. In this respect, emotion and sentiment are different mental states. Furthermore, the objects of moral sentiments, in contrast to those of natural emotions, are specifically social contexts and human behavior. We do not generate a moral sentiment toward non-sentient natural objects since they fall outside of our moral appraisal. We would, on the other hand, love our sports car or desire a fancy yacht. Moral sentiments fall into the moral realm specifically, whereas natural emotions do not. Therefore, emotion and sentiment should be separated.

Natural Desires (*yu* 欲)

Wang Fuzhi defines desire as the mind's interaction with that which is desirable: "Things like sounds and colors, goods and wealth, power and authority, achievement and success, anything that is desirable such that I would desire it, is called 'desire'" (Wang 1974a, 6:369). From this quote, it seems that the desiring and what is being desired are incorporated into the same act. What he means is that as soon as the mind perceives an object that the mind finds "desirable," the desire is already present. Desire arises at the moment of encountering a desirable object. There is no second-order judgment or deliberation. In other words, just as emotion is spontaneous and natural, so is desire. Wang Fuzhi gives the example of our desire for food and sex as a common natural desire shared by human beings.

There are, however, certain desires that are not "natural" in his view. These non-natural desires seem to be derived from prior experiences or repeated practice (*xi* 習). He gives the example of puffer fish: If one has never tasted puffer fish before, how would one possess a strong desire to eat it? (Wang 1974a, 8:570). Our experiences and our repeated practice account for how different people could have different desires that go beyond our common natural desires.

There are also certain desires that are not just "non-natural" but are morally objectionable: "Loving someone, one desires that person's longevity; hating someone, one desires that person's imminent death. These can still be called human desires. However, if one embarks on massive warfare and desires to kill others even though one bears no personal hatred against them, then these desires are simply desires of beasts" (Wang 1974a, 8:507). In other words, desires that are not prompted by natural emotions, but are motivated by other questionable motives, can easily lead to immoral deeds.

In contrast to other neo-Confucians, who advocate the reduction or even elimination of human desire, Wang Fuzhi takes a naturalistic view about the existence of human desire. He argues that as long as we are alive, we cannot avoid interacting with objects; once we interact with objects, we cannot avoid the emergence of desires. Therefore, "expecting to rid oneself completely of human desires is an impossible demand" (Wang 1974a, 6:371). According to him, our own sense of righteousness would be like a sharp axe that can divide natural desires and inappropriate ones, and thus we should not just cast away all human desire in one sweep (Wang 1974a, 10:754).[2]

Natural Talents/Capabilities (*cai* 才)

Mencius attributes the possibility of morality to our sentiments and emotions, and he specifically says that we cannot fault our natural talent/capacity (*cai* 才) with immorality. Wang Fuzhi interprets the Mencian notion of *cai* as natural capabilities pertaining to our sensory organs and our intelligence. According to Wang Fuzhi, natural talents/capacities (*cai*) are corporeal and functional attributes—what the eyes can see, what the ears can hear, and what the body can perform, and so on. *Cai* contributes to action and it is what actually gets things done. Humans are not born with the same level of natural talents or capabilities. These natural capacities, however, have nothing to do with our moral potential or our moral actuality. Natural talents belong to our *a posteriori* constitution, which Wang Fuzhi calls "the post-form (*xingerxia*) implementation." In other words, in contrast to our moral sentiments that are *a priori* endowed in us from heaven (i.e., necessarily and universally), natural talents are the result of accidental *qi* constitution in each creature. They are part of

---

2 We shall turn to this point later in this chapter.

what Zhang Zai has termed "*qi*-constituted nature." On this level are the differences in humans' natural endowments such as intelligence, temperament, and corporeal skills. Cheng Yi specifically blames *cai* and our *qi* dispositions for the origin of human immorality. According to him, "There is nothing bad in human nature. What could be not good (*bushan* 不善) is *cai*" (Chengs 1981, 204). In Chapter 5, we have also seen that Zhu Xi attributes the root of evil to humans' *qi*-constituted nature. Wang Fuzhi objects to this division between good and bad in human's natural dispositions. Humans are indeed unequal in natural capacities, but this inequality does not bring out inequality in our moral essence. There are smarter or more stupid people by birth, but, contrary to what Cheng Yi or Zhu Xi has claimed, there are no moral or immoral people by birth. Moral essence is a universal trait among us, even though we are endowed with different natural talents and capabilities.

This issue is reflected in the contemporary world as the uncomfortable question: are some humans simply born evil? The classical Confucian (Confucius and Mencius, in particular) view is that evil is the result of accumulated harmful habituation, absence of individual reflection and restraint, and the bad influences from the external social environment such as associations with the wrong crowd. The Cheng–Zhu school argues that to talk about our universal moral essence without discussing the apparent moral divergences in humans' inborn *qi* dispositions is not offering a comprehensive discourse on human nature. In principle and on the *a priori* level, all humans are endowed with the moral essence that they identify as our nature (*xing*). On the post-form side (our *qi*-constituted nature) of actual people, however, they think that some people are born good whereas some are simply born evil. Their view can be supported by current empirical speculations that there are identifiable evil genes in people's biological makeup or neurological deficiency in people's brains. Some scientists have tried to identify the so-called evil genes—variation of a gene responsible for antisocial and violent behavior, and some argue that psychopaths are born with little empathy or sympathy for others as well as a high anti-social propensity. Psychologist Dr. Kent A. Kiehl from the University of New Mexico, for example, suggests that psychopathy affects approximately 1% of the general population. He distinguishes psychopathy from "acquired sociopathy" in several "cardinal" characteristics that include goal-directed aggression, callousness, a grandiose sense of self-worth, poor response inhibition, impulsivity, irresponsibility, the need for stimulation, and a general lack of empathy (Kiehl 2006, 109–11). He cites many cognitive neuroscience studies with the finding that "the neural circuits embracing the temporal-limbic system are either dysfunctional or hypofunctioning in psychopathy" (Kiehl 2006, 122). From his own studies, Kiehl finds that psychopaths' brains "tend to have very low levels of density in the paralimbic system, the area of the brain associated with the processing of emotion, something that may be genetically determined. The result is that psychopaths tend to have impulsive personalities and show little evidence of feeling guilt, remorse or empathy."[3] Even if there is currently no direct evidence that the psychopaths' brain abnormalities or genetic aberration were present at birth, the fact that psychopathic symptoms often appear at a very young age would tend to support the hypothesis that evil is a genetic trait. The Cheng–Zhu's acknowledging genetic propensity for evil, however, is not committing to a form of genetic determinism. Both Cheng Yi and Zhu Xi advocated the possibility of transforming one's inborn *qi* disposition through learning and practice.[4] In other words, being *innate* does not equal being *immutable*.

Wang Fuzhi, on the other hand, returned to the classical Confucian conviction in the universal moral essence, and he rejected the Cheng–Zhu's attributing the root of evil to our inborn *qi* dispositions. Evil is created by men, not given by nature. He further states that evil itself does not exist—"There is nothing in the world that is the intrinsic evil; evil is nothing but the absence of good" (Wang 1974a, 575). Building on his metaphysical conviction that there is good in *qi*, he argues that our natural *qi* dispositions cannot be the source of human evil. As creatures by nature, we are alike in our moral potential in that we all share essential attributes of moral sentiments. When some people perform grossly immoral deeds without remorse, or even turn evil to the point of no redemption, they became that way partly through their lack of restraint of their emotions and desires, and partly through their life's experiences and their habituation. No one was born to be evil.

Elaborating on Mencius's remark that "immorality is not to be blamed on natural capabilities," Wang Fuzhi further argues that if natural talents cannot be blamed for our immorality, then they certainly cannot be credited with our morality either (Wang 1974a, 10:661). To fully employ one's natural disposition to be moral, one must appeal to one's moral sentiments (the moral essence) as well as one's natural emotions. Only one's natural emotions can bring about the maximization of the potential of one's natural capabilities. According to Wang Fuzhi, "Even though natural emotions have no self-essence (*zizhi* 自質), they can be readily aroused into a powerful state. If they were not moderated (*jie* 節) by moral sentiments, then one's natural capacities will … greatly deviate from one's inborn ability (*liang neng* 良能)" (Wang 1974a, 10:676). That is to say, the correct strategy is to have rectified emotions such that what one is capable of doing would all conform to propriety (*li* 禮). If the emotions are not rectified, on the other hand, then one could indulge in sensual pleasures or extravagant

---

3 http://www.telegraph.co.uk/news/science/science-news/9968753/Studying-Adam-Lanza-is-evil-in-our-genes.html (emphasis added).
4 In Chapter 8, we will explain this view as initially advocated by Zhang Zai.

pursuits and ended up misusing one's natural talents (Wang 1974a, 10:675). In the respect that Wang Fuzhi ascribes morality's motivational efficacy solely to our moral sentiments and emotions, he can be called a moral sentimentalist.[5]

Volition (zhi 志)

Wang Fuzhi claims that the will is unique to human beings (Wang 1974c; outer chapter, 55). He defines the will as "that which is motivated by the mind towards a certain direction" (Wang 1974a, 8:531). This definition shows that the will is a function of the mind. However, Wang Fuzhi treats the will as a psychosomatic state that includes both mind and body. According to him, our will is accompanied by the internal *qi* within our body. In other words, the will is not merely a mental state but an *embodied* mental state that is reinforced by some physiological reactions activated by our internal *qi*. The mind makes a decision and incites the internal *qi* to pursue the direction upon which the mind has set.

In contemporary understanding, the will is "the mental power used to control and direct one's thoughts and actions, or a determination to do something."[6] There are two opposing views on the nature of the will: while some argue that the will is "what enables the intellect to influence action,"[7] some claim that the will is determined by one's strongest desire at the time of the selection. The former can be called "the cognitive view" and the latter "the affective view." In Wang Fuzhi's conception, the will is cognitive and directive rather than affective. The will in his moral psychology is not ruled by passions and is not a blind force. The will directs our thought as well as our actions, and it has to be based on understanding and judgment. According to him, morality consists in the will's direction in accordance with *Dao*. With this prior directive, our internal *qi* can be employed in the right way. Without having any prior directive, on the other hand, we would be acting out of impulse. As a result, we could easily become distracted by our temporary desires or inclinations. According to Wang Fuzhi, "*Dao* is what sets our will straight. If we will *Dao* and appeal to *Dao* as the standard of our will, then our will can have the right foundation" (Wang 1974a, 8:537). That is to say, even though our mind's will has a directive on its own, it ought to comply with the objective moral standard. Therefore, the will must be based on the intellect's apprehending *Dao*.

---

5 We shall return to his moral sentimentalism in Chapter 12.
6 This definition of "will" comes from Cambridge dictionary (http://dictionary.cambridge.org/dictionary/english/will).
7 This definition comes from the entry on "will" in *New Catholic Encyclopedia Supplement 2012–2013: Ethics and Philosophy* (Ed. Robert L. Fastiggi). Vol. 4. Detroit: Gale, 2013. 1642–3.

On the other hand, according to Wang Fuzhi, without the aid of *qi*, our will would accomplish nothing (Wang 1974a, 8:531). The internal *qi* in this context is not simply our innate *qi* dispositions; rather, it is a moral resolve to be developed and cultivated through our own effort. The cultivation of our internal *qi* relies on "the accumulation of right thoughts and right deeds." Wang Fuzhi explains that Mencius's "flood-like *qi*" (*haoran zhiqi* 浩然之氣) is the outcome of our accumulating righteousness to cultivate this *qi* (Wang 1974a, 8:540). Just having the will set the right direction is not enough. To enhance our internal strength to support the will that was initially set in the right way, we must also repeatedly do good. The mind's function of the will is primarily the selection of a direction, and one can will toward the good or toward the bad. However, the will without the practice (*xi* 習) is empty. If our will is set in the direction of *Dao*, and we repeatedly perform moral actions to amass a flood-like *qi*, then it would be easy for us to follow the moral path. Weakness of the will results from lack of good habituation (constant practice of good thought and deeds). If we are not accustomed to being good and doing good deeds, then we will find the internal *qi* weakened day by day. The will itself, without the daily accumulation of righteous conduct, would be causally inefficacious for moral behavior. Therefore, having the intellect's apprehension of the objective moral principle (*Dao*) is insufficient to sustain moral motivation by itself. One must act on the mind's initial selection (of *Dao*) to firm up one's will to be moral.

Reflection (*si* 思)

Finally, one capacity essential to the fulfillment of moral agency is reflection (*si*). Wang Fuzhi separates the mind's cognitive functions into sense perceptions and reflection. His notion of reflection is not just the cognitive aspect of our mental activities; it is more akin to a form of moral self-examination: "Reflection is the reflection on right and wrong, and on benefit and harm" (Wang 1974a, 4:266). For Wang Fuzhi, reflection is simply moral reflection. He thinks that our sensory perceptions do not depend on reflection, but our moral cultivation does. If we think about moral principles, then we are employing the faculty of reflection; if, on the other hand, we think only about food and sex, then that form of thinking is not deemed to be "reflection." Reflection is a capacity that only humans possess and it requires individual effort: "Humaneness and righteousness are part of human nature; they are what heaven accomplishes. Reflection is the function of the mind, it is what humans accomplish" (Wang 1974a, 10:700). Without this capacity, we would simply be like other animals with merely the capacities of sensory perception and bodily motion. Thus, he says, "What separates humans from beasts, is only this" (Wang 1974a, 705).

The preceding conceptual analysis presents Wang Fuzhi's view of the mind's moral functions. At the end of this chapter, we will see his moral theory based on this moral psychology.

The Affirmation of Human Desires: The Principle within Human Desires

Wang Fuzhi departs from other neo-Confucians in his affirmation of the value of human desire. Zhang Zai advocated that scholars must have few desires (*guayu* 寡欲). The Cheng–Zhu school further emphasized that it is only with the extinction of human desires (*mie renyu* 滅人欲) that we are able to see the prevalence of heavenly principle. Wang Fuzhi argues against this kind of antithetical representation of the relationship between heavenly principle and human desires. Basic human desires are nothing but the desire for food and sex. He thinks that even the sages could not purge themselves of these desires. In his view, desires themselves are not evil; they do not stand in the way of our moral cultivation. Quite the reverse, the acknowledgment of human desires can pave the way to the understanding of heavenly principle: To cultivate one's moral self, one ought to appreciate heavenly principle inherent in human desires. "Where we see human desires, is where we see heavenly principle" (Wang 1974a, 8:520). He also criticizes that Chinese Buddhism's denunciation of human's desire for material goods is missing the point. We do not need to abandon our desire for material goods, and we should certainly not blame the objects of our desire for our own indulgence: "All desirable objects are the products of heaven and earth. To blame natural products of heaven and earth and not blaming people, is like blaming the owner for having too many treasures while acquitting the thieves" (Wang 1974a, 10:675).

In this context, we can now explain what heavenly principle stands for in Wang Fuzhi's philosophy. He takes heavenly principle to be nothing but *the moderation and fairness of desires*. In other words, for him, heavenly principle is merely a standard for regulating emotions and desires. It does not have a separate ontological content. Its content is simply human emotions and human desires. Wang Fuzhi compares principle without desires to a pond without water—it is simply vacuous. The relationship between the two can be best summarized by his famous slogan: "Without principle, desires become excessive; without desires, principle gets abolished" (Wang 1980, 212). If an individual's desires are not moderated by the individual's rationality, then they can become excessive; if the universal moral principle (heavenly principle) is not a principle that deals with human desires, then it has no content or application, and gets abolished in the end. The word "principle" in this context can be taken in two senses: a universal moral principle (heavenly principle), and the internalized moral principle materialized as the individual's rationality, what we have previously called "the principle of nature." As a contemporary scholar Liwen Zhang explains, in Wang Fuzhi's understanding, "*Li* (principle) is both the universal moral principle and the particularized form of concrete moral norms or moral principles" (Zhang 2001, 384).

Wang Fuzhi places heavenly principle within the human world, and connects the moral principle with human desires. According to him, "There cannot be heaven apart from humans; there cannot be moral principle apart from desires" (Wang 1974a, 8:519). He affirms what is essential to human existence: the need to survive. To survive, one must deal with one's physical needs. A moral agent is first and foremost a biological being; hence, there is nothing shameful or immoral about wanting to gratify one's physical needs and material desires. To reject human desires is to isolate human beings from the natural world, and to cut them off from their biological nature.

Even though desires themselves are not immoral, Wang Fuzhi does not condone indulgence in material desires. If one's desires are not moderated by the mind's reflection (*si* 思), then they would go against the objective moral principle, and he condemns them as "lacking reasonableness" (*buheli* 不合理). His notion of moderation is paired with the notion of fairness (*gong* 公): "Fairness lies in everyone's getting a share of his own" (Wang 1967, 141). In other words, if everyone's desires can be gratified, then there is nothing wrong with desires *per se*. However, one needs to be prepared to curtail or rectify one's selfish desires, so that the gratification of desire is fairly distributed (*gong* 公) among others.

The word *gong* (公) also means "public." Wang Fuzhi contrasts the public (*gong* 公) with the private or the personal (*si* 私). Just as *gong* can be used in two senses of fairness and public, *si* can also mean either "personal" or "selfish." Here we need to draw an important distinction between "personal desires" and "selfish desires." Personal desires are what everyone would want to gratify for him- or herself, and there is nothing wrong about having personal desires as long as they do not become selfish desires, which is to place one's own needs and desires over and above those of others. In other words, Wang Fuzhi does not condemn self-interestedness as long as it is not a form of egoism, an exaggerated sense of self-interestedness to the exclusion of consideration for others. The removal of selfishness is the first step toward moral fulfillment. Wang Fuzhi's proposal for moral cultivation is to transform one's personal desires to seek the gratification of others' personal desires, rather than to demand the elimination of personal desires. We shall turn to his detailed moral program in Chapter 12.

Just as Wang Yangming's condemnation of selfishness (*si*), for Wang Fuzhi the impediment to moral cultivation is also selfishness: "What one simply must not have are selfish desires" (Wang 1974a, 8:508). He also says, "One's selfish ideas and selfish desires are what obstruct the manifestation of heavenly principle" (Wang 1974a, 10:691). If everyone can have his or her natural desires gratified, then the world would be in a state of manifesting heavenly principle. Thus, he says, "What is universal in heavenly principle, is simply that everyone gets his or her desires gratified" (Wang 1974a, 4:248). When the gratification of desires can be universally obtained, then the world is the vivid manifestation of heavenly principle. This must be an ideal world indeed.

Even the ideal moral agents, the sages, must also have personal desires based on their sensory needs. According to Wang Fuzhi, "Sages have desires too; their desire approximates the principle of heaven" (Wang 1974a, 4:248). What the sages desire is nothing but the same kind of material desires that ordinary people have, but the sages can extend their own desires to sympathetically appreciate those of others. He explains, "In these sights, sounds, fragrances and tastes, one sees the shared desires (*gongyu* 公欲) of everyone, and this is exactly the common principle (*gongli* 公理) of all things" (Wang 1974a, 8:520). What the sages have achieved is the perfect harmony of reason and desire, such that they can follow their hearts' desires and never deviate from the right path. For the rest of the people on the path to moral cultivation, what is required is the guidance of reason to eliminate selfishness, and to extend the gratification of one's personal desires to the gratification of others' desires. As expressed by Wang: "Once one fully realizes moral principle, one is in accord with human desires; once one extends one's desires, one is in concord with heavenly principle" (Wang 1974a, 8:520). This "extension of desires" is the key to transforming one's natural emotions to the realization of one's moral sentiments.

Wang Fuzhi's Moral Theory Based on His Moral Psychology

Wang Fuzhi thinks that natural emotions need moral sentiments as guidance and regulation. We have explained that under his view, emotion is blithe, unchecked, and easily excessive. We need the mind's other functions to regulate our emotions. Ethical rationalists play down the role of emotions in our moral lives. Plato suggests that emotion must be ruled by reason, while Kant argues that emotion and desire have absolutely no moral vale. Morality has to be based on human reason; moral behavior must be motivated by moral reason alone. Wang Fuzhi does caution against the power of emotion, but he also praises the motivational efficacy of emotion. In his view, emotion needs to be monitored, however, the monitoring function in the mind is not moral reason, but moral sentiments. Moral sentiments can properly channel the direction of emotions and regulate their expression. This view is in accord with William McDougall's analysis of the connection between sentiment and emotion: "It is only through the systematic organization of the emotional dispositions in sentiments that the volitional control of the immediate promptings of the emotions is rendered possible" (McDougall 2001, 115). In other words, our sentiments can organize our emotions in the way that makes morality possible for us.

To Wang Fuzhi, natural emotions are "amoral": they can be credited for moral progress or blamed for immoral advancement, but they themselves do not have any moral value (Wang 1974a, 10:678). Nonhuman animals also have emotions, but they do not have any moral sentiment. Therefore, morality must be rooted in moral sentiments, and moral sentiments should serve as the guideline for emotions. At the same time, moral sentiments also need emotions to be manifested. Sentiments themselves are incipient and feeble. They arise in us, but in most cases, they are not powerful enough to motivate us to take action. This is where natural emotions come into play. According to Wang Fuzhi, "Even though immorality can be the fault of human emotions, to do good one must also rely on emotions to achieve efficacy (*gong* 功). One's heart of *Dao* (i.e., one's moral sentiments) is elusive, and it needs to build on emotions in order to thrive and propagate with ease" (Wang 1974a, 10:677). Therefore, what make morality possible are both our inborn moral sentiments and our natural emotions. For example, when we hear about people's starving to death, we spontaneously feel compassionate toward them. This is one of our inborn moral sentiments. And yet, most people simply feel sympathetic but do not take action to alleviate others' plight. If those others were their family members, however, then most people would immediately try to do everything they can to alleviate the loved ones' hunger. This is our natural emotion of love. Natural emotions have motivational efficacy and can directly lead to action. What is needed for moral behavior is thus the extension of natural emotions for the loved ones, to the enhancement of moral sentiments toward strangers. In Wang's image of moral motivation, sentiment *guides*, while emotion *assists*.

For Wang Fuzhi, our sensory perceptions correspond to our emotions, not to our moral sentiments. If, however, we can govern our perceptions with reflection (*si* 思), then even our perception of external objects can cohere with our moral sentiments: "Sensory perceptions usually react to desires; only when they are governed by reflection can they cohere with moral principle" (Wang 1974a, 10:716). In other words, if we are constantly reflecting on our emotions and desires, then we can guide them toward a moral path. If we do not reflect on whether our emotions are temperate and whether our desires are proper, then we end up indulging in violent emotions and excessive desires. This is when natural emotions and moral sentiments are sharply divorced. Therefore, Wang Fuzhi concludes, even though we should never curtail our natural moral sentiments, we must always try to restrain our natural emotions (Wang 1974a, 10:673).

According to Wang Fuzhi, our natural emotions are not just the foundation for morality; they are also the roots of immorality (Wang 1974a, 10:677). Our emotions are naturally aroused by external objects, and if we pursue external objects without checking our emotions, then we can easily be led astray. The moral sentiments are in the mind; the external objects are outside of our mind. If we go with the objects and do not reflect on the moral sentiments, then we end up smothering our moral sentiments. Therefore, moral sentiments must always accompany natural emotions.

Wang Fuzhi explains the origin of evil as the result of *a posteriori* human habituation. We have explained that he believes in the innate goodness of human nature. He argues that human nature is not separable from the *qi* that makes up human existence, and "there is nothing that is not good in *qi*" (Wang 1974a, 10:663). In other words, we are *constitutionally good*. Evil, on the other hand, is simply the lack of moderation of desires and the absence of consideration for others. Evil does not reside in emotions themselves, nor does it reside in the objects of our desires. What makes emotions and desires "immoral" is the absence of reflection (*si* 思), which leads to the lack of propriety and reasonableness, as well as the lack of good habituation (*xi* 習), which weakens our internal moral *qi*. When an object arouses our desire and we pursue it, there may be nothing immoral about gratifying our desire. When a thing or an affair stimulates our emotions, there may be nothing immoral about releasing our emotions. However, when the gratification of desires and the release of emotions become "improper" (*bu dang* 不當) because they are excessive, or because they take place at the wrong time and in the wrong circumstance, then these emotions and desires become the cause of our immorality (Wang 1974a, 8:570). When they are proper, then they are in agreement with our natural moral sentiments. Natural emotions and natural moral sentiments come together as the basis of our morality, and such a union must be accomplished by the mind's reflection. Wang Fuzhi explains the connection between reflection and morality as follows: "What makes people do evil deeds is all due to a lack of reflection" (Wang 1974a, 4:268). Therefore, our faculty of reflection plays an essential role in his moral sentimentalism.

In addition to the mental function of reflection, the mind must also exercise the will to expand (*kuo chong* 擴充) the initial moral sentiments, and extend (*tui* 推) our love for close ones to include others. Extension is simply the enlargement of one's circle of care. For Wang Fuzhi, this extension is not just a mental attitude of empathy or compassion. Extension is a *skill* that must be manifested in one's conduct. Without actually acting to care for others and to ease others' suffering, the moral sentiments one has toward others are of little worth. Extension needs external manifestation; what gets extended, however, are internal to one's mind: the moral sentiments or the heart of *dao*:

> The mind already contains the skill. [The mind itself] is complete and effectual. Expanding it, one accomplishes grandeur; fulfilling it, one achieves splendor. This one mind is what Mencius alludes to when he says, "everything in the world is contained within me." The kingly *Dao* comes from within; it is not from outside the mind.
>
> *(Wang 1974a, 8:516)*

Wang Fuzhi embraces other neo-Confucians' call for the expansion of our circle of concern to the extent of universal care. He maintains that we should desire others' wellbeing, not simply because we are compassionate toward others, but because we should see that there are, ontologically speaking, no "others." According to him, "Humans are all constituted by the same *qi*; our happiness and sorrow are all interrelated" (Wang 1974a, 8:549). When we fail to extend, we are committing not just a moral failure, but also to epistemic failure (*bu zhi* 不知) (Wang 1974a, 8:556). Once we see that all things are interconnected in their existence, it should be natural for us to wish to extend our care. Wang Fuzhi asserts that the essence of the virtue of humaneness (*ren* 仁) lies in the absence of selfishness (Wang 1974a, 10:745). Selfishness comes from the lack of reflection on the unity of all human beings. Therefore, extension is wholly dependent on the mind's reflection (Wang 1974a, 10:703).

From the above discussion, we can see that Wang Fuzhi takes the basis of morality to be our moral essence: moral sentiments that are intrinsic to our existence. He thinks humans' natural emotions and natural desires do not obstruct the development of moral agents, but they are insufficient to serve as the foundation of morality. Emotions are needed for the expansion of moral sentiments, but they are not moral sentiments. Furthermore, morality is not simply based on emotions and sentiments. One needs to employ the faculty of reflection and thinking to guide one's emotions and desires. To be fully moral, one needs to strengthen moral sentiments and to further realize them in one's actions.

In Wang Fuzhi's moral psychology, there are two affective states: sentiment and emotion. Moral sentiments are innate in us, but they are weak in motivational power. Natural emotions are based on our bodily states, and they need the monitor of sentiments to have proper expression. When the two affective states are combined, one's moral action can be easily motivated. However, in Wang Fuzhi's moral sentimentalism, morality is not simply the employment of sentiments and emotions. To qualify as a moral agent, one also needs to employ reflection. The role of reflection is not to restrain emotions, but to examine the realm of the private and the public, so that one can aim to achieve the state of *fairness*. Having emotions and desires itself is not a problem. What turns emotions and desires the gateway to immorality is the absence of reflection on our innate moral essence, and the failure to allow our emotions and desires to be in accordance with the objective moral principle *Dao*. We can see that in Wang Fuzhi's moral psychology, there is a close tie between sentiments and reason, between knowledge and action, and between thinking and feeling.

To sum up, Wang Fuzhi's moral psychology is based on his belief in the innate goodness in the essence of humans. In his view, we need to reflect on the objective truth of *Dao* and to see that *Dao* is already manifested in our own existence: our moral sentiments. Nevertheless, even with our natural moral sentiments as part of our essence, we still need to employ reflection to see that all humans are interconnected and to eliminate our selfishness. Morality is not simply being "ruled by passions"; neither is it the rejection of passions. In this way, Wang Fuzhi acknowledges the role of human emotions in the cultivation of morality, and yet his moral psychology does not turn toward the direction of any form of emotivism.

Conclusion

Wang Fuzhi's contribution to neo-Confucian moral psychology is exactly his recognition of our biological existence and his linking our moral essence to our biological existence. Moral cultivation does not require one to deny one's biological needs and material desires; on the contrary, it is based on the fact that all human beings have these needs and desires. As the contemporary scholar Liwen Zhang explains, Wang Fuzhi "treats our universal biological needs for sex and food as the content of desires. Since these desires are what humans share in common and not any individual's exotic whims, they must have their natural reasonableness [agreement with *li*]. Hence, desires do not stand against principle (*li*)" (Zhang 2001, 386).

Wang Fuzhi's theory of human nature and his moral psychology reaffirm the value of humans' natural sentiments and human desires. One does not have to go with the Buddhist credo of renouncing one's natural feelings and yearnings in order to become enlightened; one also does not need to heed the Cheng–Zhu school's teaching of eradicating human desires in order to manifest heavenly principle. His vision of a moral life is both *sensible* and *rational*, as another contemporary Chinese scholar Yun Chen puts it:

> In the philosophical consciousness of the neo-Confucian era, existence is reduced to the existence of reason, and the elimination of desires constitutes the means to one's returning to one's true being. However, Wang Fuzhi tries hard to show that only when sensibility is completely liberated can reason be truly manifested. In a humanistic sense, true being lies in the unification of both sensible and rational existence; sensibility and reason alike constitute the ontological prescript for human-as-human.
>
> *(Chen 2002, 350)*

Primary Sources

Wang Fuzhi 王夫之 1967. *Commentary on Zhang Zai's "Rectifying the Youth"* 張子正蒙注, 1685–1690. Taipei, Taiwan: Shijie shuju.

———. 1974a. *Discourse on Reading the Great Collection of Commentaries on the Four Books* 讀四書大全說, 1665. Taipei, Taiwan: Heluo tushu chubanshe.

———. 1974b. *Extensive Commentary on the Book of Odes* 詩廣傳, 1683. Taipei, Taiwan: Heluo tushu chubanshe.

———. 1974c. *Records of Thinking and Questioning (Siwen lu* 思問錄*)*, 1686. Collected in *Five Books by Lizhou and Chuanshan (Lizhou Chuanshan Wu Shu* 梨州船山五書*)*. Taipei, Taiwan: Shijie Books 世界書局), 1974.

_____ 1975. *The Extended Meaning of the Book of History (Shangshu yinyi* 尚書引義*),* 1663. Taipei, Taiwan: Heluo Books Publishing 河洛圖書出版社).

_____. 1977a (1673–1677). *A Textual Annotation on the Book of Rites* 禮記章句. Taipei: Guangwen shuju.

_____. 1977b (1655). *Supplementary Commentary on the Book of Changes* 周易外傳 Taipei: Heluo tushu chubanshe.

_____. 1980 (1685). *Textual Commentary on the Book of Changes* 周易內傳. Collected in *Chuanshan's Commentary to the Book of Changes* 船山易傳. Taipei: Xiaxueshe.

_____ 1996. *A Contemporary Interpretation of the Meaning of the Four Books (Sishu xunyi* 四書訓義), 1679. Reprinted in *The Complete Books of Chuanshan (Chuanshan quanshu)*. China: Yuelu shushe, Vols. 7–8.

Selection in English

Chan, Wing-tsit (ed.) 1963. *A Sourcebook in Chinese Philosophy*. Princeton University Press. Chapter 36.

Part III

The Cultivation of Virtue, Moral Personality,
and the Construction of a Moral World

8
Zhang Zai on Cultivating Moral Personality

Introduction

Resituating Confucian moral philosophy in the context of cognitive science and moral psychology is a relatively new endeavor. This approach appears as part of a larger movement to render ethical theories empirically warranted: ethics should be based on how humans actually are, rather than on some utopian ideals about perfect human beings. This movement has been called the empirical turn in ethics.[1] According to its proponents, ethicists should be "informed and constrained by our current best empirical accounts of how the human mind works," and ethics should become what Edward Slingerland has called "empirically responsible ethics" (Slingerland 2010, 2011b) or what has been commonly called "evidence-based" ethics.

The empirical turn in ethics also shifted the playing field for normative ethics. Empirical studies on humans' moral decision processes "call into question the psychological plausibility of the 'cognitive control' models of ethics—deontology and utilitarianism" (Slingerland 2011a, 391). Deontology and utilitarianism, two leading approaches in normative ethics in the West, treat a moral agent's moral act as constrained by her moral sense of duty or by her hedonistic calculus of the benefits for all parties involved. Virtue ethics, though a tradition dating back to Aristotle, reemerged in the second half of the twentieth century as the third major approach in normative ethics.[2] The empirical turn in ethics brought virtue ethics into the spotlight in current ethical discourse, because numerous empirical studies show that humans' moral actions are typically not the result of rational deliberation. Virtue ethics does not place unreasonable weight on humans' abiding abstract moral rules, nor does it focus on human's calculative moral deliberation conducted by reason alone.

---

1 The trend is most noticeable in bioethics, though it is not without critics.
2 See Rosalind Hursthouse 2012, "Virtue Ethics." *Stanford Encyclopedia of Philosophy* (http://plato.stanford.edu/entries/ethics-virtue/).

Neo-Confucianism: Metaphysics, Mind, and Morality, First Edition. JeeLoo Liu.
© 2018 John Wiley & Sons, Inc. Published 2018 by John Wiley & Sons, Inc.

What separates virtue ethics and other forms of normative ethics such as deontology and utilitarianism is that instead of giving act-centered normative rules, it is agent-centered: virtue ethics emphasizes the agent's virtue or the moral character of the agent. As such, it takes into account the psychological states as well as the personality traits of the agent. Instead of focusing on formulating and obeying a given set of moral rules as other normative ethicists do, virtue theorists focus on developing good moral habits and building moral character as the aim of moral education. Contemporary studies in cognitive science and moral psychology can enrich and support the theoretical hypotheses of virtue ethicists. Virtue ethics is thus the most feasible ethical approach that can collaborate with cognitive science and moral psychology. This is also the best model for our reinterpretation of neo-Confucianism, as Confucian moral philosophy is fundamentally a form of virtue ethics.[3] Zhang Zai's moral philosophy is no exception.

In this chapter, we shall reconstruct Zhang Zai's moral philosophy in the context of moral character development in cognitive science and moral psychology. The model contrasted with Zhang Zai's theory is the socio-cognitive model developed by psychologists Daniel K. Lapsley and wife Darcia Narvaez (2004a, 2004b, 2005, 2009), Daniel K. Lapsley and Patrick L. Hill (2009), Narvaez, Darcia et al. (2006), Augusto Blasi (1983, 1984, 1999, 2005), Carol Dweck and Ellen Leggett (1988), among others. The question with which these moral psychologists began is the following: "Why do some people tend to choose those actions that they consider to be moral while others do not, or not with the same frequency and consistency" (Blasi 1999, 1)? The answer, according to socio-cognitive theorists, lies in the agent's moral self-identity or the moral personhood of the agent.

Zhang Zai's moral program has a similar focus on moral self-identity and the same concern with the development of moral personality. Zhang Zai's most essential work, *Rectifying the Youth* (*Zhengmeng*), is on how to educate the youth. It can be seen as Zhang Zai's proposed program for moral as well as intellectual education. Zhang Zai separates humans' natural dispositions into "the nature endowed by Heaven and Earth" (*tiandi zhi xing* 天地之性)" and "*qi*-constituted nature" (*qizhi zhi xing* 氣質之性). The former includes our moral qualities while the latter includes all our physical attributes and personality traits. Zhang Zai emphasizes the importance of learning, and declared: "The most beneficial function of learning lies in one's seeking to transform one's *qi*-constituted nature" (Zhang 2006, 274). It is clear that Zhang Zai's

---

3 See, for example, May Sim 2007. *Remastering Morals with Aristotle and Confucius*. Cambridge: Cambridge University Press; Van Norden, Bryan W. 2007. *Virtue Ethics and Consequentialism in Early Chinese Philosophy*. Cambridge: Cambridge University Press; Jiyuan Yu 2007. *The Ethics of Confucius and Aristotle*. New York: Routledge. Other representative proponents of this trend include Philip J. Ivanhoe, Yong Huang, Stephen Angle, and Wai-ying Wong.

moral philosophy is not to simply identify certain moral precepts as normative ethical codes; rather, his interest lies in laying out a moral program that aims at transforming one's whole physical/biological personality into a moral personality. He takes the transformation to be a gradual process, which consists of repeated practice and eventual habituation. He defines "propriety" (*li* 禮) as "acting appropriately in accordance with the given situation" (*shicuozhiyi* 時措之宜) (Zhang 2006, 192). The key elements in Zhang Zai's moral program match the key features of the socio-cognitive model. In what follows, we shall begin with the introduction of this socio-cognitive model of the development of moral personality.

The Socio-Cognitive Model of Cultivating Moral Personality

The socio-cognitive model of the development of moral personality treats moral personhood as malleable to external influences. The focus of this approach is not on defining the intrinsic features of humans' psychological or moral makeup; rather, it is to acknowledge that even with some innate capacities or innate moral sense, the agent's moral personality is not complete at birth. The moral personality can be gradually cultivated in the person's lifetime; hence, the person's life experience and the multiple decisions she makes through life constitute an integral part of her moral personhood. Such a gradual development includes several steps: (i) the formation of a moral sense of the self, with the self's conception of *oughts* and *ought-nots*; (ii) the transformation of the person's goals, which can be modified as the person matures; (iii) the conception of the ideal moral personality as the end-state of an agent's moral development.

As explained in the Introduction of this book, a great challenge to virtue ethics comes from situationism, the view that there are no *global* character traits, which empirical scientists could invoke as the explanatory basis for humans' moral behavior. According to situationism, people typically change their moral behavior due to situational factors. Few people could maintain a stable moral personality from situation to situation. In other words, *situations trump character*. Therefore, the aim of virtue ethicists to cultivate moral character or robust moral traits is misguided. The socio-cognitive model, however, has a reassuring methodology for the cultivation of a reliably stable moral character.

The *character* versus *situation* debate cast the issue of moral foundations as either moral internalism or moral externalism—the determining factors of moral conduct is either one's own moral character and virtue, or the multifarious situational factors of the external context. A third alternative is the socio-cognitive theory. The socio-cognitive model takes the middle path—it advocates "reciprocal determinism" that takes in "person x context interactions" as the determining factor of one's moral conduct (Lapsley and Hill 2009, 188, 202). On this view, our personality traits are not "static, non-developmental and immutable *essences*, but are instead organizational constructs that operate dynamically in transaction with environments" (Lapsley and Hill 2009, 190, emphasis added). The socio-cognitive theory focuses on cultivating moral personhood rather than moral traits. Even though it is a version of virtue ethics, it is not a form of globalism in that it does not single out a set of robust traits that a moral person must maintain across situations. Under the socio-cognitive theorists' conception, moral personhood consisted in a holistically integrated moral personality that is flexible, malleable, and improvable.

One major assumption of the socio-cognitive model of the development of moral personality is that morality occurs in a social context. The transformation of one's moral identity is a gradual process in which one is inculcated in appropriate social contexts—family relationships, proper schooling, associations, and learning from moral exemplars. This socio-cognitive model does not necessarily rule out innate moral traits, but it emphasizes the *chronicity* of immersion in a moral atmosphere for the cultivation of moral personality. Even though both the socio-cognitive theory and situationism acknowledge the power of influences from the environment, the former sees a continual molding and consistent development in the person's moral growth, while the latter denies such consistency.

Since the socio-cognitive approach takes morality to be a developmental feat, it allows room for change from situation to situation. The moral agent's ethical goal could change throughout her life, and it could be for the better or for the worse. Social influences—whether through parental guidance, schooling, friends' influences, imitating others, or reading about moral exemplars—play an essential role in shaping the agent's moral personhood. The agent adopts different moral goals as she matures in life. As Colby and Damon puts it:

> The central notion behind the transformation of goals is that development in a person's beliefs and conduct is brought about through social influence processes that gradually transform the person's goals. The conditions for developmental change are set when social influence coordinates with individual goals in a manner that triggers a reformulation of the person's goal. We consider this process—the transformation of goals through social influence—to be a critical instigator of moral development during much of the life course.
> *(Colby and Damon 1995, 343)*

Ultimately, however, the moral transformation could be integrated into the person's self-identity in such a way that the agent's moral behavior becomes part of his or her spontaneous reaction to the situation at hand. This kind of spontaneity has often been called "automaticity" in the socio-cognitive model.

The socio-cognitive approach is similar to another prominent approach advocated by Jonathan Haidt: social intuitionism, to which we will appeal in Chapter 11 as a comparative model for Wang Yangming's moral philosophy. Social intuitionism agrees that one's moral judgment is often the result of cultural and societal influences, but it places more emphasis on the function of intuition than on reason.[4] Haidt regards moral judgments to be the result of quick, automatic moral intuitions, while reasoning serves as a *post facto* justification or rationalization on the agent's part. Haidt too emphasizes the social aspect of morality, but in his assessment, the social influence of the individual's moral inclinations come as a way of living among others. According to him, "Human beings have long been ultrasocial creatures embedded in webs of accountability…with a constant need to justify our own actions, monitor the actions of others, and persuade third parties to trust and support us" (Haidt 2010, 183). Therefore, under this view, moral reason is not *causally* relevant; it is merely *explanatorily* relevant in the agent's self-justification and in our assignment of moral praise or blame.

Social intuitionism and the socio-cognitive theory agree on the effect of cultural influences on an individual's moral decision and moral action; however, they differ on the process of moral decision that leads to actions. The socio-cognitive theory takes the individual's moral action in a given situation to be the expression of his chosen moral personality defined by what kind of person he aims to be. On the other hand, social intuitionism takes the individual's moral action to be the expression of his automatic, unreflective "gut feelings" or intuitions. Social intuitionism plays down the effect of moral reasoning and the importance of moral education. As Haidt puts it: "Because behavior is largely run by automatic processes, it is easier to make people more honest and altruistic by changing their social context, activating accountability concerns, or triggering other unconscious processes … *than by teaching them to think well on their own*" (Haidt 2010, 184; emphasis added). Social intuitionism would thus be incompatible with early Confucian moral program, since classical Confucianism's basic tenet is exactly *to teach people to think well on their own*. Zhang Zai's moral program inherits this emphasis on thinking and learning from classical Confucianism. What he proposes is shockingly similar to the main ideas of the socio-cognitive model.

---

4 What separates *social intuitionism* from Wang Yangming's *moral intuitionist* approach is that for the latter, moral insights are given as one's innate capacity, whereas for the former, moral insights are at the backend of moral development heavily influenced by society. We shall see Wang Yangming's view in Chapter 11.

Lapsley and Hill (2009) list five features of the socio-cognitive model for developing moral personality. We will summarize them as *interactions, moral identity, moral exemplars, automaticity,* and *habits*.

1) [Person—Context Interactions]: This model affirms that one's personality traits are by no means immutable essences but modifiable by social environments. On this view, one's moral personality outgrows from both one's internal traits and the external influences from one's environment.
2) [Moral Identity]: This model views one's moral identity as essential to one's self-understanding. On this model, in one's maturation process, one gradually adopts certain moral categories to construct one's moral self, and one eventually discerns the meaning of events in light of one's moral commitments.
3) [Moral Exemplars]: This model accounts for the moral preparedness of moral exemplars in terms of chronically accessible moral constructs. Moral exemplars experience "moral clarity" of their moral conviction, and their moral decisions have a felt necessity. On this model, moral exemplars are the outcomes of a long process of moral identity construction. They are likened to experts in other domains.
4) [Automaticity]: This model assumes that one's moral conduct is not always the result of an elaborate moral deliberation; on the contrary, one often acts spontaneously and intuitively. However, such automaticity is not based on any inborn moral intuition; rather, it is located on the backend of development through "repeated experience, of instruction, intentional coaching, and socialization" (Lapsley and Hill 2009, 203).
5) [Habits]: This model interprets one's moral conduct as a form of *habit,* rather than as the manifestation of a pre-fixed *character.* An integral part of moral development is practice. One's action-guiding scripts "become frequently practiced, over-learned, routine, habitual, and automatic," and this is a type of "moral expertise development" (Lapsley and Hill 2009, 204).

According to the socio-cognitive model, the most important forms of moral character formation are "grounded by the prosaic transactions in the daily family and social life of the young child" (Lapsley and Hill 2009, 204). Hence, family structure and parental guidance are crucial to the healthy development of a moral personhood. In the cultivation of a moral personality, the initial stage of a child's social cognitive development consists in early dialogues with caregivers (parents, teachers), who help children "review, structure, and consolidate memories in script-like fashion." At some point, however, these specific episodic memories "must be integrated into a narrative form that references a self whose story it is" (Lapsley and Hill 2009, 203). In other words, through daily affairs, the child initially relies on caregivers for behavioral guidance and ethical codes formation. However, the child will soon develop a conception of his or her moral self: things that he or she should or should not do on self-selected moral grounds. Conceivably, the moral maturation process would continue into adulthood, as "the question of what it means to be a moral person is a life-long concern" (Lapsley and Hill 2009, 206). In daily encounters with morally significant or insignificant scenarios, a person makes decisions partially based on his or her prior commitments and self-conception, and partially in consideration of situational variables. A moral self is an entity with rooms for development and alteration; hence, his or her action will not always be the same from one situation to the next.

Gradually, through repeated practice of moral deeds, the moral person could become a "moral expert." The socio-cognitive model explains the psychological preparedness of moral exemplars in terms of moral expertise: "Experts demonstrate how all humans can routinize repeated behaviors that subsequently operate beneath consciousness. With much practice, experts become more automatic and less aware of the processes they use in decision making" (Ericson and Smith 1991, cited by Narvaez and Lapsley 2005, 152). Possessing expertise explains how the moral exemplars would routinely perform the right acts effortlessly, spontaneously, or in the terminology of the socio-cognitive model, "with automaticity." This does not mean, however, that moral experts act without thinking or that they are merely *moral automata*. Moral expertise is the end stage of a long process of moral cultivation. When one reaches this stage, he or she is already habituated to act morally and appropriately in the given situation. One's moral insights come effortlessly without further deliberation and calculation.

Now we shall turn to Zhang Zai's moral philosophy, and see how his insights can be understood in terms of these features of the socio-cognitive model. The key concepts we will be analyzing in Zhang Zai's philosophy are: learning (*xue* 學), self-regulation (*keji* 克己), practice of good deeds (accumulation of righteousness [*jiyi* 集義]), habituation (*xi* 習), volition (*zhi* 志), moral exemplars (*shengxian* 聖賢), situational fit (*shizhong* 時中) and social norms established in rites and rules of propriety (*li* 禮). We will weave these central ideas in Zhang Zai's thought into a systematic philosophy on the cultivation of moral personality, and defend it against possible challenges from situationism.

Establishing A Moral Identity—How to Define A Moral Self through Volition (*Zhi*)

In Zhang Zai's moral philosophy, the goal is not to define some universal normative rules, to serve as guidance for moral deliberation, or as criteria for assessing moral worth. His moral philosophy is a developmental program for cultivating moral personality and moral self-identity. The importance of one's moral self lies in the fact that one's self-identity enhances one's moral decisions, even when those decisions may initially seem difficult. Under the conception of the socio-cognitive approach, it is not in virtue of any robust virtue that a moral agent will always act consistently across situations. It is also not a matter of adopting a certain entrenched moral belief or moral principle that guarantees consistent moral behavior from situation to situation. Rather, it is the agent's moral self-identity that enables her to act in accordance with her chosen set of moral beliefs. Augusto Blasi (1984) argues that the problem of moral action is a question of self-consistency, since the agent's moral identity is what mediates her moral knowledge and her practical moral decisions as well as actions. Colby and Damon also argues, "In the end, moral behavior depends on something beyond the moral beliefs in and of themselves. It depends on how and to what extent the individuals' moral concerns are important to their sense of themselves as persons" (Colby and Damon 1995, 365).

Even though Zhang Zai embraces Mencius's conviction of the goodness of human nature, he does not focus on what Mencius takes to be the proof of good human nature—the four innate moral sentiments that include the sentiment of commiseration, the sentiment of shame and disgust, the sentiment of reverence and deference, and the sense of right and wrong. What he focuses on instead, is the importance of moral transformation through studying, learning, and one's self-regulation. Zhang Zai is thus not a moral sentimentalist but a moral rationalist.

For Zhang Zai, moral self-cultivation begins with the agent's taking the initiatives by firming up her volition (*lizhi* 立志)[5] and rectifying her mind (*zhengxin* 正心). The beginning step of rectifying one's mind is to have strict self-admonishment: "One must employ one's own mind as a stern teacher, and have fear [for wrongdoings] in every act. If one proceeds this way, then in one or two years one will have developed a firm conviction, and one's mind will thereby be rectified" (Zhang 2006, 280). We may have been born with a moral disposition, as Mencius teaches, but our moral accomplishment is not guaranteed by our inborn moral essence. Morality takes effort, and effort begins with the right volition. According to Zhang Zai, "If one sets one's volition on learning, then it does not matter whether one's *qi* (*qi*-constituted nature) is good or bad. What matters is only one's volition" (Zhang 2006, 321). In other words, we are not born as fully developed moral agents. Our moral transformation has to be self-willed, and it is a lifelong endeavor.

---

5 The Chinese word *zhi* (志) is sometimes translated as "will." We choose to use "volition" instead of "will" to avoid association with the free will problem.

The goal for a moral agent can be expressed by Zhang Zai's famous four-line slogan[6]:

> Establish the volition (*zhi*) for Heaven and Earth.
> Expound *Dao* for all mankind.
> Renew ancient sages' supreme teachings that are dying out.
> Secure peace and prosperity for thousands of generations to come.
> *(Zhang 2006, 320)*

This slogan depicts the normative universal volition for all moral agents. What Zhang Zai asks from moral agents is to transform their first-order natural desire for the wellbeing of themselves as well as of their family members, by adopting this belief: *all people are related to me as my family members*. In other words, to develop an altruistic volition, one must have the appropriate belief: the belief that everyone in the world is related to one another as descendants of the same ancestors. However, Zhang Zai does not mean "ancestors" literally, since he takes our joint ancestors to be heaven and earth. We should understand him to be arguing for the equal consideration for all members of the human species as a *natural kind*, since we all have the same origin of life. Such a belief in our shared fellowship is what one learns from past sages' deeds and teachings. For Zhang Zai, adopting this belief in universal kinfolk is one of the essential moral transformations for one to rise up to be a moral agent.

The Transformation of Moral Personality through Learning (*Xue*)

Furthermore, Zhang Zai points out that even though Confucius had already set his volition on learning at the age of 15, in his old age, he still lamented about his own decline in ambition along with his aging. According to Zhang Zai, "If one stops at one's inborn nature, then why would Shun (*shun* 舜)[7] need to work tirelessly, and why would Confucius had the lamentation about his own aging and decline in ambition? From this we can see that learning can improve one's virtue" (Zhang 2006, 308). Hence, in Zhang Zai's moral program, learning and the life-long continuous effort are essential to one's moral self-cultivation.

Morality, for Zhang Zai, consists in transforming one's biological existence into a moral existence, and in elevating one's physical desires into a form of altruistic desire—desire for the wellbeing of others. This elevated moral state is called "humaneness" (*ren* 仁), an ideal virtue cherished by all neo-Confucians. Moral

---

6 This quote is from his *Recorded Sayings*. There are slightly different versions in his *Collected Work*.
7 Shun was a legendary sage who reprented the highest moral exemplar for early Confucians.

cultivation consists primarily in building a moral character, and the success is potentially guaranteed by our having an inborn moral essence—our "nature endowed by Heaven and Earth." However, the nature endowed by heaven and earth is by itself insufficient to guarantee moral success. It is also not wherein morality lies, since morality relies on one's effort to transform the qi-constituted nature: "One cannot take credit in one's having beautiful natural talents. One can only take credit in one's rectifying what is bad into good, correcting one's laziness into diligence" (Zhang 2006, 271). According to Zhang Zai, if one does not learn, one cannot avoid destroying one's inborn nature (Zhang 2006, 21). In other words, our innate moral sense is not what makes us moral agents. Morality is not given *a priori*; rather, it is cultivated through learning.

According to Zhang Zai, "What removes the bad and accomplishes the good must be from learning alone" (Zhang 2006, 24). The aim of learning is simply self-cultivation and self-transformation: "One studies diligently in order to cultivate oneself" (Zhang 2006, 269); "The great benefit of learning is to enable one to transform one's qi-constituted nature. Otherwise one will have the defect of studying in order to impress others, in the end will attain no enlightenment, and cannot see the all-embracing depth of the sage" (Zhang 2006, 274; modification of Chan 1963, 516). In other words, learning for Zhang Zai is not to acquire intellectual knowledge; rather, it is aimed for one's moral progression. If learning does not produce behavioral change and eventual personality modification, then this kind of learning is not genuine learning.

What Zhang Zai considers as leaning includes (i) reading the classics; (ii) studying the speech and conduct of past sages; (iii) discussing the essence of learning with friends. With reading, Zhang Zai says: "If one reads little, then one cannot acquire the essential teachings through confirmation and comparative studies" (Zhang 2006, 275). Reading serves two functions: one is to "keep the mind constantly active"; the other is to "remove one's uncertainty and to apprehend where one is still amiss" (Zhang 2006, 275). From reading, one gains new ideas and new insights (Zhang 2006, 321); from studying the classics, one learns the words and deeds of ancient sages. Finally, to learn well, one needs the help of friends, with whom one can discuss the textual essence to remove any quandary or incomprehension: "If one discusses [where one has doubt about the teachings] with friends one day, then one sees something different within that day. This discourse must be carried on daily, and after a while even one can see one's own improvement" (Zhang 2006, 286).

Cultivating Moral Expertise through the Accumulation of Righteousness (*Jiyi*) and Habituation (*Xi*)

Zhang Zai emphasizes the importance of making an effort in maintaining the right direction toward the good, as well as in keeping up the habit of doing good deeds. Morality is *accumulated*; it is not an overnight transformation.

There has to be intentional endeavor, which he calls "*mianmian*" (勉勉), and it requires the initial volition, the preservation of the initial intent, and constant self-examination: "One must constantly keep this intent, and even after one is familiar with acting accordingly, one still fears forgetting it [and going back to one's old ways].... If one can preserve this initial intent and never lose it, then one can make daily progress" (Zhang 2006, 266). The progress is guaranteed as long as one makes the effort, even if one does not see one's own progress: "With ordinary people's learning, they make daily progress without realizing it themselves" (Zhang 2006, 40).

The effort begins with setting up the right direction, and Zhang Zai appeals to Confucius's criterion as the goal: one must favor humaneness (*ren*) and detest whatever that is lacking humaneness. This mindset has to include both a moral preference and a moral aversion, and the latter is indispensable: "If one simply loves humaneness but does not detest inhumaneness, then one does not have a clear discernment in one's habituation, and one's behavior will not stand out" (Zhang 2006, 29). In other words, it is not enough if one simply "has an inborn inclination to be humane," as Mencius defines human nature to be. Morality must be the result of a conscious choice between the good and the bad, and one's sentiment toward the bad must be as strong as a sense of disgust or even revulsion. This strong sentiment is what protects one against situational distractions or temporary temptations. One must detest doing whatever that violates the rules of propriety. This sense of detest originates in what Mencius calls the sense of shame and disgust. It can be seen as one's moral compass, without which one could not be an autonomous moral agent, being guided by one's own moral sense. Zhang Zai calls this affective selection between humaneness and inhumaneness "the method for cultivating the mind" (*yang xin zhi shu* 養心之術) (Zhang 2006, 284).

Second, one must carry out one's intention to do good deeds and avoid bad deeds in one's daily conduct. Zhang Zai elaborates on Mencius's precept on the cultivation of flood-like *qi*: "To cultivate one's flood-like *qi*, one must accumulate righteousness (*jiyi* 集義)" (Zhang 2006, 279). He defines the "flood-like *qi*" as one's abundant moral energy, and suggests that one can cultivate this moral energy through repeated good deeds (*jishan* 集善) (Zhang 2006, 281). At the same time, to avoid moral wrongs, one must observe situational propriety, which is manifested in the social norms such as rites and rules of propriety (*li* 禮). Zhang Zai thinks this careful self-monitoring and self-regulation is what Mencius means by "shunning evil" (*xianxie* 閒邪) (Zhang 2006, 280).

From the above discussion we can see that moral achievement for Zhang Zai is a matter of volition, choice, and repeated behavior. Moral agency is not given at birth. Eventually, however, as the individual acquires moral expertise such that his or her moral effort becomes integrated into "implicit processes" of the mind, such endeavor may be no longer needed. In their study on moral exemplars, Davidson and Youniss (1991) observe that the most noteworthy thing about moral exemplars' behaviors is that they "do not come about through a logical application of well-worked-out belief systems. They are accomplished almost habitually, as if on automatic pilot. They are experienced with little doubt, hesitation, or inner struggle" (cited in Colby and Damon 1995, 363). Zhang Zai depicts the sages' psychological state as "without reflection, without effort, totally at ease and in agreement with *Dao*" (Zhang 2006, 40). In other words, after repeated practice and lifelong habituation, a moral agent gradually "internalizes" his acquired moral habits. His moral personality becomes an integral part of his self-identity. Zhang Zai calls such a stage "the realization of one's nature" (*cheng xing* 成性) (Zhang 2006, 266). One's self is thereby complete. This is the state of moral experts—the moral exemplars in our endeavors of self-cultivation and *sagehood* in Zhang Zai's conception.

Identifying the Moral Goal: Moral Exemplars and the Extraordinary Moral Commitment of the Sages

Colby and Damon (1995), through their empirical studies of people who can be considered "moral exemplars," found three characteristics common to almost all of the exemplars. The first is *certainty*: moral exemplars have exceptional clarity about what they believe is right and about their own personal responsibility to act on these beliefs. The second characteristic is *positivity*: moral exemplars have a positive approach to life and enjoyment of work. Finally, the third trait of moral exemplars is their *unity of self and moral goals*: these people place their moral goals in the central place of their conceptions of their own identity (Colby and Damon 1995, 361–2). In the Confucian tradition, the highest moral exemplars are the sages, and they share the above characteristics with contemporary moral exemplars. It is thus appropriate to associate Zhang Zai's notion of the sage with the socio-cognitive theorists' conception of moral exemplars.

To study the speech and conduct of past sages is to learn from moral exemplars, and one needs to identify oneself with the moral exemplar that one admires the most. Setting up an ideal self is based on one's conception of the moral exemplar. According to Lapsley and Hill (2009), one's moral identity may turn out to be "a kind of self-narrative that makes sense of one's being-in-the-world" (Lapsley and Hill 2009, 206). In a short essay "Western Inscription," which is commonly praised as presenting the epitome of Zhang Zai's moral image, Zhang Zai presents a form of "self-narrative" of the ideal moral agent (as well as of himself). In this narrative, the moral agent sees herself as "being in the world," having kinship with the whole human kind—including the sage, the worthy, ordinary people, and those who are underprivileged in the society:

> Heaven is my father and Earth is my mother, and even such a small creature as I finds an intimate place in their midst. Therefore, that which

fills the universe I regard as my own body, and that which rules the universe I consider as my own nature. All people are my brothers and sisters, and all things are my companions. The sages are those who identify their characters with that of Heaven and Earth, while the worthy are those who stand out from the crowd in virtue of their brilliance. Even those who are tired, infirm, crippled, or sick; those who have no brothers or children, wives or husbands, are all my brothers who are in distress and having no one else to turn to.

(Zhang 2006, 62, modifications of Chan's translation; Chan 1963, 497)

This self-narrative places the ideal moral agent in a world of global family—the moral agent is related to everyone in the world as family, and fosters the sense of universal care for everyone. Colby and Damon (1995) found that "[t]he great difference between moral exemplars and most people is that exemplars act without equivocation about matters that go well beyond the boundaries of everyday moral engagement. They drop everything not just to see their own children across the street but to feed the poor children of the world, to comfort the dying, to heal the ailing, or to campaign for human rights. It is not so much that the exemplars' orientation to moral concern is unusual as it is the range of their concerns and the extensiveness of their engagement is exceptionally broad" (Colby and Damon 1995, 364). We find exactly the same sentiment in Zhang Zai's conception of moral exemplars, the sage and the worthy (*sheng xian* 聖賢). According to Zhang Zai, the sage and the worthy have developed a universal concern for everyone's suffering. Through reflection on the common origin of humankind, one imagines that all human beings are descendants of heaven and earth, and there is thus a universal kinship among human beings. Once one gains this understanding, one would no longer have merely desires based on self-interest but would develop an extended care for all human beings.

The effectiveness of this mentality in bringing up altruism can be verified by contemporary psychological studies as well. According to Kristen R. Monroe (1998), altruists simply have a different way of seeing things. "Where the rest of us see a stranger, an altruist sees a fellow human being" (Monroe 1998, 3). What Monroe depicts here is similar to what Zhang Zai advocates. With such a mental preparedness, a moral agent can be more readily altruistic. Such an altruistic mentality requires the moral agent to enlarge her capacity for compassion and her sphere of concern. Zhang Zai here provides a rationalistic thinking for one to be inclusive of all human kind into one's sphere of family care. Such mentality has been manifested in ancient sages as well as in contemporary altruists and heroes.

Having chosen the sage as one's ultimate moral goal, one needs to find the ladder that can help one approach this goal. This is where external influences from proper environmental construction come into play.

Rites and Rules of Propriety (*Li*) and Situational Fit (*Shizhong*)

In classical Confucianism, rites and rules of propriety (*li* 禮) serve an important social regulatory function. They are the foundation of civil societies, and their restraining power goes above and beyond the constraints of law and order. According to Confucius: "Lead the people with governmental measures and regulate them by law and punishment, and they will avoid wrongdoing but will have no sense of honor and shame. Lead them with virtue and regulate them by the rules of propriety (*li*), and they will have a sense of shame and, moreover, set themselves right" (The Analects 2:3; Chan 1963, 22). Confucianism underscores the connection between an individual's moral cultivation and social norms manifested in rites and societal rules of propriety. However, it could be questioned: What role do rites and societal rules of propriety play in one's moral self-cultivation? If one acts in a certain way simply to be in accord with social norms, one's act can be regarded as socially acceptable and perhaps even morally excusable, but is it moral? What separates morality from mere conformity?

According to Zhang Zai, an individual's deference to societal rules of propriety has to come from his or her cognitive abilities: one must recognize the situation and what appropriate action is called for in that situation. In other words, we do not blindly do what we are expected to do in a given situation; rather, we do what *we* judge to be the right thing in that situation. The former is letting external rules set the norms for one's action, and we can characterize it as *world-to-mind* regulation. The latter is based on the individual's perception of the situational appropriateness and the individual's intention to do what is appropriate in that situation. We can characterize it as *mind-to-world* "self-regulation." This difference is already captured in the debate between Gaozi and Mencius on whether righteousness (*yi* 義) is external or internal (see the *Mengzi* 6A:4). According to Zhang Zai, virtues such as propriety and righteousness must fit the situational requirement—if one's morally praiseworthy behavior is not appropriate for the particular occasion, then it is no longer a moral act. He calls this requirement "situational fit" (*shizhong* 時中) (Zhang 2006, 85) or "the appropriateness of a timely act" (*shicuozhiyi* 時措之宜) (Zhang 2006, 192, 264).

Zhang Zai defines "rules of propriety" (*li*) as "the appropriateness of a timely act" (Zhang 2006, 192). He further defines "situational fit" as "having no fixed mind" (*wu chengxin* 無成心), and he declares: "Only when one forgets one's fixed ideas can one make progress with the pursuit of *Dao*" (Zhang 2006, 25). In other words, one needs to be flexible from situation to situation and be adaptable to situational requirements. To do so, one needs to let go of the four psychological states that Confucius himself has succeeded in renouncing: arbitrariness of opinion, dogmatism, obstinacy, and egoism (the *Analects* 9:4, Chan 1963, 35).

Zhang Zai often lists these four psychological states as what stands in the way in one's final achievement of sagehood (Zhang 2006, 318). Once an individual removes these mental blocks, he or she can begin to perceive the situation as it is, and be able to recognize what act would be considered *situationally fit*. If we merely perform the rituals or ceremonies without understanding their essence, then we would sometimes miss the *situational fit* (Zhang 2006, 193). When the agent acts on his or her rational and unbiased judgment that *this is what is appropriate in the given situation*, the act comes from the agent's own moral judgment and volition. This is indeed an act with moral worth.

In some cases, the act may have very little moral worth, such as the etiquette of removing one's hat upon entering a church or taking off one's shoes when visiting a mosque. Contents of particular etiquette are often contingent and conventional, and they may well lack intrinsic moral worth. If one acts in accordance with social etiquette simply because they are the established norms, then it is indeed questionable whether one truly acts out of morality. However, if one perceives the given social etiquette and yet deliberately violates it or ignores it with no good reasons, then one's behavior does become morally blameworthy. According to Zhang Zai, what is amiss is one's mentality: a lack of respect. He says, "Respect (*jing* 敬) is the vehicle for rules of propriety. Without respect, no rules of propriety can function" (Zhang 2006, 36). This shows that Zhang Zai's moral assessment is focused not on the act but on the agent's psychological state. It is an agent-centered, rather than act-centered, moral evaluation.

Having societal norms such as those manifested in rites and rules of propriety can set an objective, or at least intersubjective, standard for behaviors that are necessary for civility and harmonious coexistence in any society. One of the identifying features of Confucians is their trust in the ancient sages' institution of rites and rules of propriety. They believe that these rites and rules of propriety are not trivial or arbitrary. Rites and rituals are essential not only for the enculturation of individuals with the aim to preserving a civil society, but also for the moral transformation of individuals in their personal development. Zhang Zai especially emphasizes the latter function of rites and rules of propriety. He thinks that the rites and rules of propriety instituted by the ancient sages are "based on human nature," and thus their function is primarily "to sustain human nature" (*chi xing* 持性) (Zhang 2006, 264) and "to nourish (*ziyang* 滋養) one's virtue" (Zhang 2006, 279). According to Zhang Zai, "Rites and rules of propriety are merely the sages' established laws based on human mind. There is no *Dao* other than [what is manifested in] rites and rules of propriety" (Zhang 2006, 264). As Zhang Zai sees it, rites and rules of propriety are not mere formalistic ceremonies and arbitrary conventions. They are the manifestations of heavenly principle, as their reasonableness and functionality have been guaranteed by the ancient sages who instituted them. He also argues that a society's normative system (such as its institutions, set of etiquette, etc.) can regulate people's conduct in a way to foster certain desirable moral traits. For example, he suggests that we employ the system of building houses in the center of neighboring farmlands (*tianzhongzhizhi* 田中之制) as recorded in *The Rites of Zhou* (*zhouli* 周禮), to make "the people draw to one another as if they were siblings, … so that they would handle others' affairs as their own, and would consider the masses as their own family" (Zhang 2006, 282). This is a perfect example in which social norms not only regulate individuals' behavior but also modify individuals' mental states.

Rites and rules of propriety further act as individuals' guidance in self-monitoring and self-restraint. Zhang Zai frequently cites Confucius's motto: Do not say what violates the rules of propriety; do not do what is against the rules of propriety. The moral agent's self-check and self-admonishment is called "self-regulation" (*keji* 克己).

Self-Regulation (*Keji*) and Desire (*Yu*)

Zhang Zai has a low assessment of the moral weight of humans' self-centered desires (*siyu* 私欲): "Everyone has the self-centered desires, which work against one's moral cultivation. Therefore, scholars must learn to reduce desires" (Zhang 2006, 281). He distinguishes "desirable desires" from "undesirable desires" and calls the former "good": "[According to Mencius,] 'what is desirable is good.' [However,] what ordinary people take to be desirable is not completely desirable. Only what the sage and the worthy wish for is a desirable good" (Zhang 2006, 324). Ordinary people have lots of material desires or other self-centered desires; highly virtuous and worthy people have additional altruistic desires. The content of this altruistic desire, in Zhang Zai's construal of sagehood, would be such goals as giving universal humanitarian relief, taking care of the wellbeing of others in distress.

By Harry Frankfurt's classic distinction, "someone has a first-order desire when he wants to do or not to do such-and-such," and "he has a second-order desire when he wants to have (or not to have) a certain desire of the first order" (Frankfurt 1971, 7). The first-order desire has the direct causal efficacy on action. If the second-order desire is turned into a will, then it inherits the causal efficacy from the first-order desire. Frankfurt calls the enhanced second-order desires "the second-order volitions" (Frankfurt 1971, 10). The second-order desire needs to be combined with volition to have causal efficacy. Both self-interested desire and altruistic desire can be desires of the first-order, while what Zhang Zai advocates in his moral program is to cultivate a second-order desire for what he calls "the desire of the sage and the worthy (*shengxian zhi yu* 聖賢之欲)." A morally complete person such as Confucius could go with whatever his heart desires without ever overstepping the bounds of propriety, while what the sage and the worthy desire is simply "to learn to be like Confucius" (Zhang 2006, 324).

A moral agent, according to Zhang Zai, should want to have the desire of the sage and the worthy to be like Confucius with his moral grandeur, and she should not want to have the desire for her own self-gratification—what Zhang Zai calls "selfish desire." In other words, one would desire the alleviation of others' suffering once one has first adopted the desire of the sage and the worthy through one's volition (*zhi*). In Zhang Zai's theory of moral motivation, desire can indeed motivate moral behavior when it is a form of altruistic desire accompanied by the second-order desire to adopt the ideal personality of "the sage and the worthy." We can say that the sense of desire in this context is not the descriptive sense of "what I naturally desire," but the evaluative sense of "what is worthy of being desired" and the prescriptive sense of "what ought to be desired."

The Ultimate Goal: The Effortlessness of Moral Exemplars

For Zhang Zai, moral self-cultivation is the process of climbing a "moral ladder": one first achieves the status of "a person with moral character" (*junzi* 君子[8]), but the ultimate goal of moral cultivation is to arrive at the status of a sage. According to Zhang Zai, "The so-called sage is simply someone who no longer needs to strive hard, no longer needs to reflect, and can arrive [at the moral aim effortlessly]" (Zhang 2006, 28). His depiction of the "effortlessness" (*bumian* 不勉) and "unreflectiveness" (*busi* 不思) is exactly what the socio-cognitivists describe as the "automaticity" of moral experts. The moral expertise that the sage owns becomes a "skill," a "procedural knowledge," or an "implicit process." It is internalized by the sage, and it has become an integral part of the sage's moral personality.

In Confucius's self-narrative of his moral progression in life, he says: "After the age seventy, I can do whatever my heart desires without ever overstepping the bounds" (the *Analects* 2:4). This remark shows that even for Confucius, effortlessness is a mental state that can only be achieved at the backend of his moral development. It is certainly not a common psychological state for all moral agents. As Edward Slingerland points out: "The *Analects* clearly portrays effortless action and effortless attention as a goal to be reached *only after* a long

---

8 This phrase is often translated as "gentleman" in common translations of the *Analects*. It designates a common moral goal for Confucians.

period of intense training and personal reformation" (Slingerland 2010, 268, emphasis added). In this respect, Zhang Zai's moral program fits the spirit of the Confucian project of self-cultivation: from *effort* to *effortlessness*.

Final Assessment of Zhang Zai's Socio-Cognitive Theory in the Contemporary Discourse

To wrap up, we can say that Zhang Zai's moral philosophy is a moral program that depicts moral development as progressive, primarily cognitive, and originating in autonomous volition. Individual agents must be self-regulating in choosing the right goals; they must learn from others through reading, discussion with friends, and emulating the highest moral exemplars—the sages. Their moral development is partly the result of proper social influences (such as schooling and societal rules of propriety) and partly the realization of self-governance and self-regulation. Different individuals begin with divergent *qi*-constitutions (their intelligence, temperament, dispositions, etc.), they interact with distinct contingent situations, and they carry out their initial volition to do only good deeds with varying convictions. Therefore, people do not start on the same footing; neither do they end up on the same rung on the moral ladder. People's moral accomplishments are simply *not equal*.

We now come back to the question that socio-cognitive theorists began with: "Why do some people tend to choose those actions that they consider to be moral while others do not, or not with the same frequency and consistency?" (Blasi 1999, 1). Zhang Zai's theory gives us many clues as to why certain people are more consistent than others: they are the ones with firmer volition, with more repeated practice, with better learning habits, and with stronger self-regulatory power. Zhang Zai's moral program is normative in that it details what one ought to do in order to reach the final goal: *sagehood*. We can call the kind of moral personality as exemplified in the sage an "engrained personality," which does not succumb to situational pressures. In other words, the ultimate moral goal is to have a moral personality with robust moral traits. Naturally, not everyone would eventually arrive at this end state.

On the other hand, situationism is based on empirical studies in cognitive science that takes all subjects as *equal*. Doris appeals to statistical analyses done by cognitive scientists and social psychologists in his arguments, and this experimental evidence typically produces merely a higher percentage of certain expected behavior than its opposite, but it never produces an overwhelmingly sweeping prediction. For example, the phone booth experiment (Isen and Levin 1972) shows that 14 out of 16 people offered help to a stranger when they found a dime in the phone booth, as compared to only one person out of 25 helped when they did not find the dime (Doris 2002, 30). Even though few people acted differently from the majority, they nonetheless did act against the situational prompts. Nomy Arplay points out that in the famous Milgram experiment, not everyone obeyed the authority figure to administer painful electric shocks to the person in the other room. "Faced with the same test, some of Milgram's subjects left the experiment relatively early, some in the middle, some at the end, and a few—to my surprise—actually refuses to cooperate with the experimenters! This … is a case of different people reacting differently to the same situation: almost, one would think, a prima facie case against situationism" (Arpaly 2005, 644). The Milgram experiment shows that the majority of people would act against their conscience under situational pressures, but our interest is in *the minority who would not*. This empirical finding is compatible with Zhang Zai's theory that different people behave differently because they stand on different rungs on the moral ladder. Statistical generalization simply cannot reflect qualitative differences among different moral personalities.

Furthermore, using Zhang Zai's theory, we can offer an alternative explanation to the empirical studies that Doris cites. Zhang Zai stresses the importance of our cognitive abilities in recognizing what is appropriate for the situation or what he calls "the situational fit." People often do assess the situations in which they find themselves to decide what they should do, and sometimes they commit a cognitive error about what action is appropriate for the situation. In the Milgram experiment, for example, the subjects exhibited clear signs of mental struggles and yet they complied in administering torturous electric shocks as instructed. This proves that they did not suddenly transform into sadists due to situational pressure; rather, they committed a cognitive error in what appropriate conduct is called for in the given situation. On the one hand, they deem it appropriate to comply with the spirits of experimentation and cooperate with the gentle authority figure in the room (if the authority figure were more forceful, more authoritative, probably more people would have questioned the authority and rebelled). On the other hand, they performed acts that defied their own conscience or their sense of human decency. The experiment does not prove global personality inconsistency. At most, it proves that people prefer cooperation to rebellion under normal circumstances.

Of course, the above explanation does not dispel the fact that people sometimes do succumb to situational pressure and perform deeds that they would later be ashamed of or regret doing. However, even if the cultivated moral agents occasionally flounder under situational pressure, it does not show that there is no intra-personally (across time) coherent moral character. An important feature of the socio-cognitive theory is its emphasis on chronicity of moral development. Each moral act taken under the situational pressure, however reactionary or impulsive at the time, will be added to the agent's moral life plan diachronically laid out. If, due to situational pressure, the agent takes an action that she later deeply regrets, then the next time when a similar situation arises, she is more likely to act otherwise. In time, her moral identity will become more secured and stabilized against situational variances. We can further add that Zhang Zai's moral personality is based on *continuity* rather than *consistency*. It focuses on the long-term development of moral personality. As such, it cannot be defeated by the experimental outcomes generated on the one-time episodic basis that Doris appeals to as support for situationism.[9]

Since moral personality is cultivated and developed in the person's lifetime, each morally relevant life experience adds to making the moral agent a better or worse person. With case studies on the Auschwitz doctors and the Holocaust phenomena, Doris points out that situational pressures can turn an innocent man into a monster in time: "With the passage of time, what was once unthinkable became unremarkable; persons and nations alike are subject to 'moral drift'—a slide into evil as individuals and groups are gradually acclimated to destructive norms (Sabini and Silver 1982, 78)" (Doris 2002, 57). Zhang Zai's emphasis on *practice* or *accumulated righteousness* comes into play here. Each morally challenging situation poses an obstacle to our moral cultivation as well as a threat to our moral selfhood. We need to diligently make the right choice every time; otherwise, a "moral drift" is not far off when the world is hostile and cruel.

Ultimately, we have to answer the question Doris raises: Do situational variances have a determining effect on people's behavior over and above their personality traits or moral character? Zhang Zai's answer would be: moral character is not a given, and it is not resilient against all situational pressures. This is why our volition, our effort, our cognitive assessment of the situational fit, and our practice of righteous deeds are essential in developing our moral personhood. Situational factors affect people's behavior in an important way, but they are not determinants. People and situation interact, and what determine people's behavior are people's reactions against the situational pressures.

Conclusion

Ultimately, the evidence that Doris cites and the arguments he launches cannot defeat the kind of virtue ethics that Zhang Zai embraces. Zhang Zai's virtue ethics is about the process, not the end-result, of moral personality cultivation. It provides a feasible program for cultivating virtues; under which, moral

---

9 Doris acknowledges that the empirical data he cited cannot disprove claims of *continuity* or *intrapersonal coherence* by social cognitive theorists. However, he thinks that due to practical difficulties, evidence of continuity or intrapersonal coherence will be hard to come by without risking circular justification since it is mostly based on the subjects' self-reports. He remains skeptical about whether the account of character given by social cognitive theorists can be substantiated until such evidence is provided (see Doris 2002, 84–5).

development is progressive and gradual. The effort is primarily cognitive, and it originates in the moral agent's autonomous volition. The whole moral progress requires consistent habituation of moral deeds, and the end goal is the effortless immersion in the established moral personality. Such an accomplished moral agent simply would no longer be threatened by situational variances.

Primary Source

Zhang Zai 張載 2006. *The Complete Work of Zhang Zai* (張載集). Beijing, China: Zhonghua shuju.

Selection in English

Chan, Wing-tsit (ed.) 1963. *A Sourcebook in Chinese Philosophy*. Princeton University Press. Chapter 30.

9

The Cheng Brothers' Globaist Virtue Ethics and Virtue Epistemology

Introduction

This chapter presents the Cheng brothers' virtue ethics and virtue epistemology. As explained in the Introduction of this book, virtue ethics is the approach of ethical theories that emphasize the virtues, or moral character, of the moral agent. Virtue ethics defines the moral worth of an act in terms of the actor: A virtuous act is one performed by virtuous agents. As a form of normative ethics, virtue ethics investigates what kind of virtues one ought to cultivate, or what kind of moral character one ought to develop. Therefore, an important task for virtue ethicists is to identify the most essential moral virtues that one ought to cultivate in order to become a moral agent. The Cheng brothers are particularly interested in defining the virtues that they deem necessary for one's moral accomplishment.

This chapter further explicates the Cheng brothers' moral philosophy as a *globalist* form of virtue ethics, because they advocate certain moral virtues as the foundations for a stable moral personality.[1] According to John Doris, globalism is the view that personality is "an evaluatively integrated association of robust traits," and by "robust" moral traits, he means those traits that can help their possessors maintain stable and consistent behavioral patterns against situational pressures (Doris 2002, 23). The Cheng brothers' major objective in their moral program is to explicate the virtues that are "robust"—strong and enduring, and the one robust virtue that they both emphasize in particular is humaneness (*ren*). In the conception of globalist virtue ethicists, a moral agent with certain robust moral traits would not deviate from the behavioral patterns that manifest these traits even in trying circumstances. However, experience has taught us that it is not unusual to find honest people succumbing to the

---

1 This characterization would also apply to other Confucians, though to varying degrees. According to Eric Hutton, "For any scholar of Confucianism, it should be fairly uncontroversial that an emphasis on robust character traits is a central feature of Confucian ethics" (Hutton 2006, 40).

Neo-Confucianism: Metaphysics, Mind, and Morality, First Edition. JeeLoo Liu.
© 2018 John Wiley & Sons, Inc. Published 2018 by John Wiley & Sons, Inc.

temptation to occasionally lie or cheat, and kind people do not always manifest kindness even to those most deserving their kindness. Moral skepticism raises such doubts about the existence of any robust moral traits as well as the feasibility of globalist virtue ethics. Could the Cheng brothers' globalism withstand such a challenge? In addition to explicating the Cheng brother's moral theory, this chapter will investigate whether the Cheng brothers' virtue ethics could meet the challenge of skepticism about robust moral character.

In contrast to Zhang Zai's socio-cognitive model that stresses environmental influences and learning from others, the virtue ethics of the Cheng brothers focuses more on the individual moral agent's own intellectual virtues, psychological states and moral virtues. In their view, once the individual moral agent possesses the virtues of humaneness (ren 仁), authenticity (cheng 誠), and respectfulness (jing 敬), he or she would be able to resist situational pressures and maintain a robust moral character, and thereby possessing a consistent, stable, and integrated moral personhood. Such a moral agent would be morally complete as a sage or a "man of humanity" (renren 仁人).

Moral Skepticism and the Cheng Brothers' Globalist Virtue Ethics

Gilbert Harman is one of the strongest critics of globalist virtue ethics.[2] According to Harman (1999b), globalist virtue ethics takes virtues to be character traits possessed by ideal moral agents:

> In this view, ideally virtuous people are robustly disposed to do what they ought morally to do. Other people should try to become so disposed and should in various situations imitate virtue. In a typical situation of moral choice, an agent ought to do whatever a virtuous person would do in that situation.
>
> *(Harman 1999b, 4)*

This characterization fits the Cheng brothers' virtue ethics perfectly. For both Cheng Hao and Cheng Yi, ideally virtuous people are the humane people or the sages. A sage is one who has reached the highest moral achievement; a humane person is one who exemplifies the virtue of humaneness. These ideal moral

---

2 See Harman (2009, 2003, 2000, 1999a, 1999b, 1996). Harman acknowledges that there are many different forms of virtue ethics, and some of which do not advocate robust character traits. His skepticism of virtue ethics only applies to those that build on the assumption of robust character traits. Harman uses the characterization to depict the virtue ethics defended by Rosalind Hursthouse, a contemporary advocate of virtue ethics.

agents are "robustly disposed to do what they ought morally to do." The Cheng brothers further advocate that every moral agent should aim to reach such an ideal state of personhood. As Cheng Yi puts it, "The learning process of a moral agent (*junzi* 君子) must not stop until he or she has reached sagehood. Terminating one's effort before attaining sagehood is simply called 'self-abandonment (*zi qi* 自棄)'" (Chengs 1981, 1199). In other words, to be a moral agent, it is not enough to always aim to "do the right thing." It is further required that a moral agent ought to aim to be "robustly disposed" to do what one ought to do. The conditions of consistency and stability are already built into the requirement of moral agency.

Harman further characterizes his target theory as one that endorses the following theses:

1) It is possible to use the idea of a virtuous character to explain other moral notions.
2) Moral motivation is best understood in terms of what motivates a virtuous person.
3) There is or may be an objective basis for a single set of human virtues or character (Harman 2009, 239).

This characterization also applies to the virtue ethics derived from the Cheng brothers. In their conception of virtue, the character traits of an ideal moral agent (the sage or the humane person) can be used to explain a host of related moral notions. The virtues exemplified by the ideal moral agents are good in the absolute sense, as these virtues would never fail to be morally praiseworthy in any given situation. Furthermore, on their view, moral motivation is defined in terms of the motivations of the sages and the humane people. These moral agents are so purely motivated by moral considerations that their motivations simply *are* moral motivations. Therefore, a moral agent ought to adopt the same set of motivations that the ideal moral agents would endorse. Finally, in the Cheng brothers' conception, there is an objective basis for a single set of human virtues universally shared. This objective basis of morality inheres in humans' moral constitution—the human nature. They embrace Mencius's view that the beginning of human morality is rooted in humans' inborn moral sentiments. Since everyone shares these moral sentiments in their nature, the objective moral principle, *Dao*, is inherent in human nature. As Cheng Hao says, "*Dao* is [realized in] human nature. One is making a mistake to look for human nature other than *Dao* or to look for *Dao* outside of human nature.... One's original essence is already complete" (Chengs 1981, 1). The virtue ethics of the Cheng brothers is thus solidly grounded in their metaphysics of human nature.

In what follows, we shall first explicate this set of moral virtues and character traits. Afterward, we will turn to Harman's criticisms of robust virtue ethics and respond to them for the Cheng brothers.

The Virtue of Humaneness (*Ren*): Universal Altruism

According to Donald J. Munro, in contrast to the Western ethics' predominant emphasis on individual free will, "the core of Neo-Confucian ethics lies in reciprocal altruism, derived from close family relations" (Munro 2002, 140). What Munro means by reciprocal altruism is the concept in evolutionary biology that "the benefits are received by persons who are more likely to reciprocate or return the favor than are random persons in the population" (Munro 2002, 135). In other words, the altruistic organism is more likely to extend the helping behavior to those strangers who are similarly positioned to help out in the future. Munro argues that the essence of Confucian altruism "is that it is reciprocal" (Munro 2002, 133). He cites the example that the prince who treats his people with virtue would receive their affection and loyal services in return. Furthermore, in the five basic social relations that Confucian ethics builds upon, "each person has duties to and legitimate beneficial expectations from the other party in the set" (Munro 2002, 133).

Evolutionary biologists use reciprocal altruism to explain how non-kin altruism is possible given the dominant self-preservation tendency in natural selection. According to Robert L. Trivers, the evolutionary biologist who first suggested this explanatory model, natural selection favors altruistic behavior because altruism is beneficial to the organism performing them in the long run if it is reciprocated. Therefore, reciprocal altruism is more likely to be promoted in a smaller group of individuals who would have the opportunities to exchange favors multiple times in their lifespans. Trivers uses this model to explain general altruistic tendencies in human societies. Social biologist Edward O. Wilson argues that altruism is beneficial for kin-survival. He points out that plenty of evidence demonstrates that "cooperative individuals generally survive longer and leave more offspring." As a result, in the course of evolutionary history, genes predisposing people toward cooperative behavior became "predominate in the human population as a whole" (Wilson 1998, 253). Both Trivers and Wilson relate the evolutionary model of altruism to morality. Trivers argues that many of our emotions that enable us to function socially, such as friendship, like, dislike, gratitude, sympathy, guilt, shame, and moralistic aggression, and so on, are "important adaptations to regulate the altruistic system" (Trivers 1971, 35). Wilson also argues that the evolutionary process of altruism "gave birth to" our moral sentiments such as conscience, self-respect, remorse, empathy, humility and moral outrage (Wilson 1998, 253).

However, reciprocal altruism in evolutionary biology is defined over species development of behavioral and emotional patterns, and it is questionable whether it can be used as an ethical model for individual behavior. There are two major reservations for this ethical application: First, if an individual behaves altruistically simply because she is genetically predisposed to do so, then she could hardly take credit for her behavior. Second, if the altruistic individual selectively helps strangers who are more likely to return the favor but ignores the rest, then her altruism would seem egoistically driven and would reflect only calculated self-interest. Therefore, Confucian altruism, expressed in the Confucian notion of humaneness (*ren*), should not be regarded as a form of reciprocal altruism derived from the evolutionary model. It is better interpreted as "universal altruism," which is an attitude of caring for others' welfare when those others belong to the non-kin group, whether they could in the long run reciprocate or not.

The Cheng brothers placed particular emphasis on the virtue of humaneness. They define humaneness as a virtue that is "the summit of all good" (Chengs 1981, 283). According to Wing-tsit Chan, in neo-Confucian ethics "the highest peak is reached in this very concept": Not only is humaneness "the foundation of all specific virtues," it is also "the generative force that makes good deeds possible" (Chan 1978, 118). Can this virtue alone be the sole foundation of morality? Could the virtue ethics based on this notion meet the challenge of moral skepticism? To understand the magic of humaneness, we shall analyze this notion in detail.

The classic Chinese dictionary from the second century CE, *Shuowen Jiezi*, gives the etymological analysis of the Chinese word *ren* (仁) as follows: The word *ren* consists of two radicals—"two" and "people," and an ancient form of this word is *ren* (忎), which consists of "thousand" and "heart/mind." From this analysis, we can see that the Chinese notion *ren* is primarily an interpersonal virtue and it depicts a mental state. *Ren* is often associated with love, but it is a general form of love, not the specific love one has toward one's closest kin. In the official dictionary compiled under the first emperor of Qing dynasty Kangxi (completed in 1716), the word *ren* is given several other connotations. For example, *ren* stands for the kernel of fruit and the seed of the fruit's vitality, so it is associated with liveliness or potency. "*Ren*" also stands for the vigor of the limbs as the paralysis of the limbs is described as "not-*ren* (不仁)" in ancient medical books at least since the first century CE.

In the Confucian context, the virtue of *ren* is best characterized as a universal humanitarian concern for others' wellbeing; hence the translation "humaneness." In the *Analects*, Confucius regards humanness as the cardinal virtue that any moral agent (*junzi*) must cultivate, and those possessing this virtue are called "men of humanity." According to Confucius, "A man of humanity, wishing to establish his own character, also establishes the character of others, and wishing to be prominent himself, also helps others to become prominent" (the *Analects* 6:28; slight modification of Chan's translation, Chan 1963, 31). We can thus see that the virtue of humaneness is not merely based on the sentiment of compassion or sympathy, and it is not just accompanied by the desire to relieve the suffering of others. Rather, this virtue is built on the sentiment of empathy (placing oneself in the shoes of others), and the extent of the concern for others includes the others' self-realization and the attainment of their life goals. If one can set one's mind on developing one's humaneness, according to Confucius, then one will be free from evil (the *Analects* 4:4). In other words, the virtue of humaneness is a sufficient condition for moral agency. One only needs to will it, with proper intent and determination, and one will refrain from performing any bad deeds. In Confucius's conception, humaneness is indeed a robust character trait—those who truly possess this virtue will never deviate from it, not even for a short while: "A moral agent does not violate humaneness even for the short time required to finish a meal. He adheres to it even during times of emergency and hardships" (the *Analects* 4:5). However, Confucius also acknowledges the difficulty of keeping this virtue robust. He commented that among his students, only his model student Yan Hui could go for three months without having his heart stray from humaneness, while the rest of his students could at most last for one day or one month (the *Analects* 6:7). This shows that the virtue of humaneness is an exalted moral aim in Confucius's assessment. Now we shall turn to the Cheng brothers to see how they further developed their virtue ethics based on the notion of humaneness.

Cheng Hao thinks that the medical jargon for limb paralysis as "the absence of *ren*" best depicts the state of *ren*. If one's limb suffers from paralysis, then the limb does not feel like one's own. In his conception, a person of humanity is someone who would regard all things in the world as unified in one body with his self. Since others are related to one's self as within the same body, one is bound to be sensitive to others' needs and plights. Cultivating the virtue of humaneness thus requires recognizing the metaphysical fact that all things in the world are interrelated as parts of one whole. In Cheng Hao's famous treatise *Recognizing Humaneness*, he defines "humaneness" as "completely inseparable from other objects as belonging to the same body" (Chengs 1981, 16). From this definition, we see that in Cheng Hao's conception, humaneness is more than a moral virtue. It is also an ontological fact about the nature of our existence. If we are, as a matter of fact, inseparable from other things in the world, then we naturally would, and ought to, be able to have genuine concern for other things in the world. In other words, Cheng Hao's virtue ethics of humaneness is based on his metaphysical view of the oneness of all things in the world. Once one embraces this worldview and recognizes the inseparability of one's self from others, the sentiment of humaneness should naturally arise. Using his analogy, we can say that one's feeling the pains of others would be just like one's feeling the itch or pain of one's own limbs. The sentiment should be a natural reaction of the mind.

According to Cheng Yi, a mental preparation for the virtue of humanness is fair-mindedness or impartiality (*gong* 公). As long as one is fair-minded, one can "illuminate both objects and the self" and this is the way to cultivate humaneness (Chengs 1981, 153). Cheng Yi further identifies the absence of selfish ideas as a related mental preparation for the virtue of humaneness. Cheng Hao explains his brother's view that a sage aims at impartiality (*gong*) as follows: This decree of impartiality does not entail treating all things equally, but "treating all things befitting their respective dues in accordance with their particular principles" (Chengs 1981, 142). From this explanation, we can also see why Cheng Yi thinks "having selfish ideas" would stand in the way of one's moral cultivation. If one has any bias or prejudice based on self-love, self-importance, and self-regard, then one would fail to accurately perceive others' "respective dues." In Chapter 7, we have explained that in Chinese, the word selfish (*si* 私) is frequently set against the word fair (*gong* 公). The two words also delineate the private (*si* 私) and the public (*gong* 公). If one's concerns are always restricted to one's inner circles of acquaintances, then one cannot obtain the virtue of humaneness. To have a fair consideration for others or for the public good is the first step to cultivating humaneness. Cheng Yi thinks that fair-mindedness is a means to the virtue of humaneness, but it is not the same as humaneness because it is merely the principle (*li*) of being humane (Chengs 1981, 153). We can perhaps view fairness as a necessary but not sufficient condition for humaneness. To Cheng Yi, one's heart is like the seed of grains, and what makes the grains grow is humaneness (Chengs 1981, 183). In other words, the virtue of humanness nourishes the moral agent's heart and strengthens her determination to perform good deeds.

For both Cheng Hao and Cheng Yi, the foundation of the cultivation of humaneness is the conception of the self as part of the whole world. This idea is of course not the Cheng brothers' initiation. It can be traced to Zhang Zai's moral ideal of universal kinship as we have explained in the previous chapter. Nevertheless, in the Cheng brothers' moral philosophy, the virtue of humanness is more closely related to their metaphysics of *oneness*. It is because the moral agent has recognized the fact that he is related to other things in the world as part of the same whole, that he is able to be genuinely concerned with others' wellbeing. This intellectual recognition of the metaphysical fact of oneness is what makes universal altruism possible. What makes the sages and humane people "ideal moral agents" is their mentality of "being one with everything in the world." (Chengs 1981, 1179)[3] Since they truly embrace this metaphysical conception of the self, their humanitarian concern for others comes naturally and they can keep it up persistently.

To elaborate on their moral philosophy, we may say that the robustness of character traits or moral habits has to be grounded in a firm metaphysical conviction about one's relation to the world. Our self-conception and our

---

3 In recent years, Philip J. Ivanhoe has been developing what he calls "the oneness hypothesis" in the context of neo-Confucianism. Ivanhoe argues that the sense of "being at one with the other," as it derives from the neo-Confucian metaphysical belief in the interconnectedness of all things, can more effectively motivate people to help others. He cites Zhang Zai and Wang Yangming in particular. See Ivanhoe 2013 and Ivanhoe 2015. In Chapter 11, we will give a fuller explication of Ivanhoe's interpretation of Wang Yangming.

worldview affect our conduct. The Cheng brothers' virtue ethics of humaneness does not aim to establish the value of this virtue by itself, and it does not provide any argument for the comprehensiveness of this character trait. Rather, the whole ethics is only possible under their metaphysics of oneness and interrelatedness. Since humaneness is nothing but "oneness with other things," it is a given, not an acquired, characteristic of our existence. In other words, the virtue of humaneness is in our nature, because we are by nature related to all things in the world as one whole. Since it is not an acquired trait, it certainly cannot be lost from situation to situation. The robustness of this moral trait is derived from a committed metaphysical conception of the self. If one loses this moral trait, then one would also lose one's self-respect and even self-identity. This ethical view is fundamentally based on a self-identity model, uniquely established on the metaphysical view embraced by the Cheng brothers.

The Virtue of Authenticity (*Cheng*) and the Virtue of Respectfulness (*Jing*)

According to Cheng Hao, even after we realize that humaneness is innate in us, we still need to preserve this virtue with two other virtues: authenticity (*cheng* 誠) and respectfulness (*jing* 敬) (Chengs 1981, 16). Cheng Yi also stresses the importance of treating these two virtues as an inseparable pair. Authenticity is an important notion in the *Doctrine of the Mean*,[4] in which authenticity is used both as a metaphysical notion, representing *reality*, and as an ethical notion, representing *sincerity*. In Cheng Hao's conception, authenticity is not just an ethical or psychological notion, applicable only to sentient beings such as humans. Rather, authenticity is "the way (*dao*) of heaven" as heaven naturally accomplishes its operation, without making any effort and without reflection (Chengs 1981, 1158). In other words, what Cheng Hao means by "authenticity" is simply the way things function in the natural world. Things have their own principles, and, according to Cheng Yi, "authenticity is nothing but actual principles (*shili* 實理)" (Chengs 1981, 1169). When someone asked Cheng Yi what he meant by this statement, he replied that being authentic is nothing but "seeing clearly the right and wrong, the permissible and the impermissible, of things" (Chengs 1981, 1192). We can thus understand authenticity as an *intellectual virtue*, manifested in our cognitive and conative abilities in dealing with things. In the Cheng brothers' usage, the notion of authenticity has acquired an epistemic dimension, in addition to the metaphysical and ethical dimensions employed in the *Doctrine of the Mean*.

---

4 The *Doctrine of the Mean* (*Zhongyong*) is one of the four Confucian classics along with the *Analects*, the *Mengzi*, and the *Great Learning*. It is allegedly written by Confucius's grandson Zisi, and originally appeared as one chapter in the *Book of Rites*.

Cheng Hao explains the conceptual connection between *authenticity* and *actual principle* as follows:

> It is in virtue of its particular principle that each particular thing comes into existence. Everything has its own origin and its own conclusion. Authenticity is simply *actuality* (*shi* 實). It is because there *actually* is the principle for a particular thing that the thing *actually* comes to exist. It is because there *actually* is the thing that it *actually* has its function. It is because the thing *actually* has its function, that the mind is *actually* activated. It is because the mind is *actually* activated that there is *actually* the event. [Authenticity] is simply tracing the origination and the ending of all things".
> *(Chengs 1981, 1160, emphasis added)*

From the contemporary perspective, we can say that what Cheng Hao stated here is his *Realism Manifesto*: Everything that exists is *authenticated* by its own existence in the sense that since it truly exists, it must have its principle of existence. He states that there are no "mistakes" or "fabrications" (*wuwang* 無妄) in nature (Chengs 1981). Things are not constructions of the human mind, and the individuation of things is not created by human taxonomy and human conceptions. Natural kinds are divisions carved in nature, as each kind has its own principle that distinguishes it from other kinds. If we humans can recognize the nature (or the principle) of each kind of things and treat it accordingly, then we are being *authentic* to nature, and we thereby manifest the virtue of *authenticity*. This is why our self-insistent ideas (*siyi* 私意) would stand in the way of our possessing this intellectual virtue.

In the view of contemporary developmental psychology, authenticity is being true to one's self in all situations. According to a renowned psychologist on personality development, Erik Erikson (1902–1994), one's "concern with being authentic and true to one's self in action" constitutes a basic virtue that is "inherently tied to the development of identity" (Blasi 1984, 132). The Cheng brothers also regard authenticity as the basis of one's identity as well as a necessary condition to one's moral personhood. According to Cheng Yi:

> A scholar cannot be inauthentic. An inauthentic person cannot do good, and cannot become a morally cultivated gentleman. If one is not authentic in one's study, then one's learning is tainted. If one is not authentic in one's affairs, then one cannot accomplish anything. If one is not authentic in one's self-planning, then one is deceiving oneself and self-abandoning one's fidelity. If one is not authentic in one's interactions with others, then one loses one's virtues and incurs resentment from others.... This is why we say that authenticity is a must-have virtue for a scholar".
> *(Chengs 1981, 326)*

If authenticity is such an essential virtue, then how does one become authentic? The Cheng brothers offer the following guidance to one's cultivation of authenticity: "Authenticity is preserved by fencing off evil" and "the way to fence off evil is being respectful (*jing* 敬)" (Chengs 1981, 149, 185). What they mean by "being respectful" is a mental state of devotion, commitment, and concentration—Cheng Yi calls this mental state "being centered" (*zhu yi* 主一). The one thing on which the individual focuses her attention is not the external objects or affairs; rather, it is her own mental devotion. Therefore, "being respectful" requires the mental activity of introspection. It is looking inward and maintaining a mental calmness and purity in one's dealing with multifarious affairs in daily life. As Cheng Yi explains:

> The concentration on the mind is the concentration on being respectful, and the concentration on being respectful is being centered.... If one must devote one's mind to one thing at a time, then other things could not enter the mind, and one could not even focus on being respectful.
> *(Chengs 1981, 1192)*

If we can constantly hold our mind in a state of focused awareness of being respectful, then we can better handle the object or the affair at hand. Showing respect in what we do and how we treat objects is the way to preserve our mind in pure concentration, with no external ideas to pollute the mind. Therefore, what the Cheng brothers mean by "fencing off evil" is simply getting rid of distractions, self-persistent ideas or selfish desires. As Cheng Yi says, "Once one loses respectfulness, one's manifold selfish desires arise abundantly. This is what harms the virtue of humaneness the most" (Chengs 1981, 1179).

From the previous discussion, we can see that for the Cheng brothers, the three virtues—humaneness, authenticity, and respectfulness—are interconnected as a whole set of moral virtues with metaphysical, intellectual, and psychological dimensions. Their relations can be analyzed as follows: authenticity is a sufficient condition for respectfulness, while respectfulness is a necessary condition for authenticity. "One who is authentic would not lack respectfulness. But if one has not reached the state of authenticity, then one must foster the virtue of respectfulness to accomplish authenticity" (Chengs 1981, 1171). In other words, we can arrive at the state of authenticity through being respectful in the mind, but simply having this mental state of respectfulness is not enough to accomplish authenticity. In the Cheng brothers' conception, authenticity represents a further intellectual virtue of seeing things as they are; that is, knowing the principles of things and investigating things' *origination* and *termination*: from where things originally came, and to what things eventually lead. "From authenticity, the sage gains illuminating insights (*ming* 明)" (Chengs 1981, 331). That is to say, if one is authentic, one becomes unified with one's own principle. Since "everything in the world, from ages past to the present, including one's mind and the nature of things, all shares this same principle" (Chengs 1981, 1158), one comes to have illuminating insights on the principles of all things; or we can say, one becomes *enlightened*. This form of knowledge is the highest form of knowledge, and, in the Cheng brothers' view, it is the only form of knowledge that matters. Cheng Yi calls this form of knowledge "the knowledge derived from virtue (*dexing zhizhi* 德性之知)," in distinction from ordinary knowledge derived from sensory perception. The Cheng brothers' theory of knowledge concerns only this kind of knowledge; hence, their theory of knowledge is closely connected to their ethical theory.

According to Harman's construal of globalist virtue ethics, the ideal moral personhood incorporates not only robust character traits in motivation and action but also "robust habits of perception" (Harman 1999b, 4). In other words, an ideally virtuous person should possess not only moral virtues but also intellectual virtues. In what follows, we shall turn to the Cheng brothers' conception of "knowledge derived from virtue," including their list of intellectual virtues, their proposed methodology and their ideal state of intellectual agents.

The Cheng Brothers' Virtue Epistemology

According to John Greco's characterization of "virtue epistemology," there are two unifying themes in different approaches of virtue epistemology: First, they take epistemology to be a normative discipline; second, they take the primary source of epistemic value and the focus of epistemic evaluation to be "intellectual agents and communities" (Greco and Turri 2011). We shall see that these exact themes are also inherent in the Cheng brothers' virtue epistemology. Their theory of knowledge includes the normative conditions for the aim of knowledge, the definition of "true knowledge," and the satisfaction conditions for full knowledge. The aim of knowledge concerns the object of knowing, while the normative conditions for true knowledge and the satisfaction conditions for full knowledge are defined over the knowing agent's intellectual as well as moral virtues. Their theory focuses more on the intellectual agents than on the object of knowledge. Whether one has true knowledge is judged not by the justifications one has for one's believed propositions, nor by the reliability of one's cognitive mechanisms for knowing. Rather, it is judged by whether one has the intellectual virtues required for knowing, whether one's understanding of ultimate reality is enhanced through one's knowledge, and whether one's way of acting would change as a result of one's knowledge.

The Aim of Knowledge

In the Cheng brothers' conception, the aim of knowledge is not simply to know the nature of a particular thing or to know whether a state of affairs holds true in our world; rather, knowledge aims at one thing only: *to know the principle behind all phenomena.* Their view is similar to what Aristotle expresses in the following remark:

> In every systematic inquiry where there are *first principles,* or causes, or elements, knowledge and science result from acquiring knowledge of these; for we think we know something just in case we acquire knowledge of the primary causes, *the primary first principles,* all the way to the elements. It is clear, then, that in the science of nature as elsewhere, we should try first to determine questions about *the first principles.*
> (*Physics, 184a10–21, emphasis added*)

What Aristotle took to be first principles is of course different from what the Cheng brothers took to be heavenly principle or particular principles. Nevertheless, their ideas about the ultimate aim of knowledge seem quite similar: knowledge should aim at reaching the highest level of generality, and the knowing agents' goal should be to grasp the most fundamental and comprehensive principles of things—the first principles.

According to the Cheng brothers, the ultimate goal of knowledge is the one unifying principle of all things: heavenly principle. This unifying principle is manifested in myriad particular principles; hence, from studying particular principles, one can eventually grasp the one unifying principle. The aim of knowledge is ultimately to understand the world and one's place in it, so that one knows how to conduct oneself in the given situation. Knowledge is for *living well,* and gaining true knowledge enables one to obtain sagehood—the ideal moral personhood. According to Cheng Yi, "If in every state of affairs one observes its principle, then eventually one can comprehend the principles of all things in the world. After one comprehends the principles of all things in the world, one can then become a sage" (Chengs 1981, 316). Knowledge is thus not just for the sake of knowing; rather, it is for the sake of acting correctly and living virtuously.

We have explained that the Cheng brothers distinguish *knowledge through virtue* and *knowledge through perception.* The former is moral knowledge that is the function of the mind, while the latter includes all empirical knowledge of external things derived from our senses. Their epistemology focuses only on the former kind of knowledge. For the Cheng brothers, knowledge through virtue is the only kind of knowledge that matters. In their eyes, those who are intent on verifying details and gathering similarities or differences (such as scientists, we suppose) are merely studying the trivialities. According to Cheng Yi, "One's senses interact with objects and one thereby derives knowledge about these objects. This is what we now say about someone with a variety of skills and a broad base of knowledge. However, this is not knowledge through virtue, which does not depend on our senses" (Chengs 1981, 317). Furthermore, the only kind of knowledge important in the Cheng brothers' eyes is the study of sagehood.

This kind of knowledge is "fundamental," as opposed to the trivial knowledge about natural objects. For the Cheng brothers, the ultimate aim of knowledge is thus to achieve sagehood. However, sagehood is manifested not just in the agent's internal possession of moral virtues, but also in the agent's ideal way in handling all things. The Cheng brothers do not reject natural knowledge, but they regard natural knowledge as part of the overall requirement of sagehood. Even when we study the natural world such as learning the names of animals and plants, we do not aim to gain natural knowledge *per se*; rather, our aim is to "understand how to regulate things through knowing their facts and natures" (Chengs 1981, 1206–7). This emphasis on knowledge through virtue could be the main reason why the Cheng brothers' teachings did not generate knowledge of natural sciences. We shall see in Chapter 11 that the opposing school led by Lu Xiangshan and Wang Yangming further turned the investigation inward: to study the principle inside one's mind since *mind is principle*. Epistemology in neo-Confucianism is thus primarily moral epistemology.

The Conditions for True Knowledge

The Cheng brothers distinguish "true knowledge" from ordinary knowledge. According to Cheng Yi,

> True knowledge is different from ordinary knowledge. I have met a famer who was once injured by a tiger. When others talked about tigers' hurting people, even though everyone showed the sense of alarm, he alone showed the expression of fear much different from others.... True knowledge must be like this famer's knowledge. Therefore, when people say that they know something is not good and still do it, it is because they do not have true knowledge. If they really do know [that it is not good], they would never do it.
>
> *(Chengs 1981, 16)*

From this comment, we can derive the following distinction between ordinary knowledge and true knowledge:[5]

[Ordinary Knowledge]: *A* has ordinary knowledge iff
A believes that *p*
p is true
A is cognitively competent in believing that *p*

[True Knowledge]: *A* has true knowledge iff

---

5 The Chinese definition of "knowledge" is not necessarily in propositional form. We use the standard Western format merely to highlight the differences in the two forms of knowledge.

A believes that *p*
p is true
A is cognitively competent in believing that *p*, and
A's behavior conforms to A's assessment of *p* in relevant contexts

In other words, true knowledge requires behavioral alteration in suitable cases. Cheng Yi thinks that if one is merely doing lip service to what one has learned, one has not truly learned it. According to him,

> Principles must be actually [registered] principles (*shili* 實理); that is, they must be what one actually sees as right or as wrong. All the actually registered principles are distinguishable in one's mindset. If one merely passes on the information one hears without altering one's conduct, then one has not truly grasped it in one's mind. If one has truly grasped it, then one cannot possibly remain in one's erroneous ways."
> *(Chengs 1981, 147)*

For example, heavy smokers often acknowledge the risk of lung cancer from smoking and yet many remain smoking. In the Cheng brothers' assessment, these people do not really know that smoking is bad for health. They merely possess the information, but they do not *know*. There is thus a normative standard for knowing: only the kind of knowledge that leads to appropriate behavioral modifications can be deemed true knowledge. By their distinction, true knowledge is also distinguished from ordinary knowledge in the agent's conviction. If one is truly convinced that doing *x* is bad for oneself, then one would not continue to do it. Knowledge and virtue are in this way merged into a single endeavor. Later in Chapter 11, we will see that Wang Yangming further developed this view into his famous thesis of the unification of knowledge and action.

We might wonder whether most of our daily knowledge would be considered *ordinary knowledge* under this distinction, since we do not need to alter our behavior with respect to many pieces of knowledge we possess, such as knowing the history of Earth or learning a mathematical theorem. We can also think about the multiple pieces of information possessed by all the people who are successful in the TV show Jeopardy or in playing the Trivia games. Don't they know what they know? The Cheng brothers do not deny that ordinary knowledge is knowledge. However, on their view, this kind of knowledge does not really matter in our life. We may allow our minds to be filled with all sorts of trivial information, and yet if our existence does not become better for it, then the information is of no relevance to us. According to Cheng Yi, "This kind of information does not benefit us, and hence a moral agent (*junzi*) does not study them" (Chengs 1981, 319).

Since true knowledge must be reflected in the epistemic agent's behavior, knowledge and action are inseparable under this epistemology. The Cheng brothers seem to have two interpretations of the relation between knowledge and action. On the one hand, the kind of knowledge without reflective behavior is simply not "true knowledge." According to Cheng Yi, "If one knows something deeply, then one must be able to act on it. There has never been anyone who knows and yet could not act accordingly. If one knows but does not act [on one's knowledge], then one's knowledge is superficial [and is not true knowledge]" (Chengs 1981, 164). On the other hand, however, they also hold the view that knowing that p and acting in accordance with one's knowledge of p is the same epistemic process, and without the accompanying action (in suitable cases), the epistemic process is incomplete. Knowledge is the beginning of this process, while acting on it is the end of this process. "To finish the process of knowing is by actual practice" (Chengs 1981, 700). In other words, the Cheng brothers could be defining "know" in the following way:

Knowing = having the information that p, and acting upon this information.[6]

Thus defined, "knowledge" includes both the cognitive and the conative dimensions in its success conditions. Given this definition, if one does not act upon one's information that p, then one does not truly *know*. One's true knowledge is manifested in one's behavior; the success condition for true knowing is the genuine behavioral modification based on the acquired knowledge.

The Methodology of Knowledge: The Investigation of Things

The Cheng brothers endorse the teaching in the *Great Learning* that to derive knowledge (*zhizhi* 致知), one needs to investigate the individual principles in particular things (*gewu* 格物). According to Cheng Yi, the objects of one's investigation are not merely external things as they are, but external things as they are incorporated into our life experiences. In other words, to know an object x is to know how to properly handle x. He takes cooking for example, and explains that if we know the nature of x and y, then we know what flavor and what tastes the food will generate when we mix x and y together in the same dish (Chengs 1981, 162). The method of knowledge is thus embedded in the usage and application of objects. The best demonstration of "having the knowledge of x" in the sense of "having the proper handling of x" is probably

---

6 This view could be interpreted as being compatible with Ernest Sosa's proposal of knowledge as *performance*: to know is to perform well under the circumstances. Michael Mi (Chienkuo Mi) from Taiwan has been developing this comparative angle.

seen in traditional Chinese doctors' study of herbal medicine. To understand the nature of a root, for example, requires knowing its functionality in its interactions with other roots or plants. The same root could heal when used with some herbs, but it could also be poisonous when combined with some other herbs. To handle the root properly, in addition, the Chinese doctor also needs to know the physical constitution of his patients—while this set of herbal combination may be beneficial to some, it could also be detrimental to some others. Knowledge of one single item, the root in this example, thus requires knowledge of many other items in the relevant context. If one cannot handle x properly in all contexts, then one cannot be said to truly know the nature of x.

To the Cheng brothers, thinking is an essential component in the methodology of knowledge. According to Cheng Yi, "The method of learning must be based on thinking (si 思)" (Chengs 1981, 324). In general, if we think hard about something, we can eventually become enlightened. However, thinking cannot be the only method one uses. At times one can become stuck in one's investigation: no matter how hard one tries, one simply does not get it. Cheng Yi advises: "If one cannot think it through with one thing, then one should just change to a different thing to investigate. One must not dwell on one thing only, since people's knowledge are often obstructed somewhere, and no hard thinking could penetrate through the obstruction" (Chengs 1981, 186–7). This is why the Cheng brothers would advise investigating many particular things to learn about the fundamental principle that is of the utmost importance: heavenly principle. We must aim for multiplicity in our investigation of things, so that where there is insufficient understanding, it can be supplemented by what we learn elsewhere. We also cannot learn about heavenly principle just by pure meditation, as meditation would lead us nowhere.

In addition to thinking, the Cheng brothers also advocated the following methodologies of knowledge:

> Read books to fully understand essential teachings and moral principles, study history and assess historical figures to discern their merits and faults, and find the appropriate way to conduct oneself in one's dealing with daily affairs.
>
> *(Chengs 1981, 188)*

In other words, the Cheng brothers takes the conception of knowledge very broadly: it includes *knowing-that, knowing-about* and *knowing-how*. Knowing is not a single form of mental function, and the things one can know are also not just propositions, but the combination of propositional truth, information, and skill.

To the Cheng brothers, knowledge primarily serves a pragmatic function: To know the principle of x is to properly handle x in relevant contexts. According to Cheng Yi, "All things (*wu* 物) are states of affairs (*shi* 事). If we can exhaustively investigate how to handle each state of affairs, then there is nothing we cannot penetrate" (Chengs 1981, 143). The requirement of the exhaustive investigation of principles (*qiongli* 窮理), however, is about the depth, not about the scope, of the investigation. The Cheng brothers do not think that we must know each and every principle in order to know the unifying principle of all things. At some points, we will have accumulated sufficient knowledge to make the intellectual leap: "Investigating the principles of things is not to exhaustively investigate principles of all things in the world. At the same time, it is not to say that one only needs to exhaustively investigate one principle to comprehend all. What is required is sufficient accumulation: once one has accumulated sufficient understanding of particular principles, one sees it all" (Chengs 1981, 43).

There was a recorded discussion between Cheng Yi and a student on this methodology:

> A student asked: should we investigate the principle of each and every thing in the world, or do we only need to investigate one thing thoroughly to know the principles of all things? Cheng Yi replied: How is it possible that one could penetrate all principles with just a single investigation? Even [Confucius' prize student] Yan Hui would not have claimed that he could penetrate all principles with the investigation of one thing only. To learn, you must investigate one thing today and then investigate another thing tomorrow. Once you have accumulated sufficient practices, you will easily see how they can all be penetrated with one thread.
> *(Chengs 1981, 188)*

Why would the accumulation of our understanding of particular principles lead to our comprehension of the unifying principle? Cheng Yi explains: This is because all things share this same principle (Chengs 1981, 157). In Chapter 3, we have already analyzed what Cheng Yi means by his slogan "Principle is one but its manifestations are many." Here we see that the Cheng brothers' epistemology is grounded in their metaphysics—it is because they believe that there is one unifying principle for all particular things, that they set the aim of knowledge as this one principle. As we are endowed with this one principle in our very existence (our nature), our minds must be capable of grasping this one principle. Cheng Yi says, "Things and us share the same principle. Therefore, if one understands one's principle, then one can exhaust the principles of things; once one exhausts these principles, one can grasp the penetrating truth. This is the way to combine the internal and the external ways" (Chengs 1981, 1272).

The Cheng brothers' answer to epistemic skepticism would be the trust in our capacities. In Chapter 3, we have explicated their *normative realism*. Under this realistic thinking, the world and us are both governed by the same principle of nature. Our disposition, as a product of nature, warrants potential epistemic success. With the right attitude (i.e., be true to the world with no individual biases), habitual practices of investigation, and the accumulated verification in one's dealings with things, one can truly *know*. In other words, their reply to the skeptic on whether we could truly know lies in their trust in the virtue of the epistemic agents as well as the connection the epistemic agents have with the world. From the third-person point of view, the way to verify whether someone truly knows is to observe her character and her behavior. If the person truly knows, then her demeanor and her behavior will cohere with the nature of the things she handles. In other words, knowledge will be judged by the epistemic agent's *performance*. Even in the *evil demon* scenario where everything is fabricated in order to fool us, if the agent performs well in accordance with the nature of things in her manipulated world, then she can still be considered to have true knowledge. Of course, under the Cheng brothers' normative realism, such scenarios are not metaphysically possible.

Now we shall return to tackle moral skepticism's challenge to globalist virtue ethics and virtue epistemology.

Answers to Skepticism about Robust Character Traits

Harman (2009) presents some doubts about the existence of robust character traits. The first problem is people's lack of knowledge of what kind of person they really are. Harman cites Sartre's view that people do not have fixed characters "in the sense that they actually are in themselves any of the sorts of people they present themselves as being" (Harman 2009, 236). We may call this problem "the problem of pretense": "People merely pretend, sometimes even to themselves, to be one sort of person rather than another" (Harman 2009, 236).

The problem of pretense raises general skepticism about people's ability to self-examine truthfully and about the accuracy of people's self-knowledge. Eric Schwitzgebel argues that in terms of our self-knowledge of our personality traits and moral character, we are pretty "self-ignorant." He speculates that there is "approximately a zero correlation between people's actual moral character and their opinions about their moral character" (Schwitzgebel 2012, 194). However, even if this may be a common phenomenon among ordinary people, it should not be a problem for our ideal moral agents. In the *Analects*, Confucius stresses the importance of "knowing oneself": if one doesn't know oneself, one could not possibly know other people. Confucius's student Zengzi also emphasizes that he examines himself on a daily basis whether he performed his best when doing things for others, whether he was honest in his dealing with others, and whether he practiced what the teacher had taught him. A moral agent strives to truthfully know herself through careful and thoughtful self-examination. For the Cheng brothers, the virtue of *authenticity* or *truthfulness* is one of the essential virtues that moral agents must cultivate. Without this virtue, one cannot be said to have achieved the status of mature moral agent. Therefore, the problem of presence does not pose any threat for the ideal moral agents that the Cheng brothers portray as having the robust moral traits of authenticity and truthfulness.

Another problem that Harman points out is the problem of "the fundamental attribution error": Ordinary attributions of character traits to people "are often deeply misguided" (Harman 1999a, 316). Harman argues that there is "no empirical support for the existence of character traits" (Harman 1999a, 330), and thus the attribution of character traits to moral agents is simply committing a fundamental attribution error. Harman thinks that character psychologists and globalist virtue ethicists commit the fundamental attribution error by paying attention only to the figure and not to the ground; in other words, they look at the agent's stable disposition and ignore the situations in which the agents find themselves.

This problem of attribution error poses a big threat to the Cheng brothers, in that if character traits do not exist, then their whole project of building moral identity with robust virtues is based on a moral mirage. To disprove the charge of fundamental attribution error, virtue ethicists would have to collect evidence in carefully designed social experiments. The Cheng brothers were of course in no position to offer counterevidence. Defenders of the Cheng brothers' virtue ethics would need to gather empirical evidence in support of the existence of such ideal moral character traits as humaneness, sagehood, and the like. As we have seen in Chapter 8, such empirical evidence should not be found in psychological experiments on ordinary people. Ordinary people frequently succumb to various situational pressures; hence, their moral character traits may not be as robust as those of ideally virtuous people. The ideal moral agents, on the other hand, are *extra*ordinary exactly in their possessing stable moral dispositions and consistent moral habits.

Unfortunately, there are not many moral exemplars that we can cite as empirical evidence for the possibility of robust moral character. It is simply an extraordinary feat to reach the status of ideal moral agency. The Cheng brothers typically had Confucius in mind when they talked about the sage, and they took Confucius's prize student Yan Hui to be the exemplary man of humanity. In Cheng Hao's depiction of the character traits of Confucius, Confucius always "aimed at impartiality (*gong*)" and wanted to "exhaustively understand the principles of all things" (Chengs 1981, 142). Cheng Yi attributes ideal practical wisdom to Confucius: "Since the sage is identified with Principle itself, he has no excess or deficiency"; "The sage knew when to advance and when to back down; he knew how to survive without committing any faults" (Chengs 1981, 307, 697). Even though Confucius was *extra*ordinary, neither of the Cheng brothers took sagehood to be an unreachable normative goal. On the contrary, the self-selected goal of moral agents ought to be *sagehood*, and it is possible that everyone could eventually become a sage (Chengs 1981, 1199).

The status of humane personhood can be seen as the penultimate stage in the development of sagehood. Cheng Yi wrote a famous treatise for the admission exam of the Highest Institution of Learning (*taixue* 太學) when he was merely 20, "On What Yan Hui Preferred and What He Studied." In this treatise, he stated that what Yan Hui had studied was nothing but the way of sagehood. And what was Yan Hui's method? It was to adhere to the following normative rules: "Do not look at what is against the rules of propriety; do not listen to what is against the rules of propriety; do not speak in the way that is against the rules of propriety; do not act in the way that is against the rules of propriety" (Chengs 1981, 578). We can see that this is simply constant self-monitoring and self-disciplining. In Cheng Yi's understanding, this constant self-regulation is what ensures the robustness of ideal moral traits such as humaneness and sagehood. It is what made it possible for Yan Hui to maintain the moral trait of humaneness for three months uninterruptedly (in the *Analects*' account).

The proper psychological state in the cultivation of robust character traits is to be truthful to one's goals, to be "authentic." Cheng Yi describes this cultivation as a slow progress. According to him,

> The way to be authentic is to have a firm commitment to *Dao*. Once one is firmly committed to *Dao*, one will behave resolutely. Once one behaves resolutely, one can be steadfast in one's daily affairs. In one's mind, one never deviates from such virtuous traits such as humaneness, righteousness, loyalty and faithfulness. Even at times of hurriedness and even in destitute or hardships, one's choice of conduct and speech all must adhere to this aim. If one persists in this self-regulation for a long time and never loses it, then one becomes settled (*an* 安) in this moral trait. Everything one does will be in accord with the rules of propriety, and one will never entertain any deviant thought or corrupt ideas.
> (Chengs 1981, 577)

In other words, the stability of ideal moral personality traits is possible because this is exactly what moral agents work toward: no interruption in the development or maintenance of moral personhood and no breach of the normative rules. We might even conclude that the stability or the robustness of ideal moral traits is already contained in the conceptions of *sagehood* and *humaneness*: a sage or a humane person is simply someone who has a stable moral personality and robust moral traits of impartiality, humaneness, authenticity and respectfulness. Such people do not alter their moral behavior from situations to situations.

Cheng Hao himself lived up to his own teachings. According to a biographical note compiled by his students and friends, Cheng Hao composed a poem early in his childhood that says: "If one is firm in one's heart, then how could external affairs sway one?" (Chengs 1981, 328). This shows that even at a young age he already stressed the importance of stability of a moral disposition. Later in his teens, he studied with Zhou Dunyi, and exhaustively investigated the principle of one's inborn disposition (*xing* 性) and one's given circumstances (*ming* 命). In his dealings with others, he conducted himself "totally at ease and without internal struggles" (Chengs 1981, 328). In Cheng Hao's lifetime, he went through political promotions as well as demotions several times, but he never changed his demeanor, nor did he ever lose his composure. When he could not endorse the controversial socioeconomic reforms instigated by the Prime minister Wang Anshi (1021–1086), his political career was ruined and he devoted the remainder of his life to teaching. Even when others felt the injustice for his sake, he never stopped being his respectful, disciplined self. One student wrote: "I have accompanied the Master for thirty years, and never once did I observe any angry expression on his face" (Chengs 1981, 330). Cheng Hao's moral character was depicted as follows: "Even though he was not employed to his abilities, he was totally authentic (*cheng* 誠) toward the world. He was concerned if anything was not in its proper place, and if he saw the people suffer, he took it at heart as if he himself was suffering" (Chengs 1981, 330). One person depicts the quintessential moral trait of Cheng Hao as "authenticity (*cheng* 誠)" (Chengs 1981, 331), while another wrote: "The so-called 'perfect human being' must be like the Master" (Chengs 1981, 332).

This long narrative of Cheng Hao's personal life can serve as one counterexample against moral skeptics of robust moral traits. Let us come back to the question: Could people possess robust moral character such that they would not waver even in the most challenging situations? Without empirical evidence, we cannot answer this question affirmatively. We can, however, say at least that for the Cheng brothers, such a possibility was actuality in that they themselves were true to their own teachings: they had manifested robust moral character even in times of political oppression.

Conclusion

In summary, the virtue ethics of the Cheng brothers stresses the robustness of moral character traits possessed by ideal moral personhood and mature moral agents. The character traits in question are not ordinary character traits such as extrovertedness or shyness, which have been disputed by social psychologists. The Cheng brothers' virtue ethics does not regard these character traits as universal or inborn by any means; rather, their emphasis is that these character traits need to be *cultivated* with great resolution, and preserved with great efforts, especially at times of adversity or hardships. Possessing these moral character traits should be a normative goal for any moral agent: anyone who wishes to become a moral person ought to cultivate these character traits. These character traits are normative rather than descriptive; hence, their existence cannot be disputed by empirical findings on the character traits of ordinary people. Not many people can actually attain the state of sagehood or possess a robust humaneness. However, the sages and the humane people have incorporated these normative character traits into their self-identity, and thus these character traits have become part of their habits of thinking and acting. This is the moral program of the Cheng brothers: to stress the importance of these robust moral characters and to urge every moral agent to aim for incorporating these moral characters into their personhood. According to Harman, since there is no evidence that one can possess robust character traits, we should not waste our effort in cultivating moral character.[7] According to the Cheng brothers, on the other hand, the point of education is exactly to cultivate sagehood. Sagehood is the highest normative goal under the ethical teaching of the Cheng brothers. We shall see in the next chapter how Zhu Xi followed their teaching to develop his theory of sagehood.[8]

Primary Source

Chengs, Hao and Cheng Yi 1981. *Collected Works of the Two Cheng Brothers (Erchengji* 二程集*)*. Four volumes. Beijing: Zhonghua Shuju Chubanshe.

Selection in English

Chan, Wing-tsit (ed.) 1963. *A Sourcebook in Chinese Philosophy*. Princeton University Press. Chapters 31, 32.

---

7 Harman argues: "To the extent that we are interested in improving the lot of mankind it is better to put less emphasis on moral education and on building character and more emphasis on trying to arrange social institutions so that human beings are not placed in situations in which they will act badly" (Harman 2009, 241).
8 In Part I, the Cheng brothers and Zhu Xi were placed into the same chapter, explicated as the Cheng-Zhu school. Even though the Cheng brothers and Zhu Xi shared very similar ideas in terms of their moral programs, Zhu Xi deserves a separate chapter to highlight his specific thinking.

10

Zhu Xi's Methodology for Cultivating Sagehood: Moral Cognitivism and Ethical Rationalism

Introduction

Based on his conviction of internal moral realism (see Chapter 5), Zhu Xi suggests that moral success depend on each individual's *self*-cultivation (with emphasis on the self). His moral philosophy focuses on establishing an effective methodology for moral success. His concern was pragmatic and pedagogical rather than theoretic and idealistic. According to Siu-Chi Huang (1978), Zhu Xi's emphasis on the investigation of things (*gewu* 格物) and the extension of knowledge (*zhizhi* 致知) indicates a shift from formulating moral ideals to a concentration on the methodology of cultivating morality (Huang 1978, 176). This chapter focuses on Zhu Xi's methodology for moral cultivation, highlighting his moral ideal: *sagehood*.[1]

According to Zhu Xi, the methodology of self-cultivation is twofold: persevering in the state of reverence (*zhujing* 主敬) and exhaustively investigate principles (*quiong li* 窮理) (Zhu 2002, 14:301). The former depicts a particular mental state while the latter denotes a cognitive activity. The two appear unconnected with each other, and in particular, they seem to have no bearing with morality. However, Zhu Xi explains that although these two appear to be two paths, they are ultimately interconnected—or we may say that the former is the foundation of the latter. He says, "If one can exhaustively study principles, then one will daily advance one's cultivation of persevering in reverence; on the other hand, if one can persevere in reverence, then one will also become more and more meticulous in one's exhaustively attending to principles" (Zhu 2002, 14:301). Maintaining the mental state of reverence enables one to gain insights into the principles of external things; hence, reverence is "the foundation of exhaustively attending to principles" (Zhu 2002, 14:301). In other words, the mental state of reverence is a mental preparation for the moral agent to engage in the investigation of principles. The exhaustive investigation of

---

1 Stephen C. Angle (1998, 2009) has paid special attention to Zhu Xi's moral ideal of sagehood.

Neo-Confucianism: Metaphysics, Mind, and Morality, First Edition. JeeLoo Liu.
© 2018 John Wiley & Sons, Inc. Published 2018 by John Wiley & Sons, Inc.

principles, on the other hand, is the gateway to moral cultivation. Hence, the main feature of Zhu Xi's moral methodology is his *intellectualist* approach. He believes that moral cultivation requires moral knowledge, and thus one's moral deeds are the result of *knowing* what one ought to do. Zhu Xi's approach is both rational and epistemological, even though his primary aim is the individual's moral advancement. Allen Wittenborn puts it well, "If the ends are not entirely intellectual, the means certainly are. We should note, however, that knowledge and ethics are in no way exclusive, … the function of knowledge is present in any moral issue" (Wittenborn 1982, 32). On this basis, we will begin this chapter by exploring Zhu Xi's moral epistemology.

Zhu Xi's Moral Epistemology: The Investigation of Things for the Extension of Moral Knowledge

Moral epistemology concerns the truth and justification of our moral beliefs. What qualifies a personal moral *belief* of mine, such as "I believe that it is immoral to steal," as a moral *knowledge* that it is indeed immoral to steal? Can I ever claim to *know* what is objectively right or wrong? Am I equipped with certain special means of perception or understanding, different from the way I experience and know the external world? In neo-Confucianism, the issue of justification hardly arose. In terms of moral truths, there is no clearly drawn distinction between *belief* and *knowledge*. Zhu Xi, as well as other neo-Confucians, was convinced that moral truths are objectively true, and that we are equipped with the mental capacity to know these moral truths.

Zhu Xi's moral epistemology is based on his metaphysics as well as his view of human nature. He claims that heavenly principle is inherent in one's nature as well as in the nature of everything; thus, to know the principle, one needs to be acquainted with one's own nature as well as to investigate the nature of things. Under his view, the means by which we obtain self-knowledge is at the same time the means by which we obtain knowledge of the moral order of the world. In contemporary terms, we may say that Zhu Xi takes a cognitivist approach to the extension of our moral knowledge. In Chapter 5, we have explicated Zhu Xi's commitment to moral realism, and here we see that Zhu Xi's moral realism is associated with his moral cognitivism. Moral cognitivism is the view that moral judgments have objective and definitive truth-values that we can cognize. According to moral cognitivism, moral judgments are not the mere expression of one's emotions or sentiments, and they have objective truth-values. Moral cognitivists reject the relativist's position that all opinions could be right or wrong relative to different standards. They believe that there is an objective standard by which we can judge whether a moral judgment is right or wrong. According to David Brink, "If moral mistakes are possible, then moral argument and deliberation are intellectual activities that, at least in principle, always make sense" (Brink 1989, 30). In other words, moral judgments are *truth-apt* and moral cultivation is an intellectual pursuit. Zhu Xi is clearly implicitly committed to this view.

Zhu Xi believes that the attainment of virtue begins with the pursuit of moral knowledge, and the ultimate object of our epistemic pursuit is *Dao* or heavenly principle. We have analyzed his theory of principles in particular things in Chapter 3, and now we see how this view affects his methodology of attaining sagehood. To Zhu Xi, to be a moral agent, one needs to take an intellectual approach to apprehend *Dao*, and to apprehend *Dao*, one would have to perceive the principles in particular things so that one knows how to deal with each thing in accordance with its principle. Each kind of things has its particular principle, which is simply its nature (*xing* 性), and we need to learn the particular principle in our handling of the thing. For example, if I don't know the nature of a particular plant, then I might be watering too much with the good intention of keeping the plant constantly hydrated, and end up killing the plant. This may seem like a trivial example that has nothing to do with one's morality. However, Zhu Xi extends the demand of knowing principles of particular things to knowing the particular principle in every encounter with other people and every handling of other things in our daily life. If we know how to deal with a human relationship in accordance with the particular principle for such a relationship, then we will always know how to act properly with those involved in the relationship. If we know the principle governing a particular situation, then we will always know how to act in the right way in this kind of situation. If we learn the nature of each object that we encounter, then we will always know how to deal with it appropriately. And finally, if we know the nature of each worldly affair and can handle it accordingly, then we must be *sages*. From this, we can see that Zhu Xi's notion of particular principle is simply *the norm of conduct*—principle is the way things ought to be treated. Hence, principles of particular things set the standard for human conduct in dealing with each particular thing and affair. For any particular thing x, to know x's particular principle, is to know how to properly deal with x. As Zhu Xi puts it, "Even though [particular] principle is inherent in the particular thing, its manifestations are actually in the [human] mind" (Zhu 1986, 2:416). Zhu Xi thinks that by understanding how we should treat each particular thing and handle each particular affair, we will eventually gain the overall insight of *Dao*. The mind's cognitive function to grasp *Dao*—which Zhu Xi calls "the heart of *Dao*"—must be exercised through the investigation of particular things' principles until the mind reaches a heightened state of apprehending *Dao*.

At the same time, Zhu Xi also explains that to investigate principle to the utmost is to seek to know *the reason why* (*suoyiran*) things and affairs are the way they are. To know the whys of things entails going beyond the superficial understanding of a particular thing's nature to find its place in the grand scheme of all things. In Zhu Xi's worldview, all things are interconnected to constitute an ordered organic whole (the so-called *Taiji*, the supreme ultimate). Each thing naturally fits into the holistic scheme, and the universal *Dao* is the order of this organic whole. In other words, in his cosmology there is no cosmic chaos or randomness. There is a reason for everything—all things come into existence in accordance with *Dao*, such that their appearance and disappearance in the world all have their reasons. To truly understand something, is to "go beyond its surface structure, and perceive the deeper meaning of its existence" (Zhu 1986, 2:415–16). This is the true goal of the investigation of things: to thoroughly scrutinize the reasons for their existence. The same applies to all human affairs. It is not enough, for example, to know *that* we ought to serve our parents with respect; we also need to know *why* our parents are entitled to our respect. In terms of what we ought to do in any given situation, Zhu Xi's view is that human relationships and the moral obligations in relation to each relationship constitute an interconnected *moral web*. To know the *why* of things, we need to have deeper reflection and comprehensive awareness of our place in this moral web. Once we have the understanding of why an act is required for a certain situation, we are no longer simply following external moral prohibitions. We take appropriate actions because we truly understand why they are required in the given situation. Our moral actions will thus be self-motivated and self-regulated. Therefore, understanding the why behind all morally required actions, according to Zhu Xi, can make us autonomous moral agents.

One may of course question whether our knowing why we ought to do *x* will really lead to our doing *x*. There are the familiar problems of our weakness of will, our apathy and our inertia. One could easily be a rational amoralist who simply does not care about being moral or doing the right thing, or one may think and act the way "a sensible knave" does as Hume describes him: "A sensible knave … may think that an act of iniquity… will make a considerable addition to his fortune, without causing any considerable breach in the social union. … [He] conducts himself with most wisdom, who observes the general rule, and takes advantage of all the exceptions" (Hume 1983, Sect. 9, 22–25). The gap between our knowing and our acting is a notorious problem in ethical theories. In Zhu Xi's optimistic view, however, our understanding of the reason why we ought to do certain things or act in certain ways can make our actions "unstoppable" (Zhu 1986, 2:414)—we simply cannot act any other deviant way once we *know*. His conviction is based on his theory of human nature: human beings are inherently moral creatures, with heavenly endowed moral attributes: humaneness, righteousness, propriety, and wisdom. We are naturally inclined to do the right thing, but most frequently, we are limited by our ignorance of what the right thing is. Once we remove the ignorance, our actions will be pursuant to the dictates of our nature and our reason. In this way, our moral action would be "unstoppable." In other words, in his view the so-called weakness of the will is nothing but ignorance—a failure of the intellect.

We can now see that in Zhu Xi's moral philosophy, as in his theory of human nature, the notion principle also combines two senses: a descriptive sense and a normative sense. Zhu Xi calls the descriptive sense of particular principle "the reason why it is so" (*suo-yi-ran-zhi-gu* 所以然之故) of particular things, and he calls the normative sense of particular principle the "ought-to-ness" (*dang-ran-zhi-ze* 當然之則) of particular things. He claims that the former principle is "immutable" while the latter principle is "unstoppable" (Zhu 1986, 2:414). Both are inherent in the nature of particular things, but must be apprehended by the human mind since the manifestation of principle is in the human mind. Zhu Xi thinks that both senses of "principle" are integral to our moral pursuit: once we understand *why things are the way they are* and *how they ought to be treated*, we will no longer be perplexed as to what to do, and thus our action will never be wrong. Zhu Xi seems to believe that true knowledge of principle automatically leads to autonomous, unwavering, moral behavior in morally ready individuals—the individuals who are true to their nature (*jinxing* 盡性).

In Zhu Xi's moral philosophy, "the reason why something is so" (*suo-yi-ran* 所以然) and "the way the thing ought to be" (*suo-dang-ran* 所當然) are one and the same. According to Siu-Chi Huang, Zhu Xi is here combining the realm of *is* and the realm of *ought* in an effort to derive *ought* from *is*: "The more one investigates the principle of 'things' as objects (be they brothers, parents, friends), the better one will understand them and one's relation to them and accordingly *ought* to act according to their respective capacities. Oughtness is therefore derived from isness" (Huang 1978, 187). However, this derivation could be very problematic to those who are familiar with Hume's challenge to ethicists to explain how to derive *ought* from *is*. Is Zhu Xi conflating a descriptive notion of *fact* with a normative notion of *value*? As we have seen in Chapter 5, Zhu Xi's moral realism does not separate the realm of fact and the realm of value; rather, it places value squarely within the realm of fact. Following the Confucian tradition, Zhu Xi does not carve up the world of nature and the world of man. Human beings are part of nature, and thus human values are values of nature as well. To Zhu Xi, normative statements on how one ought to act or how a thing ought to be are not subjective or projected value judgments. In Zhu Xi's conception, these normative statements are statements descriptive of the ideal state for the world of nature and for human existence. An ideal state is nonetheless an objectively depicted state, and it should be the "end-state" of all evolution and development. The principle of a particular thing is both the reason why it is so and the way it ought to be treated, because only by being treated in accordance with the principle, could the thing achieve its ideal state.

In terms of human existence, the ideal state is when the individual fulfills his or her nature and become an ideal human being. In this way, the individual's nature dictates the right action. However, between the nature's dictate and the performance of the moral act, there is still a gap. This gap is to be filled by the intellectualist approach: the investigation of principle. Without this slow and accumulative step, moral realization is not feasible. The unity of knowledge and action is only the result of an individual's accomplished moral realization. In other words, the moral understanding of the "why" can lead to spontaneous, steadfast moral behavior only in certain ideal moral agents.

Siu-Chi Huang defines Zhu Xi's moral methodology as a form of ethical rationalism.[2] Ethical rationalism is the view that moral truths and general moral principles are self-evidently true and are knowable *a priori* by reason alone. Ethical rationalism is a fitting description of Zhu Xi's moral methodology. However, Zhu Xi does not advocate an intuitive grasp or an *a priori* understanding. From his emphasis on the investigation of things, we see that Zhu Xi does not discount the importance of empirical investigation. The goal of empirical investigation is not to merely see things as they are individually, but to see particular things as concrete exemplifications of the universal principle. To him, knowledge of the principles of particular things is a form of moral knowledge, since everything we learn enhances our moral cultivation. Such knowledge needs to be accumulated piecemeal by piecemeal, but at a certain point, one would make a leap of understanding and comprehend the universal moral truth. Zhu Xi preaches paying attention to details: From the most essential and most fundamental about oneself to every single thing or affair in the world, everything should be investigated to the utmost, and none of it is unworthy of attention. He suggests that although there may not seem to be substantial progress, after a long period of accumulation, one will be saturated with knowledge of principles and achieve an extensive harmony and penetration, without even noticing it oneself. He gives a metaphor of polishing a mirror: if one polishes a little bit on a daily basis, then the mirror would eventually become totally brilliant (Zhu 2002, 14:228).

Since each principle represents the norm of particular things for Zhu Xi, the cultivation of morality relies on the mind's having comprehensive knowledge of particular principles, and such knowledge should govern the moral agent's behavior toward each kind of things. This view takes the norms of conduct to be external to the mind and inherent in particular things. The moral agent's cognitive capacities enable her to "discover" objective standards for appropriate moral behavior in dealing with different things under various situations. The moral agent needs to *cognize* moral truths, act in accordance with *mind-independent* moral principles, and allow her actions to be assessed by objective moral standards. In contrast to the doctrine of *Mind is Principle* advocated by Lu Xiangshan and Wang Yangming, Zhu Xi's view is that the individual mind does not determine principle, and moral agents must abide by objective moral laws.

---

2 Wing-tsit Chan (1963) also characterizes Zhu's philosophy as *rationalism*.

In other words, we are not the makers of moral laws; we are simply rational followers of objective moral principles. Our moral knowledge should be knowledge of principles and our action should be action in accordance with principles. For Zhu Xi, the merit of the mind lies in its cognitive capacities, not in its intuitive grasp of moral truths. This is where we see the fundamental difference between the Cheng–Zhu school's doctrine of the Principle (*lixue* 理學) and the Lu–Wang school's doctrine of the Mind (*xinxue* 心學).

Zhu Xi's intellectualist approach to ethics could be traced to Confucius in the *Analects*. Confucius clearly believes that to conduct oneself in a morally correct way, one needs to learn about the *Dao*. The pursuit of the knowledge of *Dao* is an earnest intellectual quest for truth. According to Confucius, "If one day I could hear about [the truth of] *Dao* in the morning, then even if I had to die that evening, it would be alright" (the *Analects* 4:8). Confucius believes that there is some absolute truth beyond his personal judgment. So, what is morally right is not simply what he himself judges to be right. *Dao* is the moral standard for human conduct; *Dao* sets the moral bounds. For Confucius, intellect and virtue are inseparable—Intellect is the understanding of *Dao*, while virtue is living in accordance with *Dao*. Even Confucius himself did not feel that he could merge intellect with virtue until he had reached the age of seventy, when he could "do whatever his heart desires and not go beyond moral bounds" (the *Analects* 2:4).

Herein emerges a problem for this kind of moral epistemology: if the cultivation of virtue relies on the attainment of moral knowledge, while the attainment of moral knowledge depends on one's having the appropriate virtues, then don't we get into a vicious circle without a starting point? Neo-Confucians, and Zhu Xi is no exception, answer this question by assuming some innate moral quality of each individual. For Zhu Xi, this internal quality is analogous to the brilliance of a mirror—one only needs to polish it to return the dusty state back to its inherent brilliance. In other words, the starting point is our internal virtue. The virtue one needs in order to attain moral knowledge is primarily a "given" of our existence. This innate moral quality guarantees success in our intellectual pursuit of the highest moral principle, even though we still need the constant effort of polishing the mirror—we need to accumulate our knowledge of particular principles inherent in external things and affairs. Initially, we may not have a sharpened moral cognition to grasp the correct principle in things; ultimately, however, with enough accumulation, we will obtain the complete grasp of the highest universal principle.

Wittenborn (1982) raises a valid question to Zhu Xi's moral epistemology: How do we ascertain epistemic success from our own perspective? According to Wittenborn, "[I]f we were mistaken in the beginning we can never be completely certain that we will not be mistaken again. The logical conclusion is that we can always be mistaken, and thus it will be impossible for us to be perfectly correct all the time about our understanding of a thing and its [principle]. Or if we are correct, we can never be certain that we are, and the whole notion of [principle] is thrown into doubt" (Wittenborn 1982, 15). In other words, how could we possibly be both the student and the referee at the same time? How could we ever call our own understanding an *error* if we are already ones who are mistaken? To defend Zhu Xi's moral epistemology against this charge, we must explain what is required for epistemic success in Zhu Xi's view.

To Zhu Xi, advancement in moral understanding is a gradual process, and the subject doing the learning gets transformed through the process such that a later self is different from, and presumably better than, the former self both in understanding and in moral accomplishment. The later self could call on the former self's mistake, because she now has a better grasp of the particular principles inherent in things. Zhu Xi's moral epistemology defines moral inquiry as a form of empirical inquiry, but his empirical inquiry has a different methodology from those used in modern sciences. To *know*, in Zhu Xi's usage, is to find the pattern of the universe so as to *act* appropriately within the grand scheme. For Zhu Xi, understanding moral truth presupposes seeing oneself placed in a moral universe, a moral reality. The moral reality and moral truth is there for everyone to *observe*, but one needs proper mental preparation as well as proper behavioral preparation to actually *see* it. In other words, grasping moral reality requires one's being in attunement with it. Charles Taylor's depiction of the conception of *understanding as attunement* can be adequately applied to Zhu Xi' moral epistemology:

> We don't understand the order of things without understanding our place in it, because we are part of this order. And we cannot understand the order and our place in it without loving it, without seeing it as goodness, which is what I want to call being in attunement with it. Not being in attunement with it is a sufficient condition of not understanding it, for anyone who genuinely understands it must *love* it; and not understanding it is incompatible with being in attunement with it, since this presupposes understanding.
>
> *(quoted by Wong, Wong 1986, 103; emphasis added)*

Zhu Xi's moral epistemology is also a fusion of knowledge and attitude (though the attitude he emphasizes is not *love* as Taylor defines it). If we do not appreciate the order of the universe and our place in it, then our investigation of things and their principles would not enlighten us. The investigation of external affairs and objects are the gradual route one takes for accomplishing a higher moral plane for one's self.

In summary, Zhu Xi's intellectualist project of the investigation of things is the means to the internal transformation of the self. Zhu Xi rejects the Buddhist's methodology of sitting in meditation or Lu Xiangshan's looking into one's heart, as neither could give us enlightenment or bring us to a higher moral plane. In our daily life, we cannot avoid encountering multifarious affairs. To properly handle a single affair, one needs to master both a holistic perspective of the nature of the affair as well as its relation to other human affairs, and a profound understanding of the nature/principle of the particular things involved. Zhu Xi beseeches us to treat every affair as a chance for our self-improvement on our understanding, our virtue and our moral character. One is able to reach a total moral transformation through the piecemeal investigation of things, exactly because one's pursuit of knowledge already includes a psychological as well as behavioral modification in each case. This is called "sustained effort" (*gongfu* 功夫), which takes time to succeed. With gradual knowledge combined with mental attunement accumulated, one eventually obtains a sage-like moral insight on one's place in this *moral cosmos*.

Since Zhu Xi's moral epistemology is a fusion of knowledge and attitude, in addition to the intellectualist approach, he also emphasizes that one needs to have the right mindset to combine knowledge and insight. We may say that Zhu Xi's moral epistemology begins with his moral psychology. According to him, the essential mental preparedness one needs to possess in order to fully engage in the intellectual pursuit of moral knowledge is *jing* (敬)—reverence in the heart.[3] We shall turn to this topic next.

The Psychological Preparedness for Moral Knowledge: Reverence (*Jing*) in the Heart

Zhu Xi calls the cultivation of the virtue of reverence "the most important prerequisite into the gate of sagehood," that one needs to keep at it "without an instant of interruption" (Zhu 2002, 14:371). According to Stephen C. Angle, for Zhu Xi, reverence is "the key to finally achieving sagely ease—that state in which without exerting effort, one still does all one should do" (Angle 2011, 191). What is this virtue of reverence and why is it such an essential virtue in the cultivation of sagehood?

Zhu Xi separates the virtue of reverence into two stages: the pre-manifested stage and the manifested stage, but claims that the two are unified as one psychological state (Zhu 2002, 14:573). Before one encounters any external affair, one's mind should be in a state of alertness and clear-headedness (*xingxing* 惺惺). When one encounters external affairs, one's mind should contemplate on reverence and one's whole demeanor should be immaculate and serious. Without alertness in the mind, one would not be able to grasp the principle in things; as a result, one would fail to respect external affairs. Without an immaculate and serious demeanor, on the other hand, one's mind could not always stay

---

3 Allen Wittenborn (1982) translates *jing* as "concentration," which is derived from Zhu Xi's further explication of this psychological state: "concentrating on the one" (*zhuyi* 主一). Here we are using the literal translation of this word.

alert even if one tried (Zhu 2002, 14:571). The psychological state of reverence is to clear the mind off extraneous distractions and to concentrate on one thing (*zhuyi* 主一) with any task at hand, and the focus is not on the thing, but on the mind's operation itself. The behavioral state of reverence, on the other hand, is to maintain a neat appearance and a serious demeanor. The former is the preparation for the latter, while the latter in turn can also influence the mind to be focused and clear-headed.

In Zhu Xi's explication, reverence is a mental state that naturally manifests itself in outward appearance and conduct. Zhu Xi defines 'reverence' as "the mind's being its own master" (Zhu 2002, 14:371), "inwardly having no idle thought and outwardly having no rash behavior" (Zhu 2002, 14:372). In other words, Zhu Xi treats the virtue of reverence as an *inward* effort—the target is the self, not others. If one can constantly have reverence in the heart, one would not have any deviant thought or any inappropriate conduct. Using the analogy of "keeping a household," he explains the connections between the investigation of things, reverence and self-discipline: "Reverence is like guarding the doors, self-discipline is like warding off thieves, while the investigation of things is like studying the affairs within and without the household.... Ultimately, however, 'guarding the door' and 'warding off thieves' are one and the same thing" (Zhu 2002, 14:302). Zhu Xi advocates that one needs to be apprehensive and careful in one's self-control, and by this he means that one needs to constantly inspect one's selfish desire so as to completely remove them. The state of reverence can enable one's mind to be free of those distracting desires, and one's mind would be "brilliant with the manifestation of heavenly principle" (Zhu 2002, 14:372).

In a recent book *Reverence: Renewing A Forgotten Virtue* (2014), Paul Woodruff writes:

> Reverence begins in a deep understanding of human limitations; from this grows the capacity to be in awe of whatever we believe lies outside our control—God, truth, justice, nature, even death. The capacity for awe, as it grows, brings with it the capacity for respecting fellow human beings, flaws and all. This in turn fosters the ability to be ashamed when we show moral flaws exceeding the normal human allotment.
>
> *(Woodruff 2014, 3)*

Woodruff associates reverence with awe, a sense of humility and apprehension toward things outside our control. Zhu Xi sometimes does identify reverence with awe (*wei* 畏) (Zhu 2002, 14:372), which is often used in connection with the feeling of trepidation (*ju* 懼). Awe can inspire appropriate conduct, as for example, in the classic *Book of Documents* (*shangshu* 尚書), the ancient king Tang says, "I am in awe of god, and I do not dare to do anything incorrect" (cited in Zhu 2002, 16:2632). However, awe is typically object-oriented, and the sentiment is aroused in the object's presence. Zhu Xi's notion of reverence, on the other hand, is not object-directed; it is *an inward gaze* on one's body and mind with composure and concentration. He says, "[Reverence] is not a state of sitting alone, hearing nothing and seeing nothing, as if one were in a stupor. Rather, if one simply collects one's body and mind, be ordered and neat, without whimsical indulgence, then one is in a state of reverence" (Zhu 2002, 14:369). Being reverent means being mindful: one is mindful of one's own intent, one's own desire, one's focal point of attention, one's extraneous thoughts or ideas, one's conduct and speech, one's demeanor and even one's attire, and so on. If one is constantly in a reverent mental state, then one should be fully self-aware and self-monitored. We may even say that Zhu Xi's notion of reverence is being reverent of *how one should conduct oneself.*

At the same time, Zhu Xi also stresses cultivating the virtue of reverence from the outside in: He teaches that one should always strive to be orderly in clothing and appearance, that one's mannerism should be grave and austere, and that one's movement should be correct and dignified, and so on (Zhu 2002, 14:372). Zhu Xi instructs his students:

> Sit as though you were impersonating an ancestor, stand as though you were performing a sacrifice. The head should be upright, the eyes looking straight ahead, the feet steady, the hands respectful, the mouth quiet and composed, the bearing solemn—these are all aspects of [reverence].
> *(Gardner 1990, 172)*

One who has reverence in the heart would naturally express oneself with utmost care and scrupulous conduct; at the same time, the external appearance such as proper attire and respectful mannerism would also influence one's mental state. In the *Analects*, Confucius is depicted as someone who has reverence in the heart and seriousness in conduct: "When he went past the station of his lord, his face took on a serous expression, his step became brisk, and his words seemed more laconic" (The *Analects* 10:4, Lau 1979, 101). "When he bowed to his colleagues, stretching out his hands to the left or to the right, his robes followed his movements without being disarranged" (The *Analects* 10:3, Lau 1979, 101). In ceremonies, Confucius acted with deference and respect: "When he held the jade tablet, he drew himself in as though its weight was too much for him.... His expression was solemn as though in fear and trembling, and his feet were constrained as though following a marked line" (The *Analects* 10:5; Lau 1979, 102). Confucius was even choosy with respect to the color of his outfit for different occasions: "Red and violet colored silk were not used by informal dress" (The *Analects* 10:5; Lau 1979, 102). These sample descriptions show us how Confucius himself regarded outward seriousness as an indispensible manifestation of inward reverence.

On the one hand, we could say that these external composures are simply outward manifestations of one's inner mental state of reverence; on the other hand, however, these external ways of conducting oneself and dressing oneself will also gradually modify one's mind into a serious, respectful mental state. The influence from the outside in is undeniable. In social settings, we can easily see the effects of the internalization of external rules and etiquette. When young children are placed in a classroom environment, they initially would not understand why they had to sit still, talk only when addressed to, or ask for permission to go to the bathroom. In time, however, they learn to respect the class rules, adapt themselves to adopt the expected behaviors, and manage to learn new things in a quiet, ordered classroom. Their minds would not have been able to concentrate on the materials if their conducts were not already modified. The same is true for adults. Many companies enforce dress codes; many organizations, including the military and junior schools, require uniforms. In religious settings such as a temple, a church or a mosque, one should dress appropriately, speak quietly, and refrain from running, laughing, eating, and many other casual behaviors that are considered disrespectful. These external rules are all various means to cultivating the psychological state of reverence.

Why would such a psychological trait as reverence be so important to our moral cultivation? To Zhu Xi, the main function of this mental state is to constantly inspect one's mind and remove one's selfish desires and erroneous thoughts, and having such a pristine mental state is essential to our investigation of principles. According to him, "The exhaustive attending to principles is grounded in the mind's being empty of extraneous desire and busy thoughts" (Zhu 2002, 14:306). In Zhu Xi's moral methodology, the investigation of things must be conducted with the proper mental state. Therefore, even though the investigation seems to be directed outward, the grounding of our epistemic success is actually in the mind itself. As Zhu Xi puts it, "The mind embraces all principles and all principles are complete in this one mind. If you are not able to preserve the mind, you will not be able to investigate principles thoroughly. If you are unable to investigate principles thoroughly, then you will not be able to exert your mind to the utmost" (cited in Wittenborn 1982, 29, with modifications). If we can concentrate on our own mind, then we have all we need to succeed in our intellectual pursuit of moral knowledge. Cognitive errors result from the mind's losing its clear vision, being distracted by extraneous thoughts or wanton desires. If we can preserve the mind's intrinsic clarity, then we can be confident that our moral knowledge is not erroneous. The standard for correctness consists in one's interaction with the objects—an appropriate response to the things at hand would be considered *true knowledge*.

In contemporary classification of theories of moral epistemology, Zhu Xi's theory would fall under foundationalism—the view that all justified beliefs are either foundational or are derived from these foundational beliefs. We have explained that Zhu Xi is implicitly committed to moral cognitivism and moral realism, in that he believes that moral truths are truths about objective reality.

He also credits moral agents with justification of their moral beliefs, if such beliefs are obtained with reverence in the heart and with a thorough investigation of principles. The justification must be internal to the moral agents, such that they have sufficient understanding and reasons for each of their moral beliefs. In other words, for Zhu Xi, moral beliefs are *true* when they depict objective moral reality—the Principle or *Dao* in the world. Moral beliefs are *justified* when the individual agent has procured sufficient knowledge of particular principles in things, and can maintain a concentrated mental state free of extraneous ideas or desires. When the moral agent reaches a pristine mental state with full understanding of Principle and *Dao*, all her moral beliefs are foundational—they do not require further justification. This is the state of *sagehood*. Below this state, we have various levels of moral epistemic accomplishments. Our foundational moral beliefs are those of Principle and *Dao*. The justification of our other moral beliefs are derived from our intellectual pursuit that includes our own investigation of things and the understanding of their principles, as well as our learning from the sages through reading and mentorship. In Zhu Xi's moral epistemology, principles are self-evidently true such that as long as we understand them, we are justified in believing in them. The justification is internal to us and must be grounded in our own understanding of both the reason why it is so (*suo-yi-ran* 所以然), and the way we ought to act (*suo-dang-ran* 所當然), with respect to each particular thing.

Zhu Xi's moral epistemology encompasses knowing principles and acting upon one's acquired knowledge. He says, "moral cultivation already includes the skill and sustained effort (*gongfu* 功夫) to exhaustively comprehend principles, and the cognitive activity to investigate principles itself already comprises the skill and effort for moral cultivation" (Zhu 2002, 14:300). To him, moral motivation does not come from one's inborn moral sense, not from one's moral intuition, and not from one's sentiment or emotion. Rather, moral motivation is grounded in moral knowledge, and one's mind has the cognitive ability to know right from wrong. However, Zhu Xi's purely cognitivist and intellectualist approach could lead to a grave problem: how does knowledge lead to action? Couldn't someone be fully cognizant of certain moral truths, but do not feel so inclined to act on them? How does Zhu Xi provide a theory of moral motivation? This is our next topic.

Zhu Xi's Theory of Moral Motivation: From Moral Knowledge to Ethical Action

Zhu Xi was fully aware of the importance of action, and even though he stresses moral knowledge, he also proclaims that the end goal is action. According to Zhu Xi, "Knowledge and action always require each other.… With respect to order, knowledge comes first, and with respect to importance, action is more important." (Chan's translation, Chan 1963, 609). He thinks that knowledge precedes action, but without action, one's moral knowledge is futile. However, from knowing what one ought to do, to one's actually doing the right thing, there is a host of issues related to our moral motivation and the causal efficacy of our moral judgment. Are we in general inclined to act upon what our moral judgment deems to be the right thing to do in any given circumstance? Do we necessarily follow our own moral reasoning and moral judgment? If we fail to follow our own moral judgment on what to do and what not to do, is it a failure of our rationality or our morality? If we take moral judgments to be what the agent herself makes under the ideal epistemic condition; that is, with full knowledge of the principle in the particular affair, with total rationality and perfectly good intention, with no self-deception or self-indulgence, with no interference from her own selfish desires or mental inertia, and so on, then it would seem that moral judgment would naturally motivate the agent to act. As Connie S. Rosati puts it, "Perhaps moral judgments are such that no person would sincerely judge an act morally right or a state of affairs good, while remaining *wholly* unmoved" (Rosati 2014, 9). Nevertheless, does Zhu Xi's moral theory provide us any assurance of the claim that *knowledge motivates action*?

In contemporary metaethical debate on moral motivation, a main contention is between motivational internalism and motivational externalism. An internalist holds that moral judgment motivates necessarily; hence, an act is moral only if the agent is self-motivated to act in accordance with her moral judgment of the right deed. An externalist, on the other hand, is someone who believes that "any connection that exists between moral judgment and motivation is purely contingent, though it may turn out to rest on deep features of human nature" (Rosati 2014, 19). According to Kwong-loi Shun, Zhu Xi belongs to the internalist camp. Shun takes it that for Zhu Xi, "an act is [righteous] (*yi* 義) only if it is performed not just because it is proper, but because the agent is fully inclined to so act" (Shun 2000, 98). Chan Lee questions this categorization and suggests that Zhu Xi's ideas of moral motivation should not be cast as either internalist or externalist, because "Zhu Xi tries to restore an epistemic equilibrium to any distinction between internal and external in terms of moral motivation" (Chan 2010, 633). If we follow the above definitions, however, Zhu Xi is a motivational internalist, albeit a *weak* internalist. According to Zhu Xi, "Internal and external are simply one principle. Even though what one does is revealed externally, the whole process is actually internal to the mind. When Gaozi says that what determines righteousness is external to one's mind, he is simply wrong" (Zhu 1986, 723). What one judges to be the righteous thing to do, according to Zhu Xi, is internal to the mind. He says, "Righteousness is internal, not external. Righteousness is simply to form the judgment of whether an affair is appropriate, and it is the mind that makes this judgment" (Zhu 1986, 595). In other words, to Zhu Xi, it is the moral judgment of the agent herself that counts. A moral agent should not simply follow external conventional views to judge right from wrong. She must have her own standard of right and wrong, and once her moral judgment is made, her action naturally proceed in accordance with her judgment.

Zhu Xi believes that a moral act must be one that is motivated by the agent's moral judgment of rightness and goodness. "All principles in the world can be divided into right and wrong. It is *good* to follow the right and it is *evil* to follow the wrong.... Everything must be judged carefully as right or wrong, and one must choose what is right to act upon it" (Zhu 2002, 14:394). Here we see that Zhu Xi identifies moral good with the moral judgment of rightness, and he deems moral act to be one that is done in accordance with the agent's moral judgment. However, Zhu Xi's view is far from individual relativism. Moral judgments in his view are not subjective and not relative to individual standards; they are mandated by objective moral truths. He takes right and wrong to be polar opposites: there is no gradation of rightness or wrongness, and the assignment of value does not vary from person to person. He says, "When we discuss *yin* and *yang*, we say that where there is *yin* there must be *yang*. However, when we discuss good and bad, there would not be a single thread of mixture" (Zhu 2002, 14:395). In other words, good and bad are similar to black and white: they are sharply demarcated.

Zhu Xi's commitment to moral realism inclines him to take a moral agent's moral judgments to be *representational*: true moral judgments represent genuine moral properties such as *rightness* and *goodness* in states of affairs, and there is a fact of the matter whether some act is normatively appropriate and even obligatory. Moral properties are, we may say, "out in the world of particular things," and the objective moral standard on one's dealing with each state of affairs is simply the particular principles in things. These principles, once cognized, would move an agent to act, and the step needed is the agent's moral perception of these objective moral principles. To Zhu Xi, moral action should be a deliberate act, not a spontaneous, intuitive response to the given situation. Perception of the moral truth is aided by one's cognitive processing of the principle behind the given situation, and one's moral judgment comes as the result of this cognitive process. No further desire or conative state is required for the moral judgment to have the motivational power. Hence, he is a motivational internalist.

However, Zhu Xi should only be considered a *weak* motivational internalist, in that he does not hold a necessary connection between moral judgment and moral motivation. By Rosati's definition, weak internalism allows the possibility of overriding moral interferences: "even though, necessarily, the person who makes a sincere moral judgment will feel *some* motivation to comply with it, that motivation can be overridden by conflicting desires and defeated by a variety of mental maladies, such as depression and weakness of will" (Rosati 2014, 18). For Zhu Xi, the "overriding factors" of an agent's moral judgment are the agent's selfish desires. In cases where the agent knows what she ought to do but does not do it, we see that knowledge and action come apart. Therefore, unless the agent can remove her selfish desires, retain reverence in her heart, she would not act on her best moral judgment even if she perceives moral truths and makes the right moral judgment. In this respect, Zhu Xi is a weak motivational internalist.

Here we observe an internal gridlock for Zhu Xi's theory or moral motivation: if the agent judges that she ought to remove her selfish desire, but her desires stand in the way of her acting in accordance with her judgment, then her judgment would have no causal efficacy whatsoever. Furthermore, if she cannot even be motivated by her judgment to remove her selfish desires, then all her other moral judgments on what she ought to do are equally ineffective since her desires will always impede her moral action. So ultimately, all the investigation of principles in things that a moral agent partakes, all the perception of moral truths that she possesses and all the moral judgments that she makes, are completely useless if she cannot first deal with her own mind's thoughts and desires. She is her own worst enemy in terms of her moral pursuit. We can now see why later on Wang Yangming would come up with a methodology that focuses purely on the mind's ideas and desires. To be a genuine internalist, Zhu Xi must take moral cultivation to begin with the examination of the mind rather than with the investigation of things.

Conclusion

In this chapter, we have seen how Zhu Xi combines knowledge and ethics and takes a cognitivist, rationalist approach to moral cultivation. Like other neo-Confucians, he too believes that we are moral creatures because we have an innate moral quality that enables us to become moral agents. He does not characterize this moral quality in terms of our moral sense, moral sentiments, or moral intuition; rather, he takes it as a cognitive capacity to truly and fully investigate principles in external affairs. The methodology is meticulous, and the process is slow and painstaking. However, the question remains whether it gets us anywhere in terms of our own moral pursuit.

Primary Sources

Zhu Xi 1986. *The Classified Dialogues of Zhu Xi (Zhuzi Yulei* 朱子語類*)*.
    Eight volumes. Beijing: Zhonghua Shuju Chubanshe.
Zhu Xi 2002. *The Complete Work of Zhu Xi (Zhuzi Quanshu* 朱子全書*)*.
    27 volumes. Shanghai: Guji Chubanshe.

Selections in English

Chan, Wing-tsit (ed.) 1963. *A Sourcebook in Chinese Philosophy*. Princeton University Press. Chapter 34.

Gardner, Daniel K. (trans.). 1990 *Learning to Be a Sage: Selections from the Conversation of Mater Chu, Arranged Topically*. Berkeley, CA: University of California Press.

Tiwald, Justin and Bryan W. Van Norden (eds.) 2014. *Readings in Later Chinese Philosophy: Han Dynasty to the 20th Century*. Indianapolis, IN: Hackett Publishing Company. 168–230.

11

Wang Yangming's Intuitionist Model of Innate Moral Sense and Moral Reflexivism

> *Can you tell me, Socrates, whether virtue is acquired by teaching or by practice; or if neither by teaching nor practice, then whether it comes to man by nature, or in what other way?*
>
> (Plato, Meno 70a)

Introduction

It is an open question whether we humans are born with some moral sense or some innate faculty that enables us to become moral creatures. There is no doubt that all human societies have developed some moral systems even if the content of their moral systems may differ from society to society. One possible explanation for the universality of moral systems in human societies is the pragmatic or enlightened self-interest approach: we devised moral systems because they helped us to live harmoniously with one another, which in the long run also benefit the individuals in the society. By this account, the development of morality in human beings is a contingent fact derived from the nature of human society and the requirement of coexistence. A different approach, on the other hand, is to point to some biological or psychological makeup of human beings, and claim that human societies all have moral systems because humans are simply "the moral animal" (Robert Wright's phrase)[1]! One major topic in current evolutionary psychology is thus the investigation of our innate psychological mechanisms underlying our moral behavior.

In this chapter, we will analyze Wang Yangming's moral philosophy as a form of intuitionism. Contemporary social psychologist Jonathan Haidt defines "intuitionism" this way: "Intuitionism in philosophy refers to the view that there are moral truths and that when people grasp these truths they do so not by a process of ratiocination and reflection, but rather by a process more akin to perception, in which one 'just sees without argument that they are and must

---
1 See Wright 1994.

Neo-Confucianism: Metaphysics, Mind, and Morality, First Edition. JeeLoo Liu.
© 2018 John Wiley & Sons, Inc. Published 2018 by John Wiley & Sons, Inc.

be true' (Harrison 1967, 72)" (Haidt 2001, 814). There are other versions of ethical intuitionism, which may take certain moral principles or moral axioms to be *self-evidently* true, to be immediately perceivable, or to be intuitively known. Wang Yangming's moral philosophy is built on his theory of *Liangzhi* 良知, the faculty of knowing whether one's ideas are good or bad. He takes this faculty to be an innate capacity to immediately *perceive* right and wrong, without the aid of reasoning and reflection. His moral intuitionism emphasizes the immediate perceivability of certain moral truths pertaining to one's self-examination.

Haidt defends *social* intuitionism, whereas Wang Yangming's intuitionism should be called "*a priori* intuitionism." Social intuitionism take individuals' moral insights to be gradually inculcated by the their sociocultural environment, such that at the end of this development, individuals' judgment or behavior require no further reflection and become semi-automatic. As Haidt puts it, "The model is social in that it deemphasizes the private reasoning done by individuals and emphasizes instead the importance of social and cultural influences" (Haidt 2001, 814). Wang Yangming's moral intuitionism, on the other hand, takes moral insights to be given as one's innate capacity. His approach is more *individualistic*: everyone possesses *a priori* moral intuitions and only needs to confer his or her own moral intuitions to judge right from wrong. However, he does not think that everyone's ordinary intuition would all qualify as a morally correct intuition. Wang Yangming's moral intuitionism sets a normative standard: such moral intuition ought to be pure, not tainted with one's selfish desires or biased ideas. This moral theory is based on Wang Yangming's belief in the innateness of human morality. We must first explain this view in a broader context to show the credibility of his moral theory and the feasibility of his moral methodology.

The Innateness of Morality

In *The Descent of Man*, Charles Darwin wrote: "of all the differences between man and the lower animals the moral sense or conscience is by far the most important. This sense, as Mackintosh remarks, 'has a rightful supremacy over every other principle of human action'" (Darwin 1871, 67). Darwin takes conscience to be "a feeling of right and wrong" that is closely associated with the intellect, such that any other animal endowed with well-marked social instincts, would inevitably acquire a conscience as soon as its intellectual powers had become as well developed as in man (Darwin 1871, 68–70). According to Darwin, of all animals, only humans can be deemed moral beings with certainty. "A moral being is one who is capable of comparing his past and future actions or motives, and of approving and disapproving of them" (Darwin 1871, 85). Darwin thinks that our conscience is what makes humans moral creatures, because it is a faculty of retrospective inspection of one's past deeds: "conscience looks backward and judges past actions, inducing that kind of dissatisfaction, which, if weak, we call regret, and if severe, remorse" (Darwin 1871, 87). In other words, conscience is associated with such self-regard emotions as regret and remorse, and this self-admonishment serves as the guidance for our behavior in future similar situations. In Darwin's view, human beings are moral animals on account of their ability to self-inspect and self-regulate.

In "The Difference of Being Human: Morality," evolutionary biologist Francisco J. Ayala defends Darwin's view that "the moral sense is the most important difference between man and the lower animals" (Ayala 2010, 9018). Ayala argues that the question concerning whether the moral sense is biologically determined should be separate from the question concerning whether there are universal moral codes. According to Ayala, it is a commonly observed fact that there is no universal moral code from culture to culture; hence, "the norms according to which we decide which actions are good and which actions are evil are largely culturally determined" (Ayala 2010, 9018). However, such a fact does not disprove the claim that humans are moral beings by nature. In Ayala's opinion, morality consists of the disposition to pass value judgments of right and wrong, and humans are *Homo moralis* in our possessing a moral sense that "emerges as a necessary implication of our high intellectual powers, which allow us to anticipate the consequences of our actions, to evaluate such consequences, and to choose accordingly how to act" (Ayala 2010, 9019). According to Ayala, there are three necessary conditions for moral creatures, and they are the ability to anticipate the future, to make evaluative judgments, and the capacity for free will. Therefore, moral sense emerges in humans not as a form of *adaptation* in its own right, but as a form of *exaptation*—as an additional function or a necessary by-product of the evolution of human intelligence. Because *Homo sapiens* evolved such high intellectual powers for abstract thinking, they necessarily developed a moral sense that separates them from other animals. Such a moral sense is innate in us.

In *The Evolution of Morality*, philosopher Richard Joyce proposes that humans are moral animal in that humans have an innate proclivity to *making moral judgments*. He argues that the human mind was never *tabula rasa* in its original state (Joyce 2007, 7). What the human mind is equipped with at birth includes many innate mental capacities such as memory, emotion, perception, deliberation, will and understanding. Joyce thinks that one of our innate capacities is the capacity to make judgment about right and wrong. This is of course not to claim that humans already know what is right and what is wrong at birth: the content of our moral judgment is derived *a posteriori* from our experience and our environment. We are not born with a fixed set of moral beliefs or innate ideas. However, we have the capacity to make moral judgment and an innate mechanism for acquiring moral beliefs, according to Joyce. This is what makes us *moral animals*.

Frans de Waal (2010), on the other hand, argues that what makes humans moral is the fact that we are equipped with a sense of empathy developed through a long evolutionary history. He claims that the approach anchoring human morality in sentiments not only fits well with evolutionary theory, modern neuroscience, but is also supported by observing primates' behavior. He asks, "If morality is derived from abstract principles, why do judgments come instantaneously?" (de Waal 2010, 8). In de Waal's analysis, "empathy" is the sense of "feeling into," and the German word "Einfühlung" for empathy conveys "the movement of one individual projecting him-or her-self into another" (de Waal 2010, 64). He gives an example: "Seeing someone in pain activates pain circuits to the point that we clench our jaws, close our eyes, and even yell 'Aw!' if we see a child scape its knee. Our behavior fits the other's situation, because it has become ours" (de Waal 2010, 78–9). Such a reaction is spontaneous, pre-reflective, instinctive; in other words, empathy is *innate in us*. He cites psychologist Martin Hoffman's explanation of the connection between this instinctive sentiment and morality: empathy "has the property of transforming another person's misfortune into one's own feeling of distress." Hence, empathy "may be uniquely well suited for bridging the gap between egoism and altruism" (Hoffman 1981, in de Waal 2010, 84).

The pioneer in Chinese moral psychology is unquestionably Mencius, whose view on human nature is also the primary basis for neo-Confucian moral psychology. Even though Mencius was not thinking about the innateness of human morality in terms of the evolutionary origin of morality, he would have agreed with the above thinkers that humans possess an innate moral capacity. However, he thinks that only human beings are capable of being moral. According to Mencius, "What distinguishes humans from beasts is ever so slight, and while the common people lose it [the moral difference], moral exemplars [such as Yao and Shun, two ancient sage kings] preserve it" (Mencius 4B:19). What Mencius asserts as evidence for the innate goodness of human nature is the four inborn moral sentiments: the sense of commiseration, the sense of shame and disgust, the sense of reverence and deference, and the sense of right and wrong. He thinks that these four moral sentiments constitute the basis for human morality; hence, they are called "the four sprouts" (*siduan* 四端). To him, it is an *a priori* truth that humans are born with these four moral senses. This metaphysical claim is not derived from empirical observations or scientific data, nor is it refutable by counterexamples. To Mencius, anyone who does not have any of the moral senses is simply someone who did not *preserve* them. Hence, the existence of depraved people does not pose any threat to his claim that all humans are born with these moral senses.

All the eight neo-Confucians covered in this book embrace Mencius's metaphysics of mind, including his conviction of the innate moral sprouts in the human mind. Wang Yangming, however, is probably the only one who pushes Mencius's theory to a purely *a priori* claim about humans' innate morality.

According to Wang Yangming, "The original state (*benti* 本體)[2] of human mind is simply supremely good (*zhishan* 至善)" (Wang 1975, 2). To Wang Yangming, the innateness of human morality resides in human's having an innate capacity to immediately perceive the right and the wrong, the good and the bad, in one's own thoughts. This is his theory of *Liangzhi* (良知).

An Innate Moral Compass: *Liangzhi* (良知) as an *A priori* Moral Intuition

The term *Liangzhi* (良知) comes from Mencius. According to Mencius, "That which people are capable of doing without learning is their instinctive capacity (*liangneng* 良能); that which people are capable of knowing without thinking it over is their instinctive knowledge (*Liangzhi* 良知)" (The *Mengzi* 7A:15). Mencius gives the examples of an infant's instinctive love toward the parents and a child's instinctive respect toward the elder brother. Of course, these examples can be empirically challenged, but as we have explained, Mencius's conviction is based on his metaphysics of mind—his theory of the four moral sprouts. What Mencius asserts here is not the actual manifestation of these moral sprouts, but the "incipient tendency" as Bryan Van Norden (2008) calls them. Wang Yangming uses the same phrase "*Liangzhi*" in the *Mengzi*, however, he advances Mencius's posit of *Liangzhi* from an incipient tendency to "a fully developed faculty of simultaneous ethical insight and motivation" (Van Norden 2008, 175). Wang Yangming's complete moral theory, including his ethical goal and moral methodology, is grounded in his theory of *Liangzhi*.

In addition to being a solid moral grounding rather than just a sprout, Wang Yangming's *Liangzhi* has a different function than that of Mencius: it is not an instinctive sentiment, but an instinctive *judgment*. Mencius focused on an infant's natural love for the parents, and a child's natural respect for the elder brother, as foundations for the virtue of humaneness and the virtue of righteousness. Both of these sentiments are *affective*. We have seen in Chapter 8 that Zhang Zai deals more with the virtues of humaneness (*ren* 仁), righteousness (*yi* 義), and propriety (*li* 禮) than with wisdom (*zhi* 智). In Chapter 9, we also see that the Cheng brothers pay more attention to the virtue of humaneness and the virtue of reverence. For Wang Yangming, on the other hand, the most essential innate capacity is the moral sense of right and wrong, which is the foundation for our moral wisdom. He says, "The sense of right and wrong

---

2 Here I follow Philip J. Ivanhoe's translation. What Wang Yangming calls "the original state" (*benti* 本體) is sometimes rendered as *substance*, but it is not a substance in the constitutive sense. In other words, he is not claiming that human mind is *made up of* the supreme good, but that human mind is *originally* supremely good. Hence, the translation of *benti* as "the original state" is a better choice.

is what one knows without thinking it over and what one is capable of without having learnt it; this is the so-called *Liangzhi*" (Wang 1975, 65). According to Wang Yangming, the moral intuition we are born with is the intuitive perception of right and wrong. This perception appears as an immediate acknowledgment of right or wrong, not as a form of deliberate moral judgment. It differs from sense perception, and does not depend on empirical learning. As he puts it: "Having this knowledge is the original state (*benti* 本體) of the mind. Mind naturally knows [how to respond in the right way]" (Wang 1975, 5).

An intuition is an insight without recourse to reason and objective justification. Whether an intuition is an emotion or a judgment does not have a clear answer, and perhaps we can say that a moral intuition is a spontaneous judgment of right and wrong associated with some emotions such as like or dislike, approval, or disapproval. Herbert Spencer calls faculties of moral intuition "certain emotions responding to right and wrong conduct, which have no apparent basis in the individual experiences of utility" (letter to J. S. Mill, cited in Darwin 1871, 97). This shows that Spencer takes intuitions to be primarily affective. Jonathan Haidt defines moral intuition as "the sudden appearance in consciousness of a moral judgment, including an affective valence (good-bad, like-dislike), without a conscious awareness of having gone through steps of searching, weighing evidence, or inferring a conclusion" (Haidt 2001, 818). In other words, according to Haidt, moral intuitions are primarily instantaneous judgments of right and wrong.

Wang Yangming's view of *Liangzhi* is closer to what Haidt defines as moral intuition, but he has a further normative component: *Liangzhi* is *appropriate* response. Wang holds that we are born with an innate capacity of moral perception or intuitive moral knowledge. As long as our mind is not crowded with selfish ideas, we can immediately know right and wrong, ought and ought-not, without the mediation of learning or reasoning. According to Wang Yangming, "Our mind naturally knows. For example, upon seeing one's father, one naturally knows to be filial; upon seeing the elder brother, one naturally knows how to respond with brotherly love; upon seeing a young child about to fall into a well, one naturally responds with compassion. These are all cases of *Liangzhi*, and there is no need to look for it from the outside" (Wang 1975, 5). As we will see later in this chapter, for Wang Yangming, *knowledge* includes responsive emotions and actions in the right circumstances. If one does not respond appropriately given one's knowledge or one's judgment, then one does not *know*. This kind of knowledge (*zhi* 知) is what Wang Yangming calls instinctive knowledge (*Liangzhi*).

To Spencer, moral intuitions may be "*a priori* to the individual," but are actually "*a posteriori* to the race," and thus "as race experiences which in the individual appear as intuitions" (Hudson 1904, 63). That is to say, humans' collective past experience molds human minds, and traces of some changes are carried over to new generations before the individual acquires any personal experience.

Therefore, for the individual, some of the intuitions may precede any experience and appear *a priori*. Contemporary evolutionary psychology studies humans' internal psychological mechanisms as "adaptations"—"products of natural selection—that helped our ancestors get around the world, survive and reproduce" (Downes 2008). It could be argued that our moral intuitions are among those adaptations. If so, then they would be what Spencer deems as *a priori* to the individual but *a posteriori* to the race. What this means is that humans as a species have gone through various cultural evolutions to develop adaptations of their psychological mechanisms.

Jonathan Haidt's social intuitionism emphasizes the role of social interaction in one's developing a certain set of moral intuitions. According to Haidt, "[T]he social intuitionist model posits that moral reasoning is usually done interpersonally rather than privately" (Haidt 2001, 820). Haidt argues that people's moral judgments are typically not caused by their conscious moral reasoning, but are "the result of quick, automatic evaluations (intuitions)" (Haidt 2001, parentheses in original). These intuitions are partly the result of "a major evolutionary adaptation for an intensely social species, built into multiple regions of the brain and body" (Haidt 2001, 826). This explains why people would lack conscious access to the automatic processes that generate their moral intuitions. On the other hand, the moral intuitions are also partly the result of individuals' *socialization* process, of which Haidt lists the three related processes: the selective loss of intuitions, immersion in custom complexes and peer socialization. The "selective loss of intuitions" refers to a culture's opting for one set of moral intuitions over some others. "Custom complex" refers to a culture's customary practice and the beliefs, values, rules or motives associated with it. "Peer socialization" refers to the phenomenon that people's moral judgments are often shaped by the judgments of those around them. As a result of this socialization process, an individual's moral judgment "is not just a single act that occurs in a single person's mind but is an ongoing process, often spread out over time and over multiple people" (Haidt 2001, 828). Haidt thus concludes that moral intuition is "both innate and enculturated" (Haidt 2001, 826), and we can say that it is both *a priori* and *a posteriori*.

In contrast, Wang Yangming's moral intuitions are purely *a priori* and independent of personal or cultural experiences. Wang Yangming's theory of *Liangzhi* as a form of moral intuition differs from both Spencer's and Haidt's views. Since Wang Yangming takes these intuitions to be a form of innate knowledge possessed by individuals, he does not fall into the camp of commonsense intuitionists who appeal to collective individuals' moral intuitions for judgment of right and wrong. According to Wang Yangming, the content of our *Liangzhi*, namely, what we instinctively know without reasoning and learning, is not socially constructed or empirically conditioned. On the contrary, it has objective and absolute claim of truth since it simply is heavenly principle itself: "The *Liangzhi* in our mind is nothing but the so-called 'heavenly principle." If we can realize this heavenly principle in everything, then everything will fulfill its own principle" (Wang 1975, 37). In other words, the faculty of *Liangzhi* has a "direct tracking" of moral reality—it does not simply make intuitive judgment on right and wrong; rather, it directly *perceives* right as right and wrong as wrong. In particular, in Wang Yangming's theory, this perception is turned inward, with one's own ideas and thoughts as its object. According to Wang Yangming, "Your *Liangzhi* is the criterion for your ideas. With whatever idea comes to your mind, if it is a right idea, your *Liangzhi* will immediately see it as right; if it is a wrong idea, your *Liangzhi* will also immediately perceive it as wrong" (Wang 1975, 77). That is to say, the line between the moral rightness and wrongness of our ideas is already objectively carved, and for Wang Yangming, our faculty of *Liangzhi* can correctly make judgment that corresponds to this natural moral division. His theory of *Liangzhi* is thus grounded in his humanistic moral realism (see Chapter 6).

Wang Yangming's Moral Reflexivism

Based on his notion of *Liangzhi*, Wang Yangming's moral methodology consists in assiduous self-examination and self-correction. The implied theory of mind behind Wang's moral methodology is that one is reflexively self-aware and can truthfully introspect one's own mind. According to Jonardon Ganeri's analysis of Indian Buddhist theories of self-consciousness, reflexivism is "the thesis that self-consciousness consists in conscious mental occurrences being reflexively conscious of themselves" (Ganeri 2012, 166). Borrowing from Ganeri's terminology, we shall categorize Wang Yangming's moral theory as "moral reflexivism"—morality consists in the self's consciously reflecting on the self's mental activities and making reflexive moral judgments on the self's ideas. Reflexivism analyzes experience as having two distinct "aspects"—an object-aspect and a subject-aspect (Ganeri 2012, 169). By the same token, there seems to be two "selves" in Wang Yangming's moral reflexivism—the self that naturally produces ideas, emotions and desires, and the other self that is constantly monitoring the natural self's mental activities—"like a cat catching mice: with eyes intently watching and ears intently listening. As soon as a single [selfish thought such as the craving for sex, material goods or fame] begins to stir, one must conquer it and cast it out resolutely" (Wang 1994, 40, modifications of Ivanhoe 2002, 102). In this metaphor, the monitoring self is the cat while the monitored ideas in the mind are like mice. With such an analogy of eyes and ears, Wang seems to be positing a "higher-order perception" of the self's spontaneous flow of ideas.

The main difference between a higher-order-thought (HOT) theory and a higher-order-perception (HOP) theory of consciousness is that the former treats the higher-order mental state as a learned or trained process, while the latter treats it as spontaneous and innate. As with other HOP theories of consciousness, Wang Yangming's moral reflexivism also needs to give an account of the inner sense organ that accomplishes the inward perception. His explanation is simply that the mind's *Liangzhi* is such a mental faculty with which moral introspection is executed. Wang Yangming's teaching of *Liangzhi* focuses on the mind's intuitive *seeing* right from wrong. It should be interpreted as a form of *moral perception* or *moral sense*, rather than as thought-like moral reflection or moral deliberation. As we have seen in Chapter 6, Wang Yangming's perceptual model of ethical knowledge is grounded in his commitment to moral realism: there is a moral reality accessible to everyone and available for everyone's perception and recognition. We are equipped with the moral vision to immediately perceive the divide between good and bad, moral and immoral. No further teaching or learning is required: "This sense of right and wrong [in Mencius's teaching] is something one can know without deliberation, can carry out without ever learning. This is the so-called '*Liangzhi*.' The *Liangzhi* in everyone's mind is the same whether in the sage or in the folly. It is what is shared in common from all parts of the world and in all eras in human history" (Wang 1994, 173).

Under Wang Yangming's moral reflexivism, morality is an individual feat that could be accomplished by everyone as long as he or she is sincere with the intent and diligent with the effort. Morality is *in* us and is *our* business (borrowing Pihlström's phrase for moral realism, see Pihlström 2005, 30, italics in original). Whether we become mature moral agents is solely decided by our own efforts. According to Wang Yangming, "The sense of right and wrong is what everyone possesses and there is no need to seek elsewhere" (Wang 1994, 70). A major difference between Wang Yangming's methodology and those of other neo-Confucians before him is that he does not advocate emulating moral exemplars such as the sages. We have seen in previous chapters that Zhang Zai implores moral agents to read books written by the sages and to learn to adopt the sages' volition. The Cheng brothers, on the other hand, beseech moral agents to identify themselves with the sages, to observe their comportment and to learn to acquire their joyful (*le* 樂) mental state. Wang Yangming sternly rejects such an outward-looking approach. He says, "The others have said that one should first acknowledge the sage's comportment. But this remark lacks careful thinking. The sage's comportment is his own, so how could I possibly acknowledge it?.... My own *Liangzhi* is originally the same as that of the sage. If I can truthfully acknowledge my own *Liangzhi*, then the sage's comportment is not in the sage, but in myself" (Wang 1975, 48). Wang Yangming defends the self-sufficiency of one's inner moral compass. What one needs to do is not to learn from others, emulate moral exemplars, or be socially conditioned in the right way; rather, one needs to establish a *direct* connection with one's inner moral self, and through which to recognize heavenly principle inherent in one's own mind. Each individual has an *a priori* access to the ultimate moral reality, and one only needs to look inward to recognize this moral reality. One may want to ask: how is knowledge of moral truth possible? Wang Yangming's answer would be: moral knowledge is possible because it is already in one's mind.

Once a student came back from outside and Wang Yanming asked him what he observed. The student replied: "I saw the streets filled with sages." Wang Yangming said approvingly, "You saw all people as sages, and they too see you as a sage" (Wang 1994, 255). In Wang Yangming's assessment, sagehood, the highest moral accomplishment for all neo-Confucians, is easily obtainable because it is already an established fact that we are all born as sages. We only need to recognize this fact and reflect on ourselves to maintain our innate goodness.

In this way, Wang Yangming's methodology focuses on *introspection*, rather than extrospection. He advocates that instead of investigating or examining what is outside oneself, one ought to look inside one's mind and be in tune with one's true nature. This sole emphasis on introspection is another aspect in which he departs from the teachings of the Cheng–Zhu school. One plausible connection that Wang's theory has with the Chinese Chan school is its emphasis on *the present*. Perception is an act that can be carried out when the supposed object is present; as a result, *Liangzhi* as moral perception requires the presence of the ideas or the thoughts in question. One's having a reflexive moral perception of one's own thoughts can take place only when those thoughts in question are presented as objects. This may explain why Wang Yangming's moral methodology demands incessant self-monitoring and self-correction, "without a moment's lapse" (Wang 1994, 40).

Moral Methodology: The Method of Retrieving One's Innate Moral Intuition is to Remove Selfish Desires

Even though everyone is born with instinctive knowledge (*liangzhi*) and instinctive capacity (*liangneng*), not all people can act upon their innate knowledge. According to Wang Yangming, "Ordinary people and the sages share the innate knowledge and innate capacity in common, but only the sages are capable of actualizing their innate knowledge. This is what separates the sages from ordinary folks" (Wang 1975, 41). For ordinary people, there is a moral ladder to climb and the goal is to fulfill the inner moral compass with which everyone is born. Wang Yangming calls this process "attaining innate knowledge" (*zhi Liangzhi* 致良知)—it is the realization, or we should say the retrieval, of one's *Liangzhi*.

To talk about retrieval is not to imply that one has at any point actually lost one's *Liangzhi*, however. According to Wang Yangming, the innate perception of right and wrong is ever-present, but this capacity could be obscured by one's erroneous ideas such as one's selfish thinking or one's materialistic desires.

His typical metaphor is the cloud and the sun: The mind is likened to the sun, and the erroneous thoughts or selfish desires are like the dark clouds shielding the sun from exhibiting its brilliance. Even when the sun's brilliance cannot be seen, nevertheless, the sun has never lost its brilliance. In the same way, even in the vilest people the innate goodness is never lost; it is simply hidden from view. The goal of learning is to learn to remove these obstructions (Wang 1975, 51–2). Here the metaphor of the sun and the cloud again supports the interpretation of Wang Yangming's *Liangzhi* as a higher-order moral *perception*. We can have misperception when objects are obstructed from view; similarly, our *Liangzhi* can fail to detect our own faults when it is obstructed by our self-insistent ideas.

Wang Yangming suggests that moral methodology consists in our constant thinking about eliminating desires and preserving our innately owned heavenly principle (Wang 1975, 34). To him, human desires and heavenly principle cannot coexist—as soon as a desire arises in the mind, the original moral sense is obstructed from view. The targeted thoughts to be eradicated by the faculty of *Liangzhi* are *si-yu* (私欲), one's selfish desires. He declares: "[If one can] overcome selfishness and return to [heavenly] principle, then one's *Liangzhi* would have no more obscuration and can be fully operational" (Wang 1994, 16). What does he mean by "selfishness" (*si* 私) and why is selfishness so bad?

Some contemporary scholars (Ivanhoe 2013; Tien 2012) have taken Wang Yangming's rejection of "selfishness" to be a criticism of one's "self-centeredness." David W. Tien, for example, argues that being *selfish* "means to be almost exclusively or excessively concerned with one's own desires, though not necessarily with one's individual self"; being *self-centered*, on the other hand, "is to be almost exclusively or excessively concerned with one's individual self, though not necessarily with one's own desires" (Tien 2012, 57). Tien thinks that for Wang Yangming, it is self-centeredness, rather than selfishness, that stands in the way of one's moral cultivation.

However, it is questionable whether Wang Yangming would really find self-centeredness morally reprehensible. If self-centeredness is simply "making one's personal self the center of one's world," then it seems to be both a common and a natural human psychological trait. In ethical deliberations, we often need to start with an agent-centered perspective—locating ourselves in the world and seeing how others relate to us. The Confucian "love with distinction" requires that we place our immediate family at the center of our affection. Mencius's teaching of "extension" (*tui* 推) is an agent-centered approach that aims to extend one's love for immediate family members to a form of humanitarian care for all human beings. Wang Yangming does not seem to deviate from this teaching of "love with distinction" when he talks about "treating Heaven, earth and the myriad things as one body," since he acknowledges that there should be the distinction between vegetation and animals, between humans and beasts, or between families and strangers. He says, "We love both our immediate family members and strangers on the road. However, if there is only a bushel of food or a ladle of bean soup, with it one can survive while without it one would die, and there is no way to satisfy both, then we would rather save our immediate family members and not strangers on the road. How could the heart bear [not doing it]? It is simply what is the reasonable thing to do" (Wang 1975, 133).

In a deeper sense, the "self-centeredness" could be seen as the quintessential teaching of the Lu–Wang school. As Lu Xiangshan says, "The universe's affairs are one's own affairs. One's own affairs are the universe's affairs" (Ivanhoe's translation; Ivanhoe 2009, 90). In explaining what it means to say that man's heart or mind is the same body (*tongti* 同體) with the myriad things, Wang Yangming also says, "My spiritual brilliance (*lingming* 靈明) is the master of Heaven, earth and all ghosts and spirits…. Heaven, earth, ghosts, spirits and the myriad things, if separated from my spiritual brilliance, there would be none of them" (Ivanhoe 2009, 130). We could perhaps say that Wang Yangming advocates a "heightened" sense of self-centeredness, according to which the universality of heavenly principle lies in the individual mind, and the whole universe is centered on one's pure mind. Therefore, what Wang Yangming rejects should not be self-centered ideas but the selfish ones.[3]

We still need to understand what Wang Yangming means by "selfishness (*si* 私)" and why he condemns it. What Wang Yangming rejects as "selfishness" is not egoism or self-interestedness, but the kind of self-insistence on one's own idea (*siyi* 私意) or desire (*siyu* 私欲) that is contrary to the universal heavenly principle. In Wang Yangming's critique of the common people's moral flaws of selfishness, the first of which is "lack of moderation." Once, a student of his in residence received the family letter informing him that his son was gravely ill, and the student was so stricken with worries that he could hardly function. Wang Yangming told him: "A father's loving his son is the deepest sentiment. And yet, heavenly principle has its balance and harmony. Anything beyond it is the self-insistent idea (*siyi* 私意)" (Wang 1975, 56). His advice to the student was: "if you do not work on regulating your emotions at the time of crisis, then what is the use of studying and learning on a daily basis?" (Wang 1975, 56). This seemingly harsh admonition demonstrates the difficulty of truly getting rid of one's "self" (*si* 私). What Wang Yangming saw as a problem of the student's "selfish" behavior was not that he loved his son, but that he allowed himself to be smitten with worry to the extent of losing his own mental peace. It is *self-ish*, because this kind of mentality violates the universality of heavenly principle.

---

3 Tien himself also "readily admits that sometimes Wang uses the term in the sense of a straightforward 'selfishness'" (Tien 2012, 61).

Lack of moderation, according to Wang Yangming, is the result of thinking too much. He says, "Happiness, anger, sadness and joy, in their original state these emotions are naturally balanced and harmonious. As soon as one adds further consideration, one's emotions become either excessive or deficient. This is exactly what 'selfishness (*si*)' is" (Wang 1994, 52). From this comment, we can see that the root of the ills of "selfishness (*si*)" is one's extra consideration; in other words, the problem is simply "having one thought too many." Since Wang Yangming advocates an *immediate perception* of right from wrong in one's own ideas, the extra thinking on the agent's part obstructs one's intuitive moral perception or one's innate moral knowledge. This is why being *self-ish* is bad.

Wang Yangming's preference for immediate moral perception over moral deliberation explains why in his attack on selfishness, he focuses on one's self-insistence on one's own idea (*siyi*) or desire (*siyu*) that is contrary to the universal moral principle. In answering a student's query about why our casual thoughts are considered our own desires (*siyu*), Wang says, "if you only keep to your mind's original state, why would you have any casual thoughts? This state is exactly the unagitated, immovable, unreleased equilibrium (*zhong* 中), and this is exactly the state of fairness (*gong* 公)" (Wang 1994, 64). What he describes here is none other than our innate *Liangzhi*. The *absence of one's own ideas* and *the prevalence of heavenly principle in one's mind* are simply two sides of the same coin. This explains why Wang Yangming claims that if one can remove one's own ideas, one would immediately be one with heavenly principle. As he says, "The mind is principle. Without one's insistence on one's own ideas, one is in accord with principle; as soon as one is against principle, one's mind is the lone mind (*si xin* 私心)" (Wang 1994, 72).

The opposite of the lone mind is to be one with everything, and this is Wang Yangming's teaching of *Oneness*: "The sage's heart is to be one with everything in the world. He treats everyone impartially, with no separation of inner or outer [circle], far or near. Any living person is as dear to him as his own brothers and children, whom he desires to be safe and educated. This is how he fulfills his intent on *being one with everything*" (Wang 1994, 129). Philip J. Ivanhoe and David W. Tien have both stressed the value of the notion *oneness* in Wang Yangming's moral philosophy. Tien argues that being "at 'one' with others and other parts of the world, and even with the universe at large" constitutes Wang Yangming's conception of the self (Tien 2012, 52). In Tien's analysis, the sense of "oneness" is at once psychological and metaphysical—it is "a felt state of metaphysical unity in which one's sense of self is not much lost than expanded" (Tien 2012, 55). With this expanded sense of the self, an individual would find it natural to care for others and things in the world. Tien argues that this metaphysical conception of the self provides a strong motivational force in that "the state of oneness enables one to experience an emotional identification and a feeling of interpersonal unity with the entirety of Heaven and Earth, including other living things and even inanimate objects" (Tien 2012, 68). Ivanhoe (2013) further constructs an ethics of care based on such a notion, which he defines as "a kind of identity between self and world" (Ivanhoe 2013, 8). He argues that even though neo-Confucians share this conception of oneness, Wang Yangming renders this notion more powerful by stressing the metaphor of corporeal unification (*yiti* 一體) of the self and the world: "Great people regard Heaven, earth, and the myriad creatures as their own bodies. They look upon the world as one family and China as one person within it" (Ivanhoe 2013, 11). Ivanhoe suggests that this conception constitutes "an enlarged sense of the self" and can take individuals beyond isolated self-conception and self-concern. According to Ivanhoe, "the oneness hypothesis," as he calls it, "offers some significant advantages over the empathy-altruism hypothesis" in that it allows us to explain human concerns beyond those with whom we can empathize, such as inanimate objects or even the ecological environment at large (Ivanhoe 2013, 23). This metaphysical conception of the self thus serves as the foundation for a more holistic ethics of care.

Wang Yangming once had a long discourse with a friend on the connection between *Liangzhi* and his ethics of *oneness*:

> Heaven and earth are fundamentally all one body with me. Is there any suffering or miseries of the people that is not as dear to me as my own body's illness or pain? Those who do not see [others' pain and misery] as their own bodies' illness and pain are simply lacking in their sense of right and wrong.... As long as moral agents (*junzi*) can cultivate their *Liangzhi*, they can all share their judgments of right or wrong and their sentiments of like and distaste. They will then naturally look upon others *as if* their own self, look upon the nation *as if* their own family, and can be *one body with everything in the world.*
>
> (Wang 1994, 173, emphasis added)

In this quote, Wang Yangming explains that we already have within us the capacity to be empathetic toward others' misfortune, namely, our *Liangzhi*. As long as we can remove any extra thinking on our part, we can be one body with the rest of the world. This is clearly an intuitivist model of moral theory.

The Unity of Knowledge and Action

Wang Yangming has another thesis that is uniquely his: the doctrine of the unity of knowledge and action. He claims that an essential component of knowledge is *acting on the knowledge*: "Those who 'know' but do not act simply do not yet know" (Ivanhoe's translation; Ivanhoe 2009, 140). During his lifetime, his contemporaries already noted that this teaching was his own creation and some were skeptical of its truth. A friend wrote to him: "Up until now, former scholars all took 'study, inquiry, reflection, and discrimination' as pertaining to knowing while 'sincere practice' pertained to acting. They clearly distinguished between these two things [i.e., knowing and acting]. Now, though, you alone say that knowing and acting form a unity (*zhi xing he yi* 知行合一). I cannot but have doubts about this" (Ivanhoe's translation. Ivanhoe 2009, 123; brackets in original). In his reply, Wang Yangming made it clear that by "acting," he meant a much broader sense of action that includes any volitional "performance of some affair." Not only are bodily movements a form of acting, so are mental activities such as study, inquiry, reflection, and discrimination in the friend's examples of "knowing." Therefore, Wang Yangming's unity of knowledge and action thesis may be based on a terminological dispute with others on the scope of "knowing" and "acting." Nevertheless, by advocating this thesis so vehemently, Wang was concerned not with a revision of definition, but with altering people's mindset and conduct.

According to Ivanhoe, the kind of knowledge Wang Yangming has in mind here is moral knowledge, and the crux of his teaching of the unity of knowledge and action is that "[t]here is no real moral knowledge that does not lead one to act; one cannot really possess moral knowledge if one has not properly engaged in moral activity" (Ivanhoe 2009, 113). In other words, this thesis makes a *normative* claim in setting up the standards for "true" moral knowledge and "true" moral deeds. The question Wang Yangming raises here is: if I know what I should do, but do not do it, then do I really know it? For example, I know that I should not cheat on taxes and yet I continue to do it. Do I really know that cheating is bad? I know that it is good to be charitable to others, and yet I do not do it. Do I really know that it is good to be charitable? Wang Yangming would say that in both these cases, my knowledge is not true knowledge. True knowledge must come from one's actual doing; in other words, knowledge must come from one's *performance*.[4]

To illustrate this thesis, Wang Yangming uses the analogy of sight and smell:

> Seeing a beautiful color is a case of knowing, while loving a beautiful color is a case of acting. As soon as one sees that beautiful color, one naturally loves it. It is not as if you first see it and only then, intentionally, you decide to love it. Smelling a bad odor is a case of knowing, while hating a bad odor is a case of acting. As soon as one smells that bad odor, one naturally hates it. It is not as if you first smell it and only then, intentionally, you decide to hate it.
>
> *(Wang 1994, 10. Ivanhoe's translation, Ivanhoe 2009, 141)*

---

4 We have discussed *knowledge as performance* in the context of the Cheng brothers' virtue epistemology. See Chapter 9. For all neo-Confucians, the kind of knowledge that really "matters to us" is moral knowledge, and moral knowledge is empty without *performance*—acting on the knowledge. In other words, the success condition of "knowledge" is defined over one's actual performance.

In this analogy to sight and smell, the knowledge he has in mind is experiential knowledge. Hearsay or learning through descriptions does not contribute to genuine knowing. Wang Yangming has another example in which he describes a mute person eating a bitter melon. The mute man cannot tell you what it is like to eat a bitter melon. In order to know the quality of his experience (or we may say *qualia* in contemporary terminology of philosophy of mind), you have to eat the bitter melon yourself. In other words, to know x, one has to experience x, and as soon as one experiences x, one's spontaneous reaction to x is already formed. This is a pre-reflection, immediate, intuitive, and semi-cognitive response to things. We can see in Wang Yangming's examples of taste, smell, sight, and so on, that he employs a perceptual mode of moral knowledge. Moral perception is similar to perceptual reaction: it too is a pre-reflection, immediate, intuitive, and semi-cognitive experience. If knowing pertains to experiential knowledge, then our immediate response to the experience itself is already *acting*. The two cannot be separated.

In some other cases, Wang Yangming takes knowing and acting to be a process, with knowing as the beginning state and acting as the end state. According to him, "Knowing is the beginning of acting; acting is the completion of knowing" (Wang 1994, 11; 33). Without action to complete the process, even the initial knowing cannot qualify as *knowing*. Knowing and acting form a unity not because there are two states that are now combines as one; rather, it is because they are one and the same: "As soon as knowing is mentioned, there is already action involved; as soon as action is mentioned, there is already knowledge involved" (Wang 1994, 11). We call this knowing-acting process "knowledge" and "action" respectively, only to identify the key traits of the whole process. According to Wang Yangming, "The intelligent, conscious, refined, and discerning aspects of acting are knowing. The authentic, direct, sincere, and substantial aspects of knowing are acting" (Ivanhoe's translation. Ivanhoe 2009, 124). This statement again shows that Wang Yangming is engaged in a terminological dispute with previous scholars on the scope and definition of "knowledge" and "action" when he proposes that the two are, or ought to be, unified.

If the unity of knowledge and action is merely a terminological reclassification, then why did Wang Yangming advocate it so vehemently? Wang Yangming's motivation behind this teaching is primarily *pragmatic*, in that he wishes to transform people's attitude toward morality. When someone asked him about the unity of knowledge and action, he explains,

> To understand this you must first *recognize the purpose of my doctrine*. Nowadays people separate knowing and acting, thus even if they have a bad thought emerging, they do not prohibit it since that thought has not been carried into action. I now proclaim the unity of knowledge and action, exactly because I want people to realize that action has already taken place even at the initiation of the bad idea. If the initial idea is bad, one must

overcome this bad idea. In other words, *one needs to completely obliterate any bad idea hidden in the mind.* This is the crux of my teaching.
(Wang 1994, 207, emphasis added)

In other words, Wang Yangming's moral teaching is this: *One should not have a single thought that is not good.* His moral standard is not only on the acts, but also on the internal mental states, of the moral agent. While other neo-Confucians also emphasize the importance of acting, Wang Yangming is focusing on the thought. It is indeed true that if one only thinks with good intent but never acts on it, one cannot be considered a qualified moral agent. Wang's doctrine of the unity of knowledge and action professes something more: if one harbors any malevolent intent, selfish desire or unspeakable thought, then one is already an immoral person *even if one was successful at suppressing such urges and checking one's behavior.* We thus see that Wang Yangming's doctrine of the unity of knowledge and action renders further support for his moral reflexivism discussed earlier in this chapter. His moral theory is *perfectionism* in its purest form.

For Wang Yangming, morality is based on the individual's mentality, and much is judged before the agent even takes any action. In Wang's definition, the very emergence of an idea to do something, whether good or bad, is called "intentionality" (*yi* 意). The directed affairs in the world, is called a thing (*wu* 物). He analyzes the much discussed phrase in the *Great Learning* "the investigation of things" (*gewu* 格物) as "correction of the mind's intended affairs," "correction of the affairs of the intentionality," or "correction of the affairs of the *Liangzhi*" (Wang 1994, 168). Investigation is not an outward pursuit of knowledge of principles of particular things, as Zhu Xi teaches; rather, investigation is simply *self-scrutiny* and *self-rectification*. Wang Yangming's moral teaching beseeches one to turn one's gaze inward, since to prevent immoral deeds, one must begin with cleansing oneself of any immoral thought.

We may now see the connection between Wang Yangming's moral sense theory and his moral reflexivism. According to Wang Yangming, the original state of our mind is nothing but heavenly principle, and this is what he calls "the true self." The true self is the master of our body; it is what drives our action. Since our original mental state is this pure "true self," the more we matured and the more ideas we developed, the farther away we would be from our original purity (Wang 1994, 96). Therefore, morality is a process of *retrieval* rather than advancement: it is to retrieve our initial purity of the mind as the infant's mind. Moral cultivation is accomplished first and foremost in one's private space: when one is alone with one's own thought. Wang Yangming develops the idea of "being watchful when one is alone" (*shendu* 慎獨) in the *Doctrine of the Mean*: "[*Dao*] cannot be separated from us for a moment. What can be separated from us is not [*Dao*]. Therefore, the superior man is cautious over what he does not see and apprehensive over what he does not hear.... Therefore, the superior man is watchful over himself when he is alone" ("Doctrine of the Mean," Chan's translation with slight modifications, Chan 1963, 98). On this idea of being watchful when one is alone, Wang Yangming says, "To maintain one's true self, one must continually preserve this true self's original state. Being cautious over what one does not see; being apprehensive over what one does not hear, this is all because one dreads diminishing one's true self in any way" (Wang 1994, 96). In other words, for Wang Yangming, morality has less to do with one's action than with one's mental state. If one is impure in the mind, then even if one has not performed any immoral deed, one cannot be considered *good*. If one has genuine purity in the mind, preserving one's innate moral sense and thinking in alignment with heavenly principle, then one cannot fail to be moral both in deeds and in thoughts. One can then be said to be a *sage*.

Wang Yangming presents us with a stern moral teaching that focuses on the agent's mental states, her private thoughts and ideas, and beseeches all of us to be wholesome from the inside out. To be qualified as a moral agent, we should not desire fame and profit, food and sex. One's mind must be sterile with nothing but the direct perception of good and evil. On must question at the end: is this teaching too idealistic? Is it at all plausible? Could ordinary people really all be sages in their own minds? Furthermore, is this moral life truly a *good life*? A person who is so neurotic and sanitary with her own ideas and desires can hardly be a happy person.

Another issue that can be raised to Wang Yangming's as well as to Lu Xiangshan's teaching of moral universalism is the indisputable fact of moral disagreements.[5] Lu Xiangshan and Wang Yangming were convinced that as long as our minds are pure, we are sages and our *Liangzhi* will all converge on the same moral truths, because all sages in the past, present, and future share the same moral perception. However, it seems highly possible that even a sage with a pristine mind could still be mistaken in some moral judgments. It is also likely that two sages could diverge on their verdicts of moral truth, especially when the external circumstances call for different interpretations or variant responses. Furthermore, times are changing, perspectives vary, so how could we expect people of the past or people of the future to share the same moral perception as we do now when we don't even have a consensus among ourselves? What should be done if two apparent sages have different intuitive answers? Is there a *fact of the matter* to fall back on when people have moral disagreements? These and a host of other questions seem to remain unsolved in the Lu–Wang's idealistic image of the human mind.

Conclusion

In a nutshell, Wang Yangming's moral philosophy focuses on the agent's mental state. To encourage moral conduct and discourage evil deeds, we need to cleanse our mind of selfish ideas, immoral intent, or even the slightest bad idea. Immorality begins with the mind; hence, we need to be acting like a cat trying

---

5 I wish to thank Kam-por Yu who first raised this question.

to catch the mice—our bad ideas. A moral agent in Wang Yangming's envisioning needs to be diligent in self-examination, self-reflection, and self-correction, and the method she must first employ is introspection. As Wang Yangming puts it, "The only thing one needs to do is to exert oneself to keep this heart-mind *free of human desires* and preserve heavenly principle" (Ivanhoe's translation, Ivanhoe 2009, 138, emphasis added). We are reminded of Jesus' teaching: "What comes out of a man is what defiles a man. For from within, out of the heart of man, come evil thoughts, fornication, theft, murder, adultery, coveting, wickedness, deceit, licentiousness, envy, slander, pride, foolishness. All these evil things come from within, and they defile a man" ("The Gospel According to Mark", *the Bible*). We may call such an attitude on the sanction of the mind "moral purism." However, it is natural for us to wonder whether this moral standard is too stringent, too lofty and too impractical. If someone covets the neighbor's wife (or his best friend's girlfriend) but does not ever take any inappropriate action, is he still immoral? If someone fantasizes becoming very famous or very rich, and yet does not do anything bad to achieve this dream, is she still immoral? Shouldn't we praise people for having self-discipline, self-control, in suppressing the urge to perform any immoral act? Must we also impeach them to completely remove any selfish desire or immoral thought? According to Owen Flanagan and Amélie Rorty, "Traditional moral theories have recently been criticized for being indefensibly utopian, enjoining an impossible reconstruction of our psychologies" (Flanagan and Rorty 1990, 2). Based on his purist demand on morality, we might conclude that Wang Yangming's moral theory is also a form of *utopian* ethical theory—highly idealistic and implausible.

Primary Sources

Wang, Yangming 1975. *The Compete Works of Wang Yangming*. Taipei, Taiwan: Zhengzhong shuju.
Wang, Yangming 1994. *The Records of Wang Yangming's Teachings (Chuanxilu* 傳習錄*)*. Taipei, Taiwan: Taiwan Shangwu Yinshuguan.

Selections in English

Chan, Wing-tsit (ed.) 1963. *A Sourcebook in Chinese Philosophy*. Princeton University Press. Chapter 35.
Ivanhoe, Philip J. (trans.). 2009 *Readings from the Lu-Wang School of Neo-Confucianism*. Indianapolis, IN: Hackett.

12

Constructing a Moral World: Wang Fuzhi's Social Sentimentalism

Introduction

This chapter concludes neo‐Confucian moral theories with the socioethical program of moral cultivation suggested by Wang Fuzhi. The main idea behind this program is that to construct a moral world, it is not enough to focus only on the moral agent's *isolated* moral conscience, moral reason or moral sentiments. The individual's moral sensibility has to be integrated into the whole society, such that moral conduct becomes a social norm. Morality should not belong to only saints or sages, and the moral demands should not go beyond the common patterns in human psychology. This chapter examines how Wang Fuzhi's theory, extending from Mencius's ideas, leads to a more realistic proposal for constructing a moral world.[1]

Wang Fuzhi was most influenced by Zhang Zai's moral metaphysics, but in respect of moral motivation, he takes a sentimentalist approach rather than Zhang Zai's rationalist approach. We have seen in Chapter 8 that Zhang Zai advocates the importance of learning and studying: moral cultivation must be accomplished through education; in particular, through studying what ancient sages wrote and learning to assimilate the way they think. With the aid of moral education, one eventually transcends one's natural tendencies and becomes a purely virtuous moral agent in the company of the sages. Zhang Zai suggests that the appropriate moral belief about universal kinship, mediated by the second‐order desire to be like the sages, would be sufficient for motivating altruistic behavior. In Zhang Zai's theory of moral motivation, desire can indeed motivate moral behavior, but only when it is a form of altruistic desire accompanied by the second‐order desire to adopt the ideal personality of "the sage and the worthy." From the intellectual transformation and assimilation, one can eventually develop the volition to assist strangers in dire need. Zhang Zai's moral theory tries to expand family love into worldly care, and to generate

---

[1] This chapter is partially based on the author's previous paper. See Liu 2012.

Neo‐Confucianism: Metaphysics, Mind, and Morality, First Edition. JeeLoo Liu.
© 2018 John Wiley & Sons, Inc. Published 2018 by John Wiley & Sons, Inc.

altruistic desire on the basis of one's natural desire for the wellbeing of oneself and one's own family. The second-order desire to have "the desire of the sage and the worthy" must be cultivated by adopting the belief that everyone is related to one another as family members and that the whole world is just one large family under heaven. Under Zhang Zai's view, the genuine concern for others' wellbeing can be established in a moral agent as long as she emulates the sage.

Since Zhang Zai calls the morally justified altruistic desire "desire of the sage and the worthy," it is clear that he thinks the goal of moral education is to transform one's self to be like the sage and the worthy. Once the moral agent is so transformed, her moral beliefs alone would be sufficient to motivate the right moral deeds without the aid of desire. In his discussion on Michael Smith's theory of moral motivation, David Brink acknowledges that for the virtuous person, moral beliefs alone are indeed sufficient to motivate, "but this is only because a virtuous person is *someone with a certain well-developed psychological profile* that is structured by various cognitive and conative states" (Brink 1997, 15, emphasis added). The same can be said about Zhang Zai's rationalist theory of moral motivation. The moral belief that "I should consider all those in dire need as my brothers and sisters and render aid as much as I would to my own family members" would be sufficient to motivate a moral agent who is *already* assimilated with the sage. We might interpret Zhang Zai's moral precept of *sagehood* as an ideal metaphysical conception of oneself. This kind of moral theories emphasizes ideal personality, a goal that one aspires to reach in one's lifetime. According to Flanagan and Rorty's explanation of ideal personhood, "These ideals may be characterized by a life plan or a ground project, by an unfolding array of projects that change over the course of a life, and by a range of personal commitments" (Flanagan and Rorty, 4). For Zhang Zai, the ideal personhood is the sage, and the moral goal one should strive for is to *think, desire* and *act* like a sage would.

However, such an ideal moral agent must be exceptional. Zhang Zai's theory may have provided an explanation of the moral motivation of purely altruistic moral agents, and yet it fails to provide a practicable strategy for realizing altruism in human society. We could apply Thomas Nagel's criticism of other desire-based motivational theory of altruism to Zhang Zai's theory as well: "If one wishes to guarantee its universal application, one must make the presence of reasons for altruistic behavior depend on *a desire present in all men*" (Nagel 1970, 28, emphasis added). It is hard to believe that ordinary people all have such an ideal metaphysical conception of themselves to the extent that they would all want to cultivate the desire of "the sage and the worthy." Zhang Zai's theory would thus lack universal feasibility. The fundamental problem of Zhang Zai's theory is its overly idealistic conceptions of moral agency. We have seen in our conclusion of Chapter 11 that Wang Yangming's moral methodology is also extremely idealistic to the point of being utopian. Neo-Confucian moral methodologies would most likely all fall into the category of *utopian* moral theories. This final chapter introduces Wang Fuzhi's moral theory, which does not have such a utopian bent, and is supported by a reasonable explication of human psychology.

Wang Fuzhi's Sentimentalist Theory of Moral Motivation

In Chapter 7, we have explained that Wang Fuzhi takes morality to be rooted in moral sentiments, which are distinguished from, and preside over, our natural emotions. What makes altruism possible under his theory would be the combination of both moral sentiments and natural emotions, with the further requirement of reflection (*si* 思). It is a theory that incorporates both moral reason and moral sentiments.

With the functions of the four moral sentiments that Mencius calls the "four moral sprouts," Wang Fuzhi gives a much more detailed analysis. He points out that the sentiment of commiseration for the misery of strangers is the initial psychological readiness for the virtue of humaneness (*ren* 仁). The sentiment of commiseration and the emotion of love both involve the agitation of the mind and the urge to bestow care and concern for others; however, the two have different origins. Love originates in the biologically based parental feelings toward the child, which Wang Fuzhi calls "the emotion for sons and daughters." The sense of commiseration, on the other hand, is based on a universal, *a priori* endowment from heaven. It is not restricted to one's biological kinship. According to Wang Fuzhi, "Commiseration shows humaneness while love is simply love. Emotions (*qing* 情) and moral essence (*xing* 性) are each to its own category" (Wang 1974a, 10:674). Therefore, the altruistic act that manifests the virtue of humaneness must be motivated by our innate sentiment of commiseration for the sufferings of those who are not biologically related to us.

The sentiment of shame and disgust includes both the sense of shame for one's own wrongdoing (action) or one's failure to do the right thing (inaction), and the sense of disgust for others' wrongdoing. The sentiment of "shame" should be separated from what Bernard William calls "agent-regret," which "indicates that though one may not be at fault for failing to meet a claim, one nonetheless fees some degree of responsibility" (Sherman 1990, 151). Feeling shame is a much stronger sentiment than the passive sense of regret. It can drive one to take certain action or refrain from some foreseeable acts. Gabriele Taylor also makes an interesting distinction between *feeling ashamed*, which she identifies with regret, and *feeling shame*: "It is quite possible for a person to claim sincerely that he is feeling *ashamed* of having said or done something where this means no more than he regrets having done that thing." Feeling *shame*, on the other hand, involves "beliefs on the agent's part concerning his own standing"

(Taylor 1985, 53, emphasis added). In other words, the sentiment of shame is closely associated with the agent's sense of self-worth. One would not want to debase oneself from doing what one considers as a shameful act.

The sense of disgust should be separated from an impulsive physical reaction that is associated with hygiene or aesthetics. It is in particular a form of moral disgust, which can be interpreted as an emotionally charged attitude of "disapproval" upon seeing another's wrongdoing or inappropriate suggestion. Shame and moral disgust are closely connected. According to Zhu Xi, shame arises from the self-criticism of one's own immorality, while moral disgust has others' immorality as the target. What an individual feels a strong shame for in her own conduct and what she feels indignant about in others' doing often go hand-in-hand. Bernard Williams makes the same observation on the Greek notions of shame and moral indignation. According to Williams, the Greek word for "shame" (*aidos*), and the Greek word for indignation (*nemesis*) are a "reflexive pair" (borrowing James Redfield's term), "People have at once a sense of their own honor and a respect for other people's honor; they can feel indignation or other forms of anger when honor is violated, in their own case or in someone else's. These are shared sentiments with similar objects, and they serve to bind people together in a community of feelings" (Williams 2008, 80).

While the content of our moral disgust could be conditioned and modified by social culture, the sense of disgust itself in nonetheless an innate moral disposition of ours. According to Wang Fuzhi, this sentiment of shame and disgust is "what everyone each has within himself and cannot be passed down from one person to another" (Wang 1974a, 8:538). This sentiment is the motivational foundation for our righteous acts. Even if the context that calls for our righteous act may come through life's experience, our mind already contains the standard of righteousness (Wang 1996, 35:676).

The sentiment of reverence and deference includes a sense of observance of the social context in which one finds oneself, as well as a sense of respect for others and deference in one's attitude toward those with expertise or authority. Mencius thinks that this sentiment is the foundation for propriety (*li* 禮). Wang Fuzhi explains that the sense of reverence and deference is best illustrated in our respect for the elderly. The elderly are merely people who are a few years senior to us, and this natural fact alone would not have any moral significance. However, in human society (at least in ancient Chinese society) people naturally pay tribute to the elderly. He thinks that this is because we naturally have the sentiment of reverence and the sentiment is aroused when we encounter the elderly (Wang 1996, 35:688). So, even if the appropriateness (*zhongjie* 中節) of the behavior may depend on the objects we encounter, "the activation of this sentiment originates in our nature" (Wang 1974a, 10:670). Because of our sentiment of reverence and deference, we would aim to act appropriately in different contexts and toward different objects. Therefore, this sentiment is the motivational foundation for our acts of propriety.

Finally, the sense of right and wrong is one's ability to perceive right from wrong, which we have seen in Chapter 11 that Wang Yangming calls "*Liangzhi*." Wang Fuzhi also identifies it with *Liangzhi*. Similar to the sentiment of shame and disgust, this sense is also innate in us even if sometimes the judgment of right and wrong could shift from society to society. Having the ability to discern right and wrong is our natural endowment, not socially conditioned or culturally constructed. Wang Fuzhi claims that the mind already contains myriad principles. As long as one cultivates one's moral sentiments and preserves them in one's mind, one would unerringly judge right from wrong. This is what he calls *Liangzhi*—the innate capacity to know right from wrong (Wang 1974a, 10:686). In other words, he thinks that the standard of right and wrong consists in the objective moral principle (*li* 禮), and our own moral judgments can match the objective standard if only we know how to look within the mind.

According to Wang Fuzhi, emotions are simply humans' natural responses to external things and objects, and on their own, they have no moral value. If unchecked, furthermore, they could lead to evil. He also makes a moral distinction between the motivational force of natural emotions and the motivational force of moral sentiments—Only conduct motivated by moral sentiments can be considered ethically justified. However, Wang Fuzhi thinks that emotions can serve as the motivational foundation for moral sentiments, because emotions have the strongest motivational force for human conduct: "The sentiments of commiseration, shame and disgust, reverence and deference, as well as the sense of right and wrong, are all subtle in their original state and their power is weak. *They must ride on natural emotions* such as joy, anger, sorrow and happiness and guide the latter's discharge, so that one can be inspired to employ one's natural capacities (*cai* 才) and accomplish much" (Wang 1974a, 10:676, emphasis added). In other words, in Wang Fuzhi's sentimentalism, moral sentiments are the morally justified moral motivation, but they nonetheless rely on the power of natural emotions to sustain causal efficacy. He does not advocate the elimination of human emotions in moral deliberation and moral motivation, because emotions do make moral contributions. The influence of emotions does not destroy the epistemic warranty of our moral judgments; on the contrary, emotions help to enlist energy in us to turn judgment into action.

Emotions are tied to desires on the level of one's biological existence. Just as emotions are "spontaneous and irrepressible," desires, once agitated, are also "what cannot be stopped" (Wang 1974b, 22). Unlike Zhang Zai and many other neo-Confucians who condemned human desires, Wang Fuzhi treats human desires as a natural and blameless part of our existence. His theory of moral motivation acknowledges what Michael Slote calls "self-concern"—"concern about one's own wellbeing" (Slote 2001, 77). To Wang Fuzhi, morality begins with the recognition of one's natural desires, and what it requires is simply an extension (*tui* 推) to the recognition of the desires of others.

We have seen in Chapter 7 that Wang Fuzhi has a fundamental affirmation of what is essential to human survival—our physical needs and material desires. According to him, the highest moral principle—heavenly principle—is simply manifested in humans' desire for food and sex: "Ultimately Heaven is not a separate realm divorced from humans, and ultimately [heavenly] principle is not a separate mandate detached from human desire" (Wang 1974a, 6:519). If a moral agent does not have personal desires for material goods, then she would not even be able to relate to others and feel empathy for others' material deprivation. The foundation for altruism lies in understanding that one is a biological and social being, sharing the same basic physical needs and material desires as others. Unlike Zhang Zai's considering the only "worthy desire" as the sage's desire "to be like Confucius," Wang Fuzhi acknowledges the value of ordinary material desires. Sages have material desires too, and because they are not self-centered, they can "empathize with others' desires on the basis of their own desires (*yi yu guan yu* 以欲觀欲)" (Wang 1974a, 4:246). Wang Fuzhi takes this view from Mencius, who advised the king that if he loved material possessions and sexual gratification, then he should just share his desires with the people (The *Mengzi*, 1B:5). Wang Fuzhi explains; "In sights, sounds, fragrance and tastes, *one sees the shared desires of everyone, and this is exactly the common principle of everything*" (Wang 1974a, 8:520, emphasis added). In this statement, he succinctly rejected the dichotomy of heavenly principle and human desire that had dominated the whole moral discourse in neo-Confucianism that came before him.[2] The difference between heavenly principle and human desire, according to him, lies in "the mere distinction between being fair and being selfish, between being sincere and being disingenuous" (Wang 1974a, 6:372). In other words, moral distinction lies not in the content, but in the scope, of one's recognition of desire. Wang Fuzhi does not condemn the content of one's material desire, and draws the only moral difference in one's attitude in respecting or acknowledging the entitlement of others' desires.

Natural emotions and the gratification of one's own desires have the immediate and most powerful motivational force. From motivation to *moral* motivation, however, the required step is to recognize others' claim to the gratification of their desires. If one's love for one's close ones would lead to the violation of the objective moral principle *Dao*, then the natural emotion in that particular instance is not morally permissible. If one's self-gratification interferes with, or even deprives others from, others' self-gratification, then such a pursuit of self-interest is not morally permissible. If one can no longer express one's natural

---

2 This affirmation of the moral worth of human desire would later become a major thesis in the moral philosophy of the Qing neo-Confucian Dai Zhen (1724–77), whose work we could not cover due to the scope of this book.

emotion or satisfy one's desire in a morally permissible way, then it is no longer *good* to follow one's natural emotion and desire. In this sense, we can say that natural emotion and desire for Wang Fuzhi are a form of "conditional good."[3] They must be regulated by an external, objective moral consideration, and according to Wang Fuzhi, they are good only insofar as the pursuit of them does not violate "the principle of fairness" (*gong* 公).

Wang Fuzhi claims, "Fairness lies in everyone's *getting a share of his own* ("*du de* 獨得")" (Wang 1967, 141, emphasis added). "When human desires are each gratified, it is the great equilibrium of heavenly principle; when heavenly principle achieves great equilibrium, there is no occasional divergence of human desires" (Wang 1974a, 4:248). In other words, the moral precept is not to denounce each individual's personal desires to aim for absolute altruism, but to allow everyone a fair share of the gratification of his or her desires. The empathy for others' desires and the willingness to share is the key to transforming one's natural emotions to the realization of one's moral sentiments. "A person of humanity (*ren* 仁) is simply one without *selfish* desires" (Wang 1974a, 6:441). To be free from selfishness, one simply needs to check one's own pursuit of happiness so that it does not obstruct others' pursuit of happiness. One also needs to balance one's self-concern with the concern for others' fair share of their wellbeing. This self-examination is what Wang Fuzhi calls "reflection" (*si* 思).

Wang Fuzhi regards reflection as human's innate faculty, and its target is the distinction between right and wrong as well as the consequences of benefit and harm (Wang 1974a, 4:266). Reflection is closely related to, but not identical with, the fourth inborn moral sentiment—the sense of right and wrong. One has the innate sense of right and wrong, which is endowed by heaven, but to utilize this natural moral sense, one needs to put in one's effort: "Humaneness and righteousness are one's nature—they are what Heaven accomplishes; reflection, on the other hand, is the function of the mind—it is what humans accomplish" (Wang 1974a, 10:700). Wang thus concludes: "When people commit evil deeds, it is only because they did not reflect (*busi* 不思)" (Wang 1974a, 4:268).

To Wang Fuzhi, moral virtue is not merely the noble character of the mind. Moral action is needed. He defines "virtue (*de* 德)" in terms of "what one

---

3 This term is derived from a Kantian notion of "unconditional good": "A thing is unconditionally good if it is good under any and all conditions, if it is good no matter what the context. In order to be unconditionally good, a thing must obviously carry its own value with it—have its goodness in itself (be an end in itself)" (Korsgaard 1996, 257).

obtains (*de* 得)⁴ in the mind after one has put into action" (Wang 1974a, 1:47). In this sense, one's virtue could be either good or bad, depending on what one practices in one's life, how one conducts oneself and what actions one has taken. He takes from Mencius's point to argue that to obtain moral virtue, one needs to enlarge one's circle of care, namely, to extend one's sense of empathy. Mencius (1A:6) argues that what made ancient people far surpass the rest is that they were good at extending (*tui* 推) their deeds. Wang Fuzhi interprets Mencius's notion of extension as follows: "To extend is to propagate (*kuo-chong* 擴充), and to propagate means to realize one's sentiment of *not bearing to see others suffer* in the actual practice of *not letting others suffer*" (Wang 1974a, 8:512; emphasis added). "To say that I respect the elders in my family and I care for the youth in my family is not just that I have the intent. I must really respect and care for them. When it comes to the elders and the youth in other people's families, how could I simply have the sense of sympathy [and no action]? *There must be the realization (shi* 實) *of my sentiments*" (Wang 1974a, 8:513; emphasis added). Realization of one's moral intent is thus the ultimate goal of Wang Fuzhi's moral teaching.

Based on Mencius's theory of moral sentiments, Wang Fuzhi proposes that moral motivation begins with the simple recognition of the self and the self's emotions and desires, aided by:

1) the sentiment of sympathy for those whose basic needs and rights are gravely deprived;
2) the sentiment of shame when one does not act upon what one's sentiments call for;
3) the sentiment of conformity to what others consider to be the proper (situationally appropriate) thing to do in the given context; and
4) the judgment of the right thing to do in that context.

However, Wang Fuzhi further develops the Mencian theory of moral sentiments into a theory of *complex sentiments*: these four sentiments are not independent of one another, and they must jointly form the morally justifiable motivational force. The sentiment of sympathy, for example, needs to be checked by the other three sentiments. As he puts it: "The sentiment of sympathy and the other three sentiments branch out the same way and should be employed interchangeably. How could one allow sympathy to pour out without

---

4 The Chinese word *de* for virtue is 德 while the word *de* for obtain is得. The two Chinese characters have the same sound, but different meanings. Wang Fuzhi is here playing on the phonetic similarity to connect the two words. Kam-por Yu suggests (in the review of this book),, "The use of the word *de* (得) to explain the word *de* (德) is very common, and has a very long history in Chinese literature. It can be found, among many others, in Wang Pi's commentary on Laozi, and Zhu Xi's commentary on *The Analects*. Actually, it is exactly the definition given in *Shuowen Jiezi* (說文解字). (悳者, 得也. 內得於己, 外得於人. "Virtue" means "gaining"—inwardly gaining oneself and outwardly gaining others.)" I am grateful to him for the amendment.

any restraints?" (Wang 1974a, 8:551). The agent's sympathy could be a purely subjective mental state—whether one feels for another depends on how much sensitivity one has as well as other contextual but ethically irrelevant factors, such as the geographic distance, the age and appearance of the sufferer. However, the other three sentiments—shame, deference to others and perception of right and wrong—bring in the agent's self-awareness and her awareness of normativity set by social practices. Wang Fuzhi's theory of moral sentiments is not an *atomistic* theory of emotions that focuses only on the individual's subjective sentiment of sympathy, but is a theory of complex sentiments that include one's awareness of, and respect for, social standards. It would thus not lead to a radically subjective theory of ethics.[5]

Both Zhang Zai and Wang Fuzhi stress the importance of "recognizing the reality of others," and for them, the possibility of morality lies in the recognition of the reality of others. But they suggested different modes of imagination: Zhang Zai asks the moral agent to imagine others' being related to oneself as one's siblings from the common source of life—Heaven and Earth. It is an agent-centered approach that aims to extend one's love for immediate family members to cultivate a sentiment of humanitarian care for all human beings. Wang Fuzhi does not ask the moral agent to abandon her first-person point of-view; he does not beseech the moral agent to elevate herself to the moral status of a sage who is motivated by his universal humanitarian care for all sentient beings. Since Wang Fuzhi was a great admirer of Zhang Zai, the two views are frequently conflated and their differences often overlooked. If we read Wang's commentary on Zhang's *Rectifying the Youth* (*Zhengmeng*), we can see that Wang does not completely embrace Zhang's worldview. In "Western Inscription," for example, where Zhang Zai wrote "Heaven [*Qian* 乾] as my father and Earth [*Kun* 坤] as my mother," Wang Fuzhi's commentary explains it in terms of one's biological parents instead of the abstract Heaven and Earth:

> To be more precise, then there is no so-called *Qian*—my father is the *Qian* that begot me; there is no so-called *Kun*—my mother is the *Kun* that completed my life.... *If one tries to abandon one's parents in order to serve Heaven and Earth as parents, then even if one could expand one's heart to aim for it, there must be some hidden irrepressible sorrow.*
> (*Wang 1967, 265–6; emphasis added*)

---

5 In Marcia Lind's defense of Hume's moral sentimentalism, she argues that Hume's theory of moral sentiment should be considered a complex theory, rather than an atomistic theory, of sentiment. Lind claims, "I argue that emotion in Hume can be analyzed as a complex.... I then apply this particular idea of emotion as a complex to *moral* emotion in Hume and show that this analysis allows Hume to avoid at least the standard objection that he is committed to a radically subjective moral theory." (Lind 1990, 133; italics in original.) Here we are applying the same interpretation and argument to Wang Fuzhi's theory of moral sentiment.

This quote shows that Wang Fuzhi places individuals first and foremost in their biological families. He asks the moral agent to imagine others as being similar to herself, having similar needs and desires as she does. It is also an agent-centered approach, which asks the moral agent to extend her self-concern to the adoption of *fair consideration for others.*

Both Zhang Zai and Wang Fuzhi combine belief/reason and desire/emotion as the motivation. Zhang Zai's theory acknowledges the motivational force of emotion and desire, but employs reason as the guiding principle of emotion and desire. It is a version of the ideal personhood theory, setting up sagehood as the ideal personality. Wang Fuzhi's theory treats emotion and desire as the primary motivation for action, and advocates the balancing of one's self-concern and one's others-concern to achieve fairness (*gong* 公). The sense of fairness is rooted in reason's function of reflection (*si* 思). Hence, his theory of moral motivation is a form of sentimentalist theory with reason serving as the ultimate monitor for action. We might express the difference between the two moral motivation theories as building motivation either on *reason-based desire* (Zhang Zai) or on *desire-based reason* (Wang Fuzhi). Both reason and emotion-prompted desire are needed for the motivational force for moral behavior.

The final section of this chapter will sketch a moral motivation theory largely based on Wang Fuzhi's ideas, but expand on them to construct a moral theory that is empirically responsible and supported by contemporary psychological findings. We shall call it *social sentimentalism* in that this theory emphasizes the motivational force of sentiments, and stresses the social affectivity especially in the sentiment of shame and disgust, as well as in the sentiment of reverence and deference.

Enlarging Our Circles of Concern—Expanding on Wang Fuzhi' Social Sentimentalism

Neo-Confucians all aimed to enlarge our circles of concern for others, and the moral image they present typically involves the grand vision of "being one family under heaven" (Zhang Zai), "feeling the pain and suffering of everyone in the world" (Cheng Hao), "being one with the myriad things" (Wang Yangming). We have seen how they proposed various means to making this psychological state possible for individual moral agents: we have been urged to study and learn from the sages, to cultivate robust virtues, to maintain reverence in the heart, or to perform rigorous self-monitoring and self-rectification, and so on. Wang Fuzhi's moral program, on the other hand, begins with commonsense psychology and acknowledges ordinary people's natural emotions and mundane desires.

From empirical studies of human psychology (Hoffman 1981; Darley and Latané 1968; Latané and Rodin 1969), we learn that genuine altruistic behavior is most often a spontaneous reaction to either others' present suffering or their impending harm. These empirical studies of altruism are based on the criterion that an altruistic behavior "is behavior that promotes the welfare of others without conscious regard for one's own self-interests" (Hoffman 1981, 124). Martin Hoffman cites others' (Darley and Latané 1968; Latané and Rodin 1969) as well as his own experiments to show that people usually do not think much before lending a helping hand to another in distress. He says, "When I asked people what went through their minds when they helped someone in a real-life situation, the typical response was that they acted without thinking or because the other person obviously needed help" (Hoffman 1981, 134). Such spontaneity is a manifestation of sentiments such as sympathy or empathy. Hoffman cites many empirical studies that demonstrate people's natural empathic arousal upon observing another person in distress. He concludes:

> The findings in these studies, taken as a group, suggest that (a) empathic arousal precedes helping, (b) the more intense the pain cues from the victim, the more intense the observer's empathic arousal, and (c) intensity of empathic arousal is systematically related to subsequent behavior.
> *(Hoffman 1981, 131)*

Such empirical data shows that many, if not most, altruistic acts are prompted by empathetic sentiments. Prudential self-interest or egoistic reasoning about long-term benefits is not necessarily the foundation for altruism.

However, it is important to emphasize that the sentiment of sympathy or the sense of commiseration cannot work alone. Sympathy may be a necessary condition for spontaneous altruism (if I don't even care about other people's suffering, then I would not be motivated to assist in the first place), but it does not have sufficient causal efficacy. Take for example the calamity of the devastating earthquake and tsunami in Japan in 2011. Sympathy for those who lost their lives, family members, houses, belongings, and so on, must be a common sentiment among those who have watched the news coverage, and yet the act of donating to charity organizations is not as prevalent as the sentiment felt. How people can move from feeling sympathetic to taking the action to lend a helping hand is what social sentimentalism aims to investigate.

In a nutshell, social sentimentalism does not place motivational force on the moral sentiment of sympathy alone; rather, it advocates the combined force of the four sentiments proposed by Mencius and further developed by Wang Fuzhi. What social sentimentalism emphasizes is that the seven emotions and the four moral sentiments are to be treated as a "complex," because they jointly constitute the motivational foundation for one's moral behavior. For example, the natural emotions of anger and resentment are closely connected to the moral sentiment of shame and disgust. If one can combine these emotions/sentiments with the sense of right and wrong, and to be morally repulsed by any wrongdoing judged by one's own moral sense, then one would at least be inclined to refrain from doing it. The four sentiments include not just one's own sentiment of sympathy and one's own perception of the moral good, but also one's respect for, and one's desire to conform to, interpersonal practices in one's society, and the sense of shame one incurs from failure to perform what one considers to be socially acceptable. These four moral sentiments thus form the basis of our conforming to common ethical norms in our society. Social sentimentalism is informed by social psychologists' observation that an individual's moral behavior can be heightened or inhibited by relevant socioethical practices in apt social contexts.[6] In other words, social sentimentalism is not an individualistic, but a socioethical, program. Here are some suggestions, inspired by Wang Fuzhi's sentimentalist theory of moral motivation, on how to build a moral world.

First, to build on the sense of commiseration, we need to enhance sympathy with empathetic imagination. By common usage, "sympathy" is the compassion for another's suffering from one's vantage point, while "empathy" is putting oneself in the circumstances of the other and employing a vivid imagination of the other's suffering. Empathy requires the ability of imagination. As Adam Smith points out: "As we have no immediate experience of what other men feel, we can form no idea of the manner in which they are affected, but by conceiving what we ourselves should feel in the like situation." Our senses cannot give us direct access to others' feelings, and "it is by the imagination only that we can form any conception of what are his sensations" (Smith 2002, 11). Empathetic imagination carries more motivational force for altruism than mere sympathy does.

To enhance empathetic imagination, we need to locate the basis for a vivid imagination of others' sorrows and concerns, and family love is one of the natural passions to which we can easily relate. The empathetic imagination derived from Wang Fuzhi's theory is built on one's relatedness to one's family members and one's passion of family love. According to Gilles Deleuze, family is a natural unit of care in the state of nature: "What we find in nature, without exception, are families; the state of nature is always already more than a simple state of nature. The family, independently of all legislation, is explained by the sexual instinct and by sympathy—sympathy between parents, and sympathy of parents for their offspring" (Deleuze 2001, 39). If the basic structure in the state of nature is family relationship, then the individual's consideration from his point of view *as a member of his own family* is a natural human tendency. The function of empathetic imagination must be associated with the personal standpoint in the multi-relations of family. The next step is to extend (*tui* 推) one's feelings for one's own family to cultivate one's concern for strangers.

---

6 Examples of some social psychological experiments will be given below.

To achieve this empathetic extension, it is not required in Wang Fuzhi-inspired social sentimentalism that one love others' parents or children *as if they were one's own*, but that one imagine how others would feel if their own parents or children were in harm's way. One's considerations for strangers are not just extended from any one individual to another, but from *one-individual-situated-in-one's-family-relations* to *another-individual-situated-in-his-or-her-family-relations*. If one has sincere and deep feelings toward one's own parents, siblings and children, then one would be able to relate to these strangers not as mere strangers, but rather as *someone else's parents, someone else's siblings* or *someone else's children*. A common practice in the media can be seen as an employment of this empathetic extension. News coverage of disasters often chooses the angle of interviewing family members to talk about their loss. Implicit in this method of reportage is the assumption that family passions are sharable and relatable. If we want to enhance altruism in our society and thereby to foster an altruistic culture, then we could encourage the reportage of major calamity using family stories and personal anecdotes. When distant victims are no longer faceless strangers or sheer numbers, but the lost loved ones of someone whom we see or hear, we will be more readily moved to donate to disaster relief agencies. It may be a simple practice, but it has been proven to be effective time and time again.

Second, the sentiment of shame and disgust is a powerful tool in societal regulation and behavioral modification. Jennifer Jacquet *et al.* (2011) points out that the sentiment of shame can boost social cooperation. In a series of experiments, they demonstrate that the participants' expectation of negative (in the case of shame) or positive (in the case of honor) reputation would enforce their pro-social behavior in consideration of public goods. They hypothesized that shame might even be "more effective than honor" because the participants "would particularly seek to avoid negative exposure, and therefore contribute more to the public good" (Jacquet *et al.* 2011, 900). The experimental findings led them to conclude that "a promise to single out free-riding individuals for pubic scrutiny can lead to greater cooperation from the whole group" (Jacquet *et al.* 2011, 900). They ended with a promising note: Using the fear of being shamed as well as the sense of honor "might even help transform a crowd into a community" (Jacquet *et al.* 2011, 901).

The individual's sentiment of shame has to be matched with the sentiment of moral disgust from others. From the sentimentalist point of view, the worst enemy of a moral society is *apathy*. To build on the power of social sanction based on shame and disgust, we need to propagate the thinking that not offering a helping hand when someone is in distress is a shameful act. The murder of Kitty Genovese in 1964 sparked a series of psychological articles on the bystander apathy phenomenon. Genovese was assaulted right in front of her home. She screamed for help but no one came to her aid or called the police. The assailant came back to the scene ten minutes later and found her still lying on the ground. He stabbed her several times more. In total, 38 neighbors witnessed the attack from behind their curtains, but only one of them eventually phoned the police.[7] It was too late for Kitty Genovese. Two social psychologists John M. Darley and Bibb Latané set out to investigate why the witnesses demonstrated "such apparently conscienceless and inhumane lack of intervention" (Darley and Latané 1968, 377). Darley and Latané's hypothesis was that the more bystanders there are to an emergency situation, the less likely any one bystander will intervene to provide aid. Their experiments showed that when the subject thought she was the only witness, she was more likely to take action to assist (85% assisted when they thought they were the only bystanders in contrast to only 31% of the subjects assisted when they thought others were also witnessing the same distress) (Darley and Latané 1968). Latané and Rodin further show that "the presence of an unresponsive bystander strongly inhibited subjects from offering to help" (Latané and Rodin 1969, 194). However, an interesting discovery Darley and Latané made was that the subjects were in an emotionally conflicted state even when they did not respond to the call of distress: "subjects worried about the guilt and shame they would feel if they did not help the person in distress" (Darley and Latané 1968, 382). Darley and Latané conclude that bystanders' unresponsiveness is not necessarily a reflection of apathy or other personality deficiency (Darley and Latané 1968, 383). The bystanders were actually sympathetic toward the person in distress, but they were simply not motivated to take the appropriate action to assist or even to call for help. This observation would support the Mencian thesis that sympathy is a natural human reaction to others in distress, but it also supports Deleuze' conjecture that sympathy alone is *impotent.*

To have a moral world build on our innate sentiment of shame and disgust, we need to "shift the baselines" (J. Jacquet) for the social standard of acceptable or shameful acts. The factor of social inhibition of intervention may be a manifestation of a culture that emphasizes "minding one's own business" and "not meddling with others' affairs." Our social critique of apathetic bystanders is one of the ways to foster a more altruistic society. We need to continue our social examination of apathetic mindset and amoral inaction, and develop this sense of disgust and indignation into our social conscience. To cultivate a moral world, we need to first instill a different social attitude about human relationships and interpersonal interactions: One is *prima facie* morally obligated to assist those in distress when (i) one is able to, and (ii) there are no other overriding *morally significant* considerations. Once this normative moral principle is ingrained into the social conscience, failure to comply would generate the sense of shame from the agent and the sense of disgust from others. These sentiments would motivate the agent to do the right thing.

---

7 This report is based on the standard textbook description but it has been challenged in recent years.

One may question whether a moral program built on the sentiment of shame would be relying too much on social sanction and peer pressure. According to the Mencian sentimentalist developed by Wang Fuzhi, however, the sentiment of shame itself is not socially conditioned, but an innate disposition that we all have. According to Wang Fuzhi, "Everyone has this heart of not wanting to cut through a hole to rob someone else's house (*chuanyu zhixin* 穿窬之心)" (Wang 1974a, 10:752). "Not wanting to cut through a hole to rob someone else's house is based on the sentiment of shame…. However, even though shame is merely a sentiment within oneself, if one acts on it [to refrain from robbery] then righteousness (*yi* 義) is already present" (Wang 1974a, 10:751). In other words, what counts in one's moral behavior is *doing the right thing*, and the sentiment of shame is directly responsible for our refraining from doing the wrong thing. This sentiment is inherent in us; without it, no social pressure could have brought it on in us. We are ashamed of what we did or are about to do, not *merely* because the outside world would look upon us with contempt or disgust. We simply could not live with ourselves if we had acted that way. The sentiment of shame could be said to be the internal barricade for our own moral conduct. It sets the psychological boundary for what one would deem morally acceptable or morally outrageous in one's own conduct. It can be seen as one's *moral compass*, without which one could not be an autonomous moral agent, being guided by one's own moral sense.

Third and related suggestion is that based on our innate sentiment of reverence and deference, we can modify an individual's moral expectations of herself as well as her view of justified behavior through altering societal normativity. Both Darley and Latané 1968 and Latané and Rodin 1969 show how, when viewing someone in distress, each bystander may look to others for guidance before acting. In their experiments, other bystanders' unresponsiveness often influenced the tested subject to take no action. However, even though the presence of other bystanders inhibits intervention, the presence of observers or evaluators with an altruistic bent would have a different effect. They call this factor the "social influence" process. These studies prove that we do have the tendency to defer to others in judging what would be the appropriate action in a given situation. When others do not intervene to assist those in distress, we are more likely not to lend a helping hand. As social psychologist Ruben Orive concludes, "the likelihood of action in the similar group appears to depend not only on the intensity level of the prevailing opinion, but also on action cues that similar others provide. These external cues may act as either facilitating or restraining forces, depending on the situational inclinations of the group" (Orive 1984, 736). What is needed for a proper social influence process that enhances altruism, therefore, is a social practice that treats assisting others in need as a *norm* rather than an *exception*.

The Confucian methodology of instituting societal rules of propriety, rites and rituals, and so on, is built on humans' innate sentiment of reverence and deference. This social sentimentalism differs from other sentimentalist theories of moral motivation in that it places a strong emphasis on social sentiments and social contexts that are embodied in cultural practices and ritual propriety. According to Wang Fuzhi, we should "regulate affairs with righteousness (*yi* 義), and regulate the mind with rites and rules of propriety (*li* 禮)" (Wang 1974a, 10:754). The sentiment of reverence and deference conjoins the spheres of the public and the private. From having reverence for what others do in a given social context, one is acclimated to be in tune with social sentiments and to develop compliance with social practices. The individual's moral sentiment of reverence can thus be viewed as the psychological basis for humans' social cooperation and civil compliance. To build on our innate sense of reverence and deference, we thus need to promote the right kind of social practices and moral attitudes. Cultural practices and ethical normativity can come together, and when they do (*and only when they do*), it is good that individuals comply with social practices and conform to established norms. To construct a moral world with altruism as a social norm, we need to find the kind of social institutions and ritual propriety that would work in our society to reduce human alienation and reinforce individuals' willingness to render aid to those in distress.

Finally, with the individual's sense of right and wrong, we need to find a balance between conformity and independent thinking. Conformity to social practices and ritual propriety is not always good, as one could become lost in the herd. Hagop Sarkissian points out this dilemma: "Without participating in social rituals and conventions, a human being cannot even begin to learn virtuous conduct, yet the 'ritualistic' aspect of propriety can desensitize or blind the virtuous agent to the need for particularized response" (Sarkissian 2010, 7). The Asch Experiment (Asch 1955, 1956) famously shows that peer pressure to conform could often influence an individual's judgment. The tested subject (Asch calls it "the minority of one") was placed among a group of strangers who unanimously gave the wrong answer on a simple fact of perception. Even though the subjects initially gave the right answer, a high percentage of them (37 out of 50 in one such study) compromised and yielded to the wrong answer unanimously voiced by the majority. Asch writes,

> [The] yielding subjects ... endowed the majority with a quality of rightness or authority that went beyond the immediate question at issue, granting it a general and undefined superiority that was capable of overriding their convictions about their own rightness in the specific case.
> *(Asch 1956, 50)*

Festingei *et al.* (1952) and others (Orive 1984; Prentice-Dunn, S. and Rogers, R. W. 1980) depict the loss of sense of individuality and critical thinking as "the deindividuation effects." The deindividuation effects are sometimes needed for socialization and group assimilation, but it could lead to the loss of critical thinking and self-confidence in one's opinion as in the case of Asch's experiments. This shows that conformity to peer pressure and social norms could also destroy individuality. Therefore, the separation of public thinking and individual thinking is needed. It is important to conform to social norms only when they are good norms rather than just blindly following whatever others in the society do. One needs to have one's own moral judgment. The individual's own moral sense and moral judgment play an important role in weighing whether the communal sentiments are worth respecting. In Asch's series of experiments, there were a significant number of individuals who remained independent thinkers, and they held onto their correct answer even when they were faced with the majority's unanimous opposing view. According to Asch, "The most significant fact about them was not absence of responsiveness to the majority but *a capacity to recover from doubt and to reestablish their equilibrium*" (Asch 1955/1972, 7; emphasis added). To cultivate this capacity of self-reliance in the case of judging right and wrong, we need to strengthen the individual's "reflection" (*si* 思).

Mencius (Mencius 11:15) suggests that reflection is the faculty of the mind, and it is the employment of this faculty that distinguishes a person of grandeur (*daren* 大人) from the ordinary petty people (*xiaoren* 小人). Based on Mencius's view, Wang Fuzhi further stresses the importance of reflection. According to him, reflection is the only thing that separates humans from other animals (Wang 1974a, 705). He defines the function of reflection as the metaphysical contemplation on humaneness (*ren*) and righteousness (*yi*). It is only when one thinks about humaneness and righteousness is one employing one's faculty of reflection; thinking about material desires, on the other hand, is not "reflection" (Wang 1974a, 702). Wang Fuzhi distinguishes *reflection* from *cognition*, which is related to perceptual knowledge gained through our senses. He thinks that the objects of reflection are not perceivable things. What one reflects on, according to him, is simply the metaphysical *Dao* (*xingershang zhi dao* 形而上之道) (Wang 1974a, 701). Therefore, the faculty of reflection enables individuals to confirm the objectively right standard for judgment. The distinction of right and wrong ultimately rests on a universal, objective normative principle: *Dao*. It is not determined by social conventions or societal norms alone. Individuals must employ their faculty of reflection to discern whether or not the social practice is one that conforms to *Dao*, and one with which they ought to comply.

The importance of individual's reflection in the contemporary world can be further explicated by Owen Flanagan's analysis:

> Reflection is good in two respects: First, it can help ultraliberals to understand themselves in less atomic terms and thereby to see the grounds on the basis of which they incur communal obligations. Second, reflectiveness is good because it provides one with the critical tools needed to assess the content of one's life form so that one can judge the *ethical* basis for such communal obligations.
>
> *(Flanagan and Rorty 1990, 62, italics in original)*

With the individual's rational reflection on her moral sentiments, she is not likely to blindly succumb to communal pressure, or to do simply *what the Romans do*. As Flanagan points out, "Having communitarian sentiments is good if one's community is good, but it is obviously not good if one's community has bad values, values that one is motivated to sustain and maintain because of these sentiments. This is where the second, content-sensitive aspect of reflectiveness becomes important" (Flanagan and Rorty 1990, 62–3).

Another way to avoid blind conformity is to integrate Wang Fuzhi's emphasis on individual reflection with Zhang Zai's teaching on the importance of learning from the sage. In Zhang Zai's usage, the sage is to be seen as the ideal personality, who stands for the expositor as well as the regulator for objective universal moral principles. Zhang Zai beseeches us to learn from the sages by studying the books they wrote (he singled out the *Analects* and the *Mengzi* in particular). He thinks if someone does not study but simply employs his own intelligence to assume superiority to others, then that person is actually an idiot (*chi* 癡) (Zhang 2006, 272). "Books help us maintain our heart-mind (*xin* 心). As soon as we put down the books, we interrupt the cultivation of our virtue" (Zhang 2006, 275). To Zhang Zai, studying keeps our mind on the right path and is an essential component in our moral cultivation. Confucius emphasizes the importance of integrating studying and reflection: "One who learns without reflecting is lost; one who thinks without learning is in a perilous state" (the *Analects* 2:15). Wang Fuzhi elaborates on this claim:

> When we learn from the ancient, we see that the law and rules are already set. We thus consider them in our own mind: are the reasons for these rules completely expounded or do they need further investigation? … When we exert our mind to speculate on the principle, we also need to verify it against what the ancient people have taught and inquire whether its *dao* can be appealed to as the norm or whether it still needs amendments.
>
> *(Wang 1996, 7:301)*

Both learning from the sage and reflecting on the universal moral principle (*Dao*) constitute our moral reason. In this way, we see how moral reason supplements what our moral sentiments can accomplish: it reestablishes our individuality and independent thinking in our tendency to be socially converted.

To recap this final section: this chapter argues for a socioethical motivational theory for morality. The socioethical aspect of the moral theory is built on the complex of our four inborn moral sentiments taken together. Sympathy or empathy has been singled out by psychologists such as Hoffman as the key sentiment for moral motivation. However, sympathy alone cannot be sufficient for morality, because it is often defeated by other moral failings such as procrastination, inertia, laziness, and so on. Shame and disgust alone cannot be sufficient for morality either, since it could be accompanied by total apathy for others' suffering. Both of them need the supplement of the moral judgment that a total self-concern to the neglect of others' misery is *wrong*, and hence one can be motivated by the sense of shame to act on the sentiment of sympathy for others. Finally, in a social environment in which altruistic acts are the norm of its members' conduct, every capable member may be propelled by their sentiment of reverence and deference to adopt the same behavior that others have. The four moral sentiments form the foundation for our becoming socially as well as ethically cultivated. The mental "complex" of these four moral sentiments extends one's love for family members into a humanitarian concern. In addition, we also need to stress the importance of the individual's reflection and learning, so that his or her moral judgment does not become blind conformity to the social norm or a desensitized response in accordance with the norm.

When others are suffering, I may be moved by the sentiment of sympathy to desire the alleviation of their suffering, but such a sentiment is transient, forgettable, and consequently is often causally impotent. However, if I am situated in the society where others like me all took the action to alleviate the suffering of strangers, then I would be further propelled by my sense of shame, my desire to do the right thing, and my reverence for what is considered "proper" in my social context, to take the action. Failing to live up to one's social standards can bring up the sense of shame or disgust, and to avoid shame, embarrassment or others' contempt, one is likely to follow social norms. If altruism is a social norm, then altruistic acts will become much more prevalent than when it is not. In other words, the realization of altruism cannot be founded solely on the individual's moral sense, but must also rely on the society's moral expectations. If an individual feels *morally bound* to be altruistic, then this individual's initial sentiment of sympathy receives the further enhancement that is needed to generate altruistic acts. Private sentiment of sympathy alone does not suffice to bring out altruistic acts; what is further required is a *moral world* in which altruism is the norm rather than the exception.

Conclusion

Other neo-Confucian ethical theories have focused on the individual moral agent's moral reason, moral personality, moral character, moral volition, moral virtues, or moral intuition; in general, they focus on her ability for moral *self*-cultivation. What this chapter has suggested is that moral cultivation demands not just the individual's own effort, but also the appropriate moral culture and social context. In Wang Fuzhi's theory of moral virtue, virtue is empty without realizability, and the realization of moral virtue requires a moral culture. His emphasis on the joint functions of all four moral sentiments pushes us to see that we need to go beyond the moral agent's isolated moral conscience or moral sentiments to establish a socioethical environment, in which the individual is more likely to be influenced to take the right action. The individual conscience has to be enlarged into the society's culture, such that moral achievement is no longer considered *supererogatory*—acts that are "nice" but not morally required. When morality is integrated as a shared moral conscience in the social culture, it is no longer an idealistic feat that only the saints or sages could accomplish. We have often seen that members of particular social groups or religious organizations perform altruistic acts with fewer mental struggles, and this shows how others act in the group can affect how individuals act. Social culture is affective, and we thus need to construct a moral world in our society based on our shared inborn moral sentiments. Wang Fuzhi's social sentimentalism has supplied us with ideas of how such a moral world could be built.

Primary Sources

Wang Fuzhi 王夫之 1967. *Commentary on Zhang Zai's "Rectifying the Youth"* 張子正蒙注, 1685–1690. Taipei, Taiwan: Shijie shuju.

———. 1974a. *Discourse on Reading the Great Collection of Commentaries on the Four Books* 讀四書大全說, 1665. Taipei, Taiwan: Heluo tushu chubanshe.

———. 1974b. *Extensive Commentary on the Book of Odes* 詩廣傳, 1683. Taipei, Taiwan: Heluo tushu chubanshe.

———. 1977a (1673–1677). *A Textual Annotation on the Book of Rites* 禮記章句. Taipei: Guangwen shuju.

———. 1977b (1655). *Supplementary Commentary on the Book of Changes* 周易外傳 Taipei: Heluo tushu chubanshe.

———. 1980 (1685). *Textual Commentary on the Book of Changes* 周易內傳. Collected in *Chuanshan's Commentary to the Book of Changes* 船山易傳. Taipei: Xiaxueshe.

———. 1996. *A Contemporary Interpretation of the Meaning of the Four Books* (*Sishu xunyi* 四書訓義), 1679. Reprinted in *The Complete Books of Chuanshan* (*Chuanshan quanshu*). China: Yuelu shushe, Vols. 7–8.

Selection in English

Chan, Wing-tsit (ed.) 1963. *A Sourcebook in Chinese Philosophy*. Princeton University Press. Chapter 36.

References

Adler, Joseph A. 2008. "Zhu Xi's Spiritual Practices as the Basis of His Central Philosophical Concepts." *Dao: A Journal of Comparative Philosophy* 7(1): 57–79.

—— 1981. "Descriptive and Normative Principle (li) in Confucian Moral Metaphysics: Is/ought from the Chinese Perspective." *Zygon* 16(3): 285–93.

Angle, Stephen and Slote, Michael (eds.) 2013. *Virtue Ethics and Confucianism*. New York: Routledge.

Angle, Stephen C. 2011. "A Productive Dialogue: Contemporary Moral Education and Zhu Xi's Neo-Confucian Ethics." *Journal of Chinese Philosophy* 38: 183–203.

—— 2010. "Wang Yangming as a Virtue Ethicist." In John Makeham (ed.), *Dao Companion to Neo-Confucian Philosophy*. Dordrecht Heidelberg London New York: Springer, 315–35.

—— 2009. *Sagehood: The Contemporary Significance of Neo-Confucian Philosophy*. New York: Oxford University Press.

—— 1998. "The Possibility of Sagehood: Reverence and Ethical Perfection in Zhu Xi's Thought." *Journal of Chinese Philosophy* 25(3): 281–303.

Armstrong, David 2004. "What Is Consciousness?" In John Heil (ed.), *Philosophy of Mind*. New York: Oxford University Press, 607–16.

Arpaly, Nomy 2005. "Comments on *Lack of Character* by John Doris." *Philosophy and Phenomenological Research* Vol. LXXI, No. 3: 643–47.

Asch, Solomon 1956. "Studies of Independence and Conformity: A Minority of One Against a Unanimous Majority." *Psychological Monographs: General and Applied* 70(9): 1–70.

—— 1955/1972. "Opinions and Social Pressure." *Scientific American* 193: 31–35. Reprinted in Richard A. Condon & Burton O. Kurth (eds.), *Writing from Experience*. North Stratford, NH: Ayer Publishing, 1972, 3–11.

Ayala, Francisco J. 2010. "The Difference of Being Human: Morality." *PNAS* 107(2): 9015–22.
Bai, Tongdong 白彤東 2008. "An Ontological Interpretation of 'You' (Something) and 'Wu' (Nothing) in the Laozi." *Journal of Chinese Philosophy* 35(2): 339–51.
Behuniak Jr., James 2009. "Li in East Asian Buddhism: One Approach from Plato's Parmenides." *Asian Philosophy* 19(1): 31–49.
Blasi, Augusto 2005. "Moral Character: A Psychological Approach." In D. K. Lapsley & F. C. Power (eds.), *Character Psychology and Character Education*. Notre Dame, IN: University of Notre Dame Press, 67–100.
——— 1999. "Emotions and Moral Motivation." *Journal for the Theory of Social Behavior* 29(1): 1–19.
——— 1984. "Moral Identity: Its Role in Moral Functioning." In W. M. Kurtines & J. J. Gewirtz (eds.), *Morality, Moral Behavior and Moral Development*. New York: Wiley, 128–39.
——— 1983. "Moral Cognition and Moral Action: A Theoretical Perspective." *Developmental Review* 3: 178–210.
Brink, David O. 1997. "Moral Motivation." *Ethics* 108(1): 4–32.
——— 1989. *Moral Realism and the Foundations of Ethics*. New York: Cambridge University Press.
Chan, Wing-cheuk 2011. "Mou Zongsan and Tang Junyi on Zhang Zai's and Wang Fuzhi's Philosophies of Qi: A Critical Reflection." *Dao: A Journal of Comparative Philosophy* 10(1): 85–98.
——— 2000. "Leibniz and the Chinese Philosophy of Nature." *Studia Leibnitianna*, Supplementa 33: 210–23.
Chan, Wing-tsit 陳榮捷 1990. *Zhu Xi* 朱熹. Taipei, Taiwan: Dongda tushu gongsi.
——— 1964. "The Evolution of the Neo-Confucian Concept of Li as Principle (lide sixiang zhi jinhua)." *Tsing Hua Journal of Chinese Studies* 4(2): 123–49.
Chan, Wing-tsit 1978. "Patterns for Neo-Confucianism: Why Chu Hsia differed from Ch'eng I." *Journal of Chinese Philosophy* 5(2): 101–126.
——— (trans.) 1967. *Reflections on Things At Hand: The Neo-Confucian Anthology*. New York: Columbia University Press.
——— (ed.) 1963. *A Sourcebook in Chinese Philosophy*. Princeton University Press.
Chang, Carsun (a.k.a Zhang, Junmai 張君勱) 1962. *The Development of Neo-Confucian Thought*. Volume II. New York: Bookman Associates.
——— 1957/1963. *The Development of Neo-Confucian Thought*. Volume I. New York: Bookman Associates.
Chen, Lai 陳來 2005. *Song-Ming Neo-Confucianism* 宋明理學. Shanghai: East China Normal University Press. 2nd edition.
——— 2004. *Interpretation and Reconstruction: The Philosophical Spirit of Wang Chuanshan* 詮釋與重建—王船山的哲學精神. Beijing: Beijing daxue chubanshe.
——— 1991. *The Realm Between Something and Nothing: The Spirit of Wang Yangming's Philosophy (youwu zhijing* 有無之境). Beijing, China: Renmin Chubanshe.

Chen, Yufu 陳郁夫 1990. *Zhou Dunyi* 周敦頤. Taipei: Dongda tushu gongsi.
Chen, Yun 陳贇 2002. *Return to Authentic Being: A Study of Wang Chuanshan's Philosophy* 回歸真實的存在—王船山哲學的闡釋. Shanghai: Fudan daxue chubanshe.
Cheng, Chung-Ying 成中英 2002. "Ultimate Origin, Ultimate Reality, and the Human Condition: Leibniz, Whitehead, and Zhu Xi." *Journal of Chinese Philosophy* 29(1): 93–118.
—— 1979. "Categories of Creativity in Whitehead and Neo-Confucianism." *Journal of Chinese Philosophy* 6: 251–74.
Chengs, Hao and Yi 1981. *Collected Works of the Two Cheng Brothers* (*Erchengji*). Four volumes. Beijing: Zhonghua Shuju Chubanshe.
Cheng, Yishan 程宜山 1986. *The Chinese Ancient Yuanqi Theory* 中國古代元氣學說. China: Wubei Renmin Chubanshe.
Ching, Julia 秦家懿 1987. *Wang Yangming* 王陽明. Taipei, Taiwan: Dongda tushu gongsi.
Ching, Julia 1974. "The Goose Lake Monastery debate (1175)." *Journal of Chinese Philosophy* 1(2): 161–78.
Colby, Anne and Damon, William 1995. "The Development of Extraordinary Moral Commitment." In Melanie Killen & Daniel Hart (eds.), *Morality in Everyday Life: Developmental Perspectives* (Cambridge Studies in Social and Emotional Development). New York: Cambridge University Press, 342–70.
Dai, Jingxian 戴景賢 1981. "Zhou Dunyi's Taijin Diagram Explained (zhoulianxi zhi taijitu shuo)." In *Collected Studies on Yijing* (*yijing yanjiu lunji*), Taipei: Liming Wenhua Chubanshe. Reprinted in Shouqi Huang & Shanwen Zhang (eds.), *Collected Essays on Zhouyi Studies* (Zhouyi yanjiu lunwenji), Volume 3, 202–19, 1988.
Darley, John M., & Latané, Bibb 1968. "Bystander Intervention in Emergencies: Diffusion of Responsibility." *Journal of Personality and Social Psychology*, Vol. 8, Pt.1:377–383.
Darwin, Charles 1871. *The Descent of Man, and Selection in Relation to Sex*. New York: D. Appleton and Company.
Davidson, Philip and Youniss, James 1991. "Which Comes First, Morality or Identity?" In William Kurtines & Jacob L. Gewirtz (eds.), *Handbook of Moral Development and Behavior*. Volume 1. Hillsdale, NJ: Lawrence Erlbaum, 105–21.
De Bary, William Theodore and Bloom, Irene (eds.) 1999. *Sources of Chinese Tradition*. second edition. Volume I. *From Earliest Times to 1600*. New York: Columbia University Press.
De Bary, William Theodore and Lufrano, Richard John (eds.) 2001. Sources of Chinese Tradition, second edition. Volume II. *From 1600 Through the Twentieth Century*. New York: Columbia University Press.
De Sousa, Ronald 2014. "Emotion." In Edward N. Zalta (ed.), *The Stanford Encyclopedia of Philosophy* (Spring 2014 Edition), http://plato.stanford.edu/archives/spr2014/entries/emotion/

De Waal, Frans 2010. *The Age of Empathy: Nature's Lessons for a Kinder Society*. New York: Three Rivers Press.

Deleuze, Gilles 2001. In Constantin V. Boundas (trans.), *Empiricism and Subjectivity*. New York: Columbia University Press.

Deonna, Julien A. and Teroni, Fabrice 2012. *The Emotions: A Philosophical Introduction*. London and New York: Routledge.

Descartes, René 1644/2004. *Principles of Philosophy*. Whitefish, MT: Kessinger Publishing, LLC.

Ding, Weixiang 丁為祥 2002. "Three Ways to Understand Zhang Zai's Notion of the Great Vacuity 張載太虛三解." *Journal of Confucian Studies (Kongzi yanjiu)* 6: 44–53.

—— 2001. "Interpretation of Zhang Zai's View of Vacuity and Qi (Zhang Zai xuqiguan jiedu)". *Journal of the History of Chinese Philosophy (Zhongguo zhexueshi)* 2: 46–54. Reprinted on (http://www.lw23.com/paper_70746691/).

—— 2000. *Xu and Qi: Zhang Zai's Philosophical System and Its Evaluation* 虛氣相即: 張載哲學體系及其定位. Beijing: Renmin chubanshe.

Doris, John M. 2002. *Lack of Character: Personality and Moral Behavior*. New York: Cambridge University Press.

Downes, Stephen M. 2008. "Evolutionary Psychology." In *Stanford Encyclopedia of Philosophy*, http://plato.stanford.edu/entries/evolutionary-psychology/.

Dweck, Carol S. and Leggett, Ellen L. 1988. "A Social-Cognitive Approach to Motivation and Personality." *Psychological Review* 95(2): 256–73.

Ericsson, K. Anders and Smith, Jacqui 1991. *Toward a General Theory of Expertise*. New York: Cambridge University Press.

Feng, Youlan (Fung Yu-lan) 馮友蘭 1983. In Derk Boddd (trans.), *A History of Chinese Philosophy*. Volume II. Princeton University Press.

—— 1966. In Derk Bodde (ed.), *A Short History of Chinese Philosophy*. New York: The Free Press.

Festingei, L., Pepitone, A., and Newcomb, T. 1952. "Some Consequences of Deindividuation in a Group." *Journal of Abnormal and Social Psychology* 47: 382–89.

Flanagan, Owen and Rorty, Amélie Oksenberg (1990) (eds). *Identity, Character, and Morality: Essays in Moral Psychology*. Cambridge, MA: The MIT Press.

Flanagan, Owen and Williams, Robert Anthony 2010. "What Does the Modularity of Morals Have to Do With Ethics? Four Moral Sprouts Plus or Minus a Few." *Topics in Cognitive Science* 2(3): 430–53.

Frankfurt, Harry 1971. "Freedom of the Will and the Concept of a Person." *Journal of Philosophy* LXVIII(1): 5–20.

Ganeri, Jonardon 2012. *The Self: Naturalism, Consciousness & the First-Person Stance*. London: Oxford University Press.

Gardner, Daniel K. 1990 (trans.). *Learning to Be a Sage: Selections from the Conversation of Mater Chu, Arranged Topically*. Berkeley, CA: University of California Press.

Graham, Angus C. 1999. *Disputers of the Tao: Philosophical Arguments in Ancient China*. Peru, IL: Open Court.
Graham, Angus C. 1959/1990. "Being in Western Philosophy Compared with shih/fei and yu/wu in Chinese Philosophy." Originally in *Asia Major* 7: 79–112. Reprinted in Angus C. Graham 1990. *Studies in Chinese Philosophy and Philosophical Literature*, 322–59.
Graham, A. C. [1958] 1992. *Two Chinese Philosophers: The Metaphysics of the Brothers Ch'eng*. Originally published in 1958. London: Lund Humpries. La Salle, IL: Open Court.
Greco, John and Turri, John 2011. "Virtue Epistemology." In Edward N. Zalta (ed.), *The Stanford Encyclopedia of Philosophy* (Winter 2011 Edition), http://plato.stanford.edu/archives/win2011/entries/epistemology-virtue/).
Gu, Jun (pub.) 1980. *Collected Philosophical Essays throughout Chinese History*, Volume 2 (*Zhongguo lidai zuexue wenxuan, lianghan suitang*). Taipei: Muduo Chubanshe.
Guo, Yu 郭彧 2003. "An Investigation on the Original Form of Zhou Dunyi's Taiji Diagram (zhoushi taijitu yuantu kao)" (http://www.11665.com/Philosophy/nationalstudies/201103/49399.html).
—— 2001. "My Thought on the Study of the Origin of Taiji Diagram (taijitu yuanyuan yanjiu zhi wojian) (http://www.confucius2000.com/zhouyi/tjtyy.htm).
—— 2000. *A Collected Interpretation of Zhouyi Diagrams and Symbols* (Zhouyi tuxiang jijie). Beijing: Zhongguo Wenlian Chubanshe.
Haidt, Jonathan 2010. "Moral Psychology Must Not be Based on Faith and Hope: Commentary on Narvaez (2010)." *Perspectives on Psychological Science* 5(2): 182–84.
—— 2003. "The Emotional Dog Does Learn New Tricks: A Reply to Pizzaro and Bloom (2003)." *Psychological Review* 110(1): 197–8.
—— 2001. "The Emotional Dog and Its Rational Tail: A Social Intuitionist Approach to Moral Judgment." *Psychological Review* 108(4): 814–34.
Harman, Gilbert 2009. "Skepticism about Character Traits." *Journal of Ethics* 13(2/3): 235–42.
—— 2003. "No Character or Personality." *Business Ethics Quarterly* 13(1): 87–94.
—— 2000. "The Nonexistence of Character Traits." *Proceedings of the Aristotelian Society* 100(2): 223–26.
—— 1999a. "Moral Philosophy Meets Social Psychology: Virtue Ethics and the Fundamental Attribution Error." *Proceedings of the Aristotelian Society* 99: 315–31.
—— 1999b. "Virtue Ethics without Character Traits," http://www.princeton.edu/~harman/Papers/Thomson.html
—— 1996. *Moral Relativism and Moral Objectivity*. Blackwell.
Hanfeizi 2007. *The Collected Work of Hanfeizi* (*Hanfeiziji*). Beijing: Zhonghua Shuju Chubanshe.

Hequanzi, The 鶡冠子 2004. *A Complete Correction and Annotations of the Heguanzi (Heguanzi Huijiao Jizhu)*. China: Zhonghua shuju.

He, Zuoxiu 何祚庥 1997. "Has the Theory of Primordial *Qi* Really Influenced the Formation of the Concept of 'Field' in Contemporary Physics? (yuanqi xueshuo shifou zhende yingxiang dao jidai wulixue 'chang' de quannian de xingcheng?)." *Philosophical Investigations (zhexue yanjiu)*: 4.

Hoffman, Martin L. 1981. "Is Altruism Part of Human Nature?" *Journal of Personality and Social Psychology* 40(1): 121–37.

Hong, Jingtan 洪景潭 2008. *The Reinterpretation of "Yiwuweiben" in the Metaphysics of Wei and Jin Dynasties: Focusing on Wang Bi, Ji Kang and Guo Xiang's Philosophies (Weijin xuanxue yiwuweiben de zai quanshi)*. Ph.D. thesis. National Cheng Kung University, Taiwan.

Huainanzi, The 淮南子 1990. *A Complete Vernacular Translation of the Huainanzi (Huainanzi Quanyi)*, by Xu Kuangyi 許匡一. China: Guizhou Renmin Chubanshe.

Hu, Shi 胡適 1931. *On the Huainanzi (Huainan Wang Shu)*. China: Shanghai Xinyue Shuju.

Huang, Chin-Hsing 1987. "Chu Hsi versus Lu Hsiang-Shan: A Philosophical Interpretation." *Journal of Chinese Philosophy* 14(2): 179–208.

Huang, Siu-Chi 1999. *Essentials of Neo-Confucianism: Eight Major Philosophers of the Song and Ming Periods*. Westport, CT: Greenwood.

——— 1978. "Chu Hsi's Ethical Rationalism." *Journal of Chinese Philosophy* 5: 175–93.

Huang, Siu-Chi 黃秀磯 1987. *Zhang Zai* 張載. Taipei, Taiwan: Dongda tushu gongsi.

Huang, Yong 2014. *Why Be Moral? Learning from the Neo-Confucian Cheng Brothers*. Albany, NY: SUNY press.

——— 2010. "Cheng Yi's Moral Philosophy." In John Makeham (ed.), *Dao Companion to Neo-Confucian Philosophy*. Dordrecht Heidelberg London New York: Springer, 59–87.

——— 2008. "Why Be moral? The Cheng Brothers' Neo-Confucian Answer." *Journal of Religious Ethics* 36(2): 321–53.

——— 2007. "The Cheng Brothers' Onto-theological Articulation of Confucian Values." *Asian Philosophy* 17(3): 187–211.

——— 2005. "Confucian love and global ethics: How the Cheng brothers would help respond to Christian criticisms." *Asian Philosophy* 15(1): 35–60.

——— 2003. "Cheng Brothers' Neo-Confucian Virtue Ethics: The Identity of Virtue and Nature." *Journal of Chinese Philosophy* 30(3–4): 451–67.

——— 2000. "Cheng Yi's Neo-Confucian Ontological Hermeneutics of Dao." *Journal of Chinese Philosophy* 27(1): 69–92.

Huang, Zongxi 黃宗羲 1975. *The Scholarly Records of Song-Yuan Dynasties* 宋元學案, 1676–1879. Taipei: Heluo Chubanshe.

Huang, Zongyan 黃宗炎 1995. *Discerning the Puzzlement in the Study of [Yijing] Diagrams* 圖學辨惑. In Shi Wei & Qiu Xiaobo (eds.), *Complete Encyclopedia of*

Zhou Yi Diagram Expositions 周易圖解大典. Beijing: Zhongguo Gongren Chubanshe, 1173–92.
Hudson, William Henry 1904. *An Introduction to the Philosophy of Herbert Spencer*. London: Watts & Co.
Hume, David 1983. *An Enquiry Concerning the Principals of Morals*. Indianapolis, IN: Hackett Publishing Company.
Hutton, Eric L. 2006. "Character, Situationism, and Early Confucian Thought." *Philosophical Studies* 127: 37–58.
Isen, Alice M. and Levin, Paula F. 1972. "Effect of Feeling Good on Helping: Cookies and Kindness." *Journal of Personality and Social Psychology* 21(3): 384–88.
Ivanhoe, Philip J. 2015. "Senses and Value of Oneness." In Brian Bruya (ed.), *Philosophical Challenge from China*. Boston, MA: The MIT Press, 231–54.
——— 2013. "Virtue Ethics and the Chinese Confucian Tradition." In Stephen Angle and Michael Slote (eds.), *Virtue Ethics and Confucianism*, 1st edition. New York: Routledge, 28–46.
——— 2010. "Lu Xiangshan's Ethical Philosophy." In John Makeham (ed.), *Dao Companion to Neo-Confucian Philosophy*. Dordrecht Heidelberg London New York: Springer, 249–66.
——— 2009. *Readings from the Lu-Wang School of Neo-Confucianism*. Indianapolis, IN: Hackett Publishing Company.
——— 2002. *Ethics in the Confucian Tradition: The Thought of Mengzi and Wang Yangming*. Hackett Publishing Company, Inc.; 2 edition.
Jacquet, Jennifer, Hauert, Christoph, Traulsen, Arne, and Milinski, Manfred 2011. "Shame and Honor Drive Cooperation." *Biology Letters* (November 11): 899–901.
Jiang, Yi 2008. "The Concept of Infinity and Chinese Thought." *Journal of Chinese Philosophy* 35(4): 561–70.
Joyce, Richard 2007. *The Evolution of Morality*. Cambridge, MA: The MIT Press.
Jullien, Francois 1993. "Un yin – Un yang, C'est le 'Tao.'" In his "Figures de L'Immanence: Pour une lecture philosophique du Yi king." In *La Pensée Chinoise dans le miroir de la philosophie*. Paris, France: Éditions du Seuil, 2007.
Kang, Zhongqian 康中乾 2003. *Discerning Being and Nothingness* (*Youwu zhibian*). Beijing: Renmin University Press.
Kasoff, Ira E. 1984. *The Thought of Chang Tsai* (1020–1077). New York: Cambridge University Press.
Kiehl, Kent A. 2006. "A Cognitive Neuroscience Perspective on Psychopathy: Evidence for Paralimbic System Dysfunction." *Psychiatry Research* 142(2–3): 107–28.
Kim, Jaegwon 1984. "Epiphenomenal and Supervenient Causation." *Midwest Studies in Philosophy* 9(1): 257–70. Reprinted in Jaegwon Kim 1993. *Supervenience and Mind: Selected Philosophical Essays*. New York: Cambridge University Press.
Kim, Jung-Yeup 2011. "A Revisionist Understanding of Zhang Zai's Development of Qi in the Context of His Critique of the Buddhist." *Asian Philosophy* 20(2): 111–26.

Kim, Yung Sik 2000. *The Natural Philosophy of Zhu Xi (1130–1200)*. Philadelphia, PA: American Philosophical Society.

Korsgaard, Christine M. 1996. *Creating the Kingdom of Ends*. Cambridge, UK: Cambridge University Press.

Lach, Donald F. 1945. "Leibniz and China." *Journal of the History of Ideas* 6(4): 436–455.

Lao, Sze-kwang 勞思光 1980. *A History of Chinese Philosophy* 中國哲學史. Volume 3. Hong Kong: Union Press Ltd.

Laozi 2003. In Ames, Roger & David Hall (trans.), *Dao De Jing: A Philosophical Translation*. New York: Ballantine Books.

Latané, Bibb and Rodin, J. 1969. "A Lady in Distress: Inhibiting Effects of Friends and Strangers on Bystander Intervention." *Journal of Experimental Social Psychology* 5: 189–202.

Lau, D. C. 1979. (trans.) Confucius: *The Analects*. Penguin Classic. New York: Penguin Books.

Lapsley, Daniel K. and Hill, Patrick L. 2009. "The Development of the Moral Personality." In Daniel K. Lapsley & Darcia Narvaez (eds.) 2009. *Personality, Identity and Character: Explorations in Moral Psychology*. New York: Cambridge University Press, 185–213.

Lapsley, Daniel K. and Narvaez, Darcia (eds.) 2009. *Personality, Identity and Character: Explorations in Moral Psychology*. New York: Cambridge University Press.

——— (eds.) 2004a. *Moral Development, Self and Identity*. Mahwah, NJ: Erlbaum.

——— 2004b. "A Socio-Cognitive Approach to the Moral Personality." In D. K. Lapsley and D. Narvaez (eds.) *Moral Development, Self and Identity*. Mahwah, NJ: Erlbaum, 189–212.

Lapsley, Daniel K. 1999. "An Outline of a Socio-Cognitive Theory of Moral Character." *Journal of Research in Education* 8: 25–32.

Lee, Chan 2010. "Zhu Xi on Moral Motivation: An Alternative Critique." *Journal of Chinese Philosophy* 37(4): 622–38.

Leibniz, Gottfried Wilhelm 1896. *New Essays on Human Understanding*. New York: The Macmillan Books. Book II. Chapter 4 (of Solidity), Section 3.

Li, Rizhang 李日章 1986. *Cheng Hao. Cheng Yi* 程顥 程頤. Taipei, Taiwan: Dongda tushu gongsi.

Li, Shen 李申 2001. *A Study on Yi Diagram (yitu kao)*. Beijing: Peking University Press.

Lind, Marcia 1990. "Hume and moral emotions." In Flanagan, Owen & Rorty, Amélie Oksenberg Rorty (1990) (eds). *Identity, Character, and Morality: Essays in Moral Psychology*. Cambridge, MA: The MIT Press, 133–47.

Liu, JeeLoo 2015. "In Defense of Chinese Qi-Naturalism." In Chenyang Li, Frank Perkins and Alan K. L. Chan (eds.), *Chinese Metaphysics and Its Problems*. New York: Cambridge University Press.

―――― 2012. "Moral Reason, Moral Sentiments and the Realization of Altruism: A Motivational Theory of Altruism." *Asian Philosophy* 22(2): 93–119.

―――― 2010. "Wang Fuzhi's Philosophy of Principle (li) Inherent in Qi." In John Makeham (ed.), *Dao Companion to Neo-Confucian Philosophy*. Dordrecht, Heidelberg, London, New York: Springer, 355–380.

―――― 2005. "The Status of Cosmic Principle (Li) in the Neo-Confucian Metaphysics." *Journal of Chinese Philosophy* 32(3): 391–407.

Liu, Mu 劉牧 1995. *Diagrams Unveiling the Hidden Meaning of the Yijing's Numerology* 易數鉤隱圖. In Shi Wei & Qiu Xiaobo (eds.), *Complete Encyclopedia of Zhou Yi Diagram Expositions* 周易圖解大典. Beijing: Zhongguo Gongren Chubanshe, 1–33.

Liu, Zhaobing 2010. "The Logical Progression of the Ancient Philosophy of Primordial Qi (Gudai Yuanqilun Zhexue de Luoji Yanjin)." *Dong Yue Tribune* 31(6): 91–94.

Liu, Zongyuan 柳宗元 1979. *Collected Works of Liu Zongyuan* (*Liu Zongyuan Ji* 柳宗元集). China: Zhonghua Shuju.

Lu, Xiangshan 陸象山 1981. *The Complete Work of Lu Xiangshan* (*lujiuyuan ji* 陸九淵集). Taipei, Taiwan: Liren Shuju.

Marchal, Kai 2013a. "The Virtues, Moral Inwardness, and the Challenge of Modernity." *Dao: A Journal of Comparative Philosophy* 12(3): 369–80.

―――― 2013b. "The Virtues of Justice in Zhu Xi." In Stephen Angle and Michael Slote (eds.) (2013). *Virtue Ethics and Confucianism*. Routledge, 192–200.

Major, John S. and Queen, Sarah, Meyer, Andrew, Roth, Harold D. (trans.) 2010. *The Huainanzi: A Guide to the Theory and Practice of Government in Early Han China* (Translations from the Asian Classics). New York: Columbia University Press.

McDougall, William 2001. *An Introduction to Social Psychology*. Ontario, Canada: Batoche Books. Originally published in 1919.

McMorran, Ian. 1975. "Wang Fu-chih and the Neo-Confucian tradition." In Wm. Theodore de Bary (Ed.) *The Unfolding of Neo-Confucianism*. New York: Columbia University Press, 447–58.

Miller, Alexander 2010. "Realism." In Edward N. Zalta (ed.), *The Stanford Encyclopedia of Philosophy*, http://plato.stanford.edu/entries/realism/.

Monroe, Kristen Renwick 1998. *The Heart of Altruism: Perceptions of a Common Humanity*. Princeton University Press.

Mou, Zongsan 牟宗三 1999. *The Fundamental State of the Heart/Mind and the Fundamental State of Human Nature* 心體與性體. Shanghai: Shanghai Guji Chubanshe.

―――― 1979. *From Lu Xiangshan to Liu Jishan* (*cong luxiangshan dao liu jishan*). Taipei, Taiwan: Xuesheng Shuju.

Munro, Donald J. 2002. "Reciprocal Altruism and the Biological Basis of Ethics in Neo-Confucianism." *Dao: A Journal of Comparative Philosophy* 1(2): 131–41.

Nagel, Thomas 1970. *The Possibility of Altruism*. Princeton, NJ: Princeton University Press.

Narvaez, Darcia 2010a. "Moral Complexity: The Fatal Attraction of Truthiness and the Importance of Mature Moral Functioning." *Perspectives on Psychological Science* 5(2): 163–81.

—— 2010b. "The Embodied Dynamism of Moral Becoming: Reply to Haidt (2010)." *Perspectives on Psychological Science* 5(2): 185–86.

Narvaez, Darcia, Lapsley, Daniel K., Hegele, Scott and Lasky, Benjamin 2006. "Moral Chronicity and Social Information Processing: Tests of a Social Cognitive Approach to the Moral Personality." *Journal of Research in Personality* 40: 966–85.

Narvaez, Darcia and Lapsley, Daniel K. 2005. "The Psychological Foundations of Everyday Morality and Moral Expertise." In D. Lapsley & C. Power (eds.), *Character Psychology and Character Education*. Notre Dame, IN: University of Notre Dame Press, 140–65.

Needham, Joseph 1994. *The Shorter Science and Civilization in China*. Abridged by Colin A. Ronan, Volume 4. New York: Cambridge University Press.

Neville, Robert C. 1983. "The Unity of Knowledge and Action." *Review of Metaphysics* 36 (3):703–706.

—— 1980. "From Nothing to Being: The Notion of Creation in Chinese and Western thought." *Philosophy East & West* 30(1): 21–34.

Orive, Ruben 1984. "Group Similarity, Public Self-awareness, and Opinion Extremity: A Social Projection Explanation of Deindividuation Effects." *Journal of Personality and Social Psychology* 47(4): 727–37.

Pang, Pu 龐樸 1995. *The Tripartite One (yifenweisan)*. Shenjun, China: Haitian Chubanshe.

Perkins, Franklin 2004. *Leibniz and China: A Commerce of Light*. New York: Cambridge University Press.

Peterson, Willard 1986. "Another Look at Li." *The Bulletin of Sung and Yuan Studies* 18: 13–32.

Pihlström, Sami 2009. *Pragmatist Metaphysics: An Essay on the Ethical Grounds of Ontology*. London: Continuum International Publishing Group.

—— 2005. *Pragmatic Moral Realism: A Transcendental Defense*. Value Inquiry Book Series, Volume 171. Amsterdam; New York: Rodopi.

Prentice-Dunn, S. and Rogers, R. W. 1980. "Effects of Deindividuating Situational Cues and Aggressive Models on Subjective Deindividuation and Aggression." *Journal of Personality and Social Psychology* 39: 104–113.

Putnam, Hilary 1992. *Renewing Philosophy*. Cambridge, MA: Harvard University Press.

—— 1990. In James Conant (ed.), *Realism with a Human Face*. Cambridge, MA: Harvard University Press.

—— 1981. *Reason, Truth and History*. Cambridge, UK: Cambridge University Press.

Reber, Rolf and Slingerland, Edward G. 2011. "Confucius Meets Cognition: New Answers to Old Questions." *Religion, Brain and Behavior* 2: 1–11.
Rees, Martin 2000. *Just Six Numbers*. New York: Basic Books.
Robinson, Howard 2014. "Substance." In Edward N. Zalta (ed.), *The Stanford Encyclopedia of Philosophy* (Spring 2014 Edition), http://plato.stanford.edu/archives/spr2014/entries/substance/.
Rosati, Connie S. 2014. "Moral Motivation." In Edward N. Zalta (ed.), *The Stanford Encyclopedia of Philosophy* (Spring 2014 Edition), http://plato.stanford.edu/archives/spr2014/entries/moral-motivation/. [pdf. format]
Sabini, John and Silver, Maury 1982. *Moralities of Everyday Life*. New York: Oxford University Press.
Sarkissian, Hagop 2010. "Confucius and the Effortless Life of Virtue." *History of Philosophy Quarterly* 27(1): 1–16.
Sartre, Jean-Paul 2007. *Existentialism Is A Humanism*. [Originally a lecture given in 1946.] New Haven, CT: Yale University Press. Trade Paperback Edition.
Sayer-McCord, Geoffrey 1988. "The Many Moral Realisms." In Geoffrey Sayer-McCord (ed.), *Essays on Moral Realism*. Ithaca, NY: Cornell University Press, 1–23.
Schwitzgebel, Eric 2012. "Self-Ignorance." In JeeLoo Liu & John Perry (eds.), *Consciousness and the Self*. New York: Cambridge University Press.
Seok, Bongrae 2008. "Mencius's Vertical Faculties and Moral Nativism." *Asian Philosophy* 18(1): 51–68.
Sherman, Nancy 1990. "The Place of Emotions in Kantian Morality." In Owen Flanagan & Amélie Oksenberg Rorty (eds). *Identity, Character, and Morality: Essays in Moral Psychology*. Cambridge, MA: The MIT Press, 149–70.
Shien, Gi-Ming 1951. "Being and Nothingness in Greek and Ancient Chinese Philosophy." *Philosophy East & West* 1(2): 16–24.
Shun, Kwong-loi 2010. "Zhu Xi's Moral Psychology." In John Makeham (ed.), *Dao Companion to Neo-Confucian Philosophy*. Dordrecht, Heidelberg, London, New York: Springer, 177–95.
——— 2000. *Mencius and Early Chinese Thought*. Pala Alto, CA: Stanford University Press.
——— 1997. "Mencius on Jen-hsing." *Philosophy East & West* 47(1): 1–20.
Sim, May 2007. *Remastering Morals with Aristotle and Confucius*. Cambridge: Cambridge University Press.
Slingerland, Edward 2011a. "The Situationist Critique and Early Confucian Virtue Ethics." *Ethics* 121(2): 390–419.
——— 2011b. "Of What Use Are the Odes? Cognitive Science, Virtue Ethics, and Early Confucian Ethics." *Philosophy East and West* 61(1): 80–109.
——— 2010. "Toward an Empirically Responsible Ethics: Cognitive Science, Virtue Ethics and Effortless Attention in Early Chinese Thought." In Brian Bruya (ed.), *Effortless Attention: A New Perspective in the Cognitive Science of Attention and Action*. Cambridge, MA: MIT Press, 247–86.

Slote, Michael 2001. *Morals from Motives*. New York, NY: Oxford University Press.
Smith, Adam 2002. *A Theory of Moral Sentiments*. Cambridge: Cambridge University Press.
Sorensen, Roy 2009. "Nothingness." *The Stanford Encyclopedia of Philosophy*, http://plato.stanford.edu/entries/nothingness/.
Swartz, Norman 2009. "Laws of Nature." *Internet Encyclopedia of Philosophy*, http://www.iep.utm.edu/lawofnat/.
Tang, Chün-I (Tang, Junyi) 1956. "Chang Tsai's Theory of Mind and its Metaphysical Basis." *Philosophy East and West* 6(2): 113–36.
Tang, Yongtong 湯用彤 2001. *Essays on Wei-Jin Philosophy* 魏晉玄學論稿. Shanghai: Guji Chubanshe.
Taylor, Gabriele 1985. *Pride, Shame and Guilt: Emotions of Self-Assessment*. New York: Oxford University Press.
Tien, David W. 2012. "Oneness and Self-centeredness in the Moral Psychology of Wang Yangming." *Journal of Religious Ethics* 40(1): 52–71.
—— 2010. "Metaphysics and the Basis of Morality in the Philosophy of Wang Yangming." In John Makeham (ed.). *Dao Companion to Neo-Confucian Philosophy*. Dordrecht Heidelberg London New York: Springer, 295–314.
Tiwald, Justin and Van Norden, Bryan W. (eds.) 2014. *Readings in Later Chinese Philosophy: Han Dynasty to the 20th Century*. Indianapolis, IN: Hackett Publishing Company.
Trivers, Robert L. 1971. "The Evolution of Reciprocal Altruism." *The Quarterly Review of Biology*, Vol. 46, No. 1, 35–57.
Yu, Jiyuan 2007. *The Ethics of Confucius and Aristotle*. New York: Routledge.
Van Norden, Bryan 2014. "Wang Yangming." In Edward N. Zalta (ed.), *The Stanford Encyclopedia of Philosophy* (Fall 2014 Edition), http://plato.stanford.edu/archives/fall2014/entries/wang-yangming/.
—— (trans.). 2008. *Mengzi: With Selections from Traditional Commentaries*. Indianapolis, IN: Hackett.
—— 2007. *Virtue Ethics and Consequentialism in Early Chinese Philosophy*. Cambridge: Cambridge University Press.
Wang, Bi 王弼 1980. *Annotations to Wang Bi's Collected Works* (*Wangbi ji jiaoshi*) (ed., annotated.) Lou Yulie. Beijing: Zhonghua Shuju.
Wang, Chong 王充 1990. *A Complete Vernacular Translation of Disquisitions* (*Lunheng Quanyi*). China: Guizhou Renmin Chubanshe.
Wang, Fuzhi 王夫之 1967. *Commentary on Zhang Zai's "Rectifying the Youth"* (張子正蒙注), 1685–1690. Taipei, Taiwan: Shijie shuju.
—— 1972. *The Complete Collection of the Posthumous Works of Chuanshan* (船山遺書全集). Vols. 1–22. Taipei, Taiwan: Chinese Chuanshan Association & Liberty Press 中國船山學會與自由出版社.
—— 1974a. *Discourse on Reading the Great Collection of Commentaries on the Four Books* (讀四書大全說), 1665. Taipei, Taiwan: Heluo tushu chubanshe.

—— 1974b. *Extensive Commentary on the Book of Odes* (詩廣傳), 1683. Taipei, Taiwan: Heluo tushu chubanshe.
—— 1974c. *Records of Thinking and Questioning* (*Siwen lu* 思問錄), 1686. Collected in *Five Books by Lizhou and Chuanshan* (*Lizhou Chuanshan Wu Shu* 梨州船山五書). Taipei, Taiwan: Shijie Books 世界書局), 1974.
—— 1975. *The Extended Meaning of the Book of History* (*Shangshu yinyi* 尚書引義), 1663. Taipei, Taiwan: Heluo Books Publishing 河洛圖書出版社).
—— 1977a (1673–1677). *A Textual Annotation on the Book of Rites* 禮記章句. Taipei: Guangwen shuju.
—— 1977b (1655). *Supplementary Commentary on the Book of Changes* 周易外傳. Taipei: Heluo tushu chubanshe.
—— 1980 (1685). *Textual Commentary on the Book of Changes* 周易內傳. Collected in Chuanshan's *Commentary to the Book of Changes* 船山易傳. Taipei: Xiaxueshe.
—— 1996 (1679). *A Contemporary Interpretation of the Meaning of the Four Books* (*Sishu xunyi* 四書訓義), *1679*. Reprinted in *The Complete Books of Chuanshan* (*Chuanshan quanshu*). Volumes 7–8. China: Yuelu shushe.
Wang, Haicheng 王海成 2009. "The Analysis of the Meaning of Zhang Zai's Taixu 張載太虛意義辨析." *Tangdu Journal* 25(2): 88–91.
Wang, Robin 2005. "Zhou Dunyi's Diagram of the Supreme Ultimate Explained (taijitu shuo): A construction of the Confucian metaphysics." *Journal of the History of Ideas* 66(3): 307–23.
Wang, Robin and Ding, Weixiang 2010. "Zhang Zai's Theory of Vital Energy." In John Makeham (ed.), *Dao Companion to Neo-Confucianism*. Dordrecht: Springer, 39–57.
Wang, Yangming 1975. *The Compete Works of Wang Yangming*. Taipei, Taiwan: Zhengzhong shuju.
Wang, Yangming 1994. *The Records of Wang Yangming's Teachings* (*Chuanxilu* 傳習錄). Taipei, Taiwan: Taiwan Shangwu Yinshuguan.
Williams, Bernard 2008 [1993]. *Shame and Necessity*. Berkeley, CA: University of California Press.
Wilson, Edward O. 1998. *Consilience: The Unity of Knowledge*. 1st edition. New York: Alfred A. Knopf.
Wittenborn, Allen 1982. "Some Aspects of Mind and the Problem of Knowledge in Chu Hsi's Philosophy." *Journal of Chinese Philosophy* 9: 11–43.
Wong, David 1986. "On Moral Realism Without Foundations." *Southern Journal of Philosophy* 24(Supp.): 95–114.
Woodruff, Paul 2014. *Reverence: Renewing a Forgotten Virtue*. New York: Oxford University Press.
Wong, Wai-ying 2010. "The Thesis of Single-Rootedness in the Thought of Cheng Hao." In John Makeham (ed.), *Dao Companion to Neo-Confucian Philosophy*. Dordrecht, Heidelberg, London, New York: Springer, 89–104.

―― 2009. "Morally Bad in the Philosophy of the Cheng Brothers." *Journal of Chinese Philosophy* 36(1): 141–56.
Wright, Robert 1994. *The Moral Animal, Why We Are the Way We Are: The New Science of Evolutionary Psychology*. New York: Vintage Books.
Xiao, Jiefu 蕭萐父, and Sumin, Xu 許蘇民 2002. *A Critical Biography of Wang Fuzhi* 王夫之評傳. Nanjing: Nanjing daxue chubanshe.
Yan, Shoucheng 嚴壽徵 2000. *An Introductory Reading of Chuanshan's Records of Thinking and Questioning* 思問錄導讀. Shanghai: Shanghai guji chubanshe.
Yang, Lihua 楊立華 2008. *Qi as Fundamental State and Transformations with Unpredictability: A Treatise on Zhang Zai's Philosophy* 氣本與神化:張載哲學述論. Beijing: Beijing University chubanshe.
―― 2005. "Qi as Fundamental State and Transformations with Unpredictability: A Reinvestigation of Zhang Zai's Ontological Structure 氣本與神化:張載本體論建構的再考察." *Zhexuemen: Beida Journal of Philosophy* 6(2), http://www.phil.pku.edu.cn/zxm/show.php?id=230.
Yi, Desheng 易德生 2003. "Some Impacts and Inspirations Chinese Ancient Theory of Primordial Qi Has on Contemporary Physics 中國古代元氣論對近現代物理的影響與啓示." *Xinjiang Social Sciences Discourse* (*xinjiang sheke luntan*), 2003(6): 58–61.
Zeng, Zhaoxu 曾昭旭 1983. *Wang Chuanshan's Philosophy* 王船山哲學. Taipei: Liren shuju.
Zhang, Dainian 張岱年 1958/2005. *The Outlines of Chinese Philosophy* 中國哲學大綱. China: Jiansu Jiaoyu Chubanshe.
―― 1996. "Zhang Zai: A Chinese Materialist Philosopher in the Eleventh Century 張載 – 十一世紀中國唯物主義哲學家." In *Complete Work of Zhang Dainian*張岱年全集, Hebei: Hebei renmin chubanshe. Volume 3: 231–80.
Zhang, Dainian 2002. *Key Concepts in Chinese Philosophy*. Translated by Edmund Ryden. New Haven, CT: Yale University Press.
Zhang, Heng 2010. *Spiritual Constitution of the Universe* (*Lingxian*), http://blog.sina.com.cn/s/blog_5ddc581b0100mczx.html.
Zhang, Liwen 張立文 2001. *Authentic Learning and Creation of New Situations: The Philosophical Thought of Wang Chuanshan* 正學與開新—王船山哲學思想. Beijing: Renmin chubanshe.
―― 1985. "A Discerning Analysis of Zhou Dunyi's 'Wuji' and 'Taiji' Theory" 周敦頤無極太極學說辨析 *Qiosuo* 2. Reprinted in Shouqi Huang & Shanwen Zhang (eds.), *Collected Essays on Zhouyi Studies* (*Zhouyi yanjiu lunwenji*), Volume 3: 220–29.
Zhang, Qihui 章啓輝 2004. "Realism Labeling of Wang Fuzhi's Philosophy 王夫之哲學的實學精神." *Journal of Hunan University* (*Social Sciences*) 18(6): 14–19. [湖南大學學報 (社會科學版), 2004年18卷6期, 14–19.]
Zhang Zai 張載 2006. *The Complete Work of Zhang Zai* (張載集). Beijing, China: Zhonghua shuju.

Zhou, Bing 周兵 2006. *Neo-Confucianism's New Interpretation of the Relation between Heaven and Humans: A Study of Wang Fuzhi's Discourse on Reading the Great Collection of Commentaries on the Four Books* 天人之際的理學新詮釋—王夫之讀四書大全說思想研究. Sichuan: Bashu shushe.

Zhou, Dunyi 周敦頤 1975. *The Complete Work of Master Zhou* 周子全書. Taipei: Guanxueshe Chubanshe.

Zhou, Xuewu 周學武 1981. *An Investigation of Zhou Dunyi's Taiji Diagram Explained* 周蓮溪太極圖說考辨. Taipei: Xuehai chubanshe.

Zhu Xi 1986. *The Classified Dialogues of Zhu Xi (Zhuzi Yulei)*. Eight volumes. Beijing: Zhonghua Shuju Chubanshe.

Zhu Xi 2002. *The Complete Work of Zhu Xi (Zhuzi Quanshu)*. 27 volumes. Shanghai: Guji Chubanshe.

The Zhuangzi 莊子 1961. In Guo Qingfan (ed.), *Collected Annotations on Zhuangzi (Zhuangzi Jishi)*. China: Zhonghua Shuju.

Index

References to footnotes will be followed by the letter 'n'.

a

a posteriori nature   115, 116, 132, 160–161, 176
a priori intuitionism   132, 160, 246, 249–252
   see also Wang, Yangming
a priori nature   160–161
absolute nothingness/void   82
   see also being and nothingness debate; emptiness; formlessness; nonbeing; void
   and cosmology of Zhou Dunyi   40, 42, 45, 47, 52, 55–57
action, unity with knowledge   218–219, 258–262
Adler, Joseph A.   31, 32
altruism   195, 208–212, 275–277
   reciprocal   208–209
Ames, Roger   39
Analects, The   22, 27, 112, 132, 199, 209, 210, 222, 233, 237
Angle, Stephen C.   4n, 184n, 227n
arché (origin/beginning)   6
Aristotle   6, 109, 183, 216
Armstrong, David   18
Arplay, Nomy   201
Asch, Solomon   280–281
attribution error   223
attunement   234

authenticity (*cheng*)
   cosmology of Zhou Dunyi   58–59
   as essential virtue   222–223
   nature of *qi*   105
   and respectfulness   212–215
automaticity   187, 188, 189
Ayala, Francisco J.   247

b

Bai, Tongdong   56
Behuniak Jr, James   89
being and nothingness debate   12, 34, 38–51, 57, 72, 77
   see also void
   absolute nothingness   40, 42, 45, 47, 52, 55, 56, 57, 69, 70, 74
   concepts   38–39
   ethical application of doctrine of being   49–50
   forms   39–47
   nonbeing   39, 44–47, 52, 55
   origins of being   69–70
   School of Being   47, 50
   substance   44, 45
   wu (nothingness), as ontological basis of all existence   42, 45
being watchful when one is alone
   see *shendu* (being watchful when one is alone)

Neo-Confucianism: Metaphysics, Mind, and Morality, First Edition. JeeLoo Liu.
© 2018 John Wiley & Sons, Inc. Published 2018 by John Wiley & Sons, Inc.

beyond physical form *see xingershang* (beyond physical form)
Blasi, Augusto   184, 190
Bloom, Irene   32n
Bodde, Derk   31n, 32
Book of Changes (*Yijing*) *see Yijing* (*Book of Changes*)
Book of Documents (*Shangshu*)   133, 236–237
Book of Rites (*Liji*)   22, 162
Boundlessness (*wuji*)   51, 52, 56, 72
   see also Wuji concept (boundlessness)
A Brief Exposition of the Essence of Laozi's Teachings (Wang, Bi)   43, 45
brilliance (*ming*) *see ming* (brilliance)
Brink, David O.   228–229, 2266
Buddhism   2, 20, 22, 35, 45, 72, 77, 89, 105, 116, 234
   see also emptiness
   Chinese   1, 13–14, 163, 172
   Huayan   6

C

cai (natural talents/capabilities)   167–170, 269
cardinal virtues *see* four cardinal virtues
causation, supervenience   98–101
Chan, Wing-cheuk   76n, 82
Chan, Wing-tsit   6, 9, 10n, 13, 16, 22, 32, 34, 38, 39, 40n, 41–44, 48–49, 50n, 51, 63, 64n, 70n, 91, 95, 96, 98n, 139, 140, 141, 209, 232n
chaos, state of   55, 62–63, 79, 85, 113
Chen, Lai   53, 54, 70, 72, 92, 96, 98n, 106–107, 146
Chen, Tuan   35, 37, 38, 59
Chen, Yi   35
Chen, Yufu   38
Chen, Yun   27, 104n, 178
cheng see authenticity (*cheng*)

Cheng, Chung-Ying   10–11, 97, 108, 110
Cheng, Hao   4n, 8, 9, 12–13, 13, 17, 19, 20–22, 31, 85, 86, 86–88, 91–94, 118, 130, 131, 205–226
Cheng, Yi   8, 9, 9–10, 12–14, 17, 19–23, 31, 83, 85–94, 96, 115, 116, 118, 130, 168, 169, 205–226
   see also Cheng–Zhu school
Cheng, Yishan   61, 62n, 69, 70n, 80, 81
Cheng brothers *see* Cheng, Hao; Cheng, Yi
Cheng–Zhu school   6, 7, 8, 14, 22, 31, 82, 102, 150
   see also Cheng, Hao; Cheng, Yi
   distinguished from Lu–Wang school   139
   moral psychology   158, 168, 169, 172, 178
   heavenly principle   86, 87, 103, 233
   normative realism   13, 85–102, 117, 120, 221–222
Chinese Buddhism   1, 13–14, 163, 172
Ching, Julia   151n
classical Confucianism *see* Confucianism, classical
coherence, principle as   90
Colby, Anne   186, 190, 194, 195
Commentary on Laozi's Daodejing (Wang, Bi)   43
Commentary on the Zhuangzi (Guo Xiang)   48
compassion/commiseration   3, 141, 164–165, 175, 176–177
   see also empathy
complementarities principle   43
concrete existence   115, 116
concrete things   52–53, 92, 97, 111
   see also function, and substance
   material and immaterial things, *qi* as constituent of   76–77
   prior to formation   71–72

qi theory of Zang Zai 65, 71–72, 73, 76–77, 81
unification with *Dao* 115–117
Confucianism, classical 2, 13
  see also Neo-Confucianism
  Daoism distinguished 38–39
  ethical theories 15, 16
  and human nature 87
  Neo-Confucianism distinguished 3
  universal moral essence 169
Confucius 13, 15, 16, 19, 34, 50, 132, 161, 168, 191, 193, 196, 198–199, 209, 210, 222, 223, 233, 237, 270, 282
constitutions 32, 68, 79, 81, 127, 167, 207
  inborn/innate 125, 130, 164
  physical 126, 127, 129, 131, 159, 220
  of *qi* 77, 100, 126, 129–132, 135, 157–159, 167, 200
  yin and *yang* 11, 113
Correcting Youthful Ignorance (Zhang Zai) 20, 105
cosmic accident 12, 85
cosmic necessity *see* Necessitarian Theory of Laws of Nature
cosmic principle concept 77, 95
cosmic state, initial *see* supreme vacuity (initial cosmic state)
cosmogony 12, 67, 69
  chaos, state of 62–63n
  and cosmology of Zhou Dunyi 34, 42, 43, 48, 52, 59
  Daoist 61, 68, 69, 72, 74
  primordial *qi* concept *see* primordial *qi* concept 64–65
cosmology
  see also qi (cosmic energy)
  Confucian compared to Daoist 69
  Daoist 69, 70, 72
  initial cosmic state *see* supreme vacuity (initial cosmic state)
  of Zhang Heng 70
  of Zhou Dunyi 31–60
creation ex nihilo 55, 56
Cua, Antonio S. 4n
Cui, Jing 110

d

Dai, Zhen 116
Damon, William 186, 190, 194, 195
Dao 40, 41, 63, 112
  see also heaven and earth
  distinguished from principle 7–8, 114, 115
  heart of 133
  and heavenly principle 86, 87
  as highest moral truth 146
  life-generating process 90
  ontological layer 92
  unification with concrete things 115–117
Daodejing (Daoist text) 26, 32, 34, 38n, 40–44, 46, 75
Daoism 2, 12, 20, 22, 31, 32, 35, 45, 50, 51, 89, 90, 92, 114, 116
  Confucianism distinguished 38–39
  metaphysics 61, 92
Darley, John M. 278, 279, 2275
Darwin, Charles 246–247, 250
Davidson, Philip 193–194
Davis, Bret W. 45n
day and year, analogy of 89
De Bary, William Theodore 31n, 32
De Sousa, Ronald 165n, 166
De Waal, Frans 159
deference (*jing*) 3, 237
Deleuze, Gilles 276, 278
Deonna, Julien A. 163
deontology 5, 183, 184
Descartes, René 82, 109
descriptive dimension (how things are) 87

desires   133, 198
    affirmation of   172–174
    and emotions   134, 163
    eradicating   19, 178, 254–258
    gratification of   173–174
    and moral essence   163
    morally objectionable   167
    natural   166–167
    personal, distinguished from selfish   173, 174
    selfish   254–258
    and self-regulation   198–199
    and volition   136, 198
determinism   50n, 169, 186
Ding, Weixiang   70
Discourse on Heaven (Liu Zongyuan)   73
disgust   3, 132, 165–166
dispositions, physical and psychological   131
Disquisitions (Wang Chong)   68–69
division, problem of   68
Doctrine of the Mean   22, 31, 87n, 105n, 126, 129, 136, 212
Dong, Zhongshu   61, 62, 68–69
Doris, John M.   16–17, 201, 202, 205
Downes, Stephen M.   251
dualism   97, 98
Duan, Yucai   40, 51
Dweck, Carol S.   184

e

East Asian Buddhism   89
    see also Buddhism
Einstein, Albert   55n, 81
emotions
    amoral   174–175
    arising from contacts with external objects   163
    defined   162
    and desires   134, 163
    and moral essence   163, 177
    moral psychology (Zhu Xi)   132–135
    and moral sentiments   164, 174–177, 177
    natural   162–164, 163, 165, 169, 174–177
    seven   162
empathy   159, 176, 209, 248, 270, 271, 272, 276, 282
    see also compassion/commiseration
    empathy-altruism hypothesis   258
    lack of   168, 169
emptiness   77, 105
    see also being and nothingness debate; formlessness; supreme vacuity (initial cosmic state); void
    and cosmology of Zhou Dunyi   35, 39, 40, 42, 44–46, 45
    supreme vacuity (initial cosmic state)   71–73
epistemology
    moral epistemology   17, 18, 228–235
    virtue epistemology   205–226
equilibrium, supreme   74–76
Erikson, Erik   213
eternalism   96
ether   81
ethical rationalism   17, 174, 232
ethics
    see also morality
    empirical turn in   183
    ethical action   239–242
    ethical rationalism   17, 174
    ethical reality   147
    ethical teachings   15
    and metaphysics   94, 152, 154
evil   3, 133
    created by men   169
    good and evil, root   130–132
    innate   168
    origin   176
existentialism   157
The Exposition of the Taiji Diagram (Zhou Dunyi)   31, 33, 34, 35, 52, 53

extension
　care for others   176
　of empathy   272
　of knowledge   227, 228–235

f

fair-mindedness   210
Fang, Yizhi   80–81
Feng, Youlan   32, 35n, 59, 115
Festingei, L.   280
Five Agents   94, 95
Five Classics   25, 27, 40n
Five Constant Virtues   58–59
Flanagan, Owen   15
flood-like *qi*   193
formlessness   10, 73, 76, 79, 80, 105, 108, 110, 116
　see also being and nothingness debate; emptiness; supreme vacuity (initial cosmic state); void
　and cosmology of Zhou Dunyi   41, 44, 54
　primordial *qi* concept   62–67
　supreme vacuity (initial cosmic state)   70, 71, 73
foundationalism   238
four cardinal virtues   62, 128
Four Classics   22, 120
Frankfurt, Harry   198
free will   208
functional analysis/function
　functions of the mind   161–171
　and particular principle   128
　substance and function   44, 70n
　unification of   107–112
　teleology   109–110

g

Ganeri, Jonardon   252
"Gang of Seven in the Bamboo Forest,"   46, 48n
Gaozi   161
Gardner, Daniel K.   237

generation, problem of   68
globalism   16, 17, 205, 206
globalist virtue ethics   17, 205–226
goodness
　doctrine of the goodness of *qi*   107
　good and evil, root   130–132
　of human nature   128, 134, 190
　innate, questions as to existence   3
　of *qi*   158
　and rightness   241
Goose Lake debate (1175)   34–35, 151
Graham, Angus C.   6, 38, 39, 90, 92, 93
Grand Chaos   67
Grand Obscurity   66, 67
Grand Singularity   63
Great Element   66, 67
Great Equilibrium   105, 106
Great Incipience   67
The Great Learning   2, 22, 219
Great Ultimate   107
Great Vacuity   105–106, 108, 111, 120
　see also substance; supreme vacuity (initial cosmic state)
Greco, John   215
Gu, Jun   48, 50
Guo, Xiang   47, 48–49, 50
Guo, Yu   38, 53, 57

h

habituation   132, 160, 161, 168, 169, 171, 176, 185, 189, 203
　accumulation of   192–195
Haidt, Jonathan   15, 187
Hall, David   39
Han dynasty (206 BCE–220 CE)   39, 40n, 54n, 57, 61n, 66, 68, 70n
Hanfeizi   7, 16
Harman, Gilbert   206, 207, 215, 222, 223, 226n
harmonica universalis   82
He, Yan   42, 43, 46
He, Zuoxiu   81

heaven and earth   4, 137, 140, 172, 184, 191, 195, 257, 258, 273
  and Cheng–Zhu school   62, 90, 96
  formation   63
  and nature   69, 192
  prior to division of   53, 54–55, 64
  prior to existence of   41, 44, 62, 65, 67, 69
  between realms of   73, 77, 105, 142
  separation of   55, 67
  theory of principle inherent in *qi* (Wang Fuzhi)   107, 110, 118, 119
heavenly (universal) principle   3, 6–9, 12, 14, 103, 115, 216
  see also principle
  as Cheng Hao's conception of principle   86–88
  heaven-as-human   118, 119
  human nature   125, 134, 149, 158, 172
Heguanzi   62
Heshanggong   38
higher-order perception (HOP)   18
Hill, Patrick L.   184, 186, 188, 194
History of Jin   48n
Hoffman, Martin L.   248, 275, 282
holistic order, principle as (Zhu Xi)   94–95
Hong, Jingtan   45
Hu, Shi   65n
Huainanzi (Daoist text)
  qi theory of Zang Zai   61n, 63–70, 73, 74
  seven stages   64–67
  supreme vacuity (initial cosmic state)   70, 73
Huang, Baijia   35
Huang, Chin-Hsing   20, 151n
Huang, Siu-Chi   151, 227, 232
Huang, Yong   3, 4n, 85, 90, 184n
Huang, Zongxi   33n, 34n
Huang, Zongyan   35, 38

Huayan Buddhism   6
Hudson, William Henry   250
human nature   14–15, 125–138
  see also nature
  animals, compared with human beings   3, 126–127, 129, 175
  and classical Confucianism   87
  daily renewal (Wang Fuzhi)   157–179
  defined   125–130, 193
  dispositions, physical and psychological   131
  dynamic nature of   14
  emotion   132–135, 162–164
  four cardinal virtues   128
  goodness of   128, 134, 190
  and root of good and evil   130–132
  human essence, daily renewal and completion   15, 158–161
  and human mind   161–162
  ideal state   231–232
  as principle   159
humaneness (*yen*)   94, 119, 226
  and altruism   208–212
  human nature   128, 134, 137, 161, 171
  and inhumaneness   193
  moral cognitivism and ethical rationalism (Zu Xi)   230, 249
  moral personality   191, 193
  social sentimentalism   267, 271, 281
  virtue ethics and virtue epistemology   205, 206, 208–212, 214, 223, 224
  virtue of   208–212
humanistic moral realism   139, 144–150
Hume, David   109, 230
Hursthouse, Rosalind   206n
Hutton, Eric L.   205n

i

idealism 140, 155
  Berkeleian ontological 143
  Consciousness-Only school 143
  dynamic 139
  objective 98n
identity, moral 188, 189–191
immorality 13, 131, 169, 175, 176
impartiality 210
infinity, notion of 51
intellectualism, of Zhu Xi 228, 229, 233
intellectuals, Wei-Jin 46
intentionality 153
interconnectedness 229–230
internal moral realism 14, 125, 130, 137, 227
intersubjectivity 148
intrapersonal coherence 202n
intuition
  innate 146–149, 164–166
  moral compass 249–252
  retrieving 254–288
  moral 14
  a priori intuitionism 246, 249–252
  social intuitionism 187
Isen, Alice M. 200
Ivanhoe, Philip J. 4n, 5, 25, 134, 139–142, 144, 146, 148, 151, 153, 184n, 211n

j

Jacquet, Jennifer 277
Jiang, Yi 51–52
Jincheng, city of 21
jing see respectfulness
Joyce, Richard 247
Jullien, François 115

k

Kang, Zhongqian 45, 46, 47n
Kangxi (emperor of Qing dynasty) 209

Kant, Immanuel 9, 76, 174
Kiehl, Kent A. 168–169
Kim, Jaegwon 100n, 101n
Kim, Yung Sik 7
knowledge 18, 216, 217, 227, 228, 240
  aim of 215–217
  conditions for true knowledge 217–219
  fundamental 217
  knowing-that, knowing-about and knowing-how 220
  methodology 219–222
  moral *see* moral knowledge
  as performance 219n, 222
  self-knowledge 222, 228
  true 17, 217–219, 238
  unity of knowledge and action 218–219, 258–262
  and virtue 215, 216
Korsgaard, Christine M. 271n

l

Lach, Donald F. 86
Lack of Character (John Doris) 16
Lao, Sze-kwang 38, 55
Laozi 39, 40, 41, 42, 43, 51, 56n, 61, 67
Laplace, Pierre-Simon 76
Lapsley, Daniel K. 184, 186, 188, 189, 194
Latané, Bibb 275, 278, 279
Lau, D. C. 237
learning
  aim of 192
  importance of 184–185
  transformation of moral personality through 191–192
Lee, Chan 240
Leggett, Ellen L. 184
Leibniz, Gottfried Wilhelm 74, 81, 82, 109n
Levin, Paula F. 200
li (principle) *see* principle

Li, Rizhang   21, 22
Li, Shen   38, 55
Li, Tong   22
Liangzhi (pure knowing)   18, 250–254, 258
Lind, Marcia   273n
Liu, An   63n
Liu, JeeLoo   62n, 98n, 103n, 265n
Liu, Mu   53
Liu, Yuxi   73
Liu, Zongyuan   61n, 73
Locke, John   109, 142
love   164, 175
Lu, Dian   62
Lu, Suosan   33, 34
Lu, Xiangshan   7, 9, 14, 20, 23, 25, 33–34, 139–155, 232, 234
Lu–Wang school   23, 82, 139
see also Lu, Xiangshan; Wang, Yangming

m
McDougall, William   164, 174
McMorran, Ian   81n
Major, John S.   64n
Mandate, of Heaven   128, 131, 136
Mao, Qiling   35
Marchal, Kai   125
materialism
  desires   173
  material and immaterial things, *qi as* constituent of   76–77
  material objects   11, 78, 96, 100, 108, 115, 116
  materialistic postulates   81
  matter   104
  naïve materialism, Western   80, 104
  naturalized   80
Memoir of Chuanshan (Wang Fuzhi)   26–27
Mencius   3, 13, 15, 18, 27, 126, 129–32, 141, 159, 161, 164, 167, 169, 171, 190, 193, 207, 265

meontology   45
metaethics   165
metaphysics   4, 12–13, 91–92, 221
  common themes   12
  Daoist   61, 92
  defined   116n
  and ethics   94, 152, 154
  moral   3, 14, 85–86, 104–107, 126
  pragmatist   150–153
  of Zhang Zai   71
  of Zhu Xi   97, 228
Milgram experiments   201
Miller, Alexander   144n
mind
  see also mind is principle; School of Mind
  functions of   161–171
  innate moral sentiments   164–166
  maximizing of functions   162
  role in moral cultivation   135–137
  school of   14
mind is principle   14, 139–155, 232
  humanistic moral realism   144–150
  pragmatist metaphysics   150–153
  principle in the mind   140–143
mind-body dualism   109
ming (brilliance)   65, 127, 233, 255
Ming dynasty (1368–1644)   26
Mingdao Academy, Jincheng   21
moderation   173
Monroe, Kristen Renwick   195
moral action   3, 230, 271
  moral cognitivism and ethical rationalism (Zu Xi)   241, 242
  moral personality, cultivating (Zhang Zai)   183, 187, 190
moral agents   5, 13, 16, 133, 140, 174, 193, 211
  see also sages/sagehood
  moral cognitivism and ethical rationalism (Zu Xi)   240–241
  moral personality, cultivating (Zhang Zai)   186, 191, 194, 195, 199

moral attributes *see* humaneness; propriety; righteousness; wisdom
moral beliefs   190, 228, 239, 247, 266
moral character   4, 5, 16, 17, 226, 235, 283
  moral personality   184, 185, 188, 192, 199, 201, 202
  robust   17, 206, 223, 225, 226
  traits   223, 225
  virtue ethics and virtue epistemology   205, 206, 222, 223, 225
moral cultivation   16–17, 18
  and moral personality   191–192
moral epistemology   17, 18, 228–235
moral essence   14, 15, 115
  and emotions   163, 177
  good and evil, root   130, 131
  inborn/innate   177, 190, 192
  moral realism of Zhu Xi   130, 135, 137
  universal   168, 169
moral exemplars   17, 186, 188, 189, 191n, 193–194, 223, 248
  effortlessness of   199–200
  and sages   194–195, 253
moral expertise   189, 192–194, 202
moral externalism   4
moral goodness   134–135
moral identity   188, 189–191
moral inquiry   149–150
moral intuition   14, 18, 187, 239, 246
  defined   250
  innate   188, 250, 254–258
  a priori   249–252
moral knowledge   14, 18
  and ethical action   239–242
  extension of   228–235
  psychological preparedness for   235–239
moral metaphysics   3, 14, 85–86, 104–107, 126
  of classical Confucianism   137

moral methodology   254–258
moral motivation
  sentimentalist theory   267–274
  theory of Zhu Xi   239–242
moral objectivism   140, 144, 146, 147
moral personality   17, 183–203
  establishing moral identity   189–191
  habituation   192–195
  propriety and situational fit   196–198
  righteousness   192–195
  self-regulation and desire   198–199
  socio-cognitive model   17, 184, 185–189, 190, 199–200
  transformation through learning   191–192
moral programs   15, 18, 173, 274, 279
  of Cheng brothers   205, 226
  early Confucian   187
  of Zhang Zai   17, 184–185, 187, 191
moral psychology   14, 16, 132–135
  see also moral personality
  theories   174–178
  of Wang Fuzhi   161–171
moral realism   14, 129–130
  humanistic   139, 144–150
  internal   14, 125, 130, 137, 227
moral reflexivism   18, 252–254
moral self   125, 172, 188, 189, 190, 202, 253
  moral self-cultivation   190, 191, 196, 199, 283
  moral self-identity   184, 189, 190
moral senses   140, 248
moral sentiments   3, 132, 133, 174
  concept of sentiment   164, 166
  and emotions   164, 174–177
  innate   164–166
moral skepticism, and virtue ethics   206–207
moral transformation   186–187, 190, 191, 197, 235

moral truths   145, 147
moral universalism   144, 149
morality   2, 13
  see also immorality
  accumulation of   192
  innate intuition   164–166,
    246–249
    moral compass   249–252
    retrieving   254–288
  psychological foundation   3
  selfish desires, removing   254–258
Mou, Zongsan   70, 140
Mount Hua, *Wuji* diagram on   35, 38
Mu, Xiu   35, 38
Munro, Donald J.   15–16, 208
myriad concrete objects (*wanwu*)
  Cheng–Zhu school   92
  and pre-myriad things   53
  qi theory of Zang Zai   67, 69, 75, 76, 77–78, 104
  and supreme ultimate   96
  and Zhu Xi's theory of principle   101

n
Nagel, Thomas   266
naïve materialism, Western   80, 104
Narvaez, Darcia   184, 189
natural constitutionism   159
naturalism, moralistic   2–3
naturalized materialism   80
nature   4, 6, 12
  see also human nature; school of nature
  and heaven and earth   69, 192
  laws of nature   12, 77–80
  Necessitarian Theory of Laws of Nature   77–80, 85, 112–113
  original and material   130, 131
  qi-constituted   168
  role of humans in world of   118–119
nature–nurture debate   14–15, 161

nebular hypothesis   76
Necessitarian Theory of Laws of Nature   77–80, 85, 112–113
nomological necessity, inherent in *qi*   79
Needham, Joseph   66, 95
negation doctrine   39, 40–41, 44, 45, 46, 51
  see also nonbeing
Neo-Confucianism
  classical Confucianism distinguished   3
  concepts/definitions   2–5
  distinguished from New-Confucianism   108n
  Song-Ming neo-Confucianism   2, 21
  as "Studies of Principle,"   5
  terminology   5–19
Neville, Robert C.   25, 32, 51, 56, 58n
Newcomb, T.   280
New-Confucianism   108
no error theory   50
nomological necessity, externalist and internalist view   79
nonbeing   39, 44–47, 52, 55, 72
  see also being and nothingness debate
  School of Nonbeing   46
non-reductionism   13, 86, 91–94
normative ethics   4–5, 183, 184
normative principles   91
normative realism   13, 85–102, 117, 120, 221–222
normativity   87
nothingness *see* being and nothingness

o
On Yellow Emperor (Wang Fuzhi)   25–26
One and two   74, 75
one-body thesis (Wang Yangming)   14
Oneness hypothesis   63, 210–212, 257, 258

ontology 11, 12
  basicness 108
  ethical application of 51
  ontological foundation of
    phenomenal world 50–51
  ontological hierarchy (Cheng
    brothers) 13, 86, 91–94
  Taiji, ontological status 56
  wu (nonbeing), as ontological basis
    of all existence 42, 45
order 94–95, 113
Orive, Ruben 279, 280
ought-to ness (what ought to be
  the case) 10, 19, 148, 182,
  185, 230
  Cheng–Zhu school 90, 94, 97
  human nature 128, 129, 135

p

Pang, Pu 39–40, 41, 42, 44
passions 133, 165
Pei, Wei 47–48, 50
Penetrating the Book (of Changes)
  (Zhou Dunyi) 31, 33, 58
Pepitone, A. 280
perceptions 142, 145, 175, 216
  see also senses
performance, knowledge as 219n, 222
Perkins, Frank 2
permanence 108
personality psychology 16
Peterson, Willard 90, 96
phone booth experiment 200–201
physicalism 101
Pihlström, Sami 147, 149–153
Plato 89n, 174
pragmatist metaphysics 150–153
Prentice-Dunn, S. 280
prescriptive dimension (how one ought
  to treat things) 87–88
primary matter 81–82
primitive force concept 82
primordial chaos 55

primordial *qi*, concept 12, 56, 61,
  62–69, 72, 80
  homogeneous primordial *qi* 66, 67,
    68, 74
  quantum field theory 81
  yin and *yang* 63, 66, 67, 68, 74
principle
  actual (*shi*), and authenticity
    (*cheng*) 213
  coherence 90
  comparison of Cheng brothers and
    Zhang Zai 91–92
  concerns of neo-Confucians on 8–9
  connotations of, according to Cheng
    Hao 88
  cosmic 77, 95
  cosmos, well-placedness of 97
  descriptive and normative senses 231
  distinguished from *Dao* 7–8, 114, 115
  externalism of 115
  heavenly *see* heavenly principle
  as holistic order of the world
    (Zhu Xi) 94–95
  and human nature 159
  inherent in *qi* (Wang Fuzhi) 103–121
  li, substantial usage of term 6
  mind is *see* mind is principle
  as necessary law of the world 112–113
  Necessitarian Theory of Laws of
    Nature 77–80
  non-reductionism 13, 86, 91–94
  normative principles 91
  notion of 5–9, 13
  one principle but each one's due is
    different (Cheng Yi) 88n, 91
  one principle with multiple
    manifestations (Cheng Yi)
    88–91, 95, 96
  of particular things *see* principles for
    particular things
  qi, relationship with 97–101
  unification of descriptive dimension
    with prescriptive 87

principles for particular things   6–7, 9–10, 13, 88, 90, 94, 96–97
propriety (*li*)   3, 9, 14, 17, 47, 59, 119, 141, 193, 224, 230
  defined   185
  human nature   128, 132, 133, 137, 161, 169, 176
  moral personality   189, 193, 199, 200
  rites and rituals   193, 196–198
  and situational fit   196–198
  social sentimentalism   268, 279, 280
psychopaths   168–169
Putnam, Hilary   143, 147, 154

q

qi (cosmic energy)   11, 12, 79, 106, 107, 111
  and Cheng–Zhu school   91–94
  concepts/definitions   10–11
  as constituent of material and immaterial things   76–77
  constitution of   77, 100, 126, 129–132, 135, 157–159, 167, 200
  distribution of   11, 126, 158
  evaluation   80–83
  flood-like   193
  monist theory *see Qi*-monism
  Necessitarian Theory of Laws of Nature   77–80
  pre-object state (great vacuity)   105–106, 108, 111, 120
  pre-Qin philosophy, use in   61, 62
  primordial *qi* concept *see* primordial *qi* concept
  relationship with principle   97–101
  theory of principle inherent in *qi*   103–121
  separation of metaphysical layer of principle from physical layer of *qi*   91–92
  supreme vacuity   12, 69–71, 74
  theory of Zhang Zai   61–83
Qi-generation thesis   76
Qi-monism   11, 53
  see also primordial *qi* concept; *qi* (cosmic energy); supreme equilibrium; supreme vacuity (initial cosmic state); *Taiji* concept (Supreme Ultimate)
  theory of Wang Fuzhi   104, 120
  theory of Zhang Zai   69, 71, 76, 77, 92, 103, 107, 108, 120
Qing dynasty (1644–1911)   26, 116
qualities, primary and secondary   142

r

realism   32
  commonsense   143
  humanistic moral   144–150
  metaphysical   143
  and metaphysics of Wang Fuzhi   104n
  moral *see* moral realism
  normative   13, 85–102, 117, 120, 221–222
Realism Manifesto (Cheng Hao)   213
Reason, Truth and History (Putnam)   143n
Reber, Rolf   15
reciprocal altruism   208
reciprocal determinism   186
Recognizing Humaneness (Cheng Hao)   210
Rectifying the Youth (Zhengmeng)   184
Rees, Martin   7
Reflection (*si*)   15, 34, 116, 146, 171, 175, 230, 245, 246, 267, 272, 281, 282
  absence of   176, 177
  compared to cognition   281
  compared to sense of right and wrong   271
  importance   176, 281, 283
  lack of   131, 168, 173, 176, 177, 194, 212

moral   2, 171, 176, 253
   role of   177, 271, 274
   Reflections on Things at Hand
      (Zhu Xi)   22
   Regulatory theory   78, 85
respectfulness   164, 212–215
   lack of respect   197
reverence   3, 166, 227, 235–239
   pre-manifested and manifested
      stage   235
   Reverence: Renewing A Forgotten Virtue
      (Woodruff)   236
right and wrong, sense of   3, 190,
   212, 241
   human nature   128, 129, 134,
      164–166, 171
   mind   144, 148, 149
   moral sense and moral reflexivism
      246, 247–254, 258
   and reflection   271
   social sentimentalism   269, 271,
      273, 276, 280, 281
righteousness (*yi*)   9, 14, 16, 58, 107,
   224, 249
   accumulation of, cultivating
      moral expertise through
      192–194, 202
   human nature   128, 132, 133, 137,
      161, 167, 171
   mind   141, 148
   moral cognitivism and
      ethical rationalism
      230, 240
   moral personality   189, 196, 202
   social sentimentalism   268, 271,
      279, 280, 281
Robinson, Howard   108
robust character traits   222–225
Rodin, J.   275, 278, 279
Rogers, R. W.   280
Rorty, Amélie Oksenberg   263, 266,
   281, 282
Rosati, Connie   240, 241

S

Sabini, John   202
sages/sagehood   17, 34, 58, 172, 239
   see also moral agents
   human nature   133, 136
   mind   140, 149
   moral personality   191, 194,
      198, 200
   virtue ethics   224, 226
Sarkissian, Hagop   280
Sartre, Jean-Paul   157
Sayer-McCord, Geoffrey
   144, 145n
School of Being   47, 50
School of Mind   20
   see also mind
   debate with School of Nature
      2, 14, 139
School of Nature   13, 20, 23
   see also human nature; nature
   debate with School of Mind
      2, 14, 139
School of Nonbeing   46
Schwitzgebel, Eric   222
self-cultivation   34, 91, 192, 194,
   200, 227
   human nature   134, 135
   moral   190, 191, 196, 199
self-interest   195, 209, 245, 275
selfishness   173, 254–258
   and humaneness   210, 211
self-knowledge   222, 228
senses   92, 126, 133, 142, 174, 216,
   276, 281
   see also perception
Seok, Bongrae   15
shame   3, 133, 165–166
Shao, Yong   19n, 53–54
shendu (being watchful when one is
   alone)   261–262
Shien, Gi-Ming   56, 57
Shun, Kwong-loi   4n, 125–126, 128,
   129, 130

Shuowen Jiezi (Chinese dictionary) 51, 209
Silver, Maury 202
Sim, May 184n
singularity 62, 63
situational fit 196–198
situational pressure 201
situationism 16–17, 185
Six Classics 23, 27, 40
skpticism
 epistemic 221–222
 moral 206–207
 robust character traits 222–225
Slingerland, Edward 15, 183, 199
Slote, Michael 4n
Smith, Adam 276
Smith, Jacqui 189
Smith, Michael 266
social conditioning 3
social intuitionism 187
social sentimentalism 265–284
 expanding on 274–283
socio-cognitive model, moral personality 17, 184, 185–189, 190, 206
 automaticity 187, 188, 189
 contemporary discourse, assessment in 200–202
 five features 188
 moral exemplars, effortlessness of 199–200
sociopathy, acquired 168
Song dynasty (960–1279) 26, 53, 83, 120
Song-Ming neo-Confucianism 2, 21
Sorensen, Roy 53n, 54, 55n
Sosa, Ernest 219n
A Sourcebook in Chinese Philosophy (Chan) 13, 64n, 139
space–time framework 54–55, 57, 82, 109
Spiritual Constitution of the Universe (Zhang Heng) 66

spontaneous transformation 48
Stewart, Ian 85n
subjectivity 148
substance
 and function 44, 70n
 unification of 107–112
 material and mental 109
 nonbeing as 45
 supreme vacuity as 71
 ultimate 92
substance dualism 98, 99n
suffering, root of 13
supervenience 98, 99, 100
supervened base properties 98–99
supreme equilibrium 74–76, 82
supreme ultimate *see Taiji* concept (Supreme Ultimate)
supreme vacuity (initial cosmic state) 12, 69–71, 78, 82, 92, 105
 vacuity versus vacuum 71–74
Swartz, Norman 78, 79n, 85n

t

Taiji concept (Supreme Ultimate) 14, 32, 52–59, 69, 89
 division into pre-myriad-things and myriad things 53
 instantiation in particular things (Zhu Xi) 95–97
 interconnectedness 229–230
 motion and rest 53, 55, 57
 ontological status 56
 space–time framework 54–55, 57
 and supreme equilibrium 75
 Zhu Xi's concept of 96
Taiji diagram (Zhou Dunyi) 32, 33, 35, *36*, 38, 55
Tang, Chün-I 107
Tang, Yongtong 42, 44, 45–46
Tang dynasty (618–907 CE) 26, 61n, 73, 110
Taylor, Charles 234
Taylor, Gabriele 267–268

teleology 4, 5, 109
Teroni, Fabrice 163
Tien, David W. 143
Treatises on Heaven (Liu Yuxi) 73
Trivers, Robert L. 208
Turri, John 215

U

understanding, as attunement 234
universal principle *see* heavenly (universal) principle
universe
  whether cosmic accident or driven by eternal laws of nature 12, 85
  evolution of 67–68
  formation, primordial *qi* concept 65
  pre-established harmony 74
  space–time framework 54–55
utilitarianism 183, 184

V

vacuity *see* supreme vacuity (initial cosmic state)
vacuum 54, 55, 80, 82
  versus vacuity 71–74
Van Norden, Bryan W. 25, 184n
Veneration of Being (Pei Wei) 47
virtue ethics 15, 17–18
  agent-centered nature 184
  Cheng brothers 17
  criticisms 16
  defined 205
  forms 18–19
  globalist 17, 205–226
  and moral scepticism 206–207
  and neo-Confucian moral theories 17
  and normative ethics 4–5, 183, 184
  and virtue epistemology 205–226
  virtue ethics of flourishing (VEF) 5
  virtue ethics of sentiments (VES) 5

void 32, 39
  see also being and nothingness debate; nonbeing
  absolute 68, 71, 72, 73, 82
  complete 56, 68
  dark/lightless 66, 67, 70
  formless 64, 73
  volition 136, 170–171, 190, 198
  see also will, the

W

Wang, Anshi 225
Wang, Bi 42–47, 51
Wang, Chong 68–69
Wang, Fuzhi 7–8, 9, 13, 14–15, 18, 25–27, 70n, 80, 82, 94, 104–107, 157–179, 265–284
Wang, Haicheng 70, 71n
Wang, Robin 32, 38, 57
Wang, Yangming 4n, 7, 9, 14, 18, 20, 23, 24–25, 26, 116, 139–155, 173, 187, 211n, 218, 232, 245–263
Warring States period (475–221 BCE) 40, 62n
Wei and Jin dynasties (220–420) 42, 45, 46, 50
"Western Inscription" (Zhang Zai) 9, 20–21, 91, 194
White Deer Cave Academy 22
will, the 170–171, 208
  weakness of 230
Williams, Bernard 268
Williams, Robert Anthony 15
Wilson, Edward O. 208
Wisdom (*zhi*) 9, 14, 46, 59, 107, 119, 161, 223, 230, 249
  human nature 128, 132, 137
  mind 141, 152
Wittenborn, Allen 228, 233, 234, 235n, 238
Wong, David 145
Wong, Wai-ying 184n

Woodruff, Paul 236
Wright, Robert 245
wu (nothingness) *see under* being and nothingness debate
Wuji concept (boundlessness)
  historical controversies 12, 33–35
  and *Taiji* 51–59
Wuji diagram (Chen Tuan) 35, 37, 38

x

Xiang, Xiu 48n
Xiao, Jiefu 104n, 160
xingershang (beyond physical form) 117
Xiong, Shili 108
Xu, Shen 39, 40, 51, 54n, 57, 62n, 109
Xu, Sumin 104n, 160
Xunzi 3, 10, 33n, 161

y

Yan, Hui 19n, 223
Yan, Shouzheng 104
Yang, Lihua 70
Yangming Grotto 24
Yi, Desheng 62n, 81
Yijing (*Book of Changes*) 2, 3, 126
  Cheng–Zhu school 27, 89, 92
  cosmology of Zhou Dunyi 31, 35
  hexagrams in 4
yin and *yang* 8, 11, 78, 82, 100, 158
  Cheng–Zhu school 92
  cosmology of Zhou Dunyi 32, 52, 54
  equilibrium principle 113
  harmony between 106
  opposing nature of 75
  order 94
  primordial *qi* concept 63, 66, 67, 68, 74
  principle inherent in *qi* (Wang Fuzhi) 105
Youniss, James 193–194
Yu, Jiyuan 184n
Yu, Kam-por 116n, 262n, 272n

z

Zeng, Zhaoxu 104n
Zhang, Dainian 8, 10, 40, 62n, 70, 110
Zhang, Heng 66, 67, 69–70, 74
Zhang, Liwen 172, 178
Zhang, Qihui 104n
Zhang, Zhan 42n
Zhang, Zai 7–8, 9, 11, 12, 17, 20, 21, 22, 61–83, 85, 86, 101, 103–108, 111, 118, 120, 130, 141, 168, 183–203, 211n, 265
Zhou, Bing 160
Zhou, Dunyi 9, 12, 19, 20, 21, 22, 31–60, 72, 225
Zhu, Xi 7, 9, 10, 13–14, 17–18, 19n, 22–23, 25, 31, 33–35, 52, 58n, 83, 85, 86, 91, 94–101, 103, 106, 115–116, 116, 125–138, 139, 140, 141, 150, 151, 154, 168, 169, 226n, 227–244
  see also Cheng–Zhu school
Zhu, Yizun 35
Zhu, Zhen 35
Zhuangzi, the (Daoist text) 26, 50
  primordial *qi* concept 62–63, 64, 68